Writing and Holiness

DIVINATIONS:
REREADING LATE ANCIENT RELIGION

Series Editors
Daniel Boyarin
Virginia Burrus
Charlotte Fonrobert
Robert Gregg

A complete list of books in the series is available from the publisher.

Writing and Holiness

The Practice of Authorship in the
Early Christian East

Derek Krueger

PENN

University of Pennsylvania Press
Philadelphia

Copyright © 2004 University of Pennsylvania Press
All rights reserved
Printed in the United States of America on acid-free paper

10 9 8 7 6 5 4 3 2 1

Published by
University of Pennsylvania Press
Philadelphia, Pennsylvania 19104-4011

Library of Congress Cataloging-in-Publication Data

Krueger, Derek.
    Writing and holiness : the practice of authorship in the early Christian East / Derek Krueger.
       p.   cm. — (Divinations : rereading late ancient religion)
    Includes bibliographical references and index.
    ISBN 0-8122-3819-2 (cloth : alk. paper)
    1. Christian literature, Early—History and criticism.   I. Title.   II. Series.

BR67.K77   2004
270.2—dc22   2004042037

For Gene

Contents

"In narrative prepare for saints."
—*Gertrude Stein,* Four Saints in Three Acts

Chapter 1
Literary Composition as a Religious Activity

For Lent 382, Gregory of Nazianzus placed himself under a vow of silence. This discipline, while restricting speech, did not restrain him from writing. In fact, as his poem "On Silence at the Time of Fasting" suggests, Gregory employed writing to assist him in his Lenten practice.[1] "Hold still, dear tongue. And you, my pen, write down the words of silence and tell to the eyes the matters of my heart" (lines 1–2). In Gregory's hands, literary composition became a method for exploring his introspective quiet. While Gregory's poem documents his devotions, it also uses his writing to display and publicize his virtue. He writes, "Accept these sounds from my hand that you may have a speaking monument to my silence" (lines 209–210). On the page, readers would see Gregory performing his repentant silence. If they were reading aloud, as is likely, to themselves or to others, they would, ironically, even hear it.[2] The poem produces an image of its author as pious, dutifully engaging in the patterns of religious observance. Moreover, for Gregory, adherence to literary form highlighted the disciplinary potential of writing: composing metrical poetry could become a formative spiritual practice. "I followed the advice of holy men and placed a door on my lips. The reason was that I should learn to set a measure [μέτρα, meter], and be in control of everything" (lines 10–12). In another poem, "On Writings in Meter," Gregory states that he writes poetry "to subdue [his] own unmeasuredness."[3] Gregory uses meter not only to craft his poem, but to craft himself as well. The discipline of writing served as a powerful metaphor for the composition of a more Christian self.

In adapting writing as a tool for the cultivation of virtue, Gregory was not unique. In the course of the fourth century, Christians negotiated a distinct relationship between writing and the religious life. According to Athanasius, Antony commanded his monks to keep diaries "to note and write down" the "stirrings of [their] souls."[4] John Chrysostom called on his lay parishioners to keep a written record of their sins: "For if you write them down, God blots them out. . . . If you omit writing them, God both inscribes them and exacts their penalty."[5] It is far from clear how many of his listeners could actually write. Generous estimates for basic literacy in the period range from 15 to 20 percent. Skilled literacy, a product of grammatical and rhetorical training, may have been available only to a small, and predominantly male, 2 percent.[6] Nevertheless, each of these fourth-century bishops imagined the potential for the practice of writing, even if intended only for the intimate audience of the author and God, to discipline the writer, and thus afford an opportunity for human participation in God's act of redemption.

The power of writing to shape the Christian author flourished especially in the production of narrative literary forms. Saints' lives, in their combined ability to entertain and edify, contributed broadly to the formation of Christian practice and self-understanding. From the middle of the fourth century, Christian writers engaged in the task of representing holy people in text, offering models of the saints in narrative. But in hagiography, authors deployed narrative simultaneously for the improvement of their readers and themselves. These literary acts of the making of saints were doubly generative, producing both the saints and their authors. Composing hagiography made one a hagiographer. Thus the lives of the saints are also the residuum of a process of authorial self-production, of the making of authors. In generating a Christian authorial persona, the author was inevitably the subject of his own creative act. Indeed, the authors of early Christian saints' lives and miracle collections reconceived the production of literature as a highly ritualized technology of the religious self.

While offering models of the saints in narrative, Christian hagiographers began to pose questions about authorship. The ascetic call to humility rendered artistic and literary creativity problematic. Claiming authority and power appeared to violate the saintly practices these authors sought to promote. Writers meditated within their texts on the tension inherent in Christian acts of authorship. According to ascetic teachers such as Evagrius of Pontus in the fourth century and Dorotheus of Gaza in the sixth, Christians were to regard themselves as greater than no one and attribute all virtuous acts to the work of God. This novel and distinctly Christian valuation of humility moved far beyond Roman aristocratic ideals of modesty. Self-assertion, whether in the form of holding office or authoring a text, seemed to counter Christ's example of self-humiliation in the incarnation and obedience in the crucifixion.[7] Did writing displace the authorship of God or could it participate in it? In what ways did literary creation, an embodied practice, mark an author's own creatureliness?

This study addresses conceptions of authorship displayed in hagiographical works written between the fourth and the seventh centuries around the eastern Mediterranean, primarily in Greek. The period from the Christianization of the Roman Empire to the Arab conquest begins for modern historians as late antiquity and ends as early Byzantium, although the division between these two designations, the first primarily temporal, the second increasingly geographic, was subtle and slow.[8] During this period, new styles of authorial self-presentation emerged under the desire to bring acts of writing into conformity with Christian patterns of virtue and devotion. Drawing on literary studies, ritual and performance studies, cultural history, and the history of asceticism, this book explores how hagiographers and hymnographers came to view writing as salvific, as worship through the production of art.

Through the reading of a wide variety of saints' lives, miracle collections, and narrative hymns, *Writing and Holiness* seeks out late antique and early Byzantine answers to the question "What is an author?"[9] It illuminates the various models that Christian authors followed, considering a range of scripts according to which the performance of authorship proceeded. As writers cultivated the habits of Christian authorship, Christian literary culture constructed concepts of the saintly writer. What might it mean to be a *Christian* author, to write in a Christian context, to make writing an idiom of Christian self-expression, indeed of Christian self-fashioning through literary composition?

The thread running though the rhetorical strategies examined in this book is the attempt to integrate writing and piety. Considering late antique and early Byzantine hagiographical composition as a religious activity offers a new approach to a formative chapter in Christian literary history. Previous studies have tended to view an author's piety as a barrier to historical inquiry, dismissing miracle accounts (among other hagiographical elements) as pious fictions.[10] Positivist attempts to extract "what actually happened" (as opposed to what is narrated) from hagiographical writings have consistently underestimated the centrality of theological and literary concerns. Neglect of the religious dimensions of the act of writing arises in part from the confluence of two additional trends. First, renewed interest in late antique popular culture has highlighted the affinities between the religious life of elites and nonelites.[11] Despite the refreshing aspects of this approach, the distinctly literary contributions to the formation of piety have been overlooked. Second, traditional divisions between patristics and social history continue to exclude theology and religious composition from discussions of piety on the assumption that thought and action are separable. Since Émile Durkheim, the academic study of religion has tended to treat religion as a system of beliefs and practices. But the work of recent critics has argued that the distinction between beliefs and practices, or between thinking and ritual, tends to recapitulate Enlightenment distinctions between mind and body.[12] Indeed a rigid application of Durkheim's distinction between beliefs and practices ill serves the formative Orthodox Christianity in which these acts of authorship took place. After the councils of Nicaea (325) and Constantinople (381), the doctrines of the greater church focused on the embodiment of divine reason in the person of Jesus Christ. Confidence in the doctrine of the incarnation expressed itself bodily in a variety of practices, including baptism and eucharist. The holding of orthodox theological ideas was itself a practice of constant mental vigilance. In short, thinking was an activity, something obvious to Christians such as Gregory of Nyssa, for whom contemplation of God was virtuous motion, "eternal progress toward the divine."[13] For the late antique Greek authors considered in this study, writing was a vehicle for the expression of piety as well as a technology for its cultivation. As Chapter 7 discusses, texts themselves, the repositories of thought, were regarded as analogous to bodies. The act of writing bridged the mental and the bodily; while the written text, inscribed on papyrus or on skin, was embodied logos.

The rapid Christianization of the Roman Empire during the fourth century, and particularly the conversion of its lettered elites, meant the Christianization of Roman literary culture and traditions. New ideas about literary composition emerged in a environment where Christians also adapted the technologies of book production, revised scribal habits, and developed distinctly Christian modes of reading.[14] Habits of literary composition came increasingly to reflect and incorporate the values and practices of late Roman Christianity. To be sure, Christians, especially in the Greek-speaking East, had been writing since the first century, composing gospels, letters, treatises, sermons, and accounts of the lives of the apostles and the deaths of martyrs. The spread of Christianity among the upper classes, however, vastly increased the number of Christian orators and bishops with highly developed literary skills and the number of Christian aristocratic literary patrons with highly developed literary tastes. Despite attempts to characterize hagiography as a "low-level" genre, many saints' lives represent the work of highly literate authors for apparently sophisticated audiences.[15]

Other texts remain closer to the patterns of orality from which they derived. Nevertheless, high literary style and sophisticated biblical allusion did not preclude the more literary texts from reaching a wider, and not necessarily educated, audience.

Questions about the authoring of hagiography inevitably raise questions about genre.[16] Ordinarily discussions of genre, both in late antiquity and the present, involve the classification of texts according to literary type, form, structure, and themes. One way to think about hagiography is as a new genre that began with Athanasius's *Life of Antony*, composed between 356 and 362, and proceeded to become the dominant literary form of both the Greek and the Latin middle ages. Thus late antiquity witnessed the birth of a new Christian literature. Indeed no other literary practice was as distinctively Christian as hagiography, the representation of the lives and miracles of Christian saints in writing. But the genre hagiography did not spring forth suddenly from nowhere, and it is also possible to narrate a history of the origins of hagiography that emphasizes the debt of its forms and structures to modes of Greco-Roman biography. To a great degree, the emerging culture of Christian letters involved the Christianization of established Greco-Roman genres, and hagiography was no exception. The evangelists themselves composed the New Testament gospels following the conventions of the literary genre of the life (Greek: βίος), or biography.[17] Eusebius's treatment of the life of Origen in Book Six of his *Ecclesiastical History* and of the first Christian emperor in the *Life of Constantine* also followed ancient models for narrating the lives of philosophers and statesmen.[18] Christian funeral orations participated in the conventions of classical and contemporary pagan panegyric.[19] Hagiography was never entirely new.

These two approaches to the history of hagiography, deriving from readers' drives to classify extant texts from the outside, are not mutually exclusive. Discussions of genre internal to the earliest Christian saints' lives, however, are more problematic, suggesting generic instability rather than the simple origins of a literary type.[20] While Christian writers from the outset claimed the newness of what they were doing, they were surprisingly slow to fix its name. The term "hagiography"—literally "holy writing"—is a nineteenth-century scholarly designation. For the sixth-century theologian known as Dionysius the Areopagite, the adjective *hagiographos* (ἁγιό-γραφος) described the divinely inspired scriptures, not the lives of the saints.[21] Athanasius's *Life of Antony* presents itself as a letter. Gregory of Nyssa's *Life of Macrina*, composed in 381, also embedded in a letter, ponders what genre it belongs to. Too long for a letter, it is perhaps a "discourse," "a prose composition," or a "long-winded speech."[22] Precisely what authoring the lives of the saints entailed remained unclear. Perhaps the first moment of explicit genre-consciousness occurred as late as the 440s, when a third- or fourth-generation hagiographer, Theodoret of Cyrrhus, argued that the "lives of the saints" should take its place among the classical genres: epic, history, tragedy, and comedy. In time, the genre would be called the "lives of the saints" (οἱ βίοι τῶν ἁγίων), a retrospective label that would gather the earlier precursors.

Deferring clarity about literary form to explore conceptions of authorship enables the rethinking of the formation of Christian literature. Each of the texts examined here uses writing as a technique for the representation of holiness. Some are narrative representations of saints that facilitate emulation and veneration. Others are collections of accounts of miracles composed to publicize a shrine. The Christological hymns of Romanos the Melodist, the subject of Chapter 8, employ not prose, but poetry, and recount not the life of a saint, but the life of Christ. In each case, authorship includes reflection on the writing self. Perhaps genre can be seen from the writer's point of view as the ritualization of literary patterns and the adherence to traditions and structures as authors conform themselves to preexisting models. If so, then each of these works also belongs to a new genre, one of Christian authorship, a new way of writing that integrated literary habits with other forms of Christian life.

Christian ideas about authorship arose alongside broader theological reflection on writing and literature. Christian literary theories were closely linked to theories of signs. In contrast to the emphasis in the West, where, under the influence of Augustine, language was often seen as a consequence of the Fall and a marker of the distance between humanity and God, Eastern discourse about the nature of language was significantly more sanguine.[23] Greek theologians adapted Platonic conceptions that signs do not merely point to the things they signify, but in fact participate in the essence of the things signified.[24] Recounting the lives of the saints did not so much call attention to their absence, but rather rendered them present through narrative. In this respect, hagiographical texts functioned analogously to visual images or icons, containing the real presence of their subject.[25] Indeed a commonplace in introductions to the lives of the saints was the assertion that the text offered a verbal portrait or icon of the saint.[26] This trope, adapted from earlier Greco-Roman biography, took on additional meaning in light of Christian ethics and aesthetics.

The Greek verb *graphō* means both "I write" and "I draw." Like visual representation, narrative mimesis rendered holiness available in a copy. Hagiography strove for the representation of virtue in narrative. The Bible, with its stories of the holy men and women of old, offered the prototype, but subsequent narratives continued to produce images of the good and the beautiful. As the author of the anonymous *Life of Chariton*, probably composed late in the sixth century, explained, "Both Testaments [of the Bible], as well as the writings of the God-inspired church fathers and ascetics, all display as in a picture, by means of the written word, the virtues of the holy men, one by one, to all who wish to take heed."[27] The performance of hagiographical authorship provided images of the saints to inspire imitation and moral change, inviting readers and hearers to produce further images of holiness in themselves.

The writing life also provided key metaphors for understanding the work of God. In the early Christian gospels, Jesus reads (Lk 4:17–20) but never writes. (The scene in the Gospel of John [7:53–8:11] in which Jesus "bent down and wrote with his finger on the ground" is a later insertion.)[28] Yet the history of salvation figured as a series of scribal acts. The Gospel of John (1:14) declared Jesus to be God's Logos made flesh. *Logos* had a wide semantic range that included "oral expression," "words," "story," or "narrative," as well as "thought" and "reason." For some, the incarnation of the Logos in Jesus was a materialization of God's speech analogous to committing words to parchment or papyrus. The second-century Valentinian *Gospel of Truth* simply declared, "He put on the book."[29] Furthermore, creation might figure as a love letter. Evagrius, himself writing a letter to his friend Melania, read creation as God's epistolary communication with humanity.

For those who are far from God have made a separation between themselves and their Creator by their loathsome works. But God, out of his love, has provided creation as a mediator: it is like letters. . . . Just as someone who reads letters, by their beauty, senses the power and ability of the hand and the finger which wrote them together with the intention of the writer, thus he who looks upon creation with understanding, perceives the hand and the finger of its Creator as well as his intention, that is, his love.[30]

Scripture also participated in God's graphic habit. For John Chrysostom, God accommodated himself to humanity's limitations by willing himself to be described in scripture, taking literary form in the fleshly garments of human thought and language. The sacred writings of the Bible were also God's Logos incarnate.[31]

In salvation God wrote or emended the human text, an interpretation already present in the Pauline correspondence of the New Testament. In 2 Corinthians (3:3), the members of the congregation are "a letter from Christ," "written not with ink but the Spirit of the living God, not on tablets of stone but on the tablets of fleshly hearts."[32] Colossians (2:14) saw redemption as God's "blotting out the handwritten decree against us [ἐξα-λείψας τὸ καθ' ἡμῶν χειρόγραφον]," which he set aside by nailing it to the cross. The poet Romanos would later pray, "Blot out [my] mistakes, underwrite remission, grant amnesty; / Engrave the handwritten decree [χειρόγραφον], and free me."[33] With God portrayed as so engaged in literary and scribal activity, the performance of authorship afforded the opportunity to emulate God. Through their literary skill, the authors of saints' lives might participate in the work of creation, textual incarnation, and redemption.

So what is authorship? It is not so much a proprietary claim over literary output as a performative act, a bodily practice resulting in the production of text. Therefore its meanings are deeply intertwined with the context in which such acts are performed. Ideas about authorship, about being an author, are not static; they change and shift over time, forming in dialectic with literary and aesthetic tastes and cultural priorities.[34] In contrast, early nineteenth-century northern European images of the author as a romantic hero, notions of the writer as a tortured artist or of writing as the locus of suffering, are culturally and temporally contingent, emerging simultaneously with the valuation of such heroes in novels and poems. More modern concerns with writer's block, with anxiety about output, and with sudden breakthroughs unleashing the suppressed authorial voice belong to an age of psychoanalysis.[35] At the same time, writing is not inherently a religious activity. The new patterns of Christian literary practice that emerged in late antiquity must be seen within their cultural, religious, and theological settings. Christian authors in late antiquity rendered their writing a religious activity, specifically a late ancient Christian religious activity.

Even the apparent connection between "authorship" and "authority" is not inevitable. The common etymological root of both English words is the Latin *auctor*, a term meaning, among other things, "originator," and thus by extension, "one in authority." The word applied increasingly to authors of authoritative texts in the course of the Western middle ages, as writers such as Aristotle, the evangelists, Paul, and the early church fathers were accorded respect and deference by their readers. But the late ancient Greek vocabulary for "authorship" did not overlap with that of "authority."[36] To be sure, Greeks since antiquity accorded authority to earlier texts. But acts of authorship were not necessarily problematized as exercises of power. For many early Byzantine authors, authorship and authority came into conflict with each other because of Christological models. Christ's authorship of a new creation depended on his humility and obedience, on his renunciation of authority.

How then to go looking for the author in the text? Perhaps the most obvious way in which authors emerge in their texts is when they write about themselves. The authors of Christian hagiography often struck autobiographical poses, bringing their portraits of themselves as artists into conformity with religious ideals. In many vitae, the authorial voice is most obvious when the author addresses his audience directly. The rhetorical performances framing the central narrative of saints' lives, the prologues and epilogues, shape authorial identity.[37] Sometimes direct address also punctuates breaks in the middle of narratives. In a number of the texts considered in this study, including Gregory of Nyssa's *Life of Macrina*, Theodoret's *Religious History*, and the *Life and Miracles of Thecla*, the author is himself a character in the narrative, portrayed interacting with the saint or with the saint's shrine. Subjecting themselves to a variety of models, hagiographers depicted themselves as participants in the religious system they described and endorsed, casting themselves as emulators of the evangelists (the subject of Chapters 2 and 3), as faithful devotees of powerful holy men and women (Chapter 4), as ascetics and monastics (Chapter 5), as priests engaged in liturgy (Chapter 6), and, generally, as emulators of the saints and of Christ.

Attention to these features of hagiography does not recover uncontroverted evidence for an author's interior religious disposition. For literary studies and the study of religion alike, the question of whether an agent's intention can be determined remains vexed.[38] Observing an author performing acts of piety in his text tells more about how a writer wished to be viewed than about what he really thought. Authorial self-presentation, however, does give insight into the emerging phenomenon of Christian authorship. Greek Christian authors rendered images of themselves as such through specifically Christian acts of writing. Their performances of authorship provided no exception to, but rather exemplified emerging Christian practices of asceticism, devotion, pilgrimage, prayer, oblation, liturgy, and sacrifice. These new modes of enacting authorial voice were part of an emerging Christian discourse, a complex of "rhetorical strategies and manners of expression" that came to characterize Christian writing.[39]

What follows is a series of soundings in early Christian literature selected to reveal a wide variety of literary experiments. The Christian literary
theories uncovered along the way, while potentially compatible, were never
systematic. The chapters proceed topically to elaborate the impact of a variety of emergent forms of Christian piety on Christian conceptions of authorship, progressing toward increasingly complex theories of literary composition and toward increasingly subtle methods of weaving them into
texts. Some of the literary techniques discussed here, such as typology and
the textual performance of humility, were widespread, even ubiquitous, features of the genre. However, some of the texts I have chosen to discuss distinguish themselves more in shaping an especially articulate theology of
Christian authorship than in their immediate historical impact; these are
not so much typical as exemplary. Three chapters address the works of single authors, Theodoret of Cyrrhus, Gregory of Nyssa, and Romanos the
Melodist. Other chapters address groups of texts to illustrate the range of
performances possible in the interpretation of typical authorial roles.

One of the most distinctive features of Christian hagiography is its sustained reference to the Bible. The next two chapters consider the impact of
biblical narrative and biblical composition on the emergence of the Christian author. The first of these (Chapter 2) considers the aesthetics of biblical
correspondence by reading a single remarkable work, Theodoret of Cyrrhus's *Religious History*, written around 440. In the *Religious History*, Theodoret makes extensive allusion to biblical figures and events while narrating
the lives of fourth- and fifth-century ascetics in northwest Syria. This imitation of the Bible attests to the sanctity of his subjects by showing them to
be equal to—and even greater than—Old Testament prophets and New
Testament apostles. His typological system has implications for his own
self-understanding: he both configures his act of composition as an imitation of biblical writers, the evangelists and Moses, and understands his
product as a biblical text.

What models did the biblical writers offer for subsequent Christians
authors to imitate? Interest focused on the evangelists. As Chapter 3 reveals,
both written and artistic representations of the evangelists as writers at
work yielded a conception of writing as a sacred activity and of the evangelists as saints. Even in light of claims for divine inspiration, early Byzantine
Christians understood the sacred narratives to have resulted from a holy
person's labor. The writing itself figured as an extension of the authors' virtuous ascetic practice. Their supposed ascetic commitments and achievements dominated postbiblical lore. Human composition of the scriptures

promised divine cooperation in other human endeavors through the grace of the Spirit. Conceptions of divine inspiration yielded at once a high theology of scripture and a high regard for the embodied instruments who produced it. It was to such a model that early Byzantine authors aspired. In imitation of such figures, subsequent Christian authorship revealed its potential for holiness.

The next three chapters explore various guises of the author—devotee, ascetic, and priest—that integrate authorship with common Christian bodily practices. Chapter 4 focuses on writing undertaken in service to a saint or as participation in popular devotional forms associated with their cult. Miracle collections celebrating the efficacy of shrines dedicated to Thecla, Menas, Cosmas and Damien, and Artemios assimilate their composition to the oral acts of glorifying the saint integral to the cult. Theodoret's *Religious History* and Cyril of Scythopolis's sixth-century *Life of Euthymius* and *Life of Sabas* present composition as religious activity by employing metaphors drawn from other expressions of piety, such as asceticism, pilgrimage, and the donation of votive objects. In producing narrative, Theodoret, Cyril, and the anonymous compilers of miracle stories figured themselves *within* the cults of the saints, recasting writing not just as a record of devotion, but as devotion itself.

For many writers, the patterns of monasticism were as influential as the Bible in shaping their acts of authorship. Much hagiography not only described but imitated the ascetic life. Chapter 5 explores hagiography as an ascetic practice, particularly for monastic authors. Christian literary composition participated in an ongoing discourse about discipline, control, and authority. How should Christian writers emulate the humble and obedient Christ? In the hands of hagiographers such as Palladius in the fourth century or Antony of Choziba in the seventh, writing, like fasting or prayer, became a technology for attaining the goal of their own ascetic profession: a reconstituted self, displaying the virtues exemplified by the saints about whom they wrote. This development depended on the double meaning of the word *mimēsis,* both representation and imitation. Authors strove to emulate their subjects through mimesis, configuring themselves through the production of texts. As a genre, hagiography's purpose was to communicate virtues to an audience through narrative; as a practice, it offered an opportunity to practice humility and obedience. By representing the saints, authors hoped to resemble them. Thus authors established the place of literary production in ascetic formation.

Moving from monk to priest, Chapter 6 treats Gregory of Nyssa's *Life of Macrina*, the earliest Christian biography of a woman. Here writing becomes priestly activity analogous to early Christian liturgy. Writing shortly after his sister's death in 380, Gregory of Nyssa establishes a theological context for hagiographical composition in late fourth-century liturgical piety and practice. Situating acts of storytelling in the struggle to manage grief, Gregory uses remembering (*anamnēsis*) as a technology for rendering the absent present. Within the text, Macrina herself stresses that the goal of biography is "thanksgiving to God," modeling the proper method of Christian biographical narrative. Thus Gregory's literary production has analogues in evening prayer and the anaphora, or canon prayer, of the divine liturgy. Reflecting on the relationship between spoken and written words and between logos and flesh, the *Life of Macrina* posits a complex relationship between body and text in which Gregory's writing figures as sacrificial offering.

Devotion, asceticism, and priesthood both expressed and formed the body. By participating in these creative acts, authoring hagiography produced multiple material bodies, the saint, the author, and the text. The subsequent two chapters turn to frequent analogies between writing and embodiment to raise questions about textuality and materiality. Chapter 7, entitled "Textual Bodies," considers discourses comparing and identifying bodies with texts, delineating the relationship between the bodies of the saints and the texts that rendered them materially present. To gain leverage on peculiarly Christian approaches to textuality, this chapter reads the fifth-century Christian *Life of Syncletica* against Porphyry's life of the pagan philosopher Plotinus, written around 300. Whereas Porphyry makes an elaborate performance of his nervousness about representing a mere body, the connection between Syncletica's divine teaching and her deteriorating body highlights the difference that a doctrine of incarnation makes when considering biography as a representation of a person's body. Syncletica's teaching solidifies in the text to become nourishing food. Like Christ, she is a pedagogue feeding her flock with her instructive logos. This chapter concludes by reading the startling fifth-century account of the last judgment in the Syriac *Teaching of Addai*, where bodies rise out of their graves covered in text, their flesh inscribed with a narrative of their deeds. In this peculiar vision, Christ's judgment becomes an act of literary criticism or an archivist's work entailing the proper cataloging of books, emphasizing Christian interest in constructing connections between identities and books.

The relationship between authorship and the constitution of bodies could inscribe both authorial identity and the body of Christ. Chapter 8 marks a shift in literary genres to consider the cycle of liturgical hymns on the life of Christ composed by the sixth-century Constantinopolitan poet Romanos the Melodist. In this corpus, multiple themes of authorship as worship, asceticism, liturgy, and scripture (and thus inscription) converge. These poems dramatize dialogues between Jesus and various characters from the gospels. Serving as Christ's hagiographer, Romanos habitually inserts acts of writing into his retellings; he figures Jesus' death on the cross as an act of self-inscription where Christ signs a ransom for humanity using his body as parchment and his blood as ink. Curiously, the poet himself signs his poems by encrypting variants of the phrase "BY THE HUMBLE ROMANOS" into acrostics that determine the first letter of each stanza. While this signature is visible on the page, it could not be heard in vocal performance. The poet attaches his identity silently to his work, performing the humility he hopes to achieve. A concluding chapter reassesses literary composition as a Christian activity, rethinks adherence to genre as a form of writerly discipline, and surveys the relationship between the practice of authorship and the formation of Christian identity.

This thematic approach admittedly results in an untidy chronological sequence. To be sure, a chronological scheme, if it were possible, would hold great appeal, since in an imitative genre such as hagiography, questions of influence are bound to arise. However, with very few exceptions (most notably Cyril of Scythopolis), the trajectories into a given writer's library are very hard, if not impossible, to trace. While all hagiographers were familiar with biblical narratives, we often do not know much about which other texts they read. When they show familiarity with stories about other saints, it is by no means clear whether they learned these accounts from the texts we continue to possess, from other texts, or from oral tradition. That an author knows the story of Antony does not mean that he has a copy of Athanasius's *Life of Antony* before him.

The focus here is not on the stories about the saints in themselves, but rather on the performances of authorship displayed in texts that contain them. Too much emphasis on literary dependence occludes more defining factors. The shape of a given writer's Christian practice seems to have been more influential then other hagiographical texts in shaping his self-presentation and narrative technique. Thus I am teasing out, by largely synchronic analysis, certain strands in the variegated weave of late ancient hagiographic practice. This necessitates fixing individual texts in their historical, cultural, and often local contexts to recreate the interpretive framework in which these authorial acts took place. In a period of religious change and development, different trends in the practice of Christianity spawned different trends in the practice of authorship. What unifies these trends are the efforts to make literary composition a vehicle for piety.

A final note on sources is in order before proceeding. One of my goals has been to introduce more readers to a range of complex and fascinating texts little known outside the fields of early Christian and Byzantine studies. Most of the texts interpreted here are available in modern editions. Many have been translated into English. To the extent that it was possible, I have employed these translations, modifying them as necessary to emphasize aspects of the underlying Greek.[40] Full references can be found in the bibliography. The comparative study of ancient and medieval literatures still tends to ignore Byzantium. And yet this Christian Greek literature yields an important chapter in the history of authorship.

Chapter 2

Typology and Hagiography: Theodoret of Cyrrhus's Religious History

Christian hagiography was always already in conversation with the Bible. In narrating lives exemplary precisely in their imitation of biblical precedents, authors constructed links of varying complexity between their writings and sacred scripture. This intertextual correspondence with the Bible rendered hagiography a Christian genre. Indeed, biblical typology may be the most significant feature distinguishing Christian hagiography from pagan biographical forms.[1] Literary acts creating a text so closely resembling the Bible had implications for the understanding of authorship, offering opportunities for writers to conform themselves to the models provided by biblical authors. Most often such links remained implicit, even unacknowledged, in late antique texts. One work, however, Theodoret of Cyrrhus's *Religious History*, surfaced these implications in an especially sophisticated and reflective performance of authorship. Writing near the middle of the fifth century, some eighty years after Athanasius's *Life of Antony*, Theodoret took stock of a genre neither quite new nor yet fully theorized. What resulted was one of the most remarkable examples of Christian hagiographical practice to survive from the late antique East.

The *Religious History* reflects the interplay of Theodoret's roles as bishop and theologian, writer and ascetic.[2] Turning his literary art to the representation of Syrian holy men and women, Theodoret explored a correspondence between the world of late antique monasticism and the world of the Bible. Theodoret's primary tool for placing the deeds of the local saints into a context comprehensible to his readers was the device of biblical typology, the linking of his modern-day heroes with biblical figures. In the course of the biography of James of Nisibis, a mere fourteen paragraphs in the modern edition of the *Religious History*, Theodoret compares the hermit turned bishop with Moses, Phinehas, Elijah, Elisha, Hezekiah, the apostles generally, Peter particularly, and frequently with Christ, "his own Master"

(1.6). The saturation of the text with such allusions reveals Theodoret's sophisticated insight not only into the practices of the saints he so vividly describes, but into the practice of writing hagiography as well.

Theodoret wrote the *Religious History* (Φιλόθεος ἱστορία), subtitled the *Ascetical Life* (Ἀσκητική πολιτεία), in the year 440.[3] Later he would refer to the work simply as the *Lives of the Saints* (τῶν ἁγίων οἱ βίοι).[4] The work consists of a series of twenty-eight chapters describing ascetics active in and near the towns and villages of northern Syria from the early fourth century through his own day.[5] Theodoret organized these accounts—which he called *diēgēmata*, or "narratives"—by whether their subjects were dead or living; the former ordered by the date of their death, the latter grouped by geography and gender.[6] Despite Theodoret's claims to have avoided composing panegyric, the *Religious History* demonstrates Theodoret's extensive rhetorical and philosophical education.[7] He wrote a nuanced, atticizing Greek, eschewing both the common dialect of the western Syrian cities and the Syriac that was the native tongue of most of the holy men he describes.[8] While the didactic concerns of the work show a bishop eager to educate his flock, the text's sophisticated linguistic and rhetorical level points toward a larger audience of educated Christians, monastic and lay, throughout the Eastern Mediterranean.[9] The work apparently circulated widely. At the end of the 440s in his *Ecclesiastical History*, Theodoret described the *Religious History* as "easily accessible [ῥᾴδιον ἐντυχεῖν]" to "those who wish to become acquainted with [its contents]".[10]

Theodoret did not merely write about ascetic devotion, he practiced it; moreover, he was quite familiar with hermits and monastic communities. He was born in 393 in Antioch to wealthy and pious Christian parents who had dedicated Theodoret (whose name means "given by God") to God's service before his birth.[11] Already in his childhood, he made frequent visits to local holy men.[12] After the death of his parents, Theodoret entered the monastery at Nicerte (near Apamea), where he pursued the ascetic life and began a long career as a writer.[13] He continued his ascetic regimen even after he was elected bishop of Cyrrhus (north of Afrin in modern Syria) in 423.[14] Monastic bishops were common in northwestern Syria, and the *Religious History* provides a number of examples for Theodoret's mode of life.[15] When briefly deposed from his see in 449–51, he returned to the monastic community at Nicerte.[16] After his restoration to the see of Cyrrhus at the Council of Chalcedon, Theodoret remained an ascetic bishop for another seven years. He died around 466.[17]

The *Religious History* remains one of the most important sources for the history of Syrian monasticism. Particularly renowned for its memorable narration of the life of Symeon the Stylite, who spent most of his adulthood standing upon successively taller pillars, the work has rightly proved valuable to modern scholars for its documentation of details about the daily life of monastics and of the laity of the Syrian villages and countryside.[18] However, although often praised for its historical reliability,[19] the *Religious History* provides neither a translucent repository of historical facts nor unfiltered evidence for popularly held views.[20] Shifting concern away from querying the historicity of things described gains two advantages: it fosters appreciation of the text's literary quality and permits consideration of Theodoret's efforts to fashion a view of his world within his text. This approach necessitates paying attention to the mechanisms through which Theodoret actively shaped his representation of the ascetical life and advances inquiry into the specific aims or goals of the hagiographer. The first part of this chapter investigates Theodoret's use of biblical typology as an aesthetic technique in shaping his narratives of the Syrian monks. The second part situates this typology within the context of Theodoret's exegetical and theological concerns, while the third part turns questions about biblical figuration to Theodoret's own role as author to consider how he wished his audience to regard the work of composing saints' lives within the context of his typological scheme.

The Meaning and Function of Typology within the *Religious History*

Typological allusion was commonplace in late antique hagiography.[21] In the narrowest sense, typology refers characters and events to the life of Jesus. In practice, however, the technique was more complex, involving reading history and constructing stories to highlight correspondences between events in the world and events in the Bible, thus absorbing the world into the sacred text. Already in the second and third centuries, the task of representing the Christian heroes as types for Christ governed the composition of the *Acts of the Martyrs*.[22] In later lives of the saints, the author's purpose was to attest to the holiness of the men or women he described. Paradigms for what constituted holiness derived from the Bible. Appeal to biblical models functioned as a principle for selecting what to narrate and how to narrate it, dictating the reshaping, and even fabrication, of events. By employing typology as a structural feature, authors endeavored to sustain a close intertextual relationship with sacred history. Thus typological composition defined the hagiographical genre as a consciously postbiblical narrative form.[23]

In the majority of late ancient saints' lives, the typological construction of the narrative remains implicit. The author assumed that the audience was familiar with a great number of biblical stories and appealed to specific biblical figures by name only occasionally. While the saint's activities reenacted events of sacred scripture, authors were not generally compelled to explain to their readers which deed of Jesus the saint was imitating.

What distinguishes Theodoret's *Religious History* from the vast majority of hagiography from the early Byzantine period is the pervasiveness of explicit reference to biblical precedents, as the catalogue of names invoked in the course of the biography of James of Nisibis makes clear. In fact, Theodoret prefers explicit reference to implicit allusion in depicting his saints as resembling figures in the Old Testament, the disciples in the New Testament, and, ultimately, Christ himself. Thus Theodoret states explicitly that in their fasting Marana and Cyra emulate Moses and Daniel (29.7) and that Limnaeus "imitates the miracle-working of the Apostles" (22.3). Over and over Theodoret explains that his saints imitate their Master;[24] while somewhat more baldly, Theodoret dubs James of Nisibis a "new Moses" (1.5) and Macedonius a "new Elisha" (13.17).[25] Through constant invocation of biblical figures, Theodoret prooftexts his claims that these Christian men and women are indeed saints.

Theodoret employs biblical typology to frame an understanding of his saints' works, especially their asceticism and their miraculous powers. Throughout the *Religious History*, he parses asceticism as a combination of an adherence to biblical commands and an emulation of biblical precedents. The holy people follow Jesus' explicit commands to reject family, give possessions away, pray constantly, fast, and keep watch. Theodoret frequently cites the scriptural justification for these common practices.[26] In addition to this obedience, Theodoret depicts asceticism as mimesis, the imitation or showing forth of the Christ by enacting his resistance to temptation, his suffering, and especially his love of humanity.[27] Furthermore, Theodoret's saints heal and preach, and Aphrahat even speaks in parables (8.8). The names and the deeds of other biblical heroes also appear throughout the text as exemplars of the ascetic life. Thus, for Theodoret, Marcianus's rigorous ascetic practice renders him in a class with that most famous of Old Testament ascetics, the prophet Elijah, and with John the Baptist, recalling various Old Testament figures to whom the author of Hebrews alluded when he described those who "went about in skins of sheep and goats, destitute, afflicted, ill-treated—of whom the world was not worthy—wandering over deserts and mountains, and in dens and caves of the earth" (Heb 11:37–38; Theodoret, *Religious History* 3.1).[28] Theodoret employs biblical markers to reflect on the sacrificial aspects of the ascetic life. Salamanes's practice had rendered him so dead to this life that he could say truthfully what Paul had said in Galatians 2:20–21, "I have been crucified with Christ; I no longer live, but Christ lives in me" (19.3). And Theodoret implicitly connects ascetics' cultivation of virtues with the Israelites' offerings of first fruits (4.1). For Theodoret, the ascetic life was a biblical life.

In his understanding of asceticism, of course, Theodoret was not unique. Asserting the biblical grounding of the solitary life had long been commonplace in the literature of Christian monasticism. The invocation of such figures as Elijah and John the Baptist as models for the ascetic life features in a variety of sources representing the literary culture of Egyptian, Syrian, and Cappadocian asceticism.[29] The poet Ephrem startlingly captured the potential force of biblical figures as ascetic types within the Syrian milieu in a *Hymn on the Nativity* with which Theodoret may have been familiar.[30]

Since Elijah repressed
the desire of his body, he could withhold the rain
from the adulterers. Since he restrained his body,
he could restrain the dew from the whoremongers
who released and sent forth their streams.

Since the hidden fire, bodily desire,
did not prevail in him, the fire of the high place
obeyed him, and since on earth he conquered
fleshly desire, he went up to [the place] where
holiness dwells and is at peace.

Elisha, too, who killed his body,
revived the dead. That which is by nature
mortal, gains life by chastity,
which is beyond nature. He revived the boy
since he refined himself like a [newly] weaned [infant].

Moses, who divided and separated himself
from his wife, divided the sea
before the harlot. Zipporah maintained
chastity, although she was the daughter of [pagan] priests;
with a calf the daughter of Abraham went whoring.[31]

Here the poet's knowledge of ascetics and asceticism has conditioned his interpretation of the Bible. His exegesis highlights the prophets' control over the body as a key to their power and renders the Bible an ascetic text.[32] Such was the pervasive Christian reading of these biblical figures upon which Theodoret drew.

Perhaps the greatest cluster of biblical reference amasses in Theodoret's narrative about Symeon the Stylite.[33] Symeon began as a shepherd, like Jacob, Joseph, Moses, David, and Micah (26.2). In his youth he desired to fast forty days without food, like Moses and Elijah (26.7). And Theodoret groups Symeon's admittedly peculiar practice of standing on a pillar with the strange behavior of biblical prophets: Isaiah's walking naked; Jeremiah's wearing a loin cloth, a wooden collar, and later an iron one; Hosea's marriage to a harlot; Ezekiel's lying on his right side for 40 days and his left side for 150 (26.12). Theodoret compares Symeon implicitly with Christ crucified upon the cross.[34] When taking the biography of Symeon in isolation from the rest of the *Religious History*, scholars have tended to regard this nexus of biblical citation as apologetic, understanding Theodoret to be justifying Symeon's mode of *askēsis*.[35] Indeed, Theodoret introduces his list of eccentric deeds by writing "I do not think that this standing [on a pillar] has occurred without the dispensation [οἰκονομία] of God, and because of this I ask fault-finders to curb their tongue" (26.12), suggesting the existence of some opposition to Symeon's calling. Since similar appeals to prophetic precedent appear in the Syriac *Life of Symeon the Stylite*, composed independently of Theodoret's vignette, the germ for such a list may derive from the monastic community gathered about Symeon's pillar near Telneshe. Theodoret, however, has reshaped whatever material he has received.[36] When considered in the context of the entire *Religious History*, the prooftexting of Symeon's pillar-standing, occurring so late in the collection, strikes the reader less as a defense of anomalous behavior than as an integral part of Theodoret's larger interpretive project.[37] To the extent that Theodoret's typological exercise is apologetic, it is an argument for seeing the biblical character of the whole of Syrian ascetic praxis.

The Syrian monk's biblical *askēsis* leads to biblical gifts. As in the passage from Ephrem quoted above, the saints' control of the body results in extraordinary powers. Theodoret employs biblical examples to explain his ascetics' miracles. Lest his audience disbelieve the account of how Symeon the Elder (not the Stylite) was fed dates by a lion, Theodoret invokes, as "proofs of God's power," the crows who fed Elijah, the whale who protected Jonah, and those lions who were awestruck at Daniel (6.10–11), thereby attesting to the credibility of his account by presenting the saint as a latter-day prophet and revealing the essentially prophetic character of the monastic life.

Theodoret's saints perform healings and exorcisms resembling those of Jesus. Symeon the Stylite cures a paralytic (26.16), Julian Saba a lame man (2.19). Peter the Galatian restores sight (9.7), while the gifted Maron cures "varied diseases of every sort" (16.2). James of Cyrrhestica raises the dead (21.14), and Marcianus twice exorcizes girls possessed by demons (3.9, 22).[38] To a large extent, the saints' repertoire of cures is defined by the biblical narrative. Symeon the Elder is extolled for performing miracles "like the Apostles and prophets" (6.5).[39] Here too Theodoret follows patterns already established in Christian hagiography, of which Bernard Flusin has written, "There is no miracle without a biblical precedent. . . . That which God has accomplished, he accomplishes again."[40] And if a saint does not quite walk on water, he might nonetheless amble across the Nile submerged only to his waist like Paphnutius and his followers in the *History of the Monks of Egypt*, or, as with Amoun in Athanasius's *Life of Antony*, the holy man might be carried miraculously across the water without getting wet.[41] Thus, even when elements of the story contrast the saint's gifts with those of Jesus, they show the saint to be like Jesus, to be Christlike.

Within Theodoret's vision, justification for the typological resemblance between saints' miracles and biblical miracles comes from Christ himself. After narrating an episode in which Symeon the Stylite orders a paralyzed Saracen first to renounce his false religion, second to walk, and third to lift up his tribal chieftain—an enormous man—and carry him away, Theodoret remarks,

[Symeon] gave this order in imitation of the Master, who told the paralytic to carry his bed [compare Mt 9:6]. But let no one call the imitation usurpation, for His is the utterance, "He who believes in me will himself do the works that I do, and greater than these will he do" [Jn 14:12].[42] Of this promise we have seen the fulfillment; for while the Lord's shadow nowhere performed a miracle, the shadow of the great Peter canceled death, drove out diseases and put demons to flight. But it is the Master who through His servants performed these miracles too; and now likewise it is by the use of His name that the godly Symeon performs his innumerable miracles. (26.17)[43]

Jesus predicted the repetition of biblical miracles in the lives of the saints. Their deeds are the fulfillment of prophesy, linked to the Gospels by the same bond that links the New Testament to the Old.

For Theodoret, the task of narrating the lives of the saints lay in exploring the connection between them and biblical types. This mode of composition, so dependent on the Bible, affords insight into Theodoret's own conception of the hagiographical genre, especially when the *Religious History* is compared with his later *Ecclesiastical History*. Theodoret's choice to forgo the typological mode of the saints' lives in the *Ecclesiastical History* reveals his understanding that these works belong to different genres. Writing at the end of the 440s, Theodoret included brief stories about four of the holy men of the *Religious History* in his *Ecclesiastical History*. The renarration of James of Nisibis's involvement in the siege of that city (*Ecclesiastical History* 2.30; compare *Religious History* 1.11–13), while describing James as a man who "shone with the grace of a truly apostolic character," in fact lacks the typological themes of the earlier account. Theodoret mentions no biblical figure by name and makes no attempt to present the calling down of the plague of mosquitos as Mosaic. The *Ecclesiastical History*'s treatment of Julian Saba, Aphrahat, and Macedonius is similarly free of the typological effort so characteristic of the *Religious History*.[44] While both works tell stories relevant to the life of the church, it is proper only to the discourse of sacred biography to craft an explicitly postbiblical story.

Theodoret's Typology as Exegesis and Theology

Individual instances of typological reference in the *Religious History* adhere to patterns familiar within the corpus of late antique Christian hagiography. However, the work's saturation with explicit allusion to biblical figures exceeds the conventions of the emergent genre. This feature of Theodoret's style provides an opportunity to explore his aims in the integration of biblical and hagiographical narrative. The force of Theodoret's typological reading of the saints reveals itself within the context of Theodoret's activities as a theologian, biblical exegete, and small-town bishop in northwestern Syria.

Ironically, scholars have had little success linking one of the best-known aspects of Theodoret's career as a theologian with the *Religious History*.[45] Although the twentieth century has tended to pronounce him thoroughly orthodox, Theodoret's teaching frequently sparked controversy. On the eve of the Council of Ephesus of 431, Theodoret defended an Antiochene Christology associated with his contemporary Nestorius against the attacks of Cyril of Alexandria. Theodoret continued to support this position, and several years after he composed the *Religious History*, the "Robber

Synod" held at Ephesus in 449 deposed Theodoret from his see. In 451, the Council of Chalcedon restored him to his bishopric only after he anathematized the teaching of Nestorius and all others who "did not declare that the holy Virgin Mary was the Mother of God and divided into two the only-begotten Son."[46] To some degree, Theodoret's illustration of how his Syrian ascetics conform to biblical models implicitly attests to their orthodoxy. Nevertheless, the issues central to the so-called Nestorian controversy have left little discernible mark on the *Religious History*, even though three of the monks described in the *Religious History*—James of Cyrrhestica, Symeon the Stylite, and Baradatus—had in 434 intervened at the request of the imperial court to bring about a reconciliation between Theodoret and John, bishop of Antioch, regarding the teachings of Cyril of Alexandria.[47] It is unreasonable to conclude that this theological controversy dominated Theodoret's long and active episcopacy. Perspective on the theological concerns of the *Religious History* must develop through an exploration of other aspects of Theodoret's service to the church.[48]

Theodoret directed much of his energy toward composing extensive commentaries on the Bible, especially the Old Testament. By his own description, his biblical exegesis plotted a middle course between the often-extreme allegory associated with Origen and the perceived literalism of Theodore of Mopsuestia, who had taught in Antioch during Theodoret's youth.[49] In contrast to Theodore, who tended to see a "discontinuity between the two Testaments,"[50] Theodoret's method emphasized the unity of Christian scripture such that the Old Testament, while narrating historical events, was also to be read as predicative of fulfillment in Jesus.

Typology, of course, was a standard method of Christian biblical exegesis in late antiquity.[51] Christian commentators and apologists strove to illuminate correspondences between events narrated in the Old Testament and events in the New. Theodoret employed this hermeneutic throughout his biblical commentaries, showing the relationship between the events in the two testaments to be one between "archetype and image."[52]

This concern to demonstrate the integrity of scripture was in part polemical and needs to be considered in light of Theodoret's interaction with other religious communities. Theodoret's biblical commentaries are filled with anti-Jewish rhetoric precisely over the issue of Christian typological exegesis, and while "the Jews" function to some extent as straw men, actual Jewish communities flourished in Theodoret's native Antioch and in other cities of northern Syria into the mid-fifth century.[53] Moreover, even among local Christian populations, there were those who rejected the relevance of

Jewish Scripture. Marcionites populated villages within Theodoret's own bishopric, and in the course of the *Religious History* Theodoret recounts how he enlisted the prayers and clairvoyance of the local holy man James of Cyrrhestica in forcibly converting these villages to orthodoxy.[54] It is no accident that in relating these events Theodoret refers to James as "my Isaiah" and relies on the accuracy of his predictions (21.17–18). Isaiah was the prophet most important for demonstrating the link between the two testaments and the relevance of the Old Testament for Christians.[55]

The presence of Jews and Marcionites in the regions surrounding Cyrrhus, a constant reminder that not everyone read the events of Israelite history as Christian prophecies, stands behind Theodoret's interest in asserting both Old Testament and New Testament prototypes for fourth- and fifth-century Christian experience. The typological breadth of Theodoret's narratives of local ascetic life also bolsters arguments for the unity of scripture. When Theodoret compares James of Nisibis, Julian Saba, or Symeon the Stylite with Moses, he invokes the authority of the Septuagint, the Greek translation of the Hebrew Bible, for orthodox Christians. In this way, the theological concerns of Theodoret's biblical exegesis and his hagiography converge.

But the *Religious History*'s use of scriptural reference makes an additional claim, as the following example demonstrates. In the narrative concerning Eusebius of Teleda, Theodoret employs biblical examples to justify monks' taking on broader roles in the church. The monk Ammianus convinces Eusebius to abandon the cell where he has immured himself and lead a community of monks by invoking "the great Elijah, who pursued this life" and the "second Elijah, the famous John [the Baptist] who embraced the desert" for their service to others while pursuing the monastic life (4.4). Intertestamental biblical typology asserts the link between Elijah and John. Hagiographical typology links the ascetic to the biblical examples. John the Baptist is the second Elijah, and Eusebius of Teleda is a third. Here Theodoret reveals that the typology that connects the monks to the Bible is identical to the typology that connects the Old and the New Testaments. In the *Religious History*'s composition, a mode of reading the Bible becomes a mode of reading the saints. Theodoret's hagiographical project consists of linking archetype and image. Moreover, the typological system reaches its full potential when the Syrian ascetics become types for each other. Thus James of Cyrrhestica "emulates" James of Nisibis and in turn has become a "model of philosophy for others" (21.2).[56]

A related but potentially more surprising agenda manifests itself already in the first narrative of the *Religious History*. As stated previously, the story of James of Nisibis abounds in typological figuration.[57] Each of James's miracles prompts the invocation of at least one biblical type. Consideration of these episodes captures the flavor of Theodoret's project as well as his intent; here Theodoret consistently presents James not only replicating the work of biblical figures, but in fact doing so in a fashion more Christlike.

In one instance James chastised immodest girls who had hiked up their skirts and stared at him while doing their laundry. James turned their hair gray, thus, presumably, rendering them unattractive and incapable of licentiousness (1.4). For Theodoret, James compares favorably with biblical types: whereas Elisha had cursed impudent children, causing them to be eaten by bears (2 Kgs 2:24), James effected a "harmless correction" of "slight disfigurement" that taught the girls proper piety and good manners (1.5). While James "possessed the same power" as the prophet Elisha, his deed accorded with "the gentleness of Christ and the new covenant." This "new Moses" worked not with the "blow of the rod" but with the sign of the cross (1.5). As in his biblical commentaries, Theodoret demonstrates simultaneously the relevance of Hebrew scripture to the Christian life and the superiority of the new dispensation to the old.[58] Theodoret reiterates the saint's supersession of the biblical types in his account of how James saved the city of Nisibis (1.11), an event that invites comparison with numerous biblical figures and much rhetorical flourish. When Nisibis was under siege by the Persian army, James resembled Moses by calling on God to send a plague of gnats and mosquitoes to bite the army's horses and elephants. His defense of Nisibis also recalls Hezekiah, who defended Jerusalem against the Assyrians (2 Kgs 19).

Such are the miracles that God wrought in the case of this Hezekiah also, not inferior to those earlier ones but greater. . . . I myself am also filled with admiration at the way James, when applying a curse, did not ask for the introduction of thunderbolts and lightning, as the great Elijah did when each of the commanders of fifties came to him with his fifty [1.13; compare 2 Kgs 1:1–10].

Here, however, Theodoret does not limit himself to comparing James with Old Testament types; he goes on to assert that James's subtlety also exceeds those New Testament exemplars whom the Gospels had portrayed in a critical light (compare Mk 10:35–45). Unlike the apostles James and John who tried to effect a similar miracle in the Gospel of Luke (Lk 9:51–56), "he did not ask for the earth to gape under them nor did he call for the army to be consumed with fire" (1.13).

James of Nisibis, described by Theodoret as "full of the grace of an Apostle" (1.9), in fact, exceeds the apostles because he follows Christ's ethical example more closely. Thus, James "imitated his Master's love of humanity [φιλανθρωπία]" (1.8) in dealing with a man who was pretending to be dead and whose friends asked the holy man for money to bury him. While James prayed for the repose of the man's soul, the man actually died. In this, Theodoret explains (1.9), James resembled the apostle Peter, who consigned Ananias and Sapphira to death for lying (Acts 5:1–10). But unlike Peter, and like Jesus instead, in answer to the friends' supplications, James proceeded to raise the man from the dead. Similarly, when a Persian judge handed down an unjust verdict, rather than cause harm to people, James cursed a large stone, causing it to explode (1.6). "Here too," Theodoret explains, "James emulated his own Master . . . who did not inflict punishment" on those with whom he was displeased but rather demonstrated his power by causing "the lifeless fig-tree to whither up." Kinder and gentler than the apostles, James exhibits the virtue of divine love that his biographer wishes to instill in his readers.[59]

The desire to present James of Nisibis as a superior imitation of Christ motivates Theodoret's celebratory use of a typological method. Favorable comparison with prophets and apostles yields James a very high ranking indeed. Some of the chapters that follow, such as those on Julian Saba, Marcianus, and Eusebius of Teleda, are laden with explicit typology. In others, Theodoret uses this tool less frequently, although when he comes to Symeon the Stylite late in the work, he pulls the stops out once again. Nevertheless, once Theodoret has instructed his audience how to read the saints in light of biblical figures, the thrust of his exegesis is clear. Theodoret's performance in narrating James of Nisibis frames the whole of the work, providing his readers with an interpretation not only of James but of all the holy men and women who follow.

Typology provided Theodoret a flexible literary mode and conceptual process through which to interpret the world of Christian ascetics. His application of biblical models to his own time posited an intertwining of the biblical narrative and late antique Christian experience. Through his typological construct, the dominant principle shaping his narration, Theodoret asserted the biblical character of his own day, exposing the unity not only of the two testaments but of the experience of God's peoples in both biblical and postbiblical times.[60] In this endeavor Theodoret articulates a view of history present already in the *Martyrdom of Perpetua and Felicitas*, where an early third-century redactor presents the events of his own day as works of the Spirit analogous to those recorded in scripture. Closer to Theodoret's own time, the author of the *History of the Monks of Egypt* asserted regarding his subjects, "To this day they raise the dead and walk on the water just like Peter. And all that the Savior did through the [biblical] saints, he does in our own time through these monks."[61] Just as Old Testament narratives could prefigure the Christ and the experience of the church, so also certain events and people in Theodoret's age could point back toward the Bible. Thus, when Theodoret created a correspondence between the "lovers of God" (φιλόθεοι) living in his own age and those living in the world of the Bible, the biblical age became at once past, present, and timeless. His simultaneous retelling of ascetic and biblical history serves to demonstrate that the world of the Bible lives on in these people: the saints are like the figures in the Bible; the times in which they live, like biblical times. Moreover this biblicizing worldview extends beyond the saints to the common folk. Often minor characters within Theodoret's various vignettes, lay people also compare with biblical figures. A wealthy woman who invites the traveling Julian Saba to stay in her house emulates the hospitality of Sarah (1.17; compare Gen 18:6). The women who seek miracles from Maësymas (14.2–3) are compared with the widow of Zarephath (1 Kgs 17:9–16) and the Shunnamite woman (2 Kgs 4:22).[62] In this way, typological figuration allows Theodoret to redefine the greater society that both he and his audience inhabit. Theodoret situates his audience within a world that reenacts the Bible.[63]

The Author's Role in a World of Mimesis

What does Theodoret's typological composition contribute to an understanding of the role of the hagiographer? Theodoret's narrative reenacts the Bible in two senses. First, Theodoret interprets the stories he tells within the text as reenactments of biblical narrative. Second, Theodoret's text itself is a reenactment, a mimesis of biblical narrative. His text *as a text* stands in typological relationship to the biblical texts in the same way that his subjects stand in typological relationship to the subjects of biblical narrative. What then of the act of authoring such a text? How did Theodoret fit himself into his typological scheme?

The prologue to the *Religious History* assumes that Theodoret's composing of a text that imitated the Bible was an imitation of the biblical authors. Undergirding his formulation of his task lies a conception of the Bible as a series of stories about divine gifts with a capacity to teach virtue. Theodoret articulates this attitude at the beginning of the life of James of Nisibis, where he observes that the Bible describes "the virtue of Abel, the devotion of Enoch, the righteousness of Noah, the priestly piety of Melchizedek, the call, faith and endurance of Abraham" (1.1), each biblical figure representing a different desirable quality. Such an approach widely informed Christian use of scripture, perhaps most notably in a letter of Basil of Caesarea to Gregory of Nazianzus that cites Joseph for chastity, Job for fortitude, and so forth, and in a number of sayings of the desert fathers.[64] For Theodoret in his prologue, the sense through which the lives of the saints have impact is hearing, especially when one remembers later what he or she has heard. However, since the "memory of profitable narratives" (prol. 2) is not permanent, but subject to forgetting, it is necessary to retell stories of virtuous lives. After mentioning epic and history and registering a low opinion of tragedy and comedy, Theodoret argues that Christian biography should take its place among the literary genres. Theodoret asks rhetorically, "How would it not be absurd if we let be consigned to oblivion men who in a mortal and passible body have displayed impassibility and emulated the bodiless beings [angels]?" (prol. 2). A multiplicity of such stories is necessary because each of the holy people has received a different form of grace (prol. 8).[65] In this sense it is not the classical genres so much as the Bible that the work resembles.[66] The variety in Theodoret's narrative reflects the variety of stories within the Bible, each displaying different gifts and virtues.[67]

While this link between the parenetic mechanism of the *Religious History* and the Bible remains implicit, Theodoret explicitly compares his text to the biblical narratives under another rubric: namely, credibility. Theodoret argues that the truth of his narrative is on a par with the truth of biblical narratives. "Quite obviously, he who will disbelieve what we are about to tell does not believe either in the truth of what took place through Moses, Joshua, Elijah and Elisha, and considers a myth the working of miracles that took place through the sacred Apostles" (prol. 10). Jesus is left off the list, but in this, Theodoret is merely oblique. Theodoret's statement suffices to suggest that doubting the veracity of his accounts is tantamount to a denial of the faith. Moreover, each of these biblical figures was already commonly read as a type of Christ. Of course, Theodoret's claim to biblical authority for his text makes sense through a series of typological relationships. If the saints he tells of are like the biblical heroes, then the text that tells of them is like the biblical texts, a true account of the work of God among his holy people.

This appeal to the truth of sacred history has direct implications for Theodoret's presentation of himself as an author; for subtly he implies not only that his saints imitate Christ, but also that he himself imitates the evangelists. Again, the author does not say so in so many words, but rather veils this issue in the discussion of his own credibility as a narrator. Theodoret assumes—a rhetorical device to be sure—that he will be taken at his word regarding those holy men of whom he has been an eyewitness, but he stresses that he is to be regarded as telling the truth also about those of whom he has learned at second hand when he compares his accounts with the production of the various gospels.

Trustworthy as writers of the Gospel teaching are not only Matthew and John, the great and first Evangelists, the eyewitnesses of the Master's miracles, but also Luke and Mark, whom "the first eyewitnesses and ministers of the Word" [Lk 1:2] instructed accurately in not only what the Lord suffered and did but also what he taught continually. Despite the fact that he had not been an eyewitness, the blessed Luke at the beginning of his work says that his narration concerns facts about which there is full assurance. And we, hearing that he was not an eyewitness of these very narratives but received this teaching from others, pay equal attention to him and Mark as to Matthew and John, for each of the two is trustworthy in his narration because he was taught by those who had seen. For this very reason [τοιγάρτοι][68] we too shall tell of some things as eyewitnesses and of others trusting the narration of eyewitnesses, men who have emulated [ἐζηλωκόσιν] their life. (prol. 11)[69]

The comparison with the evangelists on the matter of trustworthiness even when relying on eyewitnesses assumes a typological connection between what Theodoret is doing and what the evangelists did.

Thus in its teaching virtue, its claim to truth, and the circumstances of its composition, the *Religious History* resembles biblical narrative. Moreover the trustworthiness of Theodoret's eyewitnesses rests on their emulation of those about whom they had spoken; they too pursued the ascetic life. Theodoret has relied on the oral testimony of the ascetic Acacius for stories about Julian Saba (2.22) and Eusebius of Teleda (4.7). He claims the witness of his pious and ascetic mother for tales of Symeon the Elder (6.14).[70] The text of the *Religious History* is the next term in the series of transmission. Theodoret, himself an ascetic bishop, stands as part of the chain of qualified narrators, his own ascetic devotion a guarantor of truth.

Both in body and in literature Theodoret imitated his saints. This interplay of emulation and representation reproduces the relationship that Theodoret attributes to the biblical witnesses and their biblical subjects. As the passage quoted above reveals, Theodoret understood those eyewitnesses of the life of Jesus who served as sources for Luke and Mark to be showing forth Christ in their lives as well as their testimony. In the evangelists, Theodoret finds types for his own enterprise.

That Theodoret also claims an Old Testament model emerges in examining the juxtaposition between the passage about the evangelists just quoted, which occurs at the end of Theodoret's prologue, and the opening of the first life that Theodoret narrates, that of James of Nisibis. Theodoret begins not by delving immediately into James's biography, but by delivering an encomium of Moses. He does so in part to invoke as a muse the same divine Spirit that inspired Moses, the Holy Spirit who, according to Theodoret's Nicene faith, had "spoken through the prophets."[71]

Moses, the divine legislator, who laid bare the bottom of the sea, flooded with water the moistureless desert and worked all the other miracles, wrote down the way of life of the holy men of old, not using the wisdom he had adopted from the Egyptians but receiving the splendor of grace from on high. . . . I too need this assistance [of the rational and divine Spirit] at present, as I try to write down the life of the glorious saints of our own time and the recent past, and seek to set out a rule, as it were, for those who wish to emulate them. (1.1)

This invocation offers further proof that Theodoret saw his composition as one created in the likeness of the Bible. If God so willed, the *Religious History*, like scripture, would be the result of divine inspiration. In this passage, the revelation of virtue in biblical narrative results not from having reliable eyewitnesses, as in the case for the truth of the Gospels, but rather from a gift of the Spirit. Following immediately on the heels of Theodoret's discussion of truth and eyewitnesses, this theology of biblical composition is surely significant. Theodoret allies himself with divine inspiration to guarantee that he conveys a biblical truth, a point further enforced by the typology of the narratives that follow, since by this mechanism Theodoret relates stories that conform to biblical narrative.

But Theodoret's characterization of Moses reveals an even richer association. Theodoret's description of the lawgiver presents him in two roles, first as the holy man who performed miracles at the sea and in the desert, and second as the author of the biblical tales of holy men: that is, as a hagiographer. The figure of Moses, both holy man and hagiographer, links the activities of the saints of the *Religious History* to the activities of its author. Theodoret imitates this second aspect of the biblical type: Moses the author.

Theodoret's act of composition thus participates in the complex typological system laid out within his text. The saints of the *Religious History* resemble Old Testament figures, the apostles, and Christ. The work that tells of these Christlike saints is like the Bible. Theodoret recapitulates the biblical authors: Moses, and by extension the other prophets, and the evangelists, all of whom are emulators of Christ. The technique of typological composition thus allows this accomplished student of scripture to claim a role drawn from the biblical world, to become a self-consciously postbiblical author. By binding himself and his saints to the Bible, Theodoret grants insights into Christian literary creation as spiritual practice.

For Theodoret, however, these themes of modeling extend beyond the realm of the author to become an invitation to his readers. In this endeavor, the metaphors shift from stories heard to images that can be seen. Throughout the work, Theodoret draws connections between narrative portraits—his stories about the saints—and visual portraits or icons.[72] Having received the "impress of all the virtue of [the holy men of old]," Theodoret's saints have made themselves "living images [or animated icons, εἰκόνας . . . ἐμψύχους] and statues of them" (prol. 2, compare 5.6). Like Olympic athletes who are "honored with images [εἰκόσι]" of their physical bodies, Theodoret honors his spiritual athletes (prol. 3). And while he does not "portray their bodily features," he "sketches the forms of invisible souls and displays unseen wars and secret struggles" (prol. 3). Hagiography is thus verbal portraiture through which the virtues of the saints become visible. Here too Theodoret echoes Basil's advice to Gregory of Nazianzus on the use of the Bible, where the "lives of blessed men" lie before the reader "like living images of God's way of life [οἷον εἰκόνες τινὲς ἔμψυχοι τῆς κατὰ Θεὸν πολιτείας] for our imitation of their good deeds."[73]

But Theodoret and the biblical authors are not the only portrait artists in this theological scheme. When Peter the Galatian encourages Theodoret's own mother to abandon wearing jewelry and makeup, Peter refers to God himself as the "sculptor and painter of our nature" (9.6). The human being is, after all, the "image of God" (9.6), and makeup ruins this image. The genitive in "image of God" here works two ways. Theodoret's mother must understand not only that she was created in God's likeness but also that God himself is an icon painter whose self-portrait is borne in each human. Theodoret no doubt understood his portraits of the saints as a mimesis of God's work: The narratives re-presented those fashioned by

God in God's image, and at the same time, Theodoret's work as an author was analogous to God's work, since both Theodoret and God were sorts of painters.

In the brief epilogue to his *Religious History*, Theodoret again draws an analogy with painting; here, however, the parallel is not between painters and hagiographers but between painters and his readers. Theodoret calls his audience to become like holy images, to show forth the saints in their own lives. "Just as painters look at their model when imitating eyes, nose, mouth, cheeks, ears, forehead, the very hairs of the head and beard, and in addition the sitting and standing postures, and the very expression of the eyes, whether genial or forbidding, so it is fitting that each of the readers of this work choose to imitate a particular life and order their own life in accordance with the one they choose" (30.7). Themes of modeling or crafting one's own life thus also draw on well-established theories of representation. The effect of hearing the lives of the saints should be the desire to bring one's own life into conformity with the lives of the saints. While Theodoret derives his metaphor from a still image, his clear intent is to effect the composition of a biography. He calls his reader to have a life story like those of his marvelous ascetics. And since these saints are modeled on biblical types, the reader is ultimately called upon to resemble the biblical stories in his or her life. With this gesture, the bishop invites his audience to participate in his typological world.

In the writing of Theodoret of Cyrrhus, ideas about authorship emerged within the context of the genre's concern to read the world through the lens of biblical narrative. In the process of producing a world intertwined with the world of the Bible, Theodoret produced an author intertwined with biblical models for composition. He thus articulated a conception of authorship always implicit in hagiography and its typological habit. But who did Theodoret and his contemporaries think *these* authors were? Not surprisingly, biblical authors had a hagiography of their own. The following chapter considers the models for authorship inherent in late antique and early Byzantine traditions about biblical authors, particularly the evangelists.

Chapter 3
Biblical Authors: The Evangelists as Saints

In 775, John IV, the non-Chalcedonian patriarch of Alexandria, authored an encomium to celebrate Saint Menas, a third-century martyr whose popular shrine lay across Lake Mareotis (now Maryut).[1] In contrast to Theodoret of Cyrrhus, who in the 440s compared himself to the evangelists somewhat obliquely, John, writing in Coptic, explicitly attached the task of narrating and lauding the saint's life and miracles to the evangelists' task of composing the lives of Jesus:

Well has the holy evangelist Luke said, "Many have begun to write things down but they were not able to reach the end of what they said about Him" [compare Lk 1:1]. And also the holy theologian, John the Evangelist has said, "There are many other things which Jesus did, which, if they were written down one by one, I say that the world would not contain the books that would be written" [Jn 21:25]. This, too, is the case of him that takes upon himself to utter the praises that befit this great champion of Christ, the holy Apa Menas, and the healing favors that God has done through him—his labor will be in vain. For many have taken upon themselves to put forth numerous encomia and martyrdom accounts, wishing to declare the glory of this great warrior of Christ, the holy Apa Menas, the soldier who renounces the soldiership of this world for the enduring soldiership of heaven.[2]

The patriarch invoked the evangelists as his precursors in Christian authorship, identifying with their inability to treat their subject completely. He also specifically claimed their literary methods in his attempt to handle his task.

While the reference to the evangelist John elevates the encomiast's limitations in the face of overabundant material, the invocation of Luke shapes the patriarch's claim to the legitimacy of his text in the face of already extant accounts. Luke's text offers an "orderly account" so that his patron "may know the truth concerning the things of which [he has] been informed" (Lk 1:3–4), a criticism directed at the "many" who had earlier attempted to tell the story of Jesus. Similarly the encomium complains that "the things that have been written about [Menas] are at variance with one another."³ The chaos of varying traditions demands a new act of authorship to sort out the true account. In contrast to previous narratives about Menas, John of Alexandria asserts, "We shall not invent and tell you ficti- tious tales but the things which our holy fathers have set forth for us from the beginning, which we have found lying in the library of the Church of the Patriarchate in Alexandria, written in Greek by the old chroniclers who lived at the time, those who saw with their eyes from the beginning and became ministers of the word [compare Lk 1:3], instructing us about his family and his martyrdom."⁴ Like Luke, who consulted those "who from the beginning were eyewitnesses and minsters of the word (Lk 1:3)," the patriarch styles himself a researcher, combing reliable accounts in the proc- ess of constructing his own. The composition of the encomium on Saint Menas thus produces not only a text claiming the model of the Gospels, but also an author claiming the image of the evangelists.

Early Byzantine hagiographers often invoked biblical authors as typo- logical precedents for their activity of narrating the lives of holy people. In the *Lausiac History* (71), Palladius alludes to Paul's writing about a journey to the third heaven (2 Cor 12:5) to explain his own wandering in the ascetic paradise of the Egyptian desert and subsequent composition. In the *Reli- gious History*, Theodoret of Cyrrhus compared his method of utilizing both his own testimony and eyewitness sources to the compositional techniques of the various evangelists (prol. 11). He also hoped that the same Holy Spirit who inspired Moses to write would inspire him (1.1). The anonymous au- thor of the *History of the Monks of Egypt* recounted a journey taken in 394–95 by seven monks from the monastery on the Mount of Olives in Je- rusalem.⁵ Like Theodoret's later *Religious History*, the *History of the Monks of Egypt* presents the world of the ascetics as a reenactment of the Bible. The author's Egypt is filled with biblical personages, men who "looked like Abraham and had a beard like Aaron's."⁶ The author's writing recapitulates the work of Moses. In the work's prologue, the author states that "[God] brought us to Egypt and showed us great and wonderful things [καὶ δείξας ἡμῖν μεγάλα καὶ θαυμαστά] which are worthy of memory and writing" (prol. 1). The first line of the epilogue recapitulates, "We also saw many other monks and fathers throughout Egypt who have performed many mir- acles and signs [πολλὰς δυνάμεις καὶ σημεῖα ἐπιτελοῦντας]" (epilogue 1).⁷ The language reverses the narrative of the Exodus (bringing the monks into Egypt rather than out of it), but the author, like Moses in Exodus, chronicles a journey through Egypt, once again a land of "signs and marvels." Jacob of Serug saw Ephrem the Syrian's composition of hymns for women to sing as a reenactment of Moses' composition of Exodus 15 for his sister Miriam and the daughters of Israel to sing at the edge of the Red Sea.[8] In short, Paul, Moses, and the evangelists provided models for Christian authorship.

Focusing primarily on the evangelists, this chapter considers some of the available models for saintly authorship in the late antique East. As Theodoret of Cyrrhus and John of Alexandria illustrate, biblical models played an important role in establishing patterns for authorial self-representation and self-stylization. Hagiographers' allusions to their biblical precursors confirm how the biblical holy writers functioned as icons for veneration and emulation. Instead of perceiving a disjunction between the composition of the Bible and their own production, many early Byzantine hagiographers understood themselves as perpetuating patterns and techniques of biblical composition. Their rhetorical efforts strove to connect their writing and their texts typologically to previous models, regarding biblical authors as holy men.

Examination of verbal and then of visual portraits of the evangelists produced in late antiquity and early Byzantium reveals conceptions of the evangelists that emerged simultaneously with broader models of saintliness. Indeed, the holy author was a variety of holy man, conforming to patterns for the display of human holiness. Moreover, to a great extent, later authors invented themselves and their biblical precursors at the same time. Or, to be more precise, they invented their ideal model of themselves twice, rhetorically creating the evangelists and rhetorically striving to emulate them as much as possible.

Biblical Writers as Holy Men in Literary Sources

In the general absence of extrabiblical vitae of biblical authors (with the exception of Gregory of Nyssa's *Life of Moses* and various *Acts of John*), early Christian ideas about biblical writers must be culled from a variety of other sources.[9] The biblical texts themselves provided some narrative details about the figures "Matthew," "Mark," "Luke," and "John," especially once the texts were connected to people named in them. This information was further supplemented by legend and speculation. The invention of identities—not merely names, but also personalities and biographical anecdotes—for each of the gospel writers was well under way by the latter half of the second century. When, late in the third century, the ecclesiastical historian Eusebius compiled information about the lives of the evangelists, he could turn to earlier traditions recorded by Papias of Hierapolis, Irenaeus of Lyons, and Clement of Alexandria. The familiar snippets of information were already well established. Matthew had been a tax collector and wrote in Hebrew. Mark followed Peter, acting as his interpreter before setting out for Alexandria. Luke, a physician, traveled with Paul. John, a fisherman, beloved of Jesus, wrote at Ephesus.[10] Scholarship on the composition of the texts of the New Testament has rightly discredited these traditions of the early church. However, these legends yield valuable insight into common perceptions of biblical authors in late antiquity. These traditions influenced conceptions of holy authorship by providing operative models.

Narrative portraits of the evangelists appear in patristic commentaries on biblical books, particularly in the sermons of John Chrysostom. Introductions composed to accompany the gospels, canon lists, and tables provided information intended to guarantee or to illustrate the authority of scripture. Combined with the traditions recounted in Eusebius, such sources flesh out traditions of the evangelists as they were available to the fourth century and beyond, allowing a reconstruction of the hagiography of the evangelists as writers in the absence of hagiographical texts.

The notable exception to the lack of hagiographical accounts of the evangelists in late antiquity is the figure of John, whose "life" received a number of treatments between the second and the seventh centuries.[11] The surviving parts of the late second- or early third-century *Acts of John* show no interest in John as writer.[12] Likely composed in Gnostic circles and treasured by Encratite and Manichean Christians, the work closely resembles other early apocryphal acts, such as those of Paul, Andrew, and Thomas.[13] With novelistic adventures, combat with pagan shrines, miraculous accounts of healing and the raising of the dead, preaching, and conversions, this *Acts of John* provides John with legends worthy of an apostle. Like the other early apocryphal acts, the work also conveys a strongly ascetic message. The impact of the text on emerging wider Christian tradition is hard to gauge. Unattested by orthodox writers before the fourth century, the work was condemned by Eusebius and Epiphanius and again in the eighth century at the Second Council of Nicaea. Fragments of the text found their way into numerous menologia, the middle and later Byzantine collections of readings for saints' days.[14] Nevertheless, the *Acts of John* demonstrates an interest from the earliest period to understand the evangelist in continuity with late second-century conceptions of early Christian heroes rather than as a different sort of holy man.

Of greater interest to the present inquiry is the *Acts of John by Pro-choros*, composed between the fifth and the seventh centuries, possibly near Antioch.[15] Its dramatic portrait of the scene of writing illustrates the tremendous promise that might lie in the emulation of the evangelists. Assigned by lots after the crucifixion to evangelize Asia Minor, John made his way to Ephesus accompanied by a certain Prochoros, the supposed author of these *Acts*. The work is action-packed with episodes typical of ancient novels and their Christian derivatives. After accounts of shipwreck, arrest, accusations of sorcery, and the separation and reunification of the principal characters, John and Prochoros find employment in an Ephesian bathhouse. John proceeds to cast out demons, raise the dead, heal the lame, and convert the followers of Artemis. Exiled to Patmos by imperial order, John and Prochoros then have similar adventures on an entirely fictionalized (and apparently quite large) version of that island. After a number of years of successful healing, preaching, and converting on Patmos, John was released from exile by another emperor.

Pseudo-Prochoros then narrates how, before returning to Ephesus, John wrote the Gospel.[16] John led Prochoros out to a small mountain called Katastasis (meaning "restoration" or "repose" but also "establishment" or "order"), where he fasted for three days, "praying and beseeching God to give the good gospel to the brethren." "Prochoros" continues, "On the third day John spoke, saying 'Prochoros, my child, go down to the city and get ink and sheets of papyrus [χάρτας] and bring them to me here, but do not tell the brethren where we are." After Prochoros returned with the ink and papyrus, John instructed him to go back to the city and return to the mountain after two more days. When Prochoros returned this second time, he found John standing and praying. John told Prochoros to place the ink and papyrus on his right. "Then there came much lightening and thunder so as to shake the mountain. And I [Prochoros] fell on my face on the ground and lay as dead." After John revived him, he told Prochoros to sit on the ground at his right. "He prayed once again, and after the prayer he said to me, 'Prochoros, my child, write on the paper everything you hear from my mouth.' And opening his mouth, John, standing and praying up toward heaven, said, 'In the beginning was the Word.'" For two days and six hours, John stood and dictated while Prochoros sat and wrote. After the composition was complete, John told Prochoros to procure good parchment and to transcribe the Gospel carefully. After Prochoros read the Gos-

pel in public, copies were sent "to all the churches." The parchment copy
was kept on Patmos, while the original papyrus was sent to Ephesus.[17]

The account's detailing of dictation and stenography on inexpensive
papyrus, the production of a clean master copy, and the subsequent publication and distribution through additional copying in this account reflect
standard ancient practices for textual production.[18] This representation of
the scene of gospel composition is singular among those dating from before
the Arab conquest in depicting an evangelist composing with the assistance
of an amanuensis rather than engaging in his own pencraft.[19] Visual portraits of John and Prochoros begin to appear in gospel manuscripts only
from the tenth century. Before that, John is depicted working alone.[20]

That the Prochoros *Acts* assigns the composition of the Gospel of John
to the island of Patmos militates against associating the text with the bur-
geoning cult of John at Ephesus. In fact, the overwhelming majority of
Christian traditions before the tenth century assign the composition of the
Gospel of John to the city of Ephesus, after which point Pseudo-Prochoros's
version of events begins to take increasing precedence.[21] Most significant,
the *Acts of John by Prochoros* does not discuss, and probably does not recog-
nize the authority of, the Apocalypse of John, which declares itself to have
been written on Patmos (Rev 1:9–10). The canonical status of the Apocalypse among Greek Christians was not established until quite late. The Cappadocian fathers did not accept the text as scripture, and the first Greek
commentaries (ascribed to Andrew of Caesarea and Oikoumenios) did not
appear until the late sixth or early seventh century. The Apocalypse of John
received its first (if ambiguous) declaration of canonical authority in the
Greek world only at the Quinisext Council in 692. That the author of the
Prochoros *Acts* knew that John had written something on Patmos likely encouraged his deviation from the more standard account of the provenance
of the Gospel of John.[22]

While the Prochoros *Acts* provides a conventional representation of
the mechanics of textual production through dictation, stenography, tran-
scription, and publication, the drama leading up to John's dictation and the
act of composition itself set this text and John's performance of authorship
apart from the ordinary, establishing both as holy. The account is a pastiche
of prophetic tropes, although none of the biblical typology is made explicit.
The withdrawal to the mountain in the wilderness recalls Moses both at
Horeb (Ex 3:1) and at Sinai (Ex 19). The fasting recalls Moses' preparation
before receiving the ten commandments at Sinai (Deut 9:9), as do the interval of three days and the thunder and lightening (Ex 20:16). (Later Byzan-

tine reworkings of the Prochoros tradition made the connection to Moses explicit. The gospel prologue known as the *Memorial of Saint John* says, "He stands as straight as Samuel [see the LXX at 1 Sam 17:16 and 28:14], and he stretches forth both his hands like Moses. . . . Horrible thunderings and fearful things and lightening continuously rend the sky, exactly as at the time of Moses.")[23] The relationship between John and Prochoros in the *Acts* recalls the relationship between the prophet Jeremiah and his scribe Baruch (Jer 36:4), who took dictation and inscribed the words of Jeremiah upon a scroll. And the whole process, from withdrawal to the mountain to the completion of the composition, takes place within a week, like the creation itself, an event also framed by the words, "In the beginning." Thus the *Acts of John by Prochoros* reads the act of gospel composition as a mimesis of earlier biblical composition, offering a prophetic model for Christian authorship in addition to a conventional account of copying and dissemination. The result is the confirmation of John as a holy man that secures the composition of the Gospel among his saintly acts.

Even before the composition of such scenes of revelation, attention turned to the evangelists' preparations and credentials for authorship. Textual evidence demonstrates a consistent interest in understanding the authors of the gospels as holy men who cultivated virtue through ascetic practice. A homily on Philemon by John Chrysostom suggests that Christians hungered for the details about the first followers of Jesus. "If only it were possible to avail ourselves of someone who could give us the history of the Apostles. I am talking not about what they wrote and discussed, but rather their other ways of life: what they ate, and when they ate, when they sat and where they walked, what they did every day, in which districts they were, into which houses they entered, and where they lodged—to relate everything with minute exactness, so full of benefit is all that was done by them."[24] This curiosity, which for Chrysostom justified the place of an apparently trivial letter about a runaway slave in the canon of scripture, ran on the assumption that the life and habits of Jesus' first followers would offer beneficial examples for emulation.

The everyday life of a holy apostle could offer a model for Christian life. Thus traditions about the evangelists reveal concern with their everyday habits, their pious practice, and their cultivation and demonstration of virtue. In one of ninety sermons on the Gospel of Matthew delivered in Antioch in 390, John Chrysostom called upon his congregants to "look continually upon the image of Virtue" (47.3) instantiated in the evangelist upon whose text he comments.[25]

Consider, if you will, this very evangelist.[26] Although we do not have his whole life in writing, nevertheless even from a few facts it is possible to see his image shining forth. As for his being humble and contrite, hear him, according to his own Gospel, calling himself a tax collector. As for his almsgiving, see him stripping off everything and following Jesus. That he was pious is evident from his teachings. His intelligence it is easy to see from the Gospel that he composed, and also his charity—for he cared for the whole world [οἰκουμένη]. [One sees] the manifestation of his good works from the throne upon which he is destined to sit [compare Lk 22:30]; and his courage, from his departing "with joy from the presence of the council [Acts 5:41]." Therefore let us be eager for this virtue and most of all his humility and almsgiving, without which one cannot be saved.[27]

Chrysostom emphasized Matthew's identity as a former tax collector, since this indicated both "the grace of the Spirit, and [his] virtue," rendering Matthew a model of the repentant sinner.[28] But the portrait is in fact a catalog of Christian virtues: humility, charity, and piety. Within this context, writing itself constitutes virtuous action with profound theological resonance. Matthew writes from his great love of humanity, sharing in God's own concern.

In late antique Christian thinking, charisma resulted from ascetic bodily practices, and the evangelists were no exception. By the fourth century, John was widely regarded to have been a lifelong virgin. Jerome claimed, glossing the Logos hymn that opens John's Gospel, "The virgin writer expounded mysteries which the married [namely Peter] could not."[29] A Latin prologue to the Gospel of John, composed in Priscillianist circles at the end of the fourth century, invoked John's virginity to enhance the authority of the text by attesting to the author's ascetic endurance.[30] Eusebius repeated a story he found in the works of Clement in which John shared with a penitent "the ordeal of continuous fasting."[31] Epiphanius of Salamis cited John together with his brother James as one of the eunuchs for the kingdom of heaven that Jesus spoke of in Matthew 19:2, supplying that they "neither cut off their members with their own hands nor married."[32] Elsewhere Epiphanius claimed that John (together with his brother James and James the brother of the Lord) did not cut his hair, refrained from bathing, avoided meat, and owned only one garment.[33] A Greek prologue to the Gospel of Luke, in circulation by the middle of the fourth century, claims Luke's ascetic devotion through celibacy. "He served the Lord without distraction [ἀπερισπάστως], unmarried, childless, and fell asleep at the age of 84 in Boeotia, full of the Holy Spirit."[34] The word *aperispastōs*, "without distraction" echoes Paul's explanation in 1 Corinthians 7:35 of how celibacy makes possible undivided devotion to the Lord. The prologue thus presents Luke as a faithful disciple of Paul's teachings as well as his fellow traveler. Matthew was an exemplar of strict food asceticism: as Clement of Alexandria asserted, "The apostle Matthew ate seeds, nuts, and vegetables, but no meat."[35] And according to a text now known as the *Acts of John at Rome* (composed sometime between the fourth and the sixth centuries), John impressed the soldiers who were transporting him from Ephesus to Rome when he did not eat for an entire week. When the week was over, he spread a linen napkin in front of himself and ate only a single date. This miraculous feat rivals, or perhaps imitates, the habits of the monks of the Egyptian desert.[36] Even the *Acts of John by Prochoros,* a work generally lacking in ascetic tendencies and knowing nothing of John's virginity, portrays John as praying and fasting on a mountain for three days before sending Prochoros to obtain paper and ink to write the Gospel.[37]

The connection between food asceticism and the production of holy text echoed treatments of Moses, whose receipt of the law and subsequent writing depended, according to Deuteronomy 9:9, on his 40-day abstinence from bread and water. In a section of his *Longer Rules,* dedicated to the question of "whether continence is necessary for one who would lead the religious life," Basil of Caesarea offered the example of Moses, who "through long perseverance in fasting and prayer received the law and heard the words of God."[38] John of Damascus in the 740s, in the preface to his magisterial theological treatise *The Fount of Knowledge,* figures himself (albeit humbly) like the monastic Moses, "who withdrew from all sight of human things and abandoned the turbulent sea of life" before engaging in theological reflection.[39] The drive to recreate biblical writers in the image of Christian monks was typical. Thus not only did Christian readers of scripture interpret the Bible through the lens of asceticism, using the text to justify an emerging emphasis on ascetic praxis within Christian life, but these readers also reread the biblical writers as practitioners of this asceticism.[40]

Eusebius's *Ecclesiastical History* offers a curious accretion to the figure of Mark, speculating that this evangelist was the founder of the Therapeutics, a first-century ascetic community that lived on the shore of Lake Mareotis.[41] The resemblance of these first-century Jewish ascetics to the Christian ascetic study groups of Eusebius's own day perhaps convinced him that these Jews described by Philo must in fact have been early Christians. Eusebius writes:

Mark is said to have been the first man to set out for Egypt and preach there the gospel which he had himself written down, and the first to establish churches in

Alexandria. So large was the body of believers, men and women alike, built there at the first attempt, with an extremely severe rule of life, that Philo decided that he must record in writing their activities, gatherings, meals, and everything else about their way of living. (2.16)

Whereupon follows a summary of Philo's *On the Contemplative Life.* For Eusebius, Mark, as bishop of Alexandria (2.24), became the founder of this ascetic group devoted to study of the scriptures. Jerome made the connection between Mark and the Therapeutics even more explicit. In *The Lives of Illustrious Men,* Jerome (presumably dependent on Eusebius) writes, "So, taking the gospel which he himself composed, Mark went to Egypt and first preaching the Christ at Alexandria he formed a church so admirable in doctrine and continence of living that he constrained all followers of Christ to his example."[42] Jerome even claimed that Philo wrote of these ascetics "under the learned Mark." For Jerome, writing in the midst of the rapid rise of monasticism, Mark became the founder of a monastery with no private property or social division, dedicated to prayer and the chanting of psalms, a life devoted to doctrine and asceticism (11), the likes of which Jerome and his contemporaries desired to imitate (11). Although the main significance of the association of Mark with Alexandria no doubt lay in establishing an early pedigree for that patriarchate and in accruing greater apostolic authority to the second gospel (generally regarded in antiquity as the weakest), the connection to Philo's Therapeutics linked Mark to an imagined foundation of Egyptian monasticism. Mark thus exemplified the model of a monastic writer, a man in Jerome's own image. Indeed, early Christian writers constructed ascetic identities for the biblical authors that then served as icons upon which they might model their own identities as ascetic authors.

Thus the evangelists became exemplars of ascetic virtues. For Origen, Christ converted his followers to self-control.[43] Matthew had been a tax collector and "undoubtedly his image was like the devil, but when he comes to the image of God, our Lord and Savior, and follows that image he is transformed to the likeness of the image of God."[44] The calling of Matthew—"Follow me" (Mt 9:9)—became for Chrysostom an object lesson in obedience, because Matthew immediately rose and followed Jesus.[45] Chrysostom cites Luke's benevolence in producing his gospel for the sake of a single man, Theophilus (Lk 1:3).[46] But among the virtues practiced by the evangelists, their modesty and humility received the most consistent attention.

The modesty of the disciple "whom Jesus loved" (Jn 13:23) most interested his golden-mouthed namesake. In one of his *Homilies on John,* Chrysostom urged this audience, "Let us imitate the evangelist, and see what it was that caused so great a love."[47] Perhaps it was John's obedience: at Jesus' command, John abandoned his father, his boat, and his net. But in this he was like the other fishermen, his own brother James and Peter and Andrew. This virtue would not have been sufficient in itself. "About the righteous deeds, for which he was beloved, [John] remained modestly silent." Chrysostom speculated that John's righteousness derived from his gentleness and meekness, the reason he rarely spoke openly.[48] Jesus loved John because of his modesty: indeed, John concealed his identity and presence both at the Last Supper and at the foot of the cross, speaking only of a beloved disciple! When explicating the Last Supper, Chrysostom compares the evangelist's refusal to name himself in this own text—"Notice also his lack of boasting!"—with Paul's oblique self-reference in 2 Corinthians 12:2—"I know a man who fourteen years ago was caught up to the third heaven."[49] When his exegesis reaches the passage on the crucifixion, the preacher remarks, "Again, John conceals himself in modesty!"[50] Nor does Chrysostom consider such humility unique to John; in the first of his *Homilies on the Acts of the Apostles* (1.3), he cites Luke's modesty for calling his own work a mere "treatise" rather than a "gospel." Furthermore Chrysostom regarded anonymous authorship as the biblical norm, observing, "Moses having written five books, has nowhere put his own name to them, neither have they who after him put together the history of events after him, no nor yet has Matthew, nor John, nor Mark, nor Luke."[51] Indeed the fact that Paul announces his identity at the beginning of his letters must be explained by epistolary conventions. On the whole, the Bible presented examples of authorial modesty.

As further evidence of this lack of authorial self-assertion, tradition depicted the evangelists as rather reluctant writers. Eusebius (*Ecclesiastical History* 3.24) explains that of the immediate followers of Jesus, only Matthew and John left memoirs, "and there is a firm tradition that they took to writing of necessity." About the composition of Mark, Eusebius relates that those who heard Peter preach were not satisfied with a single hearing of the divine message and thus "resorted to appeals of every kind to induce Mark . . . to leave them in writing a summary of the instruction they had received by word of mouth." Eusebius continues, "nor did they let Mark go before they had persuaded him."[52] This yielding to the demand of the crowd in the production of text outlines a proper motivation for composition. Chrysostom stresses that Matthew and Mark composed their gospels not from "boldness of speech" but rather in response to the requests and entreaty of their own disciples.[53] Their acts of literary composition exhibited the virtue of obedience, not the vice of arrogance. Epiphanius of Salamis ascribed similar virtues to John, whom the Holy Spirit compelled to expound his Gospel out of piety and humility, although he did not wish to write.[54]

The fragmentary annotated list of New Testament writings known as the Muratorian Canon provides another account of how John came to write a gospel. The Latin text, once thought to derive from the late second century, but now generally dated to the fourth century, probably depends on the canon list in Eusebius's *Ecclesiastical History* and may have first been compiled in Greek in Syria or Palestine around 375.[55] The fragment relates that when John's "co-disciples and bishops" encouraged him to compose a gospel, rather than dive immediately into such a project, John invited his fellow disciples to fast with him for three days in order to receive revelation. "Whatever is revealed to each, let us narrate it to one another." John's move characterizes a modest attempt to avoid authority over the composition of the text and may also endorse a pattern of seeking consensus among church leaders. Ironically, the apostle Andrew had a revelation that night that John should write the Gospel in his own name and that the others should certify (*recognos*; possibly "review") it. Despite John's modesty, the Holy Spirit had elected him to author the text.

An unrelated account in the *Syriac History of John,* whose earliest manuscript survives from the sixth century, emphasizes John's reluctance while attempting to account for the vast difference between John's gospel and the synoptics.[56] The Holy Spirit moved first Matthew, then Mark and Luke to write their gospels. Then together they wrote a letter to John (at Paul's instigation), bidding him to write as well. "But the holy man did not wish to write," worried that his significantly different account might sow dissension in the churches. Finally Peter and Paul journeyed to Ephesus to see John in person. They spent five days attempting to persuade him to write. On Sunday night, "at the time when our Lord arose from the grave," the Spirit descended and the whole place was in a flame. "And John took paper and wrote his gospel in one hour and gave it to Paul and to Peter." Just as the preparation to compose the gospel through fasting emphasizes both the connection between gospel composition and prophecy and the necessity of proper ascetic preparation before assembling a holy text, the gospeler's hesitation provided yet another model for subsequent imitation.

Another persistent theme in the lore about the evangelists emphasized their humble origins and the relationship of these origins to the humble quality of their language. John Chrysostom marveled that "tax collectors, fishermen, and tent-makers" became guides to God's commonwealth.[57] Eusebius (*Ecclesiastical History* 3.24) remarked that Christ's apostles "had completely purified their lives and cultivated every spiritual virtue, but their speech was unskilled [γλῶτταν ἰδιωτεύοντες]." They were also inspired: "The divine wonder-working power bestowed on them by the Savior filled them with confidence; and having neither the ability nor the desire to present the teachings of the Master with rhetorical subtlety or literary skill, they relied only on demonstrating the divine Spirit working with them and the miraculous power of Christ fully operative in them."[58] Of these apostles, only Matthew and John wrote gospels, and, Eusebius adds, "there is a firm tradition that they took to writing of necessity." Chrysostom reminds his audience that John came from a poor village, the son of an impoverished fisherman who fished on a tiny lake: "Nothing is poorer, shabbier, or more ignorant than fishermen."[59] Nor was this a secret, for Luke himself testified that the apostles were unskilled (*idiōtai*) and unlettered (*agrammatoi*).[60] Chrysostom stresses that John was neither rhetorician, sophist, nor philosopher—evidence that he "has the Lord of all speaking within him."[61] The gifted preacher praises the plainer language of the evangelist who teaches clear doctrines in humble speech: "For we do not find resounding sentences or pompous diction, nor excessive and useless ordering and arrangement of words and phrases."[62] This phrase is nearly an indictment of Chrysostom's failure to measure up. The ornate elaboration of the apostles' simplicity may reach its height in a Pentecost hymn of the sixth-century poet Romanos the Melodist:

Brothers, let us sing the praise of the tongues of the disciples because, not with
    elegant words,
but with divine power they caught everyone in their nets,
because they took up his Cross like a rod,
because they used words again as lines and fished the world,
because they had the Word as a sharp hook,
because the flesh of the Master of all things became for them
a bait, not hunting to bring death,
but drawing out to life those who honor and glorify
    the All-Holy Spirit.[63]

Such poetic musings on the fishers of men and their ignorant speech nevertheless betrays a Christian valuation of linguistic simplicity. In contrast to the syntactical complexity and rhetorical flourish of Chrysostom or Romanos, other writers would strive for a sparer idiom. When hagiographers claimed, as they often did, that they too were unlettered and unskilled, they were invoking for themselves the model of the apostles, molding themselves in the images of the evangelists.

The interest in the humility of the evangelists often participated in a larger and more theologically significant discourse about the inspiration of scripture. The Greek prologue to Luke describes him as "impelled by the Holy Spirit" to write his gospel.[64] Chrysostom remarks about John, "It is said that he was the last to come to writing, God [some manuscripts have "Christ"] having moved and roused him to do this."[65] Inspiration figures as an overwhelming force pushing the evangelists to write. One might think that a higher theology of biblical composition would have supplanted human agency in the production of scripture. Yet as one historical theologian has observed, "While emphasizing the divine action of inspiration and even comparing the divine author to a musician who sounds his instrument and the prophetic state to a state of ecstasy, Christian writers do not fail to acknowledge the active role of the human authors of Scripture."[66] Patristic writers' engagement in a sort of biographical criticism demonstrates that the human authors mattered. The early church subscribed neither to a modern fundamentalist nor, for that matter, to a Quranic theory of divine composition through dictation.[67] When the early second-century author of 1 Timothy 3:16 claimed that "All scripture is inspired by God and profitable for teaching, for reproof, for correction, and for training in righteousness," he referred only to the Old Testament. But the claim that God had inspired holy writ was soon applied to the entirety of the emerging Christian canon. Even while Irenaeus stressed that the earliest Christian proclamation was handed down "by the will of God" in scriptures, and that the Holy Spirit had descended upon the apostles to invest them with power from on high, he explained that "each individually possessed the gospel of God." He was interested in the particularities of the various authors, not merely in the source of their knowledge. "Matthew also published a written Gospel for the Hebrews in their own language. . . . Mark, who had been Peter's disciple and interpreter, handed down his preaching in writing to us. Similarly, Luke recorded in a book the gospel preached by Paul, whose companion he had been. Afterwards, John, the disciple of the Lord who had leaned on his breast, himself published the gospel while he was living at Ephesus in Asia."[68] Irenaeus recognized that the human authors of various biblical texts brought their observations and experiences to their writing.

Perhaps the most influential discussion of the divine inspiration of scripture lay in the fourth book of Origen's *On First Principles,* composed in the 220s.[69] Origen's convictions regarding the "divinity of the Scriptures," had less to do with a theory of biblical composition and much to do with a theory of biblical interpretation. The proof of the inspiration of scripture lay in its reading, in the fulfillment of Old Testament prophecy in the person of Christ and in the "divine enthusiasm" experienced by the reader encountering the text. This enthusiasm would convince the reader "that what we believe to be God's words are not human writings."[70] Yet in the treatise Origen also refers to the "Law of Moses," "John's Gospel," and "Paul, in his First Letter to the Corinthians." Most theories of inspiration, however, were far less mechanistic. In the writings of the sixth-century mystic known as Dionysius the Areopagite, the speakers or writers of biblical text are almost always their human authors. He does not apply his conception of inspiration uniquely to scripture, but rather conceives a more general inspiration, a grace cooperating in many gifts of the Spirit.[71] Such a theory of inspiration allows a writer such as Theodoret to invoke the Spirit for his own authorship.

By the fourth century at the latest, liturgical practice itself emphasized the human authorship of the biblical texts, introducing each lection with the formula "A reading from the Gospel according to Matthew."[72] For Chrysostom, such repeated patterns demanded that the congregation attend to the contingent aspects of each scriptural passage, composed by a given author at a particular time under specific circumstances. Chrysostom berated his congregation for not listening when the reader began "From the Prophecy of Isaiah"[73] even though the deacon had cried out, "Let us attend." "Every week these things are read to you twice or even three times. And when the reader goes up, he says first whose book it is, perhaps by a certain prophet, or apostle or evangelist, and he says what he says so that it may be more intelligible to you, and that you may know not only the contents, but also the occasion of the writings, and who said them."[74] Thus within the liturgy, the only context in which the vast majority of Christians encountered the inspired writings, the word of the Lord maintained its connection to human authorities.

Even the highest theology of biblical composition did not obliterate interest in the human author who produced the text. Chrysostom's second homily on John illustrates a tension inherent in the recognition of a dual agency involved in the production of the gospels. Chrysostom declares:

If John were about to converse with us, and to say to us in his own words, it would be necessary to speak of his people, his country, his education. But since it is not he, but God through him, that speaks to humanity, it seems to me to be superfluous and distracting to inquire into these matters. And yet even thus it is not superfluous, but rather very necessary. For when you have learned who he was, and where he was from, and who his parents were, and what he was like, and when you hear his voice and his complete wisdom, then you shall know well that these [teachings] are not his, but of the divine power moving his soul.[75]

Precisely because it is God who converses with the church in John's gospel, Chrysostom proceeds to investigate the evangelist's life and conduct. That the Holy Spirit transformed a poor, uneducated fisherman into an instrument of God's revelation renders John a model for emulation. The goal of every pious Christian was to become an instrument of the Holy Spirit in the world.

Thus the biographical details not only illustrated the divine power that propelled the writer's activity but, indeed, indicated the possibilities for all the faithful. Far from simply asserting that God wrote the Bible, theories of inspiration assumed a model of human cooperation in the divine will. Since God was the source of all goodness, the virtuous action of biblical composition signaled human participation in the work of God. Biblical composition exhibited only one species of human participation in the work of the divine. Late antique Christians' interest in the evangelists did not set these authors apart from other virtuous agents, but rather placed them high on a continuum of human cooperation in divine endeavors. Divine inspiration did not erase scripture's human authors, but rather elevated them. Writers such as Chrysostom and Theodoret placed the evangelists among the saints.

Visual Portraits of the Evangelists as Saints

Visual representations of the evangelists augment the conception of the biblical authors as holy men. Like the written sources we have been considering, some of the pictorial images dating from before the iconoclasm of the eighth and ninth centuries also stressed that while God spoke to the church through the scriptures, the texts themselves did not represent unmediated communication from another realm. As has been widely observed, Byzantine artists portrayed the evangelists in a variety of poses, including standing and seated types.[76] The portraits of evangelists seated and engaged in writing in particular conveyed a theology of the composition of scripture that

Figure 1. A sixth-century pilgrim's flask discovered at Antioch depicts on opposite sides a standing and a seated evangelist. Similar ampullae discovered near Ephesus connect this object with the cult of Saint John the Evangelist at Ephesus. Terracotta. 6.9 × 4.8 cm; thickness 1.9 cm. Photo: Department of Art & Archeology, Princeton University.

stressed the possibility of divine cooperation in human activities. Representations of the evangelists engaging in the act of authorship reveal that the holy writings were not alienated from the labor that produced them, but rather resulted from specific persons' labor.

The connection of the evangelist as saint to his act of literary composition emerges in the iconography of the cult of Saint John at Ephesus, where a pilgrimage center flourished from the late fourth century.[77] Clay ampullae obtained at the shrine survive impressed on both sides with images of the evangelist. Mass-produced in the sixth or seventh century to hold and transport holy oil or a miracle-working dust called "manna" from the saint's martyrium, these pilgrims' souvenirs are pierced with holes on either side of the neck to allow the pilgrim to suspend the portable blessing from a string.[78] On one side of an example found at Antioch, now in the Princeton University Art Museum, a bearded John, who is not identified by an inscription, stands facing the viewer clutching a codex incised with a cross and flanked by cypress trees (Fig. 1).[79] The frontal posture is typical of the representation of miracle-working saints on pilgrims' ampullae and identifies the contents as the *eulogia,* or "blessing," of St. John. This icon of the evangelist renders him available to the viewer as the object of veneration, the recipient of prayer, and the dispenser of succor. It is common for the iconography of saints to include elements from their legends, in part to assist in their identification by viewers, such as that of Thecla flanked by the lions who rescued her, or Menas by the camels who refused to budge while transporting his corpse thus determining the site of his martyrium.[80] In this frontal image, the codex decorated with the cross is John's attribute, conveying sufficient information to identify him as the author of the gospel book he holds.

The image on the reverse supplements the gospeler's identity by shifting his pose. On the opposite side of the Princeton flask, the writer sits in a chair holding a stylus, bending forward as he writes in a book that rests on his knees. The truncated fluted column at the right recalls the architectural frames of other, mostly later, evangelist portraits, but seems to serve here as an inkstand or lampstand.[81] If the frontal image conveys the saint's holiness and power, using the book to identify him, the seated figure draws attention to the saint in action, engaged in the activity of composing the Gospel. The pairing of the two distinct iconographic types, the standing evangelist and the seated evangelist, serves to emphasize that the saint's holiness derives from his work at literary composition.[82] This interest in the author at work shaped pilgrims' itineraries while they visited Ephesus. In addition to the earlier martyrium of St. John (rebuilt by Justinian in 535/536) marking the spot where John had died, pilgrims from the sixth century on also visited an oratory at the top of the hill identified with the inscription "the Holy House of the Apostle" where, it was said, John had written the Gospel.[83] This second shrine linked the composition of the Gospel of John to a human personage writing in a specific time and location.[84]

A more elaborate theology of the composition of the gospels is embedded in the mosaics of the Church of San Vitale in Ravenna, which include the earliest surviving monumental portraits of the evangelists.[85] Completed in 547 under the patronage of Justinian and Theodora, the cycle of images covers the entire sanctuary. The four evangelists appear in the presbytery, high on the north and south walls of the vaulted space that leads up to and includes the high altar (Fig. 2 [north wall]; Fig. 3 [south wall]). In contrast to the small flasks that focus attention exclusively on John and his cult, the compositional arrangement of images at San Vitale affords a complex view of the gospels and the acts of writing that produced them within a liturgical context. Here the entire iconographic program serves as a stage set for the

Figure 2. The mosaics on the north wall of the sanctuary of the Church of San Vitale in Ravenna, 547. The upper register depicts John (*left*) and Luke (*right*), with their gospels, seated beneath their mystical symbols, the eagle and the ox. The lunette in the lower register depicts the hospitality of Abraham and Sarah to the three angelic visitors and the sacrifice of Isaac. In the middle register, Jeremiah reads from his scroll (*left*), while Moses (*right*) receives the law on Mount Sinai as a scroll from the hand of God. Scala/Art Resource, N.Y.

Figure 3. The mosaics of the south wall of the sanctuary of the Church of San Vitale in Ravenna, 547. The upper register depicts Matthew (*left*) and Mark (*right*), seated beneath their mystical symbols, the angel and the lion. The lunette in the lower register depicts the offerings of Abel and Melchizedek. In the middle register Moses (*left*) unties his sandal on Mount Horeb before the burning bush; the prophet Isaiah appears at *right*. Scala/Art Resource, N.Y.

liturgy performed, defining the ritual practice and interpreting it. Earlier scholarship has demonstrated the centrality of eucharistic and sacrificial themes in the church's decoration.[86] The large lunettes beneath the evangelists depict scenes of Old Testament sacrifice, typological precedents for the eucharistic offering. The north wall shows the hospitality of Abraham and Sarah and the sacrifice of Isaac. The south wall illustrates the offerings of Abel and Melchizedek. But the divine liturgy joins two services. Before the gifts—the bread and wine—can be offered, consecrated, transformed into the body and blood of Christ, and distributed to the faithful, God must be offered the Liturgy of the Word. This service of reading includes not only the texts containing the Old Testament narratives depicted on these walls, but, of course, the gospels as well. The treatment of the gospel writers and their placement within the church program illuminates another sixth-century understanding of the evangelists and their labors. The composition of the Gospels figures as yet another type of sacrifice.

Each of the evangelists sits in a rocky landscape, a well-watered wilderness with shrubs, wading birds, and even fish. Matthew (Fig. 4) and Mark (Fig. 5) flank the arcades on the south wall; Luke (Fig. 6) and John (Fig. 7) on the north. The visionary landscape, the desert of abundance, suggests the "Paradise of the Fathers," both the heavenly home that the *Apocalypse of Paul* assigns to the Old Testament worthies and the earthly milieu of much early Christian ascetic endeavor.[87] Each evangelist holds a codex containing his composition. Three are labeled in Latin—"Secundum Marcam" and so forth. Matthew inscribes his book in an alien script, reminding the viewer that the former tax collector composed in Hebrew. The images include various items that call attention to the act of writing. John, Mark, and Matthew sit before desks bearing quills, knives, and inkpots with their lids, the tools of pencraft necessary for the work of inscribing word on parchment. Such elements assert that the gospel texts resulted from human production.

In contrast to the others, who are obviously in the process of composition, Luke handles his text as a precious object, only through a handkerchief or the folds of his robe. And yet there is evidence of his labor as well. A *scrinium*, a latchable basket containing scrolls, lies both at Matthew's feet and across the vault beside the figure of Luke. These dossiers of texts preserved in an earlier bookmaking format attest another aspect of the evangelists' act of literary composition, namely research. In their gospel texts, both Matthew and Luke quote extensively from Old Testament scripture, and the baskets in these images portray the writing of these Gospels as the result of a careful searching of the Jewish scriptures to present Jesus as the fulfillment of Hebrew prophecy. Indeed in the compositions below the images of the

Figure 4. The evangelist Matthew from the Church of San Vitale. Matthew inscribes his gospel; he is seated before a writing desk containing a quill, a knife, and an inkpot. At his feet is a basket filled with scrolls. He makes eye contact with the angel (*upper right*), both his symbol and his inspiration. Scala/Art Resource, N.Y.

Figure 5. The evangelist Mark from the Church of San Vitale. His symbol, the lion, is above him. Writing implements are on his desk. Scala/Art Resource, N.Y.

Figure 6. The evangelist Luke from the Church of San Vitale, with a basket of scrolls. His symbol, the ox, is above him. Scala/Art Resource, N.Y.

Figure 7. The evangelist John from the Church of San Vitale. His symbol, the eagle, is above him. Writing implements are on his desk. Scala/Art Resource, N.Y.

evangelists, Isaiah (beneath Mark, Fig. 3) and Jeremiah (beneath John, Fig. 2) hold similar scrolls in their hands as they prophesy the incarnation and the passion, key events in the gospel narratives. This lower register assists in conveying the theological relationship between the writing of the Old Testament and the New. In addition to Isaiah and Jeremiah, the images beneath Matthew and Luke depict scenes from the life of Moses. This third prophet and author stands before the burning bush, below Matthew, and at Sinai, beneath Luke. The placement of the seated evangelists above these earlier writers depicts the new dispensation literally superseding the old. Matthew's and Luke's baskets filled with scrolls represent the intellectual effort involved in the production of sacred text articulated in the intertextual relationship between the evangelists' writing and the literature of the prophets.

When during the service a deacon intones, "The reading from the Holy Gospel according to Matthew," the evangelist's image reinforces the connection of text to author. The image of Matthew, however, also indicates the dual source of the evangelist's output (Fig. 4).[88] At the same time that the mosaic presents the composition of the Gospel as a human endeavor, the image calls attention to the divine inspiration motivating Matthew's effort. Surmounting each of the evangelists are their mystical symbols: John with the eagle, Mark with the lion, Luke with the ox. Above Matthew flies "one with the form of a man," a winged angel. Irenaeus first associated these symbols, based on the "four living creatures" of Ezekiel 1 and 10 and Revelation 4 that guard the throne of God in heaven, with the Gospels in the second century.[89] These pairings would eventually make their way into gospel prefaces and catechetical instruction.[90] Irenaeus defined the zoomorphic beasts as images of the Gospels themselves, not of their authors, although in time they came to represent some elision of the distinction between the two. Their earliest monumental representations survive in the late fifth-century apse mosaic of the church of Hosios David in Thessalonica[91] and the church of Santa Pudenziana at Rome (perhaps as early as 390). While the combination of these iconographies would later become canonical, especially in the West, San Vitale represents the earliest extant composition combining portraits of the seated evangelists and images of the zoomorphic beasts. The mystical symbols supplement the image of the writers by emphasizing the divinity of their literary output.

In three instances, the associated animal stands on a rocky plateau above the evangelist's head, the topography defining a separate zone between the human author and divine creature. But the angel above Matthew (Fig. 4) breaks the craggy border that separates the evangelists from their symbols in the other mosaics. He represents not only the Gospel of Matthew but, in a second function, also serves to represent the divine inspiration that gave rise to Matthew's book. The angel's open hand reaches down from the sky and touches the holy writer's halo. Their eyes meet. This arrangement of writer and heavenly being recalls depictions of pagan poets inspired by their muses and suggests that the origins of the evangelist portraits lie in Hellenistic portraits of authors.[92] Within the context of the Church of San Vitale and the emerging theology of the evangelists, however, this gesture of inspiration configures Matthew's labor and the text he produced as media for divine communication with the Christian church.

Hands signifying divine communication appear twice in the register immediately below the evangelists in scenes from the life of Moses. Beneath Matthew on the south wall (Fig. 3), as Moses unties his sandal in the presence of God at the burning bush, a hand gestures from the clouds in the upper-left-hand corner of the scene, at which the prophet looks directly. Below this, Moses tends his flock on Mount Horeb, a symbol of the congregation, while holding a scroll. On the opposite wall (Fig. 2), beneath the figure of Luke, Moses receives the Law at Sinai. God's communication with Israel figures as a heavenly hand presenting Moses with a scroll. As Moses receives divine revelation, the children of Israel wait at the foot of Mount Sinai to receive the sacred instruction. These two hands communicating with Moses at Sinai and the burning bush render a context for the angel's gesture toward the writer Matthew. Like Moses, Matthew—and by extension, the other evangelists as well—conveys the voice and teachings of God to humanity. Moses' flock at Horeb and his Israelites gathered at Sinai figure as types for the faithful congregation of the church itself: they stand in the sanctuary beneath the images of the evangelists, waiting to receive instruction. The mosaics construct the communion of viewers in the act of receiving the Word.

The mosaics of San Vitale depict a theology of scripture in which the word of God is mediated through the work of human authors. In their acts of writing, the evangelists, like the prophets before them, convey divine teachings to the people of God through literary activity. Their research and composition serve as conduits for revelation. These themes of textual mediation downward from the realm of God to the realm of humanity complement the themes of sacrifice through which humanity renders its offerings upward to God. The evangelists sit in a medial zone, above Old Testament themes of both revelation and sacrifice. Thus the evangelists and their gospels emerge as nodes in the interaction between divinity and humanity. High above the evangelists, at the top of the vault, four angels offer up the lamb of God, the divine sacrifice revealed. Performed under the canopy of this vault, the liturgy points ever toward the eternal sacrifice, always already offered before the throne of God the Father. Through their composition,

Figure 8. The mosaic of Justinian with members of his court and palace guards (*left*) and clergy (*right*), on the north wall of the apse of the Church of San Vitale in Ravenna. In this depiction of the Little Entrance of the Divine Liturgy, Justinian processes with a golden paten containing bread to be offered in the eucharist. The bishop Maximianus carries a jewel-studded cross, while the deacons who precede him carry a censer and a jeweled gospel book. Scala/Art Resource, N.Y.

the evangelists not only participate in God's revelation, they also participate in acts of sacrifice. Their writing becomes an offering, like the sacrifices of Abraham, Abel, and Melchizedek below and of Christ above.

On the side of the apse, behind and to the north of the altar, one of San Vitale's most famous mosaics depicts the procession of gifts toward the altar (Fig. 8). Justinian himself carries a gold paten with bread for the eucharistic sacrifice. The archbishop and clergy accompany him on his left, carrying other items necessary for the conduct of the service: a cross (a symbol of Christ's offering), a censer (for burning incense, itself a symbol of the offering of prayers), and a jeweled gospel book. The scene represents the offertory of the First (or Little) Entrance, the liturgical procession with the gospel book before it is read to the congregation.[93] The book composed by the evangelists figures as part of the offering. As producers of offerings for the liturgy and the church, the evangelists of San Vitale write in a mode of sacrifice. The evangelist portraits capture their subjects in the act of producing and presenting the logos.

A final detail of the Ravenna portraits returns attention to the practice of virtue in the performance of biblical authorship. Each of the evangelists is depicted by himself. The three portraits that include a writing desk and implements assert that the authors engaged in their own pencraft, inscribing their works themselves. Luke's *scrinium* reinforces the idea that he too worked alone. However, the most common method of literary composition in antiquity was by dictation. Inscription itself was regarded as menial.[94] Persons of high standing employed servants or slaves as scribes. Other writers depended on patrons to supply the financial resources necessary to compose. This applied to Christians as well as classical pagans. Paul regularly employed an amanuensis when composing his letters.[95] When Paul does otherwise, he calls attention to the fact that he is writing in his own hand.[96] According to Eusebius, while Origen worked on his biblical commentaries, he dictated to "more than seven shorthand-writers, who relieved each other at fixed times" and employed as many copyists "as well as girls trained for calligraphy," paid for by his friend Ambrose.[97] With the rise of asceticism, Christians would invert this hierarchy. According the Gerontius, in the early fifth century, Melania the Younger not only "read the Old and New Testaments three or four times a year, she copied them herself and furnished copies to the saints by her own hands."[98] In the fourth century, monasteries were already becoming centers for the copying, collation, preservation, and dissemination of texts.[99] In the ascetic life, performing the act of inscribing the words on parchment or papyrus cultivated and expressed humility.

When the evangelists take up their own pens to compose their gospels, they engage in a valued self-abasement. Of all our late antique and early Byzantine evidence, only the *Acts of John by Prochoros* depicts an evangelist employing a secretary. And although the image of John dictating to Prochoros became increasingly common in Middle Byzantine gospel miniatures, for the early Byzantine period, the Prochoros *Acts* is the exception that proves the rule.[100] Art historians have long noted that Byzantine portraits of standing evangelists derived from statues of classical orators and portraits of seated evangelists followed models for the representation of poets and philosophers. Images of the evangelists both seated *and writing*, however, lack classical precedents.[101] As one scholar has observed, "Classical authors are never represented as scribes; authors meditated, composed, and dictated" but did not engage in their own pencraft.[102] Although images of the evangelists seated and writing proliferated from the late ninth century, the scarcity of pre-iconoclastic images demands some caution in interpretation.[103] Nevertheless, the

Ravenna portraits together with the image of John on the Princeton flask suggest that late antique Christians saw biblical writers differently from the authors of the classical canon. Engaged in the humble task of inscribing their own books, the evangelists participated in a Christian ideal. Authorship, even in the case of the most exalted evangelists, could take place within the context of the Christian valuation of humility. Like the incarnate Christ himself, the inscribing evangelists took on the form of a slave.[104] Indeed the very humility of these authors was part of what made them holy.

*   *   *

The examples of biblical authors marked the formation of Christian attitudes about authorship, even as the gospelers' identities were formed, circularly, by emerging Christian values and emerging conceptions of Christian literary composition. Christian authors such as Theodoret and John of Alexandria modeled themselves on these saintly authors, regarding them as precursors in the task of conveying the lives of holy persons. Moreover, in submitting to the authority of these ideal models, writers attached their writing to traditions of literary composition already regarded as holy. Indeed one's practice as a writer was holy to the extent that it was legible as cohering to a model regarded as holy. Like the saints they described, hagiographers also followed their exemplars. The habits of Christian authorship performed a mimesis of emerging patterns for the holy author, the writer as saint. While Moses, Paul, and especially the evangelists provided identities to emulate, the virtues ascribed to them became critical elements of authorial performance. Plain speech, humility, obedience, and especially ascetic achievement were prerequisites to becoming a conduit for divine communication with humanity.

Both verbal and visual portraits of the evangelists presented models for inspired authorship. By calling attention to human participation in the generation of holy writings, both media asserted biblical models for authorship. Human authors had mediated the divine word, conveying divine doctrine and ethical instruction; subsequent Christian writers recounted tales of the virtuous life and presented them to the church for edification and emulation: hence the interest on the part of hagiographers, in prose and in hymns, to invoke their predecessors. The acknowledgment of a canon of writings and the generation of accounts about its creators provided authors a tradition with which to align themselves. Biblical identities scripted the performance of authorship in the early Christian East. Chapter 5 will address more attempts to present hagiographical authorship within these patterns. But first we turn to another aspect of Christian literary composition in late antiquity and early Byzantium in which the author figures himself as the saint's devotee.

Chapter 4

Hagiography as Devotion: Writing in the Cult of the Saints

This chapter and the following two address three different but interrelated modes of authorial performance in early Greek hagiography. Having established the pervasive power of biblical models for literary composition, I turn to attempts to integrate writing with common types of late antique ritual practice. Correlating authorship with religious practice yielded a variety of writing identities. Exploring in turn analogies between hagiography and devotion, asceticism, and liturgy, these chapters chart the conception of the author as devotee, as monk, and as priest.

From the fourth through the seventh centuries, Christian authors promoted cults of saints by illustrating the ascetic labors and miraculous powers of holy men and women. Although much evidence for these cults derives from literary saints' lives and miracle accounts, genres that emerged simultaneously with the cults, scholars have overlooked the role of the hagiographer as devotee. Literary composition belongs within the economy of devotion. The four texts considered in this chapter proffer models for the integration of writing into patterns of devotion both to living saints and to posthumous shrines. For the sake of illustrating the cultic function of the production of these texts, the presentation does not proceed chronologically, nor does it group their discussion by subgenre, separating biography from miracle collection. Instead, the discussion takes up progressively more complex levels of interaction between author and cult in order to articulate a range of ways in which authorship could participate in the veneration of the saints.

The first work to be treated, the *Miracles of Artemios*, is at once the latest and the most straightforward. This seventh-century collection from a Constantinopolitan shrine reinforces the centrality of narrative to the cult of the saint and situates its author as a participant in the acts of testimonial publicizing the shrine, doing in writing what others do orally. A colorful text, the *Miracles of Artemios* provides access to the early Byzantine cult shrine, a world of miraculous healing, desperate supplicants, and the dissemination of stories. The next two works, Theodoret of Cyrrhus's *Religious History* (the subject of Chapter 2) and Cyril of Scythopolis's *Lives of Euthymius and Sabas,* represent self-consciously literary attempts to integrate text and cult. Dating respectively from the 440s and 550s, these texts conceive composing saints' lives as spiritual practice. These talented early Byzantine hagiographers figured the act of writing not only as promoting popular devotional forms but also as participating in them. While other writers also exhibit this convergence of promotion and participation, Theodoret and Cyril do so particularly well. Both authors present the composition of saints' lives as religious activity by employing metaphors drawn from other aspects of piety such as asceticism, pilgrimage, the receiving of miracles, and the offering of votives. In producing narrative, Theodoret and Cyril configure themselves within the cults of the saints, recasting writing not just as a record of devotion, but as devotion itself.

The fourth and longest discussion takes up the now-anonymous *Life and Miracles of Thecla,* also a work of the 440s, associated with the shrine at Seleucia in Isauria dedicated to the first-century protomartyr and apostle. In addition to offering aid and protection to Christian women, especially monastics and travelers, Thecla had earned a reputation as a patron of letters. For this reason, the fifth-century author of her *Life and Miracles* strove for a particularly tight integration of literary composition and cult. Like the others examined here, this text has as a goal the glorification and promotion of the saint. It also employs writing to intertwine the author's own reputation with that of saint. The text thus establishes not only Thecla, but also the author. The authorial persona as constructed in text, while less appealing than the personae offered by Theodoret and Cyril, offers an opportunity to consider larger questions about writing and authority within the context of cult.

Cult and Narrative in the *Miracles of Artemios*

According to his own testimony, recounted in the *Miracles of Artemios,* a certain Stephen, deacon of the Church of Hagia Sophia in Constantinople, suffered a terrible hernia shortly after the death of the emperor Heraclius in 641.[1] By his own reckoning, the rupture into his scrotum was caused either by lifting a heavy weight or by "shouting acclamations," lifting his voice in praise of God during the liturgy. Within the text, Stephen explains that his shame was so great that he carefully plotted the times when he could bathe alone so that no one would see his diseased testicles. After visits to doctors gave him no definitive cure, the deacon, still greatly ashamed, would slip secretly into the shrine of the holy martyr Artemios in the Church of St. John the Baptist in the Oxeia district of Constantinople (the hill on which the Süleymaniye Mosque now sits) to slather the oil of blessing on his genitals. Very late one night, he passed the church and discovered the doors still open. He explains, "This was the doing of the martyr in his desire to pity me. I stretched out face down on the holy coffin, straddling it and thus contrived to rub the corner of the same holy tomb on the spot where I was ailing" (21). Stephen reports that having mounted the tomb he entreated the saint, "Holy Artemios, by God Who had given you the gift [of cures], no doctor on earth will ever touch me again. So if it pleases you, cure me. But if not to your [everlasting] shame I will live thus without a cure." Some days after his nocturnal frottage with Artemios's coffin, the deacon was once again bathing at the crack of dawn. "Entering the hot chamber, I noticed that I still had the injury. But upon exiting, I had no injury." In a moment, the holy Artemios had removed the deacon's shame—and staved off the threat of his own.

This miraculous healing resulted not only in physical health but also in narrative. As testimonial to the efficacy of the shrine, the deacon told aloud what he had once kept secret: "Recognizing the act of kindness on the part of God and the martyr . . . in thanksgiving I glorified them as is proper and I do now glorify them proclaiming their deeds of greatness throughout my whole life" (21). Glorifying God and saint includes narrating their works as an act of pious gratitude. Stephen's continual retelling publicizes the shrine by disseminating news of its power. Moreover, his storytelling employs narration as a form of piety: that is, as doxology, the ascription of praise and glory.

Among the various healing saints, Artemios was a specialist. His clientele was predominantly male, among them clerics, tradesmen, craftsmen, and stevedores from the docks of the Golden Horn downhill from the church. Women occasionally visited the shrine seeking cures for their infant sons. Artemios's particular talents lay in the treatment of testicular hernias and other diseases of male genitalia.[2] The historical Artemios had been dux of Egypt in the 350s responsible for destroying images and votives in the Temple of Serapis in Alexandria. According to the legend that was well known at the shrine, while traveling in Syria he protested Julian's persecution of Christians in the emperor's presence. His brutal execution included being crushed by quarry stones until his eyes popped out and his privates (κρύφιοι) became unstrung.[3] At one point, the text's narrator exclaims, "Lord, Who among the gods is like unto You? Who is glorified among the saints like unto You Who are admirable in glory for working miracles? Precisely because Your servant suffered in his [privates], he seems through those parts to be distinguishing himself by cures."[4] After his death, Artemios's body was placed in a lead casket and sent to Constantinople, where it became the focus of a major cult in the early seventh century.

Upon first entering the Church of John the Baptist, suppliants would prepare a votive lamp with oil and wax, which they could keep burning throughout their petition. In the crypt, below the main altar of the church, additional oil lamps hung above Artemios's coffin.[5] Those seeking cures drank the oil from these lamps or, more often, collected the residue to use as a salve, smearing it on their afflicted body parts.[6] This wax salve was also distributed to sufferers during the Saturday-night vigil (33). Those seeking cures slept, sometimes for only a few days, but often for months or even years (5, 35), in the north aisle of the church. To incubating patients, Artemios appeared in dreams, often in disguise. Although he usually appeared as an aristocrat or official, on occasion he came in the form of a butcher (25) or blacksmith (26). He also appeared as himself, presumably looking just as he was represented in an image above the stairs leading up from his crypt.[7] With remarkable access to his patients' bodies, Artemios often healed with some violence, either real or dreamed, lancing pus from a diseased scrotum or shoving distended guts back up into the abdominal cavity.

If Stephen's ailment and its cure typify events associated with Artemios's shrine, so does his response. Throughout the text, the cured begin immediately to proclaim the glory of God. One resident of Constantinople, originally from Amastris, came to the shrine with a boil on his testicles. After three increasingly painful days at the church, the priests of the church gave him a wax salve concocted from oil of the lamps of John the Baptist and of Artemios, which he applied to his scrotum. "This took place at the fourth hour, but at noon the servant of God stood near him and, pretending to touch him, made an incision with a scalpel and all the holy house was filled with a stench" (3). Those who smelled the malodorous effluvium and witnessed the miracle then brought warm water and sponges to clean the sore. Thus after a comparatively brief visit, the text relates, "The Amastrian was restored to health and went away glorifying God Who had cured him through the holy martyr" (3).

The proclamation of God's glory in response to healing features as a persistent trope in the narration.[8] A certain 20-year-old named George, a bureaucratic official (χαρτουλάριος) of the imperial fisc, developed seven sores on the tip of his penis that doctors could not cure. (The doctors ruled out surgery on the grounds that the sores would return the following "ulcer season.") In a dream, Artemios demanded that the young man lift his robes. Upon seeing the diseased penis, the saint exclaimed, "There are seven sores. Big deal! Just consider what an insignificant disease the doctors puzzled over!" Artemios then prescribed applying a rag moistened with vinegar and salt. The sores vanished after two days of treatment. The text then remarks, "The man who had experienced this still survives proclaiming and recounting the glory of the martyr and many who have succumbed to the same disease, not only men but women also, he enjoined to employ the same treatment" (20). Thus the proclaiming of the martyr's glory involves telling the story of the disease and its cure.

Frequently, as in the cases of deacon Stephen's and young George's tale, the text glosses the phrase "glorifying God" to include recounting the story of illness and relief, as in the following examples. The infant son of a woman who managed a bathhouse connected to a hospital developed a hernia that caused him to bawl constantly. Because her duties made her unable to leave the baths, she prepared a votive lamp to Saint Artemios in the bathhouse. After Artemios appeared to her as a patron and praised her trust in God, her son was healed. Then, "taking a candle and oil and whatever she had at hand for an offering, she went [to the church] and gave glory [ἔδωκεν δόξαν] to God Who exalted the martyr, and related the incredible miracle to all" (11). Her storytelling accompanies her votive oblation, an element of its spoken content. She brings candle, oil, and narrative to the shrine. The liturgical character of this offering in gratitude is made clearer at the end of a story about a monk in a monastery on the nearby island of Plateia (one of the Princes' Islands in the Sea of Marmara). After realizing that Artemios had visited the island to perform a cure, the monks "sounded the board [calling the monks to prayer] and performed the evening doxology [ἐπιλύχνιον δοξολογίαν] celebrating and thanking the Savior of all men Christ for the miracles which He performed through the martyr Artemios and continues to perform beyond belief" (39). Glory and thanks are offered as prayer.

In other cases, the wording of the text posits an even more intimate connection between "glorifying" and telling of the miracle, suggesting that "glorifying" itself consists of narration. A 45-year-old man with tremen-

dous pain cried out in his sleep when Artemios, appearing in a dream in
the guise of a physician, squeezed his testicles "so that the man screamed
out in pain in his sleep 'Kyrie eleison! Lord have mercy!'" awakening others
with his shouting. The text explains, "Awakening and touching himself,
since he was still in the throes of pain, he found himself healthy; and glorifying God he narrated [δοξάσας τὸν θεὸν διηγήσατο] to them the vision
and the miracle of the martyr" (2). The shrine, a place of particularly intimate contact between the human and the divine, seems to have been an
especially noisy place, filled both with the cries of the afflicted and the recounting of miracles. The connection between miraculous healing and glorifying narration pervades the text precisely because narration was integral
to the ritual of receiving healing.[9]

Narrative responses to cures facilitated the shrine's reputation. Many
left the shrine "extolling the saint's miracles and thanking God and the miraculous power of the holy martyr" (37). Reports of successful encounters
spread far and wide. When a healed merchant from the island of Chios
sailed home, "he proclaimed God's greatness to all those there" (5). And
George, a shipowner from Rhodes who had suffered from testicular hernias
for many years, "returned to his own country . . . rejoicing and feeling ec-
static and relating to everyone the marvels which Christ does through his
beloved martyr Artemios" (35). Infectious enthusiasm for the curative
power of God spread though retelling. "Hearing about the miracles of St.
Artemios" prompted the desire to visit the church in search of a cure (33).

Within the collection of the *Miracles of Artemios*, the shrine produces
both healing and stories. What then to make of the text itself, which recapitulates the storytelling, and the act of composition through which the accounts of healing were enshrined? The author (or authors) knew the cult
and its traditions well and must have been associated in some way with the
Church of St. John in the Oxeia.[10] The text was probably read aloud, in
whole or in part, during the Saturday-night vigil.[11] Moreover, the *Miracles*,
as they have come down to the present, reflect two stages of development.
The original core of the text dates from between 658 and 668. The brief
introduction and the first sixteen (or perhaps seventeen) miracles appear to
constitute a compositional unit that is unified by their simple structure and
general brevity.[12] Most of these episodes of healing maintain a simple structure: the patient suffers and seeks a cure, he performs certain activities to
receive relief, and Artemios cures him.[13] The patient then glorifies God and
the saint.

At the same time that these stories publicize the saint's deeds, the generic conformity of these episodes reflects the imposition of order upon oral traditions. The author has standardized the pattern of narrative. Reading the *Miracles* in the quasiliturgical context of the Saturday vigil employed the written text to provide a model for subsequent oral testimony. Those attending the service seeking a cure would gain confidence in the shrine's power to heal, learn the various methods by which they might be healed of their afflictions, and absorb the proper form for glorifying God through recounting their cure when it happened.

As the oral traditions about the shrine's successes grew, so did the text. Scholars disagree about whether the remaining twenty-nine miracles were composed by the original author or were added a couple of generations later, sometime after the Quinisext Council of 692. In addition to many more, generally longer and more complex, miracle stories, this expansion interspersed the healing narratives with antiheretical (32) and anti-Jewish (32 and 38) diatribes as well as a sermonette about the Jordan River (34).[14] These generic deviations almost certainly derive from instructional talks given to visitors at the shrine and underscore the text's connection to the Church of St. John's oral culture.[15]

The text of the *Miracles of Artemios* mimics the oral testimonies out of which it evolved in publicizing and celebrating the shrine's efficacy. Storytelling was very much a part of the dynamics of the cult, and to that extent, the text's composition participates in prescribed activities. At times, the text explicitly represents its close connection to the oral through the use of first-person narration, supplying testimonial through quotation, as in the case of the story of Stephen the deacon.[16] In other places, the textual narration cues appropriate responses to these stories, prompting listeners to extol God's glory not for their own healing, but upon hearing a tale of someone else's healing, as in the story of a boastful youth named Plato. He bet his friends that he could lift a large stone, thus rupturing his intestines. After instructing the young man in a dream to cease making wagers, Artemios trod on his stomach. The text explains, "Thanking God and the martyr for this turn of events, he departed for home rejoicing. Whoever had learned of his misfortune, seeing him restored to health, glorified God Who had sped His mercy upon him" (7). As in the case of the monks of Plateia, narratives of Artemios's miracles compel an additional pious performance by prompting doxology on the part of all hearers.

The cult of Artemios, "who is universally celebrated in song and hymn and who is recognized to the ends of the earth through Christ our God Who empowers him" (34), depended on narration and included narration as an element of the cult. Like the oral testimonies, the text's composition flows directly from the healing, an integral part of the cult, becoming ritualized and liturgical. The text itself participates explicitly in the task of glorifying God. In the brief introductory paragraph the author explains his goal:

For in our desire to write an account [διήγησιν ἀναγράψαι βουλόμενοι] of the many miracles of the holy martyr (miracles most astonishing!), of which we have the knowledge of some by sight itself and others by hearsay, we are quite naturally at a loss to recall all of them since they are boundless in their multitude. As many as we were able to collect which were done in our own generation, these we aim to proclaim to those who love Christ, in order that the wondrous Deity might be glorified [ἵνα δοξασθῇ] through them among His saints.[17]

In his goal (σκοπός) of glorifying God through collecting and recounting narrative, the author of this paragraph situates the production of text in continuity with the oral narratives so integral to the reputation and practice of the cult.[18] Thus, writing figures as a devotional activity through which the stories of healing are preserved and disseminated and at the same time participates in the cult through the performance of piety, the glorification of God through recounting the miracles of Saint Artemios.

The *Miracles of Artemios* is a relatively simple work with few literary ambitions beyond reporting the stories already in circulation at a popular Constantinopolitan shrine. Nevertheless, it both encodes and deploys a theology of narration. Assumptions about the relationship between cult and narrative require writing to be a cultic activity because of the relationship between writing and orality. The remainder of this chapter considers much more self-consciously writerly texts in which the possibilities for integrating literary composition and piety reflect both the writer's sophistication and the repertoire of his own ritual practice.

Narration for Blessing in the *Religious History* of Theodoret of Cyrrhus

Chapter 2 explored Theodoret of Cyrrhus's use of typology, through which he situated his saints and himself in a world of close correspondence to the biblical narrative. Here, attention turns to other aspects of the *Religious History*—its narrative forms and its implicit autobiography—to consider Theodoret's composition of saints' lives as a search for blessing. The monastic bishop composed the *Religious History* in 440.[19] Its twenty-eight narratives celebrate ascetics active in northwest Syria since the early fourth century.[20] Theodoret illustrates in terms both heroic and biblical the practice of men such as Julian Saba, who dwelled for a time in a cave eating barley bread only once a week (*Religious History* 2.2–4); Eusebius of Teleda, who immured himself in a windowless cell and spent forty years bedecked with an iron belt and collar (4.3–6); and James of Cyrrhestica, who lived exposed to the elements (20.3). Perhaps most spectacular is the well-known account of Symeon the Stylite, who stood atop progressively taller pillars on a hill about two days' journey from Antioch.[21] By their disciplines, these solitaries dedicated themselves to lives of constant prayer and received miraculous powers.[22] The *Religious History* also yields a vivid portrait of the veneration of these holy men and women by local clergy and laity, who depended on Christ's athletes for blessings (εὐλογίαι) in the form of healings, exorcisms, and advice.[23]

The vivid accounts of Theodoret's amazing subjects, however, should not eclipse Theodoret's own presence in the *Religious History* both as the narrator and as a character.[24] Theodoret intertwines his own life tightly with the lives of his ascetics. Long before he composed the *Religious History*, Theodoret actively involved himself in the cult of the saints he would eventually narrate. As a child, Theodoret made weekly visits at his mother's insistence to reap blessing from Peter the Galatian (9.4).[25] This monk once divided his flaxen girdle and tied one half around the young Theodoret to cure an illness (9.15). As an adolescent, Theodoret and his mother made a pilgrimage to receive Aphrahat's blessing (8.15).[26] A few years later, Theodoret and a group of friends spent a week on retreat with the monastic community at Teleda (*Religious History* 4.10–12).[27] While a young lector in the church, Theodoret questioned Zeno (once a student of Basil of Caesarea) about "philosophy"; that is, the monastic life (12.4). And as bishop of Cyrrhus, Theodoret made frequent journeys to local monks, celebrating the eucharist for them (20.4), encouraging them to relax their regimen in times of illness (21.8), and bringing them food (21.11). Theodoret weaves himself into the fabric of his narrative: his *Religious History* is at times as much autobiography as biography. This self-presentation as a pious Christian devoted to the holy men provides a context for his work as an author.

Theodoret's reflections on the act of hagiographical composition befit the great learning and intellectual achievement displayed throughout his literary corpus. His archaizing Greek prose style and command of a remarkable range of classical texts, quoted in such works as his lengthy Christian apologetic treatise *A Cure for Pagan Maladies*, evidence the finest school-

rooms of Antioch, a renowned center of rhetorical learning and biblical exegesis. Theodoret channeled much of his training into the interpretation of
scripture, his primary scholarly and pastoral activity.[28] Biblical allusion in-
fuses the *Religious History*, allowing Theodoret to find models for fourth-
and fifth-century ascetics in the lives of biblical figures such as Moses, Elijah, John the Baptist, and Jesus himself. A biblical self-consciousness also
underlies Theodoret's introspection about what it meant to write saints'
lives within a Christian theological context. As we have seen, Theodoret is
well aware of his own biblical precursors, namely the evangelists and Old
Testament prophets, including Moses, whom he invokes for "writing down
the way of life of the holy men of old" (*Religious History* 1.1).

Biblical typology not only renders Theodoret an authorial model, it
also affords a framework for him to understand himself as a recipient of
divine grace. Theodoret narrates the miraculous circumstances of his own
birth, a story that highlights the intercessory power of holy men by alluding
to the story of Elisha and the Shunammite woman (2 Kgs 4:16–17). His parents had remained childless for many years, and Theodoret's father bade
various monks to pray for him to have children. The celebrated barley-eater
Macedonius, whom Theodoret's mother regularly fed, promised that this
would happen. After three years without success, the holy man suggested
that Theodoret's mother dedicate the child to God, whereupon she conceived (13.16–17). The reenactment of biblical stories of a barren woman's
conception interprets his mother's experience in light of Sarah, Hannah,
and Elizabeth and provides Theodoret with a biblical gloss on his whole
life.[29] Some years after Theodoret's miraculous birth, Macedonius re-
minded him of his mother's vow and charged him to "perform, speak, and
desire those things alone that serve God"; in narrating this, Theodoret reflects humbly that he does not "display this exhortation" in his deeds and
remains dependent on the holy man's prayers (13.18). Yet writing, because
it honors the saints, becomes a strategy for Theodoret to realize some of his
biblical promise.

Integrating writing and devotion to the saints to a degree not found in
earlier Christian hagiography, Theodoret situates his writing within the
larger spiritual economy of the cult of the saints in which the faithful rever-
ently visited ascetics and cared for them, hoping to receive blessings for
physical and spiritual well-being. The *Religious History* demonstrates the
wide range of the early Byzantine concept of the *eulogia*, whose primary
sense of "blessing" or "benediction" came by extension to signify any conduit for transferring the saints' power to others.[30] Theodoret, his mother,

and many other devotees described throughout the text visit the holy men in order to reap blessing in the form of a prayer said on their behalf. But the concept of *eulogia* became concrete in physical matter such as the bread of the eucharist, holy water or oil, and more mundane objects that a holy man had consecrated or blessed.[31] For years after Peter the Galatian cured the young Theodoret with a girdle, this charm was shared among family and friends, until it was stolen (9.15). More than souvenirs, these *eulogiai* were pieces of "portable sanctity,"[32] as effective as verbal blessing itself in transferring benefit for the faithful. A saint did not even need to be actively involved in blessing the substance; the blessing might transfer passively by his mere contact or proximity. Such was the curative power of the mountain where James of Cyrrhestica had once stood. Theodoret writes, "So great is the blessing [that the mountain] is confidently believed to have received that the soil on it has been quite exhausted by those coming from all sides to carry if off for their benefit" (21.4). By a similar logic, the populace sought blessings from saints' garments and eventually their corpses.[33]

Within the stories of the *Religious History*, the narrator is a full participant in the practice of venerating the holy men for the sake of a blessing (εὐλογία) that the text seeks to describe and promote.[34] Narrating his own service to the saints, the bishop presents himself—not just his saints—to his congregants and more distant readers as an example for emulation, a devotee of the holy men and women of his region. Moreover, Theodoret integrates writing itself into his pious performance.

One finds Theodoret's devotion not just in the autobiographical elements, but also in his articulation of his literary efforts and in his use of narrative techniques. The *Religious History* embeds a rhetoric of piety in its very structure. In the final sentences of each short narrative, Theodoret advances the understanding that he writes in the hope of receiving blessing. His account of the otherwise obscure Zebinas, Polychronius, and Asclepius ends thus: "So concluding at this point my account of these men, and asking in return for the gift of their blessing [εὐλογία], I shall proceed to another narrative" (25.2). Closing his treatment of the ascetic Zeno, Theodoret writes, "I myself, after begging him as well to intercede for me with God, shall turn to another narration" (12.7). Each of Theodoret's chapters concludes similarly, as he steps back from the events in the past to speak in the present and request the saints' help. In the narratives' final lines, he calls variously on the saints' "blessing" (εὐλογία) eleven times, "intercession" (πρεσβεία) five times, "assistance" (ἐπικουρία) three times, once for the saints' "remembrance" (μνήμη) before God, and once for "divine help [ῥοπή] through [the saint's] prayer [προσευχή]."[35] In this manner Theodoret expresses a connection between his act of narration and the veneration of the saints.

To be sure, these remarks signaling breaks between narratives are formulaic, and modern critics might overlook them as mere conventions or tropes, or dismiss them as rhetorical flourish. But repetitious use of liturgical vocabulary prompts their consideration as canonical gestures, like reciting the doxology at the end of a psalm or making the sign of the cross. For through these concluding forms, Theodoret links his writing to the more commonly understood acts of devotion described throughout the narratives and in which Theodoret himself participated: pilgrimage, offering of food to the saints, and quests for healing and intercession, for blessing. Thus Theodoret reveals the cultic purpose of his writing when he closes one account explaining that he has not separated Abraham, the ascetic, from the company of the saints "in my desire to receive blessing from this source as well" (17.11). This notion of transferring of sanctity from the saint to the devotee through *eulogiai*—both in words and in objects—links the devotional activities described in the text to the activity of composing the text. Theodoret writes seeking blessings.

The analogy between writing and devotion appears perhaps most vividly in the chapter on Maron, whose tomb had become a popular healing shrine. Here Theodoret remarks, "We ourselves reap his blessing even at a distance; for sufficient for us instead of his tomb is his memory" (16.4). That is, recalling the saint through narrative is the equivalent of pilgrimage, the principal activity in which Theodoret engages as a character within the text. Moreover, telling of the saints renders service to the saints while conferring both blessing and holiness upon the author. Concluding an account of hermits in the vicinity of the village of Imma (some twenty-five miles east of Antioch), he writes, "May I too share in assistance from these men, having sanctified my tongue by recalling them" (7.4). Theodoret is sanctified through narration, and so comes to resemble his saints.

The act of narration itself yields liturgical benefits. Completing his discussion of Macedonius, he writes, "We, on bringing this narrative to an end, have reaped the fragrance [εὐωδία] that comes from narrating it."[36] This association of narrative and fragrance, conflating the sense of hearing with the sense of smell, recalls the psalmist's equation of incense and prayer (Ps 141:2) and Paul's notion of the dissemination of the gospel as the church spreading "the fragrance of the knowledge of God" and the church itself as the "aroma of Christ" (2 Cor 2:14).[37] In its redolence, narrative functions both as oblation and as repository of the odor of sanctity.

Theodoret understood that just as narrating the lives of Syrian ascetics brought him blessing, hearing such narratives similarly conveyed assistance to his audience. Theodoret believed that his stories had the power to effect moral transformation by presenting examples of the virtuous life. The memory of Maron is as useful as his tomb; when the text is read, the hearer also participates in this remembrance. Thus in writing Theodoret not only reaps benefit, he also transmits it. To this extent, the hagiography is itself an *eulogia*, a conduit conveying the blessings of the saints to its audience. Theodoret's narratives function much like Peter the Galatian's healing belt (9.15) in their curative power.

Through the formulaic endings of his vignettes of the holy men and women of northwest Syria, Theodoret puts forward a complex understanding of the place of hagiographic composition within an emerging late antique system of devotional practice. For Theodoret, writing the *Religious History* serves the saints and brings their blessing on the author, who at the same time serves his readers in his act of literary oblation, conferring on them the blessing of the saints.

Writing, Miracle, and Votive in the Works of Cyril of Scythopolis

A century after Theodoret explored writing as blessing, and a century before the *Miracles of Artemios* connected writing and doxology, Cyril wondered at the miracle of writing. Cyril of Scythopolis (modern Beit She'an in Israel) lived from 525 to 559. His works include the *Life of Euthymius* and its companion, the *Life of Sabas*. These works, composed in the 550s, remain the most important literary sources for the history of monasticism in Palestine.[38] They relate the lives of Cyril's heroes and recount the history of the most important monastic communities of the Judean desert, including the monastery of Euthymius, the Great Lavra of Sabas (known as Mar Saba), and Sabas's New Lavra, places where Cyril had lived.[39] Cyril narrates the posthumous miracles and the origins of the cults of Euthymius and Sabas centered on their respective tombs.[40] He also chronicles the theological controversies that convulsed the world of the Palestinian monks in the fifth and sixth centuries, battles over Nestorianism, Monophysitism, and, perhaps most important, Origenism, to which the precocious Cyril had been initially attracted.[41] Like Theodoret's *Religious History*, Cyril's writings afford an understanding of hagiography as not merely a description of a religious world, but as an artifact that participates in that world.

Cyril's *Lives* also yield information about his own biography.[42] Cyril's father held an office in the bishop of Scythopolis's household and appears to have been highly educated.[43] When he took his six-year-old son to visit Sabas at the monastery of Procopius the Martyr, this ascetic claimed Cyril as his disciple and instructed Cyril's mother, herself a devout "servant of God," to teach her young boy to chant the Psalms, an early stage in preparation for the monastic life (*Life of Sabas*, 180). At some point during his adolescence, Cyril received tonsure and became a reader in the church (*Life of Sabas*, 181). Later he professed his vow of renunciation and took the habit in the presence of George, priest and superior of the monastery at Beella, near Scythopolis, at whose bidding Cyril later composed his *Lives* of Euthymius and Sabas.[44]

Through his own works Cyril emerges as a monastic intellectual and significant participant in the Christian literary culture of sixth-century Palestine. Cyril's writing attests the high quality of monastic education available in Palestine and provides insight into the contents of monastic libraries.[45] Extensive research has revealed Cyril's literary dependence on a surprisingly wide range of Christian works. In addition to the Bible, Cyril employs material, without attribution, from Athanasius's *Life of Antony*, the *Apophthegmata Patrum*, Palladius's *Lausiac History*, the first Greek *Life of Pachomius*, the *Life and Miracles of Thecla*, and various theological treatises. Cyril's works contain no fewer than nineteen instances of direct borrowing from Theodoret's *Religious History*, evidently a work he greatly admired.[46] Cyril displays training in standard rhetorical techniques and a sensitivity to generic conventions.[47]

Cyril brings his writing into conformity with the practice of the virtues, particularly humility and obedience, a topic considered at length in the following chapter. In the dedication of the companion biographies, Cyril submits that he "employs a style that is artless and without knowledge of secular culture" (*Life of Euthymius*, 6; compare 83). And, despite his display of Christian learning, the works indeed appear to lack direct quotation from non-Christian writers.[48] Cyril's contemporary Dorotheus of Gaza distinguished two sorts of humility: the first involved "holding my brother to be wiser than myself, and in all things to rate him higher than myself . . . to put oneself below everyone," and the second involved "attributing to God all virtuous actions."[49] By striving toward self-deprecation and relying on "the help of God" and the saints in his writing (*Life of Euthymius*, 6),

Cyril practiced humility and combated vainglory and pride. Through these conventional rhetorical patterns, Cyril attempted to bring himself into conformity with a well-established set of Christian ideals. Far from meaningless clichés, these expressions of humility carried great meaning for Cyril, helping to situate the act of writing within the religious life. This literary emulation of the saints attests to the author's piety and to his texts' credibility and usefulness to the faithful.

In addition to presenting writing as virtuous practice in its conformity to ascetic ideals, Cyril configures his endeavor as dependent on the saints' intercession. In the epilogue to the *Life of Euthymius*, Cyril relates the circumstances under which he composed the text. He had been interested in writing accounts of the lives of Euthymius and Sabas for many years and had collected stories, recording them "higgledy-piggledy on various sheets in disorganized and jumbled accounts" (*Life of Euthymius*, 83). He remained unable to craft these fragments into a flowing narrative, despite his teacher George's charge that he write these lives. After much prayer, Cyril fell asleep and had a vision in which Euthymius and Sabas appeared to him. Sabas said to Euthymius, "Here is Cyril. He holds your pages in his hands and displays intense eagerness, and yet despite his great and painful labors, he is unable to begin writing." Euthymius replied, "How can he write about us when he has not yet received the grace of opening his mouth in fitting speech?" (*Life of Euthymius*, 84). The holy men then performed a miracle on Cyril's behalf; Euthymius took a jar of ointment from his cloak and placed three drops of oil into Cyril's mouth. When Cyril awoke, still tasting sweetness, he "immediately began the preface" of the *Life of Euthymius*. Cyril, who humbly claimed to be "ignorant of the divine Scriptures and also slow of speech," attributed this gift of eloquence to the "God of marvels" who "makes the speech of stammerers distinct" (*Life of Euthymius*, 83). In this last phrase, Cyril quotes Isaiah 36:6 and alludes, as Theodoret had, to Moses (Ex 4:10–11). This biblical model had halting speech, but nonetheless he petitioned Pharaoh and, like Cyril, composed narratives of holy men. Furthermore, this gesture toward the preparation of the mouths of Isaiah (Is 6:5–8) and Ezekiel, whose ingested scroll tasted "as sweet as honey" (Ez 3:3), asserts the prophetic character of hagiographical composition, a theme Cyril may have derived from his familiarity with the *Life and Miracles of Thecla*, to which we shall turn shortly.

By relating the miracle that led to the production of his texts, Cyril places himself and his work within the context of the cult of Euthymius and emphasizes his dependence on Euthymius's miraculous power. Cyril's writings abound in miracles, quite possibly more than any other biographical works from the early Byzantine period.[50] The description of the miraculous vision that gave rise to Cyril's text follows a lengthy series of accounts of posthumous miracles associated with the tomb of Euthymius at the monastery of Euthymius, outside Jerusalem. This cult site, which Cyril promotes by writing, was renowned for its powers accessible either through contact with the tomb itself or by chrismation with oil from its silver crucible (*Life of Euthymius*, 61). Before narrating his own benefit from Euthymius's oil, Cyril tells of physical ailments relieved, robbers exposed, impure spirits exorcized, barbarians converted, moonstruck women brought to their senses, tongues untied, and tin curse tablets removed from the bellies of the afflicted through the powers of the tomb, the oil, or Euthymius's appearance in visions (*Life of Euthymius*, 68–82). The miraculous circumstances surrounding the composition of the *Lives* mirror other miracles received by ascetics and laity in the Judean desert who petitioned Euthymius for help. By juxtaposing his own story with the catalog of wonder-working, Cyril guides his reader to regard the text of the saints' lives as a token of the saints' miracles and as a sign of Euthymius's power and grace.

A posthumous miracle of Sabas, however, most closely resembles Euthymius's and Sabas's assistance to Cyril. According to the *Life of Sabas*, Genarous, a woman from Scythopolis, had organized a group of women to weave curtains for the churches at the coenobium at Castellum and the coenobium of The Cave, both founded by Sabas. When the weavers reneged on their promise to make the veils, Genarous was "very upset." Sabas, however, appeared to her in her sleep, telling her to send for her weavers the following morning, and comforting her: "Do not be upset, for your offering will not be hindered" (*Life of Sabas*, 186). Sabas also appeared to the weavers that night, and they assembled the next day to carry out their work, relating their visions. As in the miracle Cyril received, the saint intervened at a point where artistic production of offerings to the saint had stalled and provided the solution that allowed the votives to be pieced together.[51] The connection between creating texts and textiles is ancient and embedded in several languages, including Greek.[52] Like the church veils, the narratives about Euthymius and Sabas are offerings of devotion meant to adorn the saints' numerous monastic foundations. In this environment, the religious motivation for both activities takes the forefront. Having received the saints' grace in the ability to compose, Cyril follows Theodoret's precedent and calls on Euthymius and Sabas "to intercede on [his] behalf and to beg propitiation for [his] offenses" (*Life of Euthymius*, 84). Crafting his text, Cyril presents himself both as ascetic imitator and devotee of the saints.

Like Theodoret, Cyril displays considerable literary training and talent. In contrast to the *Miracles of Artemios*, their works display an introspective consciousness of the writing self. Nevertheless, all of these writers employ rhetoric drawn from early Byzantine Christian practice to pattern the composition of saints' lives in continuity with other devotional forms. Figuring the writer in the image of venerator, ascetic, pilgrim, supplicant, and even mediator between the saints and an audience ritualized the compositional act and cued readers to understand writing as pious performance. These authors thus expanded participation in popular devotions into the textual realm.[53]

Saint as Patron of Letters in the *Miracles of Thecla*

A similar, if more audacious, intertwining of text and cult governed the composition of the *Life and Miracles of Thecla*, a work of an unknown author that dates from between 444 and 448.[54] If Cyril's monastic humility led to an elegant integration of writing and piety, this secular priest deployed assertions of repeated miraculous intervention on his own behalf to shore up his authority. His self-presentation as an impresario of cult reveals a writer also engaged in petty rivalries with other local teachers and ultimately in conflict with his ecclesiastical superiors. The performance of authorship on display here is in part an elaborate act of self-positioning, using various textual strategies to negotiate the writer's standing both among his literary peers and within the church.

A teacher of rhetoric and self-identified "Man of Letters" (ἐλλό-γιμος), the author of the *Life and Miracles* had been a devotee of Thecla's shrine and a recipient of her miracles for many years before his ordination to the priesthood.[55] Introducing some of the miracles that Thecla performed on his own behalf, he writes, "This miracle concerning me (there were one, two, three of them!) I blush to tell, lest someone charge me in writing [γράψαιτο] with boasting and lying. I will speak nonetheless, relying on this martyr who healed me" (*Miracles of Thecla* 12). Mindful of his enemies, the author fears most that he will be written against, indicted. Performing a mix of textual modesty and awe in the face of abundant grace, he deploys Thecla's patronage to invoke his authorial license, the power and freedom to speak. Late in the text the author makes an extraordinary claim about his authority, linking his handling of his ecclesiastical duties and his production of text to Thecla's persistent help.

> After I had been judged worth of admission into the priestly synod and catalogue of preachers and priests, [Saint Thecla] remained present with me most of the time. And she appeared at night always handing [ὤρεγεν] to me some book [βιβλίον; scroll] or sheet of paper, which always was and appeared to be a sign to me of complete approval. If, on the other hand, while I was preparing to say something, I did not see anything, the result proved to be clearly the opposite. (*Miracles of Thecla* 41)

This confession offers more than a self-disclosing window on a preacher's anxiety while preparing to preach and an admission that his preaching does not always hit the mark. While he acknowledges that Thecla does not always provide such assistance when he prepares to speak, he presents her assistance as ongoing. As a general rule, Thecla herself enables his performance. When she appears, her approval is absolute.

Moreover, Thecla's regular presentation of scrolls situates the author within a biblical paradigm, namely that of prophet. As with the taste of sweetness in Cyril of Scythopolis's mouth, these visions link the author's preaching to the commissioning of Ezekiel (Ez 2:9–3:3):

> And I [Ezekiel] looked, and behold a hand was stretched out toward me, and a scroll of a book [κεφαλὶς βιβλίου] was in it; and he spread it before me; and it had writing on the front and on the back. . . . And he said to me, "Son of man, eat this scroll. . . ." So I opened my mouth and he gave me the scroll to eat. And he said to me "Son of man, your mouth eats and your stomach is filled with this scroll that I give you." Then I ate it: and it was in my mouth as sweet as honey.[56]

Ingesting the heavenly scroll enables Ezekiel's prophecy, both spoken and written. Divinely proffered text authenticates and licenses the production of additional text, serving to establish the authority and the credibility of Ezekiel's preaching. Through announcing his own visions of scrolls or sheets of paper, the *Life and Miracles of Thecla*'s author accesses this biblical model of authority. Although he does not eat his texts, the claim to receive them asserts enough; coming as it does late in the text, this passage authenticates not only his oral preaching but the entirety of his written work. This author presents himself both as Thecla's devotee and as her chosen prophet.

Falling into two parts of roughly equal length, the *Life and Miracles of Thecla* combines a narrative biography of the legendary first-century apostle with a collection of miracles associated with her shrine at Seleucia in the province of Isauria (modern Silifke) on the southeastern coast of Asia Minor. The text's first section, the *Life of Thecla*, depends heavily on the second-century *Acts of Paul and Thecla*, a romance of sorts about the apostle to the Gentiles and his female companion.[57] According to that popular noncanonical work, after hearing Paul preach, Thecla, a young virgin, converted to a particularly ascetic form of Christianity and became a wandering charismatic preacher, traveling in men's clothing to avoid harassment. By the end of the fourth century, her cult was well established at Seleucia. The pilgrim Egeria visited in the spring of 384, ascending a hill just outside of town to a large complex of buildings that included a church with a shrine of Saint Thecla and a great number of monastic cells for men and women.[58] Egeria attests the use of texts at the site to interpret the shrine, remarking, "We read the *Acts of Saint Thecla*."[59]

In reworking the apocryphal *Acts of Paul and Thecla*, the mid-fifth-century author supplemented the narrative of Thecla's life to include traditions about her time in Seleucia. Here, according to his *Life of Thecla*, she routed the pagan demons, taught, and baptized. Although the author regards her as one of the first martyrs of the church, second only to Stephen, in the end, she did not die a martyr's death. Instead, mysteriously, "she sank, still living, and entered into the earth" on the outskirts of Seleucia.[60] On that spot stood an altar for the celebration of the liturgy surrounded by a circular peristyle, the focus of fifth-century pilgrimage and supplications.[61] Indeed, this composition, tying Thecla closely to the cult site, seems intended not merely to supplement but to replace the earlier *Acts of Thecla* as a repository of the shrine's lore.

The second part of the work recounts the subsequent marvels wrought at the shrine under the aegis of the holy Thecla. Like the *Miracles of Artemios*, the *Miracles of Thecla* narrates the posthumous works of a martyr-saint in service of her cult (if indeed "posthumous" is the right word in Thecla's case). If Artemios's shrine tended to be patronized by men, Thecla's devotees included a significant percentage of women.[62] Among her numerous female devotees, the text tells of Tigriane and Aba, whose broken legs were healed (Miracle 18); the wife of a general whose husband had been cheating on her (Miracle 20); a wet nurse whose child had lost an eye (Miracle 24); and an illiterate woman named Xenarchis, whom Thecla taught miraculously to read the Gospel (Miracle 45). Thecla had, however, also earned a reputation as a patron of rhetoric and literature, and she bestowed much of her favor on men of letters, including the author.[63]

The *Miracles of Thecla* provides a portrait of writerly piety not only because the author used writing to express his devotion but also because the act of literary composition depends on the saint's intervention. The text intertwined these themes even before the passage in which the writer casts himself as the regular recipient of Thecla's scrolls. The prologue to the author's *Life of Thecla* presents a number of overlapping motivations for the production of his two-part text. He wishes to fulfill a personal vow and at the same time to respond to the repeated requests of his pious friend Achaios, whose prompting he describes as "a divine voice" that he later attributes to Thecla herself.[64] In humility he dedicates his "small and paltry abilities . . . to the great martyr, who in her greatest goodness is pleased by the smallest gestures."[65] His humble participation in the life of the cult shrine also establishes his authority to recount its miracles. In the prologue to the second part of the text, the author explains that he has included both "those [accounts] agreed upon by many" and those of which he has a more personal knowledge, either because he heard directly from the one to whom it had happened or because they had happened to him.[66]

While the author classes himself among Thecla's devotees, he also displays his eagerness to class himself as one of the regional literati. He frequently slips in quotations from Homer, tagged with the phrase "as Homer said," lest they be missed by a less-sophisticated audience, as well as references to Plato.[67] Intended to demonstrate his command of the classical literary canon, these pedantic references reveal a second-rate rhetorician striving to win the estimation of others.[68] This self-credentialing provides a second line of defense, after Thecla's aegis, for the writer's (and the text's) authority. Toward the end of the text, the author groups miracles illustrating Thecla's patronage of literary men, teachers of grammar and rhetoric, and orators, including both himself and some of his rivals.[69] Marking the transition to this compositional unit, the author employs a clever, if precious, literary conceit, personifying words themselves as agents of protest against his neglect.

And so will not the words [οἱ λόγοι] denounce us and call out for help on behalf of the learned [ἐλλογίμους] among men, if they alone should be overlooked by us, and especially since these things are not overlooked by the martyr? For in fact, she has often brought about miracles for wise and learned men. Come therefore, and let us speak that which we have come by now to learn, so that, for us, the words [οἱ λόγοι] also might be grateful that in this manner even they themselves are deemed worthy of this blessed chorus [χοροστασία] of miracles.[70] (*Miracles of Thecla* 37)

The author's verbal materials themselves call the author to shame, crying out to be used fittingly. If the human recipients of saintly assistance ought to express their gratitude, so too the words in which their stories are re-counted should be grateful to participate in glorifying God and the saint.

Acceding to the demand of his properly grateful words, the author turns his literary talent and skill to narrating Thecla's deeds on behalf of the guardians of language.[71] These tales reinforce Thecla's identity as a patron of letters while framing appropriately pious responses on the part of the lettered. The text recalls that a local teacher of grammar (γραμμα-τιστής) named Alypius fell gravely ill and his doctors regarded him as beyond hope. He took refuge at the martyr's shrine, "whence the martyr hastened" to deliver him from danger (Miracle 38). Before explaining how the miracle occurred, the author supplies that Thecla is "a lover of literature [φιλόλογος] and a patron of the arts [φιλόμουσος], who always takes delight in the more eloquent [λογικώτερον] praises of her." Perhaps this is why she responded so well when Alypius quoted Homer for her when she appeared to him at night in a dream. When she asked him what he suffered from and what he wanted, he responded, "You know; since you know, why must I tell you all this?" (*Iliad* 1.365). The author explains in a teacherly manner, "This was from Homer" and opines that perhaps it was more appropriate when Achilles spoke it to Thetis. Thecla, however, was thoroughly charmed by the repartee and handed Alypius a beautiful pebble (ψηφίς) with curative power and told him to tie it to his throat. When Alypius awoke from his dream empty-handed, he felt he had been cheated "and that the dream was merely a dream." Then his son Solymios, also a lover of literature (φιλόλογος), arrived after teaching his morning lesson with a colorful stone that he had found on the road the night before. The father recognized the perfect sphere, veined in white and purple, as the gift that the martyr had placed in his hand. He was immediately cured.

Thecla's passion for letters was practically indiscriminate, extending well beyond her Christian devotees to prominent nonbelievers. Having dealt with Alypius and his family of grammar teachers, the text proceeds to sophists (σοφισταί), the teachers of rhetoric. Apparently a significant percentage of teachers in the region working at this higher level of education were pagans and remained so even after they received cures from the shrine. When Thecla healed Isokasios, who had come to a church dedicated to her outside the town of Aigai in Cilicia (northeast of Seleucia) for rest during an illness, she scolded him for his unbelief (Miracle 39).[72] And Aretarchos the Sophist, whom the author compares to Plato's Gorgias, persisted in attributing his cure for a painful kidney infection to the god Sarpedon, refusing to acknowledge Thecla's handiwork (Miracle 40). The text sneers sarcastically at Isokasios's irregular job history and calls Aretarchos the Sophist both witless (ἄσοφος) and faithless (ἄπιστος). The author's tone in describing his professional peers suggests that these men were also his rivals for academic prestige. To say the least, Thecla demonstrates greater charity toward these men than does her devotee.

The saint's gracious assistance to pagan professors should not be interpreted as religious tolerance. Despite her appreciation of Homeric quotation, Thecla showed little patience with the traditional cults or their adherents. Early in the enumeration of miracles, the author presents Thecla's (and her shrine's) victory over the seaside oracle of Sarpedon (Miracle 1) and a sanctuary of Athena on a nearby mountain (Miracle 2). Thecla runs the demons Aphrodite and Zeus out of town (Miracles 3 and 4).[73] With the region cleared of pagan deities, Thecla reigns supreme as the protectress of the city and surrounding towns, healing local inhabitants as well as pilgrims from distant places. This routing of paganism gives rise to one of the author's stated goals: to compete with accounts of pagan gods' miracle tales. He insists that the stories of Zeus at Dodona, Apollo at Delphi, Asclepius at Pergamum and Epidaurus (*Miracles of Thecla*, prol.) and the like are fables and inventions, in contrast to his true narratives of Thecla's miracle-working power. Thecla dismisses the gods, and the author dismisses their stories. In the assault on paganism, the author and Thecla are in cahoots. Yet Thecla's patronage, like the author's love of the classical canon, respects the ancient literary traditions and the educators who transmit them.

Despite his rival sophists' paganism, the author presents himself as more like these men than different. Immediately after the stories of Isokasios and Aretarchos, the author turns to himself, grouping an account of how he was cured of an ear infection with these other miracles depicting Thecla as a lover of literature (φιλόλογος). His self-presentation by guild demonstrates that the author's identity lies as much—or perhaps more—with his profession as with his Christian religion or his devotion to Thecla. And, as the text makes clear, the author's professional success arises from Thecla's regular intervention. Thus the performance of authorship on display includes not only a demonstration of mastery over key texts of the ancient educational canon and various literary techniques (the tools that mark him among the literati), but also a self-inscription of the author as devotee and beneficiary of the cult, precisely in his professional capacities. He has placed his talents in the saint's service: writing in fulfillment of a vow, the author applies his literary training to the task of celebrating Thecla in written narrative. The textual votive returns his literary gift to its source.

The author's efforts to secure his identity as a man of letters provide a context in which to consider the three specific miracles that Thecla wrought on his behalf. In these accounts, he not only illustrates the extent of his dependence on the saint, he also narrates incidents in which both he and his authority were under attack. On a variety of fronts, this was a man under siege. The twelfth miracle in fact combines two incidents in which the author himself benefited from Thecla's assistance. It seems our author had developed a dark spot on his finger: anthrax!! The Greek word "anthrax" (ἄνθραξ) means "coal" (hence our anthracite). Ancient doctors diagnosed "anthrax" as a malignant pustule, a coal-colored mark on the skin (although it remains unclear whether this "coal mark" should be understood as what is now called cutaneous anthrax or rather as the first blemish of an infectious pox).[74] Our text concurs with ancient medical literature in describing anthrax as "a thoroughly burning and inflaming illness, which," the author explains, "is how it got the name 'anthrax [coal]'" (Miracle 12). This painful and deadly condition manifested itself "on one of the fingers of one hand, the one situated just next to the thumb." Despite the author's specificity regarding his index finger, he does not specify which hand is afflicted. Is it the right hand or the left? Does the condition threaten his ability to apply pressure upon the top of a stylus, and thus to write? Since the miracle that follows explicitly concerns his right hand, the text leaves the impression that both stories involve the same part of the body. If the anthrax in fact involved his left hand, his vagueness permits the reader to shift it to the more important side, to read it as a threat to the writer's manual dexterity. And in any case, this narrator, identified for the reader through the work of his writing hand, has been diagnosed with a fatal condition. Whichever hand is marked, the black lesion on his finger indicates the impending death of the author.

With both patient and doctors fearing that the condition would spread all over the author's body and kill him, the doctors determined that the best course of action was to amputate the diseased digit the following morning. That night, the narrator continues, "In terror and tears, I had a dream." Just on the verge of dawn, at the moment when night gives way to the beginning of day, and thus suspended between life and death, he saw simultaneously both "light with darkness and darkness with light, and I saw many ferocious wasps [σφήκας]." Their stingers, like spears, were at the ready as they prepared to attack. "But," he continues, "I also saw the virgin entering the place where I slept." In the peculiar manner of dreams, the author suddenly discovered himself at Thecla's shrine. "It seemed that I was sleeping in the atrium of the church," near a bowl (φιάλη) bubbling over with water that flowed into a pool under a plane tree.[75] Seeing the author threatened by the wasps, the saint took the end of the himation that covered both her head and the rest of her body[76] and, "whirling her hand around, she drove that whole swarm of wasps away, killing them and trampling them under foot. And thus she freed me from these terrible enemies." He concludes matter-of-factly, "And this is the vision that happened to me." When morning came and he awoke, our writer found himself free of pain, "smiling and brightened after the blessed vision." The anthrax was gone! When the doctors arrived in haste, "knife in hand," they admired and celebrated the martyr's miracle, although as they went away, they also complained that they been cheated out of their fee.

Hands figure throughout this account of early Byzantine anthrax: the author's spotted finger, the doctors' hands prepared to amputate, and Thecla's hand, which needs only to shoo the wasps to save her devotee. By the power of her hand, the saint saved the author's hand and thus his writing. His index finger, his life, and his authorial power depended on the saint's intervention.

But the manifestation of coal itself may be as significant as the appendage it afflicted. Like the scrolls that would later be offered to him at night, anthrax has prophetic overtones. Burning coal features in the heavenly visions of Isaiah and Ezekiel on the altar of God (Is 6:6) and in the fiery glory of the four living creatures (Ez 1:13). The Book of Isaiah associates this heavenly coal with the license to speak or to write. The prophet (Is 5:4–6) finds himself before the throne of God while the seraphim sing the antiphonal prayer, "Holy, holy, holy Lord of hosts, the whole earth is full of Your glory." Isaiah remarks on his own inadequacy to witness this scene, "Woe is me! For I am lost; for I am a man of unclean lips" (Is 6:5). The prophet must be purified. The account continues, "Then one of the seraphim flew to me, having in his hand a coal [ἐν τῇ χειρὶ εἶχεν ἄνθρακα] which he had taken with tongs from the altar. And he touched my mouth, and said, 'Behold, this has touched your lips, your guilt is taken away, and your sin forgiven'" (Is 6:6–7). Having had a touch of "anthrax," Isaiah is now prepared to prophesy.[77] While burning coal cleanses the biblical prophet's lips, in the *Miracles of Thecla* it marks the writer's hand, the mechanism of his composition. By such a textual strategy the author establishes his own authority, preserved as he is from a swarm of enemies.

While the coal invokes biblical typology to link the author to the Old Testament prophets who spoke by divine license, the dream's wasps point in another direction: they parody a stereotypical revelatory event in the lives of pagan authors. Bees (as opposed to wasps) recur as a topos in anecdotes about the early years of Pindar and Plato (among others), whose texts were studied in the late antique educational curriculum. According to Aelian's *Historical Miscellany*, a compilation of the third century C.E., the infant Plato's mother laid him among thick myrtles on Mount Hymettus. "As he slept a swarm of bees laid some Hymettus honey on his lips and buzzed around him, prophesying in this way Plato's eloquence."[78] This tale recurs in ancient catalogues of portents and in the sixth-century *Anonymous Prolegomena to Platonic Philosophy*.[79] Elsewhere in his text, Aelian writes, "Bees made their wax on Plato's lips. And Pindar, exposed outside his father's house, was fed by bees, who gave him honey instead of milk."[80] A *Life of Pindar* that may date from the fifth century cites an earlier Hellenistic tradition that the poet had fallen asleep on Mount Helicon: "As he slept a bee landed on his mouth and built a honeycomb there," upon which he decided to write poetry.[81] The *Miracles of Thecla* itself attests to Plato's place in the school tradition familiar on the southeastern coast of Asia minor in the fifth century. Knowledge of and admiration for Pindar was also widespread among educated Christians of the fourth through sixth centuries.[82] Similar stories of portentous bees circulated about Homer and Hesiod, signifying the favor of the Muses.[83] Later in the text the author of the *Miracles of Thecla* uses the arrangement of some of his own miracle stories with those of the local literati to establish his academic status; here, with his own flying insects, the author associates himself indirectly, and somewhat comically, with the greats of the classical literary tradition. That said, wasps registered as a terrible omen. In contrast to bees, which could be good luck or bad luck, depending on the profession of the dreamer, the second-century *Interpretation of Dreams* by Artemidorus of Daldis states bluntly, "Wasps are inauspicious for all, for they signify that [the dreamer] will encounter men who are evil and cruel."[84] And this dreamer did indeed have human enemies.

The author's authority was contested; he was not merely paranoid. The story of anthrax and the vision of the wasps is followed by another story in which the author is threatened by a more potent enemy—the local bishop. Here again hands play a prominent role as symbols of authority. At some point after the initial composition of the *Life and Miracles* and after Basil of Seleucia's consecration as bishop in 448, for reasons that are never made clear, Basil briefly excommunicated the author, forbidding him contact with the consecrated elements. In the wake of his troubles with Basil, the author added this additional narrative to the text of Miracle 12.[85] The incident still quite obviously upsets the writer, whose vitriol pervades his rhetoric. He employs techniques familiar in classical invective, a staple of the school curriculum and thus one of the rhetorical modes he must have taught to his students.[86] His writing discloses serious conflict with Basil's episcopal authority.

Basil of Seleucia is otherwise known by a number of homilies on biblical and liturgical themes that have come down to modern times and by his role in the controversies leading up to the Council of Chalcedon in 451. These works reveal a man of rhetorical talents and classical learning, although the ninth-century bibliophile Patriarch of Constantinople Photius criticized Basil's excessive use of rhetorical figures.[87] Perhaps the minor clergyman who wrote the *Life and Miracles of Thecla* found himself engaged in a generational conflict with a younger and more talented superior.[88] In any case, our author had run afoul of the man he calls "that pipsqueak [μειράκιον] Basil." The author sneers, "I shall leave aside for now [the question of] how he became bishop and took hold of the church, entirely unworthy of the stage [τὸ μηδὲ σκηνῆς ἄξιον]," and proceeds to explain that from the moment of his "most evil ordination [χειροτονία: literally, a 'laying on of hands']", Basil began to slander the author, apparently in retaliation for having opposed his election to the episcopacy.[89] According to the text, Basil concocted an accusation, presumably of heresy, and "shut [the author] out of the divine mysteries."

Once again dreams figure prominently in a time of crisis. On the night before the sentence of excommunication was pronounced, the author had a premonitory vision in which he saw a little Ethiopian man named Zamaras, apparently a local beggar and drunk. In the convergence of ideas about race and demonology typical in late antiquity, little black men were a terrible omen.[90] In the dream, the man, "entirely dark and gloomy," approached the author and handed him a coin, a *trimision*, a third of a *nomisma*, "also tarnished and blackened." Against his will, the author accepted the coin, knowing it boded ill. The next day, while he was pondering his dream, Basil, whom the author terms "our white Zamaras" and accuses of drunkenness, excommunicated him. According to the text, in response to the charge, which was brought without the testimony of a single witness, there was "tumult, confusion, and disorder throughout the church and the city," with everyone (so the author claims) "astonished at the shamelessness of the affair." With swollen rhetoric, the author recounts how his parents and friends protested the injustice. He displaces his own anger into the mouths of his friends, explaining how his ally, the saintly Thomas, accused the bishop and his crony Euboulos of "the most ridiculous left-handedness [σκαιωρία; by extension 'mischief'] . . . irrational falsehood, mindless calumny, [and] brazen perfidity." In a rehearsal of the author's rage, the text has shifted abruptly from praising the glorious Thecla to inveighing against the local bishop and the "shameless and disgusting" Euboulos.

Nevertheless, Thecla once again intervened on the author's behalf with an auspicious dream. On the second day of his excommunication, at nightfall, after having cried tears and prayed to God and having called upon the martyr for help, the author dozed off to see a "shuddering and blessed spectacle." "The martyr was standing by me in a young girl's clothing and a white cloak." Then, taking the author's *right hand*, "she placed in it that which Basil . . . had taken away," namely the eucharistic host.[91] " 'Hold [this] and be of good cheer my child,' she pronounced to me," before flying off in a hurry to Macedonia "to help a woman in danger." Upon waking, the author found his hand "full of an extraordinary fragrance." Pure and worthy to handle the body of Christ, the author and his orthodoxy received saintly certification. Reassured by the holy odor, the author exclaimed to his friends, "Today, whether he wants to or not, Basil will revoke my excommunication." And thus on the third day, Basil lifted his sentence against the author, without—the privileged narrator points out—the saint having ever appeared to the young bishop. Unrelenting in his opinion of his ecclesiastical superior, he ends this story by contrasting Basil's evil-working (κακουργία) with Thecla's miracle-working (θαυματουργία).

As the modern editor of the *Miracles of Thecla* demonstrates, the bulk of the text dates from before 448, the year of Basil of Seleucia's elevation to the office of bishop and thus before the author's ecclesiastical troubles. The second part of Miracle 12, the narrative of excommunication and restoration, represents a second stage of composition.[92] Why did the author insert the story of his temporary deprivation of the sacrament after the story of his anthrax, rather than at the end of the text?[93] Obviously he wished to group the miracle of his deliverance from excommunication with another miracle about himself. But again, why here with the miracle of his deliverance from anthrax and not with Miracle 41, which tells of his rescue from an ear infection on the night before he was scheduled to preach?

The connection seems to be in the hand. In both these stories, hands symbolize authority and power—ecclesiastical, divine, and writerly. By the authority conferred upon him by the laying on of hands, the bishop prevented the author-priest from touching the sacrament. (This excommunication is presaged by a dream in which Zamaras hands the author a dark coin.) By Thecla's hand, the author once again contacts the eucharistic elements. The license to touch the divine body manifests itself in his hand as the odor of sanctity. By this perfumed member, the author both consecrates the host and produces text. Having endured his triduum deprived of the sacrament, all the works of his hand are sanctified. Thecla sides with him, and not with his bishop. Moreover, the connection between this narrative and the story of anthrax with its purification of the writer's index finger recalls the liturgical use of coal in the burning of incense. This hand is a veritable thurible! Touched by coal and redolent of incense, the hand indicates its own license. With his authorship and authority under Thecla's protection, the fact of the text itself manifests the saint's power.

The third, and last, of the writer's own miracle stories recounted in the text illustrates the author's ongoing and intimate debt to Saint Thecla and her thaumaturgy. Here he joins his roles as prophet, priest, and rhetor. Classifying himself among his professional peers (and having just revealed their faithlessness), the author opens with the acclamation, "See indeed how the martyr is a lover of literature [φιλόλογος] and delights in these praises accomplished with words [διὰ τῶν λόγων]!"[94] In this case, Thecla's desire for writing enables liturgical performances in her honor. Once, at the time appointed for the annual feast (πανήγυρις) of Saint Thecla, our author was preparing a short speech for the festivities, "not so as to say anything remarkable or truly worthy of her, but to capture something of the martyr's goodwill, since she knows to respond to the slightest honors with great [benefits]." The day before he was "to speak and to declaim the speech [ἐπιδείξασθαι τὸν λόγον]," he narrates, using technical rhetorical vocabulary, he developed a "troublesome and grievous" earache, "so that my entire ear was swollen" with sharp jabbing pain and violent pounding in his head.[95] He thought (a bit melodramatically) that he was going to die and feared that he would be unable to deliver his speech. But Thecla came to his rescue: "She appeared by night, and took me by the ear and shook it violently," causing a little pus to drain out, relieving the problem.

This timely healing affords the author an occasion to cast himself in the image of Christ. In a turn of phrase admittedly self-conscious, the writer compares his cure to the scene at Jesus' tomb on Easter Sunday: "When [the blockage] was 'rolled away' from the innermost sanctuaries, so to speak, of my ear canal, I appeared at the pulpit"[96] and began to speak. The verb "to roll away" (ἀποκυλίω; here ἀποκυλισθέντος) quotes Matthew 28:2, Mark 16:3–4, and Luke 24:2, describing the stone rolled away to reveal the empty tomb, an innermost sanctuary indeed.[97] With his own stone dislodged, he appears to many; after the sickness unto death, he is risen to new life. "And thus the martyr offered her hand and her grace [τὴν χεῖρα καὶ χάριν], so that I both was and seemed to be speaking fairly well." At this time, the author had not yet become one of those who preached regularly in the church, and his novelty afforded a second opportunity for Christological allusion, this time to Christ's first preaching at Nazareth. He relates that he "roused up great wonder with his words," as he had never done before. The passages recalls Luke 4:22, where the inhabitants of Nazareth heard Jesus preach and "wondered at the gracious words which proceded out of his mouth."[98] It is while preaching in Nazareth that Jesus declares himself a prophet.[99] Thus the author identifies his own speech with a Christological marvel before revealing the persistence of the saint's favor in the explanation discussed above, the recurrent visions in which Thecla continues to hand him a scroll. It is Christ the prophet that he emulates.

Interweaving his dependence on the saint into his chronicle of the martyr and her shrine, the author of the *Life and Miracles of Thecla* inscribed himself both as devotee and authority. He established this identity by recounting stories of his prophetic preparation with scrolls and coal and of his priestly license in the redolence of his right hand. Even his competative jockeying with local literati serves as part of a larger plan to establish himself as author. These self-referential elements of the text deploy a range of rhetorical strategies in order to establish for the writer an authorial identity. His narrative strives to render the work credible and its author in control, both of his text and of the shrine's narrated memory.

Despite all his efforts to secure his identity, however, his authorship was ultimately erased. In one of the great peculiarities of Byzantine textual transmission, these works later circulated not as the work of their author, but rather as the work of the author's archenemy. While the *Life of Thecla* circulated independently in a number of manuscripts dedicated to lives of the saints, the *Miracles of Thecla* survives only in three manuscripts ranging from the tenth to the twelfth centuries.[100] In each of these examples, the *Life* and *Miracles* appear together. Fragments of both the *Life* and the *Miracles* also survive in a fragmentary palimpsest penned in the tenth century that includes the title page. Every copy of the *Life and Miracles* together, as well as all those of the *Life of Thecla* alone, attribute these works to Basil, bishop of Seleucia. Considering this implausibility, the text's modern editor has proposed possible explanations.[101] Perhaps early in the text's transmission a copyist accidentally credited the text to Seleucia's most famous man of letters. Or perhaps the misattribution was a sort of *damnatio memoriae*, suppressing the identity of a difficult priest, rendering him anonymous ever after.[102] Whatever the reason for the misattribution, inauthentic transmission ironically erased the authorial identity so strenuously asserted in the *Life and Miracles*. The modern habit of referring to the text as the work of Pseudo-Basil of Seleucia only perpetuates this erasure; this author surely never intended to pass himself off as his "pipsqueak" bishop. The name of the man at pains to present himself as one whom Thecla so consistently remembered has been forgotten. Perhaps, in an ironic sense, this befits a writer so concerned to establish his own authorial identity yet so willing to suppress the authority of the early second-century *Acts of Paul and Thecla* by subsuming the contents of that text into his own, effectively supplanting its authorship.[103]

* * *

The four texts considered here offer a range of models for the integration of literary composition into the cult of the saints. Even in the text where the authorial self-positioning is least thematic, the *Miracles of Artemios*, the performance of authorship figures as a cultic act, a written rehearsal of oral acts of glorification. Inscribing the excited testimonials lauding the saint and his shrine, the text underscores the centrality of narrative to cult. In the works of Theodoret, Cyril, and Thecla's protégé, the author participates in the cult, both within the narrative and in the act of writing itself. In these texts, writing functions both as an act of supplication and a votive of gratitude—not only the record but also the result of the miraculous intervention of the saints. Far from conceiving of the hagiographer as a mere observer, these writers expected that narrating the lives of the saints constituted participation in their cults. Like other devotees, writers sought and benefited from the saints' miracles and intercession. While not all early Byzantine hagiographical writings engage in such a sophisticated level of reflection on the creative act, the metaphors for the writing life that Theodoret, Cyril, and even Thecla's celebrant employed were paradigmatic. The theological grounding for acts of literary composition arose side by side with the range of other Christian practices described in these texts.

At the same time, in inserting themselves as characters into their texts, the authors of the *Religious History*, the *Life of Euthymius* and the *Life of Sabas*, and the *Life and Miracles of Thecla* engage in autobiography, a self-inscription that calls attention to themselves as models of piety. The *Mira-*

cles of Thecla, in particular, reveals how much the performance of authorship can be an assertion of authority. In his self-positioning as the recipient of saintly favor, the author attempts to secure for himself the license to narrate. If this agenda obtrudes, this is because he governs his magisterial voice less deftly than Theodoret and Cyril, for whom identity and authority are less contested, but just as inextricably linked. In the final analysis, each of these texts connects narrative authority to saintly power. Narrating about the saints becomes a tool to secure and to sanctify authorial identity.

In narratives promoting the cult of the saints, authorial identities are bound up in the narrators' relationships with the saints. These relational identities produce the texts, but are themselves also the product of the texts, emerging in the stories that the authors tell in authoring both the saints and themselves. Such texts produce their authors as inevitable by-products. To the extent that writing itself becomes a form of devotion, writers are themselves the product of their devotional writing. What then of a system of practice that problematized the assertion of self, that preferred humility to boastfulness and demanded obedience to authority? What if the values that the saints themselves embodied were inimical to the practice of authorship? The next chapter charts a reconfiguration of the relationship between authorship and power among monastic writers as ascetic ideals reshaped the idea of the author.

Chapter 5

Hagiography as Asceticism: Humility as Authorial Practice

In the prologue to the *Life of Daniel the Stylite*, the anonymous sixth-century author contrasted his literary skill with the glory of the saint.[1] Daniel, a Syrian of the fifth century, had received the actual mantle of the great Symeon the Stylite, journeyed to the Bosporus, and proceeded to stand on a pillar not far from the imperial capital at Constantinople. Yet the highly competent author claimed that he was unequal to the task of recounting the tale, writing, "I thought good to take in hand to recite the labors of the holy Daniel, yet I do so with fear; for this man's way of life was great and brilliant and marvelous, whereas I am but witless and unskilled [ἰδιώτης]" (*Life of Daniel* 1). The modern reader may register embarrassment or suspect a disingenuous author. But self-deprecating statements appear frequently in prologues and epilogues of saints' lives. In narratives that call the readers to a life of sanctity, the language of authorial self-denigration constitutes an aesthetic choice bearing moral value. Preparing to narrate the obvious goodness of the saint, the author's own humble gesture subtly models a Christian virtue.

The composition of Christian hagiography in the late ancient Eastern Mediterranean involved the representation in narrative of the pious performances of holy men and women. Authors offered the saints as models for emulation and reflection. The previous chapter considered authorship as a mode of venerating the saints. But hagiographers did more than merely participate in the saints' cults as suppliants, beneficiaries, and celebrators of their shrines. They also sought to imitate the saints, remaking themselves through their own observance of ascetic conventions in the production of texts. In seeking to portray virtues in action, late ancient Christian hagiographers strove to practice virtues through writing. By representing the saints, authors hoped to resemble them.

This chapter explores ways in which Greek hagiographical writings dating from the fourth to the seventh centuries bear marks of their authors' own *askēsis*. As the number of texts considered here shows, such conventional features of hagiographical composition were both widespread and various. Through a variety of techniques, authors inscribed themselves into their writing at the edges of their narratives. Rhetorical strategies deployed in the prologues and epilogues of saints' lives permitted authors to model the core values expressed in the body of their text. Here hagiographers configured the author in the image of the ascetic and represented the act of composition as formative spiritual practice. Moreover, the ascetic transformation of hagiographical authorship paralleled the remaking of biblical authorship considered in Chapter 3. Many of the ascetic virtues attributed to the evangelists, especially humility and obedience, became central to the authorial ideal.

Recent scholarly discussion points to an ascetic impulse in many facets of late antique Christianity. Between the fourth and the seventh centuries, the complex of technologies for the refashioning of the self, including controlling diet; renouncing sex, wealth, and power; regulating sleep; punctuating time with prayer and liturgy; and even standing atop pillars, articulated the growing religion's moral ideals.[2] According to early Christian ascetic theories, these spiritual exercises produced a perfected self through the practice of virtues. The ascetic renouncers' performances reshaped both body and mind to cultivate impassibility (ἀπάθεια) through temperance, continence, charity, courage, patience, justice, obedience, and—perhaps most distinctively Christian among the virtues—humility.[3] With God's help, the various techniques might result in a new Christian person.

Late antique asceticism was in its essence a creative project. Asceticism, as one historian has observed, "transcends the natural and resembles an act of literary or artistic creation."[4] If the production of an ascetic self is like the work of artistic creation, can the work of artistic creation be a form of asceticism? Indeed many hagiographers saw making a text as a means of personal reformation.

Texts played a crucial role in the promulgation of ascetic beliefs and practices. Oral traditions and written texts often served as road maps toward this new identity. Fittingly, the perfected self conformed to models embedded in writings.[5] Exegetes drew ascetic lessons from scripture, reading patriarchs, prophets, and apostles as models of moral rectitude and self-control.[6] In Jesus' temptation in the desert, monks found a script for their own discipline. Monastic teachers generated numerous handbooks to guide aspirants.[7] Reading, copying, and even owning books played salvific roles in the monastic life.[8] According to Athanasius, Antony the Great encouraged his monks to keep diaries, to employ writing as a tool through which to monitor the movements of their souls and assist in their formation.[9]

Hagiographical composition similarly textualized an ascetic's work by fashioning images of the saints through a type of narrative that mimicked "the repetitive performative gestures of the subjects of their gaze."[10] For those separated from a saint's holy flesh by space or time, a saint's life offered for instruction a text in place of a saint's body. However, the reception of hagiography by readers was not the only way in which the texts realized their salvific potential; the production of hagiography might also figure in the ascetic program of its author, a tool in the formation of his own ascetic identity.

Literary Composition in Monastic Life

An example from the end of antiquity demonstrates how a well-educated monk might understand the integration of composing hagiography into the activities of the ascetic life. In the introduction to the *Spiritual Meadow*, still incomplete at his death in 619, John Moschus explained to his companion Sophronius, later patriarch of Jerusalem, that ascetic intellectual activities include literary composition. He wrote, "For the virtuous life and habitual piety [τρόπος σεμνότητος] do not merely consist of studying divinity; not only of thinking on an elevated plain about things as they are here and now. It must also include the description in writing [ἀναγράφεσθαι] of the way of life of others."[11] For Moschus, composing (and not just reading) saints' lives was part of the contemplative life, a companion to theology and philosophy. He situated the motivation for hagiography squarely within the larger ascetic program for pious activity, revealing a monastic conception of what it might mean to be an author.

Employing a different strategy for linking the ascetic life to the production of text, Leontius of Neapolis, writing in the 640s, conceived a continuum for the practice of virtue that subordinated his writing to the glorious and richly embodied asceticism of Symeon the Fool.[12] "Since therefore I am unable to present instruction and the image and model [εἰκόνα καὶ τύπον] of virtuous deeds from my own life . . . I shall today unveil for you a nourishment that does not perish," namely the narrative served up in Leontius's text (*Life of Symeon*, 121). Those who can't do, write. Yet Leontius's deft rhetoric features a writerly sleight of hand, for his composition indeed presents the "image and model of virtue"; his text functions in the stead of a living saint, much as pilgrim narratives function for those unable to travel.[13] Moreover, he substitutes this narrative for his *own* body as a place from which to illustrate virtuous deeds. And, conversely, Leontius figures the ascetic's life itself as a presentation of instruction; the ascetic's life is conceived as an edifying text.

For the anonymous author of the *History of the Monks of Egypt*, the connection between writing saints' lives and more conventional modes of asceticism rested on the multivalence of the word "*mimēsis*," where a mimesis of the saints could be either an imitation of them or a representation of them.[14] Introducing his account of travel among the desert ascetics in the mid-390s, this author confessed his "unworthiness to undertake such an exposition," but believed he would derive benefit from his literary exercise.

I have therefore trusted in [the monks'] prayers and presumed to apply myself to the composition of this narrative so that I too should derive some profit from the edifying lives of these monks through imitation [μιμησάμενον; that is, representation] of their way of life, their complete withdrawal from the world, and their stillness, which they achieve through the patient practice of virtue and retain to the end of their lives. (*HME* prol. 2)

Availing himself of the terminological slippage inherent in the notion of mimesis, the author "imitates" the saints. In producing hagiography, he works at writing in the hope of self-improvement: illustrating the saints is creative activity through which the author refashions himself. The author thereby produces a likeness of the saints, not only in his narration, but in himself.

The Virtue of Humility in Textual Performance

Hagiographical composition participated in the ascetic life because it cultivated virtues. In fact, language configuring writing as a virtuous practice appears regularly in the prologues of saints' lives. The works of Cyril of Scythopolis, composed during the 550s, record the lives of the most famous ascetics of the Judean Desert, the founders of monasteries in which Cyril himself lived and practiced.[15] Cyril wrote not only at the request of his superior but also with the miraculous help of the saints themselves. Rather than divorcing the activity of literary composition from his ascetic labors, Cyril, like John Moschus, understood his writing as integrated with that practice. In Cyril's self-portrayal, the writing of saints' lives exemplified the performance of Christian virtues of humility and obedience. In the dedication to his *Life of Euthymius*, Cyril wrote to his teacher Abba George,

Even if I fall short of the worthiness [ἀξίας] of the venerable father I am praising, I have nonetheless judged it right rather to fall short of his worthiness, while moved by good will, than to give up the whole attempt in ill will and thereby disobey Your Fatherhood; in addition I am afraid of the terrible rebuke of the wicked and slothful servant who hid his talent in the ground. This is why I have been so bold, employing a style that is artless and without knowledge of secular culture, as to begin with the help of God the following account (*Life of Euthymius,* 6; compare 83).

In this passage, Cyril employs a literary commonplace familiar not only to students of early Byzantine hagiography but also to students of Eastern and Western medieval literature more generally; he claims his inadequacy as a narrator and directs attention to the lowliness of his style. A.-J. Festugière regarded passages such as the one just quoted as "protestations of humility" and "false declarations."[16] Indeed, it is widely recognized that Cyril's writing displays considerable rhetorical skill and learning.[17] But few scholars have reflected seriously on such ubiquitous features of late antique hagiography beyond assessing their validity.

This and other such passages found throughout the genre are not empty tropes: they portray an image of Christian authorship formed within the context of late antique Christian ascetic theory and practice. Recent scholarship on early Christian asceticism has been particularly attentive to the function of self-consciousness as a tool through which the ascetic imagined and formed himself anew.[18] In such a context it may be less relevant whether these statements are true; what matters is that claims of inadequacy are ascetic performances, expressions of piety achieved through rhetoric. Rather than a rhetoric of false modesty, it might be more accurate to speak of a rhetoric of longed-for humility.

Pairing two passages in Cyril's *Life of Sabas* illustrates the significance of the author's rhetoric of humility. In the prologue to this work, Cyril expresses that he writes "without ignorance of [his] own unworthiness and deficient education" and "fearing the danger of disobedience" (*Life of Sabas,* 86) to his mentor George, who had received Cyril into the monastic life, casting the act of composition within the framework of the practice of humility and obedience.[19] Shortly thereafter, once the narration of the life of Sabas is under way, Cyril informs his reader that Sabas made "humility [ταπεινοφροσύνη] and obedience [ὑπακοή] the root and foundation"

(*Life of Sabas,* 92) of his spiritual life.[20] In light of this description of his hero, whom he sets before his reader as an example to be emulated, Cyril's prologues are the very places where the author presents himself as an emulator of his subjects, practicing ascetic virtues. Cyril employs the introductions to the texts as occasions for writing about himself writing. Here he presents a virtuously formed image of himself in the hope of achieving his ideal. Cyril had devoted himself to pursuing the monastic life; far from protestations, his gestures of humility and of obedience to his superior in his prologue constitute repetitions, ritualizations designed both to express and to produce these virtues.[21]

Of all the virtues cultivated in the ascetic program, humility posed the greatest problem for authors of texts. The teachings of late ancient ascetic theorists provide perspective on the hagiographer's dilemma. As Evagrius of Pontus observed, the demons of vainglory and pride might lure an ascetic into a sense of satisfaction with his labors.[22] More than a matter of self-checking, the practice of humility was, for the author of the Macarian homilies, the essence of the piety itself:

The more [that successful ascetics] apply themselves to the art of growing in perfection, the more they reckon themselves as poor, as those in great need and possessing nothing. This is why they say: "I am not worthy that the sun shines its rays upon me." This is the sign of Christianity, namely, this very humility.[23]

If this goal held for the production of a perfected self, it also had implications for the production of a polished text, and for the relationship between an ascetic author and his labor. Pride in one's product, output, and creation constantly threatened.

The act of writing provided an opportunity for Leontius of Neapolis to emulate Symeon the Fool, his somewhat atypical holy man, and share in his humiliation. Of himself, Leontius wrote, "For we know that to the most senseless and disdainful we seem to be relating something incredible and worthy of laughter" (*Life of Symeon,* 122). The *Life of Symeon the Fool* relates the story of a particularly accomplished monk who, after twenty-nine years of ascetic labor in the desert, decided to leave his hermitage for the city of Emesa. There he pretended to be insane, defecating in public, waking about naked, raving in taverns, and devouring huge quantities of baked beans and raw meat on fast days, all the while performing secret miracles and reforming the populace. To the "more impassioned and more fleshly, Symeon seemed to be a defilement, a sort of poison, and an impediment to the virtuous life on account of his appearance" (*Life of Symeon*, 122). In fact, however, Symeon debased himself in order to save souls (*Life of Symeon*, 142).

Through writing, Leontius imitated his eccentric saint by similarly seeming to be foolish. Just as Symeon risked derision in order to instruct, so too Leontius risked appearing foolish in assembling his tale. In composing a risible narrative, Leontius recapitulates both Symeon's noble motivation and his scandalous modus operandi. The author too plays the fool for Christ's sake by telling a seriously silly story, and thus participates textually in his saint's ascetic performance. Leontius even shifts from learned rhetoric to a humbler, colloquial style at precisely the point in the narrative where Symeon begins his ribald antics.[24]

While Leontius's text, and not just his hero, makes a spectacle of self-humiliation, the *Life of George of Choziba*, written by his disciple Antony, works in a more earnest fashion, providing a poignant example of rhetorical groveling that nevertheless identifies the author with his subject.[25] Addressing his readers in an epilogue, Antony wrote, "I beg your indulgence, blessed servants of Christ. Forgive my deficiencies and feebleness of expression [ἀσθένεια τοῦ λόγου], my ignorant and unskilled [ἀμαθῶς καὶ ἰδιωτικῶς] attempt at setting down a few of the things from the many that I both saw and heard concerning the old man's way of life" (*Life of George* 58). This textualized performance of monastic virtue surely befits the narrative to which it is appended. Composed in 631, the *Life of George* tells of a wealthy Cypriot who, after a pilgrimage to Jerusalem, fled to the monastic life in the Judean desert. In addition to a vivid account of the travails of Palestinian monks during the tumultuous Persian invasion of 614, Antony, himself a monk of the coenobium at Choziba, recounts a handful of George's miracles and enumerates his ascetic achievements. George's diet consisted of a week's worth of crumbs and table scraps—vegetables, beans, and bones, sponged off the tables in the monastery's refectory—ground together in a mortar and formed into balls, which he dried in the sun. These powdered meals George ate alone in his cell, reconstituting them with a bit of water. Some of these desiccated balls, Antony notes, even survived the Persian assault (*Life of George* 12). George's extreme asceticism finds an appropriate frame in the self-abasing language of Antony's epilogue.

Principal among George's teachings was humility, which Antony terms "the mother of virtues" (*Life of George* 9). So central was this message that Antony has George deliver not one but two sermons on the topic (*Life of George* 14, 38–39). (At a later point in the text's history, a scribe interpolated yet another sermon on humility [*Life of George* 44–56].)²⁶ In Antony of Choziba's portrait of George, humility becomes explicitly Christological. Antony's George teaches that when the monk practices humility, he imitates Christ, who said "I am gentle and humble in heart" (*Life of George* 39, quoting Mt 11:29). Whereas arrogance drags the monk down, George preaches, "Humility has a height: the only Son of God, 'who humbled himself even unto death, death on the cross' (Phil 2:8). Know then, beloved, how great is the indescribable humility by which God descended even unto death" (*Life of George* 14). The pre-Pauline Christian hymn embedded in the Letter to the Philippians offers Antony a rubric through which to interpret the holy man's work. Like Christ, this noble monk lowered himself in service to others. In addition to his usual duties, George took on menial tasks, always assisting in the bakery, "lighting the oven two or three times a day—frequently on the day the slave was expected to work" (*Life of George* 23). The biblical allusion here would not be lost on Antony's monastic audience. By taking on the work of a slave, George emulated Christ, who according to Philippians "took on the form of a slave" (Phil 2:7).

The moral lessons at the core of Antony's text guided his activity at its conclusion. In the sermons of the *Life of George*, the saint teaches the dangers of self-righteousness and boasting. Thus the self-abasement of the author's epilogue demonstrates that he strove to be a good disciple. In writing as he does, Antony is doing humility. This enactment couples an evaluation of Antony's literary skill as "deficient and feeble" with a humbling assessment of his whole self. Later in the epilogue, echoing his first plea (quoted above), Antony wrote,

I beg your indulgence and entreat you, honored fathers and brothers, forgive me a little for so boldly and shamelessly begging you to make entreaty for me, a sinner and the least of your servants. . . . I prostrate myself [προσπίπτων] before your concordant belief, blessed servants of Christ, so that you, like the best physicians, might teach me some of the signs of humility—in which are life and light and joy and peace—and how not to denigrate my neighbor. For in these two virtues, I believe, are the full profession of our monastic habit and the kingdom of God. Our love for God is fulfilled in humility and in not despising our neighbor and in our love for him. (*Life of George* 60)

Modeling his own text's major themes, Anthony's epilogue uses liturgical language of entreaty and prostration to integrate the author into the system of virtuous practice.

Such parallelism appears throughout the text. Much as George had controlled his need for food, Antony would temper his craving for praise and superiority. A monk's manual labor in a garden, cellar, or bakery was his "ministry" or "office" carried out with humility;[27] Antony rendered his writing a similarly monastic labor. Just as his fellow monks tended their gardens, Antony made use of his text to cultivate piety.

The textual character of Antony's ascetic performance ensures that his asceticism will have an audience. In his epilogue, Antony invites his readers to observe his textual prostrations. As recent studies have argued, all asceticism has an audience, even if the audience is merely the self.[28] Authors of hagiography not only carefully watched themselves, but, especially in their prologues and epilogues, they invited audiences to observe them in the practice of virtue. Thus their act of narration—of textual production—was analogous in its visibility to the work of the saint described in the core of their text.

While Antony's direct address to his readers in the epilogue displays humility explicitly, the body of the text—by its very nature—implicitly documents the author's humility. Ostensibly, within the narrative *George* teaches humility in word and deed. But the story itself is also a lesson in humility, the work of an author who wishes to instruct. For is it not *Antony* who teaches virtue through the composition of the *Life of George*? In the course of the work's sermons, Antony displaces his teaching into the mouth of George. This ventriloquism models humility, since Antony does not claim the teaching of virtue as his own but attributes it to another. Antony emulates his master by carrying forward the great man's instruction and models the virtue he seeks to convey in the process. Subtly, the medium becomes the message.

Humility and the Problem of Agency

The practice of hagiography made moral use of the genre's most basic feature, the presentation of instruction through third-person narration. As the *Life of George of Choziba* demonstrates, an author might enact humility through the displacement of voice such that the saint speaks and enacts the teachings that the author wishes to convey. With additional rhetorical devices, however, an author might go so far as to enact the displacement of authorship itself. To combat pride, Dorotheus of Gaza distinguished two sorts of humility. The first involved "holding my brother to be wiser than myself, and in all things to rate him higher than myself . . . to put oneself below everyone."[29] This first strategy combated the problem of vainglory, in which the monk imagined himself better than others, hence writers' claims of inadequacy, as in the cases of Cyril of Scythopolis and Antony of Choziba above. Dorotheus's second type of humility had even more sweeping implications for the production of texts, for it involved "attributing to God all virtuous actions."[30] Paradoxically, the performance of humility demands the renunciation of agency in one's own asceticism, in one's own virtuous work.

This goal led some ascetic writers to renounce agency in their act of writing. In contrast to the autobiographical self-inscription practiced by Cyril and Antony, this ascetic impulse tended toward a writerly self-effacement. The *Man of God of Edessa,* a fifth-century Syriac text, tells of a Roman aristocrat who renounced his position and identity to live anonymously as a beggar on the steps of a church in Edessa.[31] Appropriately, the author of this work remained intentionally anonymous, erasing his identity just as the subject of his writing had. The author of the *Life of Daniel the Stylite* may also have concealed his identity as an act of humility.

For others, renouncing agency in one's good works meant implicitly or explicitly ascribing authorship to God. The epilogue of Athanasius's *Life of Antony the Great,* surely one of the most influential saints' lives, provides a striking example of this technique.[32] In a dense passage seemingly both pious and playful, Athanasius reveals awareness of some of the hazards of publicizing or publishing one's virtuous activity. Athanasius's work furthers Antony's fame, already spreading throughout the empire. In his epilogue, Athanasius says of the saints,

Although they do their work in secret and though they wish to remain obscure, yet the Lord shows them forth as lamps to all, that thus again those who hear of them may realize that the commandments can lead to perfection, and may take courage on the path to virtue. (*Life of Antony* 93)

Though they hide themselves and strive to live away from the world, God makes them known and spoken of everywhere because of their own goodness and because of the help they give to others. (*Life of Antony* 94)

True saints seek anonymity, yet God wills their works to be "shown forth" such that they can be known to the faithful. The secret virtue of the saints renders the ascetic author's act of publication problematic. The reader understands, of course, that it is the hagiographer who brings the holy people's virtue to light in narrative so that others can hear of it. Athanasius is the one who has done the work of "showing forth Antony as a light to all men," effecting God's call to virtue. But in this passage, it is not just the saints who wish to remain obscure; the author also wishes to obscure himself, eliding his agency, ascribing the "showing forth" that occurs in his hagiography to "the Lord."[33] Because the composition of beneficial texts constitutes virtuous action, this action must be the work of God. By eliding himself in this passage, Athanasius has begun to conform to the model of humility. Moreover, the act of composition becomes an analogue for Antony's asceticism, which in Athanasius's incarnational perspective involves Antony's "complete domination by the Logos."[34] Athanasius's textual mimesis of the saint fashions the author also as God's instrument.

In such a manner, performances of humility in the prologues and epilogues of late antique and early Byzantine saints' lives often involve placing limitations on authorship, renouncing authority with regard to the act of writing, and suffering God to work in and through the hagiographer. Cyril of Scythopolis relied on the assistance and intercession of the saints about whom he wrote in order to complete his work (*Life of Euthymius*, 83–84).[35] The often-self-promoting Jerome, writing in Latin from Bethlehem in 391, opened one work with "Before I begin to write the life of the blessed Hilarion, I call upon the Holy Spirit dwelling within in him that He who has bestowed upon him such abundant virtues may grant me the power to describe these virtues, so that my words may equal his deeds."[36] Theodoret of Cyrrhus also called upon the inspiration of the Holy Spirit for help in writing the *Religious History*. Ironically these two biblical scholars tempered their agency in authorship by placing their text in the same category in which current theories of divine inspiration had placed the Bible.[37] With the Holy Spirit at work, what then is an author? In effect, the author surrendered power over the text. Turning the writer's agency into ascetic performance resolved tensions between authorship and pride. The act of composition folded into God's act of creation.

The Denigration of Style

In addition to humiliating himself, the author could also humiliate his style. When combating vainglory, the ascetic reconceived the hierarchy between himself and others. The possession and display of literary talent—especially in a world of limited literacy—could easily become a form of self-assertion. Thus, a great many works include passages where the writer presents himself as unworthy or inadequate to undertake the task of composition, but nevertheless does so out of obedience to a superior, at the request of his comrades, or from a sense of religious calling or duty. The denigration of style not only provides an opportunity for a humiliation of the author, it also calls attention to the text itself, ritually humiliating the text.

Attempts to adjudicate claims about style in early Byzantine literature introduce a number of difficulties. Students of Greek philology identify linguistically and grammatically distinct stylistic levels available to early Byzantine authors.[38] Although the majority of late antique Greek saints' lives are written in a "middle" style, employing neither a "high" style of artificial Atticism nor a "low" style of popular dialect and colloquial expression, there are important exceptions. Theodoret of Cyrrhus wrote in a elevated style even though he claimed in his *Religious History* that "The account will proceed in narrative form, not following the rules of panegyric but forming a plain tale of some few facts" (*Religious History*, prol. 9). Athanasius composed fine rhetoric, although he claimed that his *Life of Antony* was a hastily drafted letter (*Life of Antony*, prol.). Some saints' lives mix levels within a single text, employing a more rhetorically and syntactically complex "middle" texture in the introductions and epilogues, while shifting to a lower, more colloquial style for narrating the story. Such is the case of Leontius of Neapolis's *Life of Symeon the Fool*.[39] And in his *Life of John the Almsgiver*, Leontius declared, "We have recounted our story in a prosaic, unadorned, and humble style so that even 'the unlearned and illiterate' [Acts 4:13] can benefit from these words," a claim about style that is demonstrably true.[40] However, even when a text maintains a lowered style throughout, it usually cannot be determined whether this represents a renunciation of an author's abilities or a reflection of his limits. Cyril of Scythopolis claims to write in a style "artless and without knowledge of secular culture" (*Life of Euthymius*, 6), yet his use of unattributed quotations from a rich variety of earlier Christian literature suggests a great deal of book learning. Fortunately, determining the actual linguistic level of a text is not central to an investigation of the motivation for these statements that call attention to the abasement of literary style. The habitual claims to write in a denigrated style in themselves reveal much about the piety that gave rise to the writing.

The prologue to the *Life of Daniel the Stylite*, quoted at the beginning of this chapter, provides a classic instance of the humility topos that furthers inquiry into the aesthetic and theological values of style. Using language borrowed from Act 4:13—where it describes the apostles—Daniel's hagiographer claims to be "witless and unskilled" in order to contrast himself and his writing with the great brilliance of his elevated hero (*Life of*

Daniel 1). But elsewhere in the *Life*, the author offers a possible point of comparison. His claim for a simple style gestures toward the mode that, according to our author, Daniel himself employed. In one of the climaxes of the *Life of Daniel*, after the translation of the remains of Symeon the Stylite to a spot near Daniel's column, both the emperor and the archbishop have come from Constantinople together with "the whole populace" to Daniel's enclosure in order to receive his blessing. Here Daniel instructed them, "saying nothing rhetorical or philosophical" (*Life of Daniel* 51). The artless style is a saintly style. Subordinate to the saint, the author nevertheless strives to imitate him.[41]

A lowered style might do more than imitate a saint, it might imitate the Savior himself. Palladius, the author of the *Lausiac History*, conceived of a simple literary style as an imitation of Christ.[42] In a prefatory letter to his patron, Lausus, chamberlain of the court of Theodosius II, Palladius explained that Jesus "did not use fine language" when teaching his disciples, but was rather "meek and humble of heart" (*Lausiac History*, epist. 3, quoting Mt 11:29). In the prologue to the work he reiterated, "It is not the aim of God's teaching to speak in learned fashion" (*Lausiac History*, prol. 4). Thus the treatment of style inscribes a particular Christology.

Remarks denigrating style draw attention to the author's prose, rendering it an object for reflection. The text itself—on the page and as spoken—records the author's own *askēsis*. It has become a relic of his performance of the virtue of humility, his imitation of the saints and Christ. As an instrument of ascetic praxis, the text functions as an extension of the author's body. Mortified, stigmatized by its own remarks about its inadequacy, the text suffers humiliation in order to save. The author's denigrated discourse, what Antony of Choziba called the "feebleness of [his] logos [ἀσθένεια τοῦ λόγου]," imitates the denigration of the divine Logos incarnate in Christ.[43] Through the humiliation of style, the text is transfigured to become an icon of God.

The Hagiographer among the Saints

Palladius expected that the work of the hagiographer would stand in continuity with the work of the saints and even the Savior. While asserting that teaching is not merely words, but rather "consists of virtuous acts of conduct" (*Lausiac History*, epist. 2), Palladius included in such acts Christ's speaking to the disciples, thus invoking a paradigm for his own deeds of narration. Palladius's vignettes about various ascetics teach lessons in a manner akin to the parables.

Palladius also invokes biblical authors as precedents. Paul wrote about his traveling to Jerusalem to see the apostles, just as Palladius writes of his own travels to see the saints in the desert (*Lausiac History*, prol. 6). Just as those "who wrote down the lives of the Fathers, Abraham and those in succession, Moses, Elijah, and John, wrote not to glorify them, but to help their readers" (*Lausiac History*, prol. 7), Palladius produces an edifying text to help his patron fend off evil influences. Thus at the same time that Palladius invokes biblical models for his ascetic heroes, he invokes acts of biblical composition as precedents for his literary effort.

At the end of his lengthy series of accounts of holy men and women he visited in the Egyptian desert, Palladius appends a description of himself, about whom he speaks obliquely in the third person. Here Palladius follows the model of the apostle Paul, who wrote in the third person of his apocalyptic vision of being "caught up into Paradise" (2 Cor 12:3).[44] "I know a man in Christ who fourteen years ago was caught up to the third heaven" (2 Cor 12:2), wrote Paul, in order to refrain from boasting. Palladius writes of himself in the third person,

> I shall be finished with my *historia* after I have said a few words about the brother who has been with me from youth until this very day. I know that for a long time he has not eaten from desire nor fasted from desire. I suspect that he has overthrown the lust for riches, which is the biggest part of vainglory. (*Lausiac History* 71.1)

He has rebuffed demons and received food from angels. He has traveled widely—as the body of the work itself suggests—but has had "no traffic with a woman, not even in a dream, except in resistance." In short, the author has been a model ascetic. Quoting Paul directly, Palladius exclaims "On behalf of such a one I will boast" (*Lausiac History* 71.4; 2 Cor 12:5), not on his own behalf, but on behalf of Christ working in him. While the modern reader might worry that this passage is boastful, and indeed Palladius's use of the third person signals a nervousness about self-aggrandizement, Palladius's greater purpose lies in setting a context for literary composition. By writing in the third person, Palladius is able to rehearse his credentials for authority and authorship, for his journey to the paradise of the desert coupled with his ascetic rigor have yielded a license to speak.

Palladius's work as an author is not merely a part of his ascetic practice, but results from his ascetic practice. Shifting to the first person, Palladius continues, "Now for me it is enough that I was deemed worthy to commemorate all these things which I have now put in writing" (*Lausiac History* 71.5). More than a matter of Lausus's patronage, being "deemed worthy" relates to divine providence: "For not without God's knowledge was your mind moved to prescribe the composition of this book to commit to writing the lives of these saints" (*Lausiac History* 71.5). Much as the ascetic labors of the saints led to godly gifts in the form of miracles, Palladius's ability to write the text figures as a sign of divine grace.[45] As a writer, Palladius counts himself among the saints.

*   *   *

Late antique Christian hagiography provided textual models for emulation and invited an audience to conform to the patterns of virtue narrated. While the body of these texts recounts the saints' piety, the margins of these texts enact the authors' piety. Humiliation and the renunciation of power and authority take place at the edges of the text, in dedications, prologues, and epilogues. These practices frame the act of narration itself as pious performance. Significantly, humility, the reluctance to write, and the awareness of linguistic limitations were precisely the same attributes that Christians increasingly attributed to biblical authors, as we saw in Chapter 3. The ascetic author drew on both the saints and the evangelists as mutually reinforcing models.

Hagiographical prologues and epilogues *are* the locus of commonplaces. Yet the recurrence of certain topoi signals not only their conventionality, but also their meaningfulness as conveyors of ideals within a system of religious practice. These habits of hagiographical composition are ritualizations, repeated patterns. Employing a rhetorical trope, after all, involves conforming to a model; and this too is an asceticism of sorts. Using vocabulary drawn directly from ascetic teachings on humility, obedience, and charity, these authors patterned the act of composing saints' lives in continuity with other ascetic activity.

In the hands of hagiographers, writing, like fasting or prayer, became a technology for attaining the goal of their own ascetic profession: a reconstituted ascetic self, displaying the virtues exemplified by the saints about whom they narrated. Authors strove to emulate their subjects through representation, configuring themselves through the production of texts. As a genre, hagiography's purpose was to communicate virtues to an audience through narrative; as a practice, it offered a window on the models for behavior deemed appropriate for ascetic authors. By ritualizing acts of composition as acts of humility and using writing to cultivate virtue, hagiographers constructed a Christian theology of literary composition, an ascetical poetics, and established the place of literary production in ascetic formation.

Hagiography as Liturgy: Writing and Memory in Gregory of Nyssa's Life of Macrina

The reconception of literary composition within patterns of devotion to the saints and the rhythms of asceticism underscores the impact of Christian ritual life on the formation of authorship. Largely deferred in our discussion to this point, however, have been some of the most central early Christian ritual practices, namely the recitation of daily prayers and participation in the eucharist. This chapter shifts focus to a single work of the late fourth century, Gregory of Nyssa's *Life of Macrina,* to witness an ingenious assimilation of hagiography and liturgy. Both evening prayer and the eucharist employed memory as an instrument of thanksgiving. A recounting of God's work was offered as a narrative sacrifice. In the course of remembering his sister's life, Gregory rendered Christian biography an analogous oblation. The result was a liturgical theology of authorship.

In the summer of 380, after attending a synod of bishops in Antioch, Gregory of Nyssa made the long journey north across Asia Minor to visit the family home at Annisa, in Pontus near the Black Sea.[1] He would see his sister Macrina for the first time in eight years (15). Not a moment too soon, he arrived at the manor-turned-monastery to find his sister on her deathbed. He recounts the scene in his *Life of Macrina.* Lying on a pallet on the floor of her house on the day before she died (17), Macrina began to tell the story of her life beginning with her childhood and her parents (20). Gregory remarks that she told of her life "just as if in prose composition" (καθάπερ ἐπὶ συγγραφῆς). "The point [σκοπός] of her narration," Gregory explains, "was thanksgiving [εὐχαριστία] to God" (20). Within the text, Macrina's autobiographical narration, occurring roughly at the midpoint, serves as a doublet for Gregory's own narration, even retelling some of the same information Gregory sets out to tell in the earlier chapters. What is the function of this repetition? This episode, implicitly connecting Gregory's own writerly practice to Macrina's saintly speech, signals Gregory's own efforts to construct a theological understanding of Christian hagiographical composition. Sitting with his sister in her final days, Gregory would begin to learn about the nature of memory and the cultic function of Christian narrative.

The authors of early Christian saints' lives fashioned written images of an idealized other. Their memorializing narratives of holy men and women sought to fill the gaps created by death. Like a monument placed at the saint's tomb marking a point of access to the saint's power, hagiography sought to make present in narrative a holy essence that might otherwise be irretrievably absent. As he observed regarding the festivals of the martyrs in his *Life of Gregory the Wonderworker*, the bishop of Nyssa expected that celebrating the saints, "rejoicing at [their] memory," worked to transform Christian lives.[2] As we have already seen, in presenting saints as models for emulation, hagiographers employed narrative to articulate Christian ideals and might even use hagiography as a tool to cultivate virtue in themselves, to develop humility and obedience.[3] But while composing narrative could figure as an ascetic practice, it could also be integrated into acts of worship. Hagiography thus afforded an opportunity to practice a third virtue, namely gratitude.

Gregory of Nyssa was especially well disposed to explore the theological implications of writing a saint's life. Born in Neocaesarea in Pontus between 335 and 340, he was the youngest of the three Cappadocian fathers, the late fourth-century bishops of towns in a remote and mountainous region of central Asia Minor.[4] Together with his brother Basil of Caesarea and their friend Gregory of Nazianzus, Gregory of Nyssa articulated a doctrine of the Trinity that would define Christian Orthodoxy. He had perhaps the greatest theological mind of the fourth century. Gregory had been ordained a reader in the church at age twenty, but renounced this office to marry and pursue the study of rhetoric. He returned to the service of the church when Basil ordained Gregory bishop of Nyssa in 371 or 372, although it was not until after Basil's death in 379 that Gregory devoted increasing energy to theological writing. As a scriptural exegete, he used biblical texts as a point of entry to contemplative philosophy. In the course of his refutation of the Arian theology of Eunomius of Cyzicus, he explored the metaphoric nature of religious language.[5] As this chapter demonstrates, Gregory brought his theological and literary sophistication to writing a saint's life. Allowing Macrina to model the practice of narration, Gregory introduced a distinctly liturgical theory of hagiographical practice.

Remembering Macrina

According to Gregory's prologue, the composition of the *Life of Macrina* fulfilled a request for a written account of his sister's life. After Macrina's death, Gregory had embarked on a pilgrimage to Jerusalem. On his way, he met in Antioch a certain Olympius, an old acquaintance, with whom Gregory talked about his sister at some length. According to Gregory, Olympius suggested "that a history [ἱστορία] of her good deeds would be useful, because such a life should not be forgotten with time, nor should she be passed over in silence without profit, concealed [συγκαλυφθεῖσα]" (1). Gregory's text thus presents itself as a retrospection on and revelation of the life of the holy Macrina, intended to preserve her memory and the moral benefit of her example for those who did not know her and for posterity. In the process, Gregory produced the earliest surviving biography of a Christian woman.[6]

Gregory situated the production of hagiographical narrative in the struggle to manage grief.[7] For this reason, the *Life of Macrina* employs narrative to explore the function of Christian memory. Before discerning the function, it is useful to consider the content of this memory. Gregory authored the *Life of Macrina* within two or three years of his sister's death.[8] Nearly all the details known about Macrina derive from this text.[9] She was the first of ten children born to prominent and wealthy Christian parents in the province of Pontus.[10] Her maternal grandfather had been martyred under Diocletian. Her brothers included some of the most prominent leaders and thinkers of the fourth-century church, including Basil, bishop of Caesarea, and Gregory, bishop of Nyssa, the author of her biography.[11] In contrast to her brothers, who received classical educations, Macrina learned reading and morals from the Bible (3) and gained skill in weaving, an activity deemed especially appropriate for aristocratic women (4). When Macrina was twelve, her father arranged her engagement to a young man who died before they could be married. Already intending sexual renunciation, she refused all subsequent offers of marriage on the grounds that in light of the promise of resurrection, the man was not dead, but living in God (5). After her father's death, Macrina persuaded her mother to join her in living an ascetic life. Together they abolished rank in their household and lived as equals with their servants.[12] Their home at Annisa became like a double monastery, with the women of the house under the direction of Macrina and her mother, and the men of the household under Peter, Macrina and Gregory's brother (7, 12).[13]

In Gregory's hands, Macrina becomes an exemplar for a life of ascetic piety and devotion to prayer. Her story presents a model for aristocratic renunciation of wealth in the quest for Christian ideals. Macrina had dedicated herself to strict ascetic practice. She became for her mother "a guide towards the philosophical and unworldly way of life" (11). Together they achieved a "standard of simplicity," sharing the same food and lodging as the rest of the community. Living in imitation of the angels, she participated in a life of utmost virtue.[14] According to Gregory's idealized portrait, "Among them was no anger, no envy, no hatred, no arrogance, or any such thing; neither was there in them longing for foolish things like honor and fame and vanity nor a contempt for others; all such qualities had been put aside" (11). Dedicated to continence and poverty, the monastic community devoted itself to "constant prayer and an unceasing singing of hymns distributed throughout the entire day" (11). Patterns of worship dominated Macrina's life. With her own hands, she baked bread for the altar (5).[15] Her ascetic practice punctuated the day with the liturgy of the hours, praying the psalms and reading scripture.[16] "She was especially well versed in the Psalms, going through each part of the Psalter at the proper time: when she got up or did her daily tasks or rested, when she sat down to eat or rose from the table, when she went to bed or rose from it for prayer, she had the Psalter with her at all times, like a good and faithful traveling companion" (3). Her daily schedule of prayer matches the program described by her brother Basil, a compiler of rules for monastic life.[17] In short, her mode of life was a living liturgy. One of Gregory's tasks was to represent this liturgical content of Macrina's life within her vita.[18]

Christian biography, beginning with the Gospels, is a theological enterprise, an effort to understand the subject within the religious vision of the author.[19] In composing the *Life of Macrina,* Gregory gave his sister's identity a didactic purpose, much as he did in his dialogue *On the Soul and Resurrection.* In that roughly contemporaneous work, Gregory purports to reconstruct a philosophical conversation he had with Macrina during the hours before her death.[20] With Plato's *Phaedo* as a model, Gregory employed Macrina in much the same way Plato had used Socrates, as a mouthpiece for his own philosophy, a modified version of the doctrines of Origen.[21] (At the same time, Gregory constructs a complex intertextual relationship with Plato's *Symposium,* playing Socrates to his sister's Diotima, and thus rendering her an ambiguously gendered font of wisdom.[22]) Gregory's dialogue explored the relationship between the material body and the immaterial soul (2) and the elusive condition of the immortal soul after

its separation from the body at death (4, 9). Just as he constructed an identity for Macrina in the dialogue, so too in her biography. The text of the
Life itself makes claims for its subject's value as a model of "the highest
peak of human virtue" achieved through the love of wisdom (1). Gregory
presented Macrina as a narrative model for others to follow.

The need to learn from Macrina's example arises, however, not merely
from the quest for intellectual insight but also from visceral anguish at her
loss. Within the narrative, Gregory invokes memory's power to comfort
shortly after his sister's death. After their superior died, the women of Macrina's monastery could not contain their grief, which Gregory describes as
"affecting their souls like a consuming fire" (26). The women began to cry
out, "as if they were torn away from their hope in God or the salvation of
their souls." Nor was Gregory a mere observer of this elaborate and ritualized performance of grief; Gregory joined with them, giving himself "over
wholly to lamentation." As Gregory was well aware, mourning has the potential to disorder the self. After some time, however, the mystical theologian recalled his soul from the depths and rebuked the virgins, "Look at
her," Gregory shouted, "and remember [ἀναμνήσθητε] her precepts, by
which she taught you to have order and good bearing in every circum-
stance. Her divine soul sanctioned only one moment for our tears, com-
manding us to weep at the moment of prayer. This command we can obey
by changing the wailing of our lamentation into a united singing of psalms"
(27). This first call to remembrance, to *anamnēsis*, to move from grief to
prayer, emerges in a postmortem crisis.

Thus after "recalling his soul from the depths" (27) of desperate lamentation, Gregory the bishop reassumes his pastoral role. His advice to the
women, of course, exemplifies a stock response to the bereaved. For example, another Cappadocian bishop, Gregory of Nazianzus, offered similar advice in a letter to monks and nuns mourning the superior of their monastery. The death of a saintly Christian, he declared, offers "an opportunity
for thanksgiving, not for tears."[23] Thus the bishop of Nyssa, while fully con-
fessing his own loss of self-control, invokes a proper Christian response to
death combining memory and worship. Gregory's charge to recall the holy
woman's divine soul, and especially her teachings, initiates a liturgical process, shifting attention from the finality of her corpse—"Look at her!"—to
the lasting wisdom of her moral example. Recollection itself, a process that
will prove ultimately and inevitably narrative, leads seamlessly to prayer.
Gregory invokes his sister's memory to call the community of mourners to
a proper liturgy for the bereaved. Writing the *Life of Macrina*, which in-

vokes Macrina's teachings and moral example, extends the process, converting anguish to spiritually beneficial memory.

Memory and the Narrative Logos

Gregory's approach to memory during the initial wave of lament recapitulates Macrina's own pastoral example concerning the management of grief. The deaths of various family members had already served as her crucible: "The loftiness of her thoughts had been thoroughly tested by successive attacks of painful grief, to reveal the unadulterated and undebased quality of her soul" (14). The day before her death, while Gregory's soul had been "overwhelmed by the anticipation of sorrows" (19), Macrina faced death bravely by discoursing about the blessings of her life. In doing so, she treated her own death much as she had treated the passing of others. Years earlier, after the death of her brother Naucratius, their mother was overcome with passionate grief: "breathless and speechless" (9), she even fainted. Macrina set reason against passion, "becoming the bulwark of her mother's weakness" (10). Through "her own reflections [λογισμοί]" (10) she moved beyond the tragedy and provided an example of courage to her mother. She would exhibit a similarly philosophical approach while discussing the life and death of Basil during Gregory's own visit (17, 18). In a pointed reversal of established gender roles, Macrina is masculinely steadfast, while Gregory is womanishly weepy.[24]

By analogy with his sister's example, one function of Gregory's hagiographical narration is the management of his sister's memory. Acts of memory strive to make present again through narrative that which has been lost.[25] In fact, the text recounts a number of acts of remembering, raising questions about the relationship between narrators and the stories they tell. In the course of the work, Gregory and Macrina reminisce about their brother Basil, Macrina narrates about herself, a nun recounts how a tumor on Macrina's breast was healed, and a Roman soldier retells one of Macrina's miracles in a narrative that contains a renarration of a story told by his wife. All of these recountings are retold in Gregory's own narration about his sister. Paying attention to narration as an activity represented within this narratologically complex text offers clues to Gregory's self-conception as narrator, or more precisely as rememberer, since each of the narrators within the narrative are engaged foremost in the act of remembrance.

The discourse about memory embedded in the narrative includes con-

cern to understand the transition from grief to story, the mediation between biographical narration and ethical reasoning, and the relationship
between speech (or logos) and writing. In the prologue, Gregory discusses
how he and Olympius, "in the course of the conversation [λόγος] came to
the memory of the life [εἰς μνήμην βίου] of that esteemed person [Ma-
crina]" (1.14). He describes Macrina in the prologue as "the virgin about
whom we reminisced [μνημονευθεῖσα]" (1.21), the object of memory. Episodes narrated from the course of Macrina's life articulate the proper effect
of Christian remembrance. Macrina demonstrates that the remembrance of
holy people affords an opportunity for philosophical discourse. When
Gregory first finds her on her deathbed, they talk about Basil, who had died
within the past year.[26] While the memory saddens Gregory, who begins to
cry, Macrina uses the memory to explore the human condition and disclose
the divine plan hidden in human suffering. As their conversation (λόγος)
"recalled the memory [μνήμη]" of their brother Basil (17.18), "Macrina was
so far from being downcast by our sorrow that she made the memory
[μνήμη] of the saint a starting point toward the higher philosophy" (17.23).
Gregory describes her in this mode twice "as if she were inspired by the
Holy Spirit" (17, 18), that is, by the divine force that had breathed into the
authors of the narratives of sacred scripture and who is ever present in the
life of the Church.[27] Gregory was convinced that the act of Christian remembering participates in God's communication with and sustenance of
the Christian community, or, to put it more theologically, that Christian
anamnēsis participates in the divine logos.

Most important for Gregory's own enterprise as hagiographer, Macrina engages in remembering her own life, providing Gregory with both a
content to repeat and a form to model. Gregory writes that she "took up
the memory [μνήμη] of her life since birth as if it were a prose narrative
[συγγραφή]" (20.3, compare 20.5). Gregory notes that Macrina's speech is
like writing, and thus serves as an analogue to Gregory's own prose narrative, in which Macrina's is embedded. Gregory has referred to his own composition as a "prose narrative [συγγραφή]" only two paragraphs earlier
(18.13). As if to underscore the peculiarity of this simile of a speech being
like a prose narrative, Gregory does not quote Macrina's speaking as first-
person discourse, but rather reports about the content of Macrina's speech
in the third person, thus representing her speaking with a prose narrative.
As written, the description of Macrina's discourse seems doubly removed
from speech.

The image embedded at the core of the text, then, is of a dying woman willing herself into prose, easing her own transition from life to memory. As if in response to her savior's willingness to have his Logos enfleshed, Macrina's speech makes her flesh logos. Describing her speech as writing, Gregory emphasizes the peculiar materiality of her logos, as if Macrina is striving to leave behind a permanent record.[28] In renarrating her logos, in fleshing out her story anew, Gregory himself effects the repetition and distribution of this narrative. Like a priest presiding over the eucharist, Gregory repeats the offering of Macrina's logos for the nourishment of others.

The peculiar attempt to blur or even collapse the distinction between speech and writing extends to Gregory's own presentation of his written text. In the prologue, Gregory reflects on the work's proper genre. Titled, and addressed to Olympius, as a letter, the text nonetheless has grown beyond the conventions for epistolary communication. It is worth recalling that at the time Gregory was writing, Christian biography had not yet developed into a generic tradition. Athanasius's *Life of Antony*, written in 357, also presents itself as a letter.[29] Other contemporary Christian biographical narratives took the form of encomia, such as Gregory's own *Life of Gregory the Wonderworker*, or funeral orations, such as those by Gregory of Nazianzus.[30] Funeral orations and encomia were oral to begin with, their written form recording a speech; while letters explicitly substitute for speech, a means of communication in which the writer and addressee are separated by space.[31] In letters, the speaker becomes a writer and the listener a reader, but the writing itself continues to function as an image of speech.

In the *Life of Macrina,* the writing has expanded beyond the letter form, but not beyond ostensive reference to oral communication. Indeed, Gregory confesses, the writing has "extended itself into a lengthy narrative [literally: prose-compositiony] discourse [εἰς συγγραφικὴν μακρηγορίαν]." Gregory's choice of words here is both significant and peculiar. He employs an adjective derived from *syngraphē*, a prose composition, a word Gregory uses at other key points in the text to describe narration about his saintly sister and, as observed above, to describe his sister's own writerly narration. Within the immediate context of the prologue, Gregory's use of "*syngraphikē*," "prose-compositiony," signals that the work has taken on the form of the genre of narrative history.[32] Gregory's written text resembles Macrina's autobiographical speech in rehearsing its content; Macrina's speech resembles Gregory's text by mimicking its form in being like a prose composition. In Gregory's prologue, his writing is a representation of speech (as is the case in letters), and this represented speech becomes an image of writing: the speech represented is like a written text.

The odd use of the adjective "*syngraphikē*" also calls attention to the noun that follows. Gregory terms his work a *makrēgoria*, literally a "long discourse," but the word itself is rare, and here is surely intended as a pun on the name Macrina.[33] By its etymology and usage, a *makrēgoria* is always oral, a long-winded *speech*. Thus, Gregory calls his composition a "written Macrina-speech," its own genre, a history masquerading as a letter, written words imaging oral words, a text devoted to recalling Macrina into being in the absence of her flesh. Occurring as it does at the beginning of the text, the significance of Gregory's terming his work a mix of speaking and writing emerges only in retrospect, when Macrina's speech is described similarly. Just as Macrina's speech is like writing, Gregory's writing is like speech.

What can be made of Gregory's play regarding the categories of speech and writing? The difference between speech and writing for Gregory was analogous to that between presence and absence, and also analogous to that between impermanence and permanence. Gregory was strongly influenced by Plato's discussion of writing in the *Phaedrus*, a classic of the ancient rhetoric curriculum.[34] With Plato, Gregory held, first, that writing was the image of speech and, second, that writing was predicated on absence. Gregory conceived writing as the image of speech, subordinate to speech, but made necessary by separation from the addressee by time or space. As Gregory explained in his second treatise against Eunomius, "We declare thought equally by speaking and by writing, but in the case of those who are not too far distant we reach their hearing by voice, but declare our mind to those who are at a distance by written characters."[35] The composition of letters is the example par excellence of writing, for letters reveal the degree to which writing assumed the reader's own absence, with the writer and reader separated either by space or time, or both. Significantly, the *Life of Macrina* presents itself as a letter, highlighting the reader Olympius's absence as well as the absence of its subject, Macrina.

This observation introduces a third idea about writing: writing is not only the image of speech, but is also the image of its subject. Writing down direct quotation provides a visual and material record of spoken language. A third-person narrative about someone is merely the next remove. Just as a painting of Macrina might record her image, so too the *Life of Macrina* reproduces her image in words. It materializes its subject, concretizing a memory, making the story of Macrina indelible. Thus, as in the case of letters, biography intends to compensate for absence.

The *Life of Macrina* explores the connection between writing and memory within a Christian context. In contrast to the interlocutors in the *Phaedrus*, who (despite being embedded in a written dialogue) attempt to keep writing both distinct from and subordinate to speech, Gregory's Christianity—his liturgical practice—celebrates the materiality of the Logos, the Word made flesh. Confidence in the incarnation deconstructs the opposition of speech and writing. Similarly, Gregory hopes that the (relative) permanence of his written text will compensate for the absence of its subject. The saint's biography is a narrative signifier pointing toward the saint signified. It is when we consider Gregory's attitude toward biography as a type of sign that Platonic theories of signification give way to Christian doctrine. In Platonic terms, all signifiers point toward the things they signify but are not the same as the things signified: writing points toward speech without being speech.[36] In this sense, one would expect that there is always a difference or gap, what Gregory called a *diastēma*, between writing and speech.[37] Macrina's autobiographical speech, however, tends toward a written record, while Gregory's own writing is like a speech. More than accepting the fact of her absence, the conceit collapsing speech and writing invokes Macrina's real presence.

Gregory's document is a logos sent forth into the world. As a physicalization of speech, the text strives to be an analogue both of the incarnation and of the eucharist. In the incarnation, God materialized divine speech, rendering himself present and accessible in Jesus. In the eucharist, the *diastēma* between speech and writing breaks down because the signifier is transformed into the signified: the bread and wine become the body and blood of Christ. God's own Logos becomes truly present.[38] In *On the Soul and Resurrection* (2), Gregory compared the immateriality of the soul with the immateriality of the divine essence. Like the incarnation and the eucharist, the *Life of Macrina* renders the immaterial physically present. Extending his hagiographical logos into the gap between Macrina and the living church, Gregory hoped to make Macrina fully available for emulation, a logos that could be consumed by those assembled to hear it.

A final way in which Gregory's text assumes Macrina's speech concerns literary style. Closing his prologue, Gregory registers a last observation about his writing before proceeding to his observations about Macrina. The *Life* attempts to tell the story of Macrina "in a narrative both lacking artifice [ἀκατάσκευος] and simple [ἁπλοῦς]" (1). In its claim to simplicity and lack of adornment, the text strives to resemble Macrina herself, an ascetic who renounced the trappings and sophistications of the world (5). The work is free of quotation from classical pagan authors, mirroring Macrina's own Bible-based education, although some of its philosophical discourse contains echoes of Plato.[39] Gregory's characterization of his style also reflects Macrina's preferences about language. As he relates, when their brother Basil returned home from school, "he was excessively puffed up by his rhetorical abilities" and filled with vainglory; but Macrina quickly won him over to "philosophy"—that is, asceticism—so that he "withdrew from worldly show and began to look down upon acclaim through oratory" (6). Aware of a tension between rhetoric and piety, the *Life of Macrina* adopts an ascetical approach to literary aesthetics, a style appropriate to its subject.[40]

Thanksgiving and Contemplation

Gregory's concern with writing and piety encompasses more than a refiguration of literary practice as a path of access to the virtues of a saint; Gregory also seeks to inscribe narration itself as a pious activity. While Gregory presents Macrina's autobiographical narrative as a conflation of the oral and the written, he also connects her speech to forms of liturgy, such that Macrina's act of narration figures as an act of worship. Concerning Macrina's speech from her pallet on the floor, Gregory explains, "The goal [σκοπός] of her narration was thanksgiving [εὐχαριστία] to God" (20). Early Christian biblical interpreters stressed the importance of determining the *skopos* of a given text, to read it in light of its aim or intended significance.[41] Similarly Macrina perceives the point of narrating her life's story in the opportunity to give thanks. Biographical narration is framed as an offering of thanksgiving. Gregory's observation about Macrina's purpose in relating her life story had necessary implications for Gregory's work as an author and for a conception of the genre of hagiography. Like his sister's Macrina-discourse, Gregory also has as his *skopos,* or object, the offering of thanks.

In this deathbed scene, Gregory relates that Macrina recalled with thanksgiving the religious history of her family. During the persecution earlier in the century, their paternal grandparents' property had been confiscated because they were Christians. Their maternal grandfather had been martyred. The narrative of the family's piety pointed to the work of God in their relatives' history.

What she stressed in the life of our parents was not so much their being outstanding among their contemporaries because of their prosperity, but their having been enhanced by divine favor. . . . Their life was so exalted on account of their faith that no one had a greater reputation among people of that time. (20)

When her wealthy parents had divided their estate, Macrina had donated her portion to the church. By God's providence, she never ceased using her hands in fulfilling the divine commandments. She turned away no one who asked for help, while seeking no benefactors herself. "Rather, God, in his blessings, made her little resources grow like seeds into a full-flowering harvest" (20). Thus Macrina's autobiographical discourse incorporates a narrative about the works of God in her life and in the life of her family. A Christian narrative is also the story of God.

Gregory's own text underscores the centrality of thanksgiving in acts of Christian narration. At a certain point in Macrina's story, Gregory interrupts and begins to talk about himself. "I told her of the difficulties in which I had been involved" (21). He complained about how the Emperor Valens had driven him into exile and about the controversies within the church concerning which he had been called upon to make disputations. But Macrina cut his whining short, admonishing him, "Will you ever stop ignoring the good things that come from God? Will you not remedy the thanklessness [ἀχάριστον] of your soul?" (21).[42] Scolding her brother for missing the work of divine providence in his life, Macrina tries to teach him to narrate like her, to recount biography with thanksgiving.

Christian biography, then, has as its object detecting, declaring, and giving thanks for the work of God in a Christian life. A litany of divine love, Christian biography renders itself an occasion for gratitude and thus comes to resemble prayer. This episode at Macrina's bedside ends when Macrina sends her brother off to the church for the office of "thanksgiving for the light [αἱ ἐπιλύχνιοι εὐχαριστίαι]"—that is, for evening prayer or vespers—while she herself "withdrew to God in prayer" for the rest of the night (22).[43] Thus this day progresses from one form of thanksgiving to another.[44]

On the following day, Macrina took up her autobiographical discourse again and this time was transformed. As an ascetic, Macrina lived in imitation of the bodiless angels (11); at her end, while reciting her life, she was joined to their image. On this day that she would die, once again Gregory visited his sister, and her narration continued:

She philosophized with high intelligence about what she had chosen for this life from the beginning until her last breath, so that it seemed no longer to be part of human realities. It was as if an angel had by some providence taken on human form, an angel who had no relation with or similarity to the life of the flesh and for whom it was not at all unreasonable to remain detached since the flesh was not part of her experience. (22)

Oddly, the reflection on her life, as she speaks herself into text, materializing herself as a prose composition, recasts her in an angelic body, a soul without flesh. The act of biography that grounds her story in time and place also subtly "loosens her from the chains of the body" (22). Like her ascetic practice, her narration anticipates the dissolution of the soul and body in death. At the same time, her history becomes philosophy, moving ever upward from events to ideas, from the realm of matter to that of pure thought. In doing so she makes the same transition from *historia* to *theōria,* from narrative to the contemplation of the inner meaning of the story, that characterizes the two separate halves of Gregory of Nyssa's *Life of Moses,* which renarrates Moses' biography according to Exodus before seeking allegorical meanings and divine truths. As in scriptural interpretation, Macrina moves from the body of the narrative to its spirit.[45] Now her writerly speaking takes the form of a self-reading, an anagogical exegesis of her life.

As her tale progresses and her flesh is transcended, Macrina's audience shifts as she offers a prayer to God. Her narrative "made clear to those present the divine and pure love of the unseen Bridegroom," toward whom Macrina had run the course of life. No longer addressing those gathered around her bed, she began to speak directly "to that very One toward whom she looked with steadfast eyes" (23). Now thanks-filled biography turns explicitly into prayer. In her lengthy deathbed devotion, Macrina recalls her dedication to God and reminds God of her participation in his crucifixion. She presents her soul as a spotless offering to God (24). With the fading light, Macrina recited evening prayer. "When she had completed the thanksgiving [εὐχαριστία] and indicated that the prayer was over by making the sign of the cross, she breathed a deep breath and with the prayer her life came to an end" (25). By moving from narrative to prayer, the *Life of Macrina* grounds hagiographical composition in the expression and production of the virtue gratitude.

In the *Life of Macrina,* Gregory constructs himself both as the narrative voice and as a character in the action. In the inevitable way of family history, the story of Macrina is also the story of her brother Gregory and thus, on another level, an autobiography. The text functions both as a memorial to his sister's life and as a means of demonstrating her influence upon him.

Gregory the narrator employs narrative to express virtues that Gregory the character had not yet learned within the time frame of the events he records. As he portrays himself in his own text, Gregory is not a quick study. Although Macrina has demonstrated to him the point of biographical narration, and while it is obvious that thanksgiving is a more proper response than grief, Macrina's funeral leaves him "downcast and tearful, thinking of the good of which [his] life had been deprived" (36). Fortunately there are other characters within his text who use narration correctly as a joyful and grateful response to life and to death.

Once again on the road after Macrina's funeral, Gregory meets a high-ranking soldier.[46] Like the centurion of the Gospels who is able to declare Jesus' identity after the crucifixion (Mt 27:54), this military official attests Macrina's holy identity. To the grieving Gregory, the soldier recounts a miracle that Macrina once performed (37). The soldier and his wife had brought their young daughter, who had been blinded by an illness, to Macrina's monastery. Once inside the compound, the husband and wife separated, he to the men's quarters and she to the women's. While the wife and daughter visited with the abbess, Macrina bade them stay for supper in return for a medicine to cure the girl's eyes. After the meal, the soldier, his wife, and their daughter went on their way (38). He told his wife all he had seen and heard among the monks, and she told him about her experiences in the company of Macrina.

Gregory's prose at this point is of particular interest. The soldier reports that his wife "narrated systematically [ἐκδιηγουμένη], as in a history [καθάπερ ἐφ' ἱστορίας], and did not think to leave out the smallest details." Furthermore, "She was telling everything in order, as in a prose composition [καθάπερ ἐπὶ συγγραφῆς]" (38). Significantly, Gregory describes the soldier's wife's narration with the same phrase that he used to describe Macrina's deathbed autobiography, once again making an analogy between oral storytelling and historical writing.

Much as Gregory's own composition does, the soldier's wife's prose speech narrates her encounter with the saint. Perhaps it is her systematic attention to the details of her account that alerts the woman to something she forgot; for in fact, the soldier, his wife, and his daughter had left the monastery without the salve Macrina had promised. Interrupting her narrative, the soldier's wife exclaimed, "What have we done? How did we forget the promise, the medicine for the eyes?" The soldier dispatched one of his men to return to the monastery before the mother had a chance to take a good look at the child, nestled in her nurse's arms. "Fixing her gaze on the child's eyes," the mother noticed that they had been healed. "Nothing of what was promised to us had been omitted, but the true medicine that heals diseases, the cure that comes from prayer, this she [Macrina] has given us, and it has already worked." Thus the soldier's narrative becomes a tale of thanksgiving for the miraculous cure of his daughter through prayer.

Through the soldier's tale, Gregory highlights the power of memory. The soldier's wife's systematic act of narrative memory works as a stay against forgetfulness, reminding her of Macrina's promise. Moreover, the tale of healing itself has the power to cure; for the effect of the soldier's narration is to comfort the grieving brother.[47] The soldier's narrative offers Gregory an occasion to discover blessing, to shift from lamentation to re-membrance, and through remembrance to find a cause for prayer. In the soldier's tale, Gregory underscores the functions of hagiographical narra-tive. Gregory's narrative, in contrast to the tale of the soldier's wife, is not complete or exhaustive. He mentions, but does not narrate, other miracles, healings, exorcisms, and prophecies, judging his history to be sufficient without them (39). Nevertheless, his story cures again, both by comforting those still grieving and by presenting a path to virtue, a tale to improve Christian lives.

Cultic Aspects of Hagiographical Narration

Gregory's writing integrates itself with his subject's patterns of life. Macrina devoted herself to prayer, while in Gregory's hands her vita becomes a prayer. Macrina gives license to Gregory's act of narration by giving biogra-phy an explicitly religious purpose. She teaches him how to do Christian biography by providing him, in her own narration, a model to imitate. Conceived as an act of thanksgiving, biography becomes an act of piety. Macrina's biographical, indeed hagiographical, speech, which has thanks-giving as its object, breaks off for the office of thanksgiving at the lighting of the lamps. Just as her life centered on the liturgy, her life—both as lived and as she narrates it—ends with the liturgy. The pervasive influence of prayer throughout Macrina's narrated life affects Gregory's assembling of his sister's hagiography; the text itself takes on a liturgical character, punc-tuated by the liturgy and assimilated to it.

Gregory's figuration of hagiographical composition as a form of wor-ship draws an analogy between the living of a saintly life and the narration about a saintly life, both of which produce a holy identity. The connection in the *Life of Macrina* between Macrina's life and her recitation of a narrative about her life illustrates a metaphoric relationship between living and textual production that Gregory articulates more directly elsewhere. In an earlier work, his *Treatise on the Inscriptions of the Psalms*, written sometime in the late 370s, Gregory compared the Christian life to the recitation of a psalm. Gregory explored the harmonious connection between the rhythm of a religious song's melody and the meaning of its words. The melody alone cannot convey a song's message; only when the words are sung out can the musician employ the song to articulate virtue. He compares the words and the music to two sorts of virtuous agents and Christian life to a spiritual song.

Some who devote their mind to the speculative and contemplative philosophy of reality establish a virtue which is unclear to the majority, since they confine the good to their own conscience. But the moral character of life is zealously perfected at the same time by others. These make the rhythmical order of their life known publicly, as if it were a verbal statement [λόγος], by their decorum concerning the visible world.[48]

Here the virtuous life is like a logos, an act of speech, set fittingly to music. Moreover, this analogy between living and speech occurs in a discussion of the prayerful psalms, the core of the Christian liturgy of the hours. The life as song Gregory has in mind is both liturgical and biblical in character: Gregory presents Christian living as pious psalmody directed toward God.[49]

In Gregory's figuration of life as a speech act akin to the recitation of a psalm, Gregory raises the possibility that hagiography—that is, written narration about a life lived as worship—is a representation of such speech. The Platonic relationship between speech and writing holds, such that a saint's vita constitutes an image of a lived liturgy. Gregory ties biographical speech explicitly to the life of its subject in the prologue to another saint's vita, the *Life of Gregory the Wonderworker*, where the bishop of Nyssa invokes the Holy Spirit for assistance in his writing since "the same ally must be called upon for help as the one through whose aid he achieved virtue in his lifetime."[50] The Holy Spirit is instrumental both in the production of a holy life and a holy vita.

Given the close association between liturgy and narration, an exploration of the *Life of Macrina*'s cultic features depends on understanding the cultic figuration of Macrina's own body. At the same time that Gregory anchors his text as a reflection of Macrina's own life and narration (and her life *as* narration), Gregory connects his writing to Macrina's body. Gregory's Macrina-discourse, like the lives of saints more generally, meditates upon her body, establishing it within the conventions of early Christian piety and practice. Macrina's asceticism had rendered her both an angel and a martyr. In her ascetic rejection of luxury, wealth, and comfort, she, together with her monastic sisters, "imitated the existence of angels" and, although living in the flesh, developed "an affinity to the bodiless powers" (11).[51] Even more startling, on the night before he arrived at Annisa, Gregory had a dream. Three times he saw the same portent; Gregory writes, "I seemed to be carrying relics of the martyrs in my hand, and a light seemed to come from them" (15). While the dream predicts his sister's impending death, it also posits the ambiguity of the virgin saint's living body, already poised between life and death through her ascetic practice.[52] Later, while in the presence of his sister, he understands this dream to mean that Macrina had *already* died to sin while "illuminated by the grace of the indwelling Spirit" (19).[53] That is, the living Macrina's body was already a martyr's relic, a holy witness to the work of God. Such bodily transcendence prompts a liturgical response. After her death, the virgins of the monastery held a night-long vigil, singing hymns, "as is the custom," Gregory supplies, "in the praise of martyrs" (33).

Despite Gregory's physical contact with Macrina's remains in his vision, contact with her real body after death is apparently superfluous. Macrina entrusted her corpse to Gregory to treat in accord with custom (25). She had requested that he be the one to shut her eyes. He relates, "So I placed my hand, deadened by grief, upon her holy face so as not to seem to disregard her request," although, in fact, she had died with her eyes closed and had managed already to be arranged in the proper position, so that there was "no need for any arranging hand" (25). Thus in her death, Gregory finds himself not only unnecessary but, at least with regard to his "deadened" hand, assimilated to Macrina's dead body. The hands that he had seen carrying the portentous relics became corpselike in the presence of the holy relic itself, the body of the saint.

Gregory asserts privileged and intimate knowledge of Macrina's body through touch and gaze. Even in the dark robe that Gregory and one of the nuns use to cover the corpse, "the body glowed." Gregory remarks, "The divine power added such grace to her body that, as in the vision of my dream, rays seemed to be shining forth from her loveliness" (32). The flesh itself bears marks of suffering, and Gregory sees them. While Gregory and the nun Vetiana dress Macrina's body for burial, the woman shows him a scar on his sister's breast, the reminder of a terrible sore that God had cured in response to prayer (31). While in life, Macrina's modesty had prevented her from showing the diseased breast to a doctor, Gregory looks directly at it. This peculiarly intimate knowledge of his sister's body empowers Gregory; it gives him authority to describe her in narrative.[54]

If the dream interpretation that Gregory shares with his readers makes explicit sense of the shining remains in the vision as a figure for Macrina, it leaves the significance of their being held in Gregory's own hands implicit. As the vision reveals, Gregory holds possession of and control over the relics. He handles her remains: first her body and later her memory. As the author of the text, Gregory holds authorial control over her story, manipulating her identity.[55] Physical relics are the remains witnessing to the work of the indwelling Spirit in the life of the saint. Gregory's narrative offers an analogue, a narrative remembrance of the saint attesting her holiness, lest her virtue be forgotten. In the end, the text of the *Life of Macrina* is itself a relic, a witness to her saintly life, held in the author's hands. Materializing her memory, text substitutes for body.

Sacrifice and the Liturgy of Memory

Gregory holds Macrina like bread in the hands of a priest, while his mouth his full of her narrative. Macrina figures not only as angel and martyr, but also as sacrifice. Gregory describes her as "an offering of first fruits" from the womb of his mother (1), recalling both ancient Israelite dedications of children to God (Ex 13:2) and Elizabeth's exclamation about the Christ-child within the pregnant Mary (Lk 1:42).[56] Describing their mother's death, Gregory relates that she dedicated her first and tenth children, Macrina and Peter, to God, offering them as votives (13). And on her deathbed, Macrina offers her own soul to God "as an incense offering [θυμίαμα] before Your face" (24). Here Macrina quotes from Psalm 141, already becoming a standard element of the rite of evening prayer: "Let my prayer be counted as an incense offering before your face, and the lifting up of my hands as an evening sacrifice" (Ps 141:2; LXX 140:2).[57] Macrina presents herself as the essence of prayer, a sacrifice of worship. She has become the service itself.

If Macrina is a sacrificial offering, so too is her story, both Macrina's oral and Gregory's written logos. Exploration of the idea of narration as sacrifice rests on the conception of narrative as a mode for *eucharistia*, thanksgiving. Macrina teaches Gregory that the object of biographical narration lies in giving thanks to God. Like her own prose narrative, Gregory crafts his text into a thank-offering. Connecting narrative to *eucharistia,* Gregory provides an opportunity to understand hagiographical composition within the context of modes of Christian worship. By the late fourth century, *eucharistia* had gained a wide semantic range in Christian usage and had complex liturgical overtones. The term might denote the various prayers offered throughout the hours of the day: the morning prayer recited at rising, prayers at bedtime, grace after meals, or, as in the deathbed scene in the *Life of Macrina,* the evening prayer recited at the lighting of the lamps.[58] In addition, the term regularly described the formal service of the eucharist, especially the prayers offering and consecrating the bread and wine, also referred to by the Greek term *"anaphora," "*offering."[59] In some sense, of course, each of the lesser thanksgiving rites of the liturgical hours pointed toward the Great Thanksgiving, the sacrificial cultus at the center of Christian life and worship.[60]

As liturgical historian Robert Taft has observed, what the liturgy of the hours shared with the eucharistic sacrifice was the theme of *anamnēsis,* the offering of memory.[61] The church fathers understood the eucharistic liturgy to combine an act of thanksgiving (εὐχαριστία) with an act of commemoration (ἀνάμνησις) of God's redeeming action in the life and death of Christ. In enumerating what the community was thankful for, the rite recounted sacred history.[62] The narrative aspect of liturgical offering appears in the earliest surviving forms for the anaphoral rite. The eucharistic prayer in the early third-century *Apostolic Tradition* of Hippolytus of Rome lists the deeds that God accomplished through the inseparable Logos: creation, virgin birth, suffering, death, and resurrection before reenacting the Last Supper with its call for *anamnēsis:* "Do this to remember me."[63] Hippolytus presents the prayer not as a script to be used uniformly in churches but rather as a model to be followed.[64] The key elements involving the renarration of sacred history characterize subsequent anaphoral prayers.

And what of the liturgical prayers that Gregory himself as a bishop offered in the eucharist? The precise form of the anaphoral liturgy that Gregory knew and celebrated cannot be known. The eucharistic prayers contained in the liturgy conventionally assigned to his brother, *The Liturgy of Saint Basil,* while certain to contain large elements composed or adapted by Basil, derive from a later date.[65] However, similar thematic elements of thanksgiving, narration, and offering structure the *Liturgy of Saint Basil* as it is transmitted in the ninth-century manuscript tradition and likely derive from a Cappadocian liturgy.[66] Fortunately, extant fourth-century sources confirm the narrative character of the liturgical offering. The dominant liturgical form in Asia Minor and in Constantinople in the late fourth century had its origin in the West Syrian type celebrated at Antioch, known from the *Apostolic Constitutions* and from the sermons of John Chrysostom. These influences soon became the rule for the liturgy promulgated from the imperial capital.[67] Chrysostom affords insight into both the structure and the meaning of the liturgy in the late fourth century, roughly at the time of the composition of the *Life of Macrina*. His remarks about the eucharistic liturgy, embedded in a homily on the Gospel of Matthew preached in 390, assist in articulating the narrative aspect of the act of thanksgiving, the connection between *eucharistia* and *anamnēsis*. Chrysostom asserted the thanksgiving's ability to make the absent present. The eucharistic prayer used memory to draw the community into the real presence of God. Chrysostom declares, "Thanksgiving itself adds nothing to Him, but causes us to be nearer to Him."[68] He elaborates,

For this reason Paul also said, "Be thankful." For the best safeguard of any benefit is the remembrance of the benefit, and a continual thanksgiving. For this reason even the mysteries, so awesome and full of abundant salvation, which are celebrated at every communion [σύναξις], are called a thanksgiving [εὐχαριστία], because they are the commemoration of many benefits.[69]

Chrysostom then lists the events to be recalled in the thanksgiving prayer: the virgin birth of Christ, his death by crucifixion, and its connection to his institution of the "spiritual feast and banquet." This recalling in gratitude of the birth and death of Jesus, a biography in miniature, intertwines the themes of memory, prayer, and narrative.

Similarly, in one of the *Homilies on First Corinthians*, Chrysostom glosses the eucharistic offering in explaining Paul's discussion of the "cup of blessing." Imagining Paul's own voice, Chrysostom writes, " 'For when I call it "[the cup of] blessing" [1 Cor 10:16], I mean thanksgiving, and when I call it thanksgiving I unfold all the treasure of God's goodness, and call to mind those mighty gifts.' " The preacher continues, "Thus we too, recounting over the cup the unspeakable mercies of God and all that we have been made partakers of, draw near to Him and communicate; giving Him thanks that He has delivered from error the whole race of mankind."[70] Returning thanks involves remembrance, a calling to mind events of the past, and is thus fundamentally narrative. It is the telling of history rendered a liturgical practice.

If the connection of biography to Christian cultus remains implicit in

Macrina's instruction to Gregory that the goal of remembering is thanks-giving, Macrina's lengthy final prayer (24) reveals the obvious, that narra-tive and memory are at the core of liturgical offering. The prayer exhibits Gregory's own literary and liturgical abilities.[71] Here, Gregory has Macrina integrate her own biographical narrative into the narrative of her savior. Its direct address to God with the familiar "You" recalls the form of Psalm 74:12–23 (LXX 73:12–23), and much of the language of that psalm appears here in Gregory's composition.[72] As a whole, the prayer is a "fabric of bibli-cal citations."[73]

O Lord, You have freed us from the fear of death;
You have made the end of life here the beginning of a true life for us.
For a time, You give rest to our bodies in sleep and You awaken us again with the
    last trumpet [compare 1 Cor 15:52]. (24)

Gregory has also made use of numerous liturgical formulas: in mentioning the works of God and asking for the forgiveness of sins, he employs ele-ments associated with rites for evening prayer. Moreover, particularly in the second half of the prayer, he borrows from liturgies for the dead: the call on the assistance of angels, the reference to the bosom of the patriarchs, the pardoning of both voluntary and involuntary sins.[74] Perhaps most impor-tant for the present discussion, in its work of *anamnēsis* and its conclusion with a sacrificial offering, Macrina's prayer recalls the anaphoral ritual of the Divine Liturgy. First, the prayer recalls the major events of biblical nar-rative. Macrina remembers God for the act of creation, for his act of re-demption "from the curse and from sin," and for his opening "for us a path to the resurrection" (24). This invocation of creation, redemption, and consummation constitutes a renarration of salvation history, such as we find in the early anaphoral prayers.

Macrina's prayerful offering also includes autobiography. A second section of the prayer turns from narrating a history of God to a narration of Macrina's own history, a narrative gesture that ultimately inscribes Ma-crina's story in God's.

O God everlasting, towards whom I have directed myself from by mother's womb
    [compare Ps 22:9; LXX 21:11],
Whom my soul has loved [compare Song of Songs 1:7] with all its strength,
To whom I have dedicated my body and my soul from infancy up to now,

Prepare for me a shining angel to lead me to the place of refreshment where is the water
of relaxation [compare Pss 23:2 (LXX 22:2); 66:12 (LXX 65:12)] near the bosom of
the holy Fathers [compare Lk 16:22]. . . .
Remember me also in Your kingdom [compare Lk 23:42–43],
For I, too, have been crucified with You [compare Gal 2:19], having nailed my flesh
through fear of You and having feared Your judgments [compare Ps 119:120 (LXX
118:120)]. (24)

In these phrases, Macrina merges her own narrative with that of Christ, recalling her participation in his passion, presumably through her own asceticism. Finally, having moved through grateful remembrance of the work of God, both for all humanity and in her own life, and having joined her own suffering body to God's body and her life's narrative with God's narrative, Macrina ends by offering herself as a sacrifice:

Do You who have power on earth to forgive sins [compare Mt 9:6; Mk 2:10] forgive
me so that I may be refreshed [LXX Ps 38:14] and may be found before You once I
have put off my body [compare Col 2:11], having no fault in the form of my soul,
but blameless and spotless [compare Eph 5:27] may my soul be taken into Your
hands as an incense offering [θυμίαμα] before Your face [compare Ps 141:2 (LXX
140:2)]. (24)

Her immaterial soul figures as the smoke of an incense offering.[75] The imagery here is surely fitting: like Gregory's own text, the incense stands for Macrina's presence without the body.

As night fell, the lamp was brought in, and, although her voice was failing, Macrina fulfilled her desire to recite evening prayer, moving her hand and her lips "in keeping with the impulse within her" (25). In Gregory's somewhat idealized death scene, Macrina completes the prayer with a final sign of the cross. "With the prayer," Gregory writes, "her life came to an end" (25). As Gregory remembers it, Macrina's prayer and life cease together because they were essentially equivalent.[76] The implications for narration about such a life are clear. Hagiography repeats the act of prayer.

* * *

In the *Life of Macrina*, Gregory questions the proper form and aim of Christian biography. He is well aware that when the body is gone and the immaterial soul is dispersed, what remains are the stories. Gregory presents these stories as an opportunity for philosophical, specifically ethical, reflection. But literary composition, for Gregory, occurs in a world in which it is right and just to give God thanks. Various forms of liturgy, including evening prayer and the eucharistic service, provided models for offering narrative itself as part of a thanksgiving sacrifice. By its nature as a written text, the *Life of Macrina*, the work of Gregory's hands, shares two important features with the physical Logos of the eucharist: like the bread, the *Life of Macrina* is distributable, and, like its consecration, repeatable. The impact of Christian liturgical piety and practice offered Gregory a eucharistic model for hagiography: the narration of Macrina's life is a thank-offering and sacrifice to God.

Gregory's conception of authorship as liturgy punctuates our survey of models for the writing life that late antique writers derived from other modes of Christian practice. The variety displayed among these literary performances of veneration, self-discipline, and prayer suggests that no single theory of authorship obtained in the period. At the same time, these three chapters have emphasized the degree to which authors sought to integrate writing into their religious lives, and the inventive and particularly Christian ways that they found both to be and to become authors.

Gregory's intertwining of theological and liturgical themes is exemplary, perhaps unique among the era's hagiographers. However, in theorizing hagiography's potential to render the absent present and to materialize the saint in text, Gregory's *Life of Macrina* raises questions about textuality and materiality that persisted in late antiquity, influencing the ongoing discourse about logos and flesh. The remainder of this book, therefore, turns to questions of textuality to explore the interplay between bodies and texts and to see literary composition as a generative matrix producing in text both the author and his subject.

Chapter 7

Textual Bodies: Plotinus, Syncletica, and the Teaching of Addai

The materiality of texts rendered writing akin to bodies. The crafting of a text, like the ascetic stylization of the body, yielded an identity produced as the subject of the power exerted. Gregory of Nyssa's *Life of Macrina* illustrates how vitae of holy men and women display these saintly identities after death, offering their presence in narration in the absence of their bodies. The textual body was never fully disembodied, and writers participated in the creation of matter. This chapter explores three strategies for coping with the relationship between text and body. The *Life of Plotinus*, composed around 300, expresses anxiety about representation, positioning the author as an ironically disobedient disciple, even as he works to preserve his master's identity. Written sometime in the fifth century, the *Life of Syncletica*, which posits a strong dichotomy between the physical and the spiritual, offers text as a union of opposites in its preservation of the saint's teachings. And the *Teaching of Addai*, compiled in the second decade of the fifth century, looks to the joining of text and body at the end of time.

Because texts might substitute for bodies, texts did not provide an opposition to the body. Attempts to construct an analogy such that texts were to bodies as spirit was to matter faltered on the ambiguous character of texts: both material and immaterial, both created and potentially immortal. The tenuous analogy between texts and bodies shaped the very teaching of rhetoric. In the *Phaedrus*, Plato has Socrates say, "Every discourse must be organized like a living being, with a body of its own, as it were [δεῖν πάντα λόγον ὥσπερ ζῷον συνεστάναι σῶμά τι ἔχοντα αὐτὸν αὑτοῦ], so as not to be headless or footless, but to have a middle and members, composed in fitting relation to each other and the whole" (246c). Thus, although writing may confer immortality upon the writer (*Phaedrus* 258c)— and, one might add, biography may confer immortality upon the narrated subject—it does so through a type of bodily production. In writing, the *logos* has, or perhaps is, a *sōma*. From the perspective of late antiquity, the connection between logos and body always already underlies the craft of composition; the practice of writing is the embodiment of the logos.

For Christian writers, this trajectory in ancient thought was, not surprisingly, further influenced by the prologue of the Gospel of John. The claim, uncontroversial to middle Platonism, that "In the beginning was the Logos, and the Logos was with God, and the Logos was God" (John 1:1) received a distinctive augment in the phrase, "And the Logos became flesh [ὁ λόγος σὰρξ ἐγένετο] and dwelt among us" (Jn 1:14). The discourse that is God became not merely *sōma* (body) but *sarx* (flesh), as if to emphasize the materiality of God enfleshed. The implications for the production of text unfolded in the course of early Christian literature.[1] Authorship could perform the incarnation of discourse. Writing became a vessel for holiness. Meanwhile holy men and women made Christ legible in their bodies— made their bodies text. Implications for the performance of authorship differentiated Christian from non-Christian literary efforts.

This chapter first considers two philosophers' portraits, one pagan— Porphyry's biography of Plotinus—the other Christian—the anonymous and lesser-known *Life of Syncletica*. Writing, in these texts, inhabits a gap between the material and the immaterial and, as such, becomes the object of scrutiny. Like Gregory of Nyssa's *Life of Macrina*, the literary portraits of Plotinus and Syncletica are both indebted to the Platonic tradition and are haunted by the ghost of Socrates. Or, more properly, both authors are haunted by Plato and the problem of representation, particularly the representation of the body in text. These two works employ the genre biography as a strategy to articulate and disseminate the teaching of a holy sage. In faithfulness to Platonic tradition, both texts emphasize the contrast between transient body and enduring wisdom. At the same time, both texts invest themselves in ideas about writing that blur the difference between flesh and thought and between the timebound and the timeless. Both texts understand themselves to be producing textual bodies, but with differing senses of appropriateness to this material production. One question to ask is whether the doctrine of the incarnation makes a difference to the self-positioning of the writer, modifying the practice of authorship. The chapter then turns to a more complete integration of text and body available in the eschatology of the *Teaching of Addai*. In this vision of the joining of text and body at the end of time, one Christian tradition offers a resolution to the questions regarding the materiality of texts.

Fleshing Out Plotinus

Porphyry's *On the Life of Plotinus and the Order of His Books* highlights the relationship between biography and body and between life and text.[2] The pagan Neoplatonic philosopher Plotinus lived from 205 to 270. Porphyry wrote in 301 to introduce an edition of his teacher's complete written works. This biography and canon list frame Plotinus's corpus, attaching it to an authorial identity, placing it in a historical context, and giving it shape and form. The text then attempts to integrate Plotinus's writing with the story of Plotinus's physical body: to attach the life of the body to the life of the mind.

Porphyry's ideas about the body, however, make the very act of biography, the fixing of an identity in time and space, problematic. The narrative itself sets up a tension between the desire for an embodied subject (which gives rise to the text), and a subject, namely Plotinus, who would prefer to escape embodiment. As portrayed by Porphyry, Plotinus refuses to be the willing subject of narrative. The *Life of Plotinus* opens with the observation that "Plotinus, the philosopher of our times, seemed ashamed of being in the body. As a result of this state of mind he could never bear [ἠνείχετο] to talk [διηγεῖσθαι: that is, "narrate"] about his race or his parents or his native country" (1). From the outset of his biography, Porphyry depicts Plotinus as resistant both to his own embodiment and to verbal representation. Porphyry's narration therefore figures itself as a transgressive act, a deed carried out against the ethos and wishes of its subject.

Porphyry indirectly stresses this point by relating a story about an attempt to create a visual portrait of the master. Plotinus "objected so strongly to sitting for a painter or a sculptor" that he said to Amelius, another disciple, "Is it not enough to have to carry the image in which nature has encased us [that is, the body], without your requesting me to agree to leave behind me a longer-lasting image of the image, as if it was something genuinely worth looking at?" (1).[3] Despite Plotinus's objection, Amelius arranged for a famous painter named Carterius to attend Plotinus's school for a while to develop a mental picture. Later, Carterius "drew a likeness of the impression which remained in his memory" and produced "an excellent portrait of Plotinus without his knowledge." This surreptitious portrait functions as a cipher for Porphyry's own enterprise, the drawing of a narrative likeness of the impression that remained in his memory, in violation of the teacher's explicit desire.

In the *Life of Plotinus*, Porphyry carries out the verbal portrait of a man who would not narrate himself. The description of Plotinus's body, which follows the anecdote about the secret painting, illustrates the human corpus as an object of corruption and shame. Plotinus "suffered from a disease of the bowels" but could not "bear [ἠνέσχετο] an enema" (2). He avoided the public bath, although he received daily massages. After his masseurs died of a plague, he contracted a most savage case of sore throat, possibly diphtheria. His voice worsened, his sight blurred, and his hands and feet ulcerated. Finally, most of Plotinus's friends avoided him completely, shunning physical contact with him, since it was his insistent custom to accost his visitors with a kiss. Plotinus was not the only one rejecting his body. In prose both vivid and morbid, Porphyry renders Plotinus's body a grotesque spectacle. If Carterius's painting proffered an excellent likeness pleasing to the viewer, Porphyry's words sketched the unpleasant. The body conjured in the text problematized the art of narrative. This man Plotinus, who would not reveal to anyone his birthday lest others celebrate him with a sacrifice or feast, ultimately lost control not only over his body but also over the memorialization of his life and the representation of his self.

Porphyry situates Plotinus's rejection of mimesis, or representation, in the philosopher's shame regarding his body. Plotinus rejects sitting for a portrait, terming it "the image of the image." Plotinus already regards his body as a mere debased image of his soul; the body is only a representation of his true and permanent identity. A painting of his body involves a second level of remove from the original, and thus he abhors the copying of the image. Moreover, painting and biography tamper with the impermanence of the body by fixing it in time and causing it to endure or persist. Bodies are acute; portraits are chronic.

Biography's power to materialize its subject by making his image present vies with its subject's own will. Porphyry's authorial voice takes command of its subject only in resistance. The opening paragraph aches with irony. The anecdote about the painting declares that this biographical text derives its authority, its power to represent, through circumvention and ultimately through a gentle betrayal of its hero. The audience for the verbal likeness is also implicated in the prank, especially in its own desire to read and hear Porphyry's text.[4] But the pranks themselves—the painting and viewing of the surreptitious portrait, the writing and reading of the mischievous narrative—serve to underscore the degree to which Plotinus lacks control over the body and the various downward and mimetic emanations of his soul.

Porphyry links Plotinus's wariness about the body and its representation to his master's wariness about textuality and writing. The man who *could not bear* to talk biographically about himself (1.3) and *would not bear* to have an enema (2.2) also *could not bear* to look at his own writing once he had written something down (8.2). Plotinus's tense relationship with the physical body recapitulates itself in his initial and long-standing unwillingness to produce writing and his eventual aversion even to his literary corpus. Porphyry's presentation of these three aversions—all described with forms of the verb ἀνέχομαι, to hold up, bear, or endure—integrates Plotinus's unwillingness to defecate, his reluctance to write, and his final aversion to looking at what he had produced.[5] This convergence reveals writing as embarrassingly bodily and connects this textual form of embodiment with shit.

Porphyry was not the first to attempt a literary representation of Plotinus's teachings. For many years Plotinus taught while writing nothing, a point Porphyry repeats (3.33, 36). This philosopher's literary constipation did not prevent his students' attempts to transcribe his thought. Porphyry relates that the lectures, which proceeded from student questions, lacked order and were full of pointless chatter (3). Early on, Amelius (who had desired Plotinus's portrait), assembled nearly 100 volumes of notes from these sessions, which he later presented to his son. Based on scholia and dependent on chaotic classroom practices, Amelius's compilation must have lacked clarity and focus, two goals Porphyry set for himself in arranging his own edition of Plotinus's thought. (A different edition of Plotinus's work by another student, Eustochius, does not survive.) In contrast to his portrait of Plotinus's disordered physical body, Porphyry argued for the superior organization and integrity of his version of Plotinus's intellectual corpus.

In contrast to Amelius's notes, the record of Plotinus's thought that Porphyry introduced derived from Plotinus's own hand. Nearing fifty, Plotinus had begun for the first time to write about topics discussed in his school (4).[6] When Porphyry arrived nine years later, Plotinus had written twenty-one treatises, but these circulated only very narrowly among those whom Plotinus had judged worthy to read them (4.17). The writing itself mimicked the production of an image from memory. "He worked out his train of thought from beginning to end in his own mind, and then, when he wrote it down, since he had set it all in order in his mind, he wrote as continuously as if he was copying from a book" (8). The writing represented his thought. This method of composition, incidently, finds its closest analogy in Carterius's portrait, a painting executed entirely from memory.

Even so, Plotinus's representation of his own ideas provoked anxiety. His manner of composition maintained his aversion to writing. "When Plotinus had written anything he could never bear [ἠνέσχετο] to go over it twice; even to read it through once was too much for him, as his eyesight did not serve him well for reading" (8).[7] In Porphyry's writing, Plotinus abhors his own production of text, cannot suffer subjecting it to his own gaze. Like his own body, he treats it with a measure of neglect and shame. Porphyry explains that Plotinus had poor penmanship, forming the letters without regard to their appearance. He did not divide his syllables correctly, and he "paid no attention to spelling." Concerned, according his biographer and editor, "only with thought" (8), Plotinus recapitulates a dualism between mind and body in the gap between ideas and text. The philosophy was beautiful, but the writing was misshapen, debased, and ugly. Like Plotinus's body, Plotinus's texts were disheveled. And the text suffered subsequent corruption: since the master gave no titles to his work, they circulated among various headings in a disordered fashion.

Porphyry sets out to fix the literary body, but the results are ambiguous because of the analogy between textuality and embodiment. Written texts are like bodies, images and copies, subject to the same corruption. An edition, like a biography or portrait, strives to standardize the corpus. In preparing his edition, Porphyry reproduced or oversaw the reproduction of Plotinus's texts. With spelling regularized, the treatises were copied in a neat and legible hand. In listing and ordering the names of the treatises, Porphyry produced a touched-up document of Plotinus's works, giving them a coherent intellectual shape. Within the *Life*, which serves as a biographical introduction to Plotinus's writings, Porphyry lists the titles of the treatises twice. First, he attempts to gives Plotinus's body of writing a proper chronology, assigning works to periods in the philosopher's life (4–6). Linking the treatises to Plotinus's history connects the potentially disembodied ideas to the a narratable identity, a person living through time and in space. In his second list (24–26), a table of contents for the edition, Porphyry imprints a different sort of order on the corpus, grouping the treatises by topics into an elegant structure of six groups of nine that he called *Enneads*, from the Greek word for "nine." To get the numbers to work out, Porphyry had to divide some of the longer treatises, underscoring the editor's artifice, which, like the biographer's, demanded creating coherence and meaning out of chaos. This second list, like the edition itself, moves ever upward from treatises on ethics and the natural order to disquisitions on the soul, the intellect, and ultimately on Being itself. This second narrative, the narrative implicit in the ordering of the treatises, moves anagogically from the shameful body upward toward the One. Porphyry's *Enneads* are thus a biography of the soul's progress in abandoning the life of the body. The dualist contrast between the two lists—the first list tied to chronology, time, and the body, the second plotting the movement away from the body and ultimately beyond time—manifests Plotinus's own preference for philosophy and the life of the mind over biography, the narrative of embodiment. The gap between these two lists further complicates Porphyry's literary task: given the flight from the body, why bother with narrative?

The problems raised by Porphyry's act of narrative representation merit consideration within the Neoplatonic system itself. Porphyry ascribes to Plotinus the idea that he resisted being represented on the grounds that it would produce "a longer-lasting image [εἴδωλον] of the image, as if it was something genuinely worth looking at" (1). For Porphyry, this statement assumes an opposition between the downward movement of mimesis, the production of images removed from their archetype, and anagogy, the upward motion of an image toward its archetype: movement away from the One and movement toward the One. But the quoted statement rejecting representation does not entirely reflect Plotinus's view of representation as conveyed in the *Enneads* themselves, where the treatment of images is consistently more nuanced.[8] Plotinus recognized the asymmetry of the relationship between a likeness and the thing of which it was a copy.[9] However, he taught that the discursive level of representation was a necessary result of the more real insofar as the real could be apprehended only through images. Arguing against Gnostic Christians, Plotinus defended the goodness of the sensible cosmos as an image of the intelligible: if one were to hate the image, why would you seek out the original?[10] And writing on intelligible beauty, Plotinus affirmed the role of art in producing the image of beauty through which beauty can be known (5.8.1–2). "But if anyone despises [artists] because they produce their works by imitating nature, we must tell him, first, that natural things are imitations too" (5.8.1). The beauty of the artistic image leads the mind back up the chain of emanation to the beauty of the thing represented. Moreover, to the extent that representation begins with the contemplation of something intelligible, the artist himself is a contemplative (5.1.8).

Similarly qualified valuation accrues to writing. Regarding discursive representation of the One, Plotinus writes, "Plato says, 'it cannot be spoken or written,' but we speak and write impelling towards it and wakening from reasonings to the vision of it, as if showing the way to someone who wants to have a view of something."[11] Speech and writing provide an image of the One necessary to our pursuit of it. The epistemological value of writing is confirmed: ultimately, a representation was not only an emanation of the thing represented but also a reflection of it.

Within the *Life of Plotinus*, Porphyry ascribes to Plotinus shame regarding embodiment. This literary portrait may derive more from Porphyry's own conception of the body than from those of Plotinus discernible in the *Enneads*.[12] For Plotinus, the body was not the problem, but rather the soul's concern for it.[13] Plotinus even asserted the value of bodily beauty in leading to the contemplation of higher beauty.[14] On the other hand, Porphyry's treatise, addressed to his wife Marcella, composed while he was away on a long journey, provides leverage on his views regarding embodiment and identity. Porphyry reminds Marcella that philosophy taught her to believe that "I am not this person who is tangible and susceptible to visible appearance, but rather a being completely separate from the body, without color and without form, totally incapable of being touched by hand but rather comprehended by thought alone."[15] Absent from her in body, Porphyry asserted in a manner unlikely to have been fully comforting, "You have not benefitted at all from the presence of my shadow [σκία] and visible form [εἴδωλον], nor from its absence,"[16] although he concedes that "The absence is painful to you as you train yourself to flee from the body."[17] This idea of fleeing from the body confirms that the body is not the locus of identity: it is not one's real self, but rather a mere image. Like the husk surrounding grain, the body is to be shucked on the ascent toward the divine.[18] For this reason, Porphyry instructs his wife that it does not matter whether her body is male or female, since gender is a property of the body and therefore not fundamentally constitutive of identity.[19] The separation of the soul from its representation stands in particularly tense relationship with ideas about the benefits of images.

Within the Neoplatonic system, body and writing can function as analogues. For Plotinus, the body is the image of the soul. But writings are also the image of the soul, since they are a record of the soul's thoughts, a memory of ideas. If the body itself does not constitute identity, what can be said about the textual body, or perhaps the textual bodies: the descriptive narration, the corpus of philosophical treatises, both of which are "images" of Plotinus? While Plotinus, following Socrates in the *Phaedrus*, likely thought that the real person resided in his ideas and not in his biography, the view that Porphyry ascribes to Plotinus regarding writing and images may diverge from Plotinus's own view. In fact, it diverges from Porphyry's view as well. Obviously, Porphyry saw value in the narrative representation of his teacher, in much the same way that he saw value in the "excellent portrait" painted by Carterius.[20] Nevertheless, Porphyry problematizes his own act of narration, complicating his performance of authorship. The result dramatizes the tension in Neoplatonic ideas about representation. The production of images extends downward, tending toward materiality. The problem is not that matter is evil or bad, or that pictures and stories have no value; rather, that the act of representation itself moves in the wrong direction. Once complete, of course, the representation tends to help others ascend.

But ideas about embodiment govern ideas about the exercise of authority in the production of text. Within the *Life of Plotinus*, the representation of the soul in the body, in a description of the body, or in writing the ideas of the mind into a body of writing each carry the taint of moving from the realm of thought to the realm of matter. While the materiality of a text may play an important role in the edification of others, the production of textual matter remains an object of concern. The practice of authorship is necessarily at odds with the ascent of the soul, even while it might facilitate it.

Materializing Syncletica

While Porphyry the Neoplatonist cast suspicion on writing as a species of embodiment, Christian intellectuals revalued writing as the incarnation of the word. For Nicene Christians, not only had God the Logos "taken to himself a body, and that no different than our own,"[21] God also reproduced his bodily presence in the eucharist. In Christian ritual practice, God's Logos materialized, Word become solid. The materialization of the Logos affected the way words solidified on the written page. The *Life of Syncletica* affords an opportunity to chart this difference. Its anonymous fifth-century author held no illusions about the stability of the physical body.[22] The text ends with a lengthy and often-gruesome description of the corruption of its heroine's body. The devil so hated her virtue that he "wreaked savage vengeance on her" (104). And while he had attacked Job upon the surface of his flesh, the devil assailed Syncletica from within, "breaking her lung up bit by bit with the phlegm she coughed up," "wearing her body away like a file" (105), "burning her innards as if in a fiery furnace," destroying her body slowly over three and a half years (106). An abscessed molar spread infection to her jawbone, eventually eating a hole in her face. "Putrefaction and a very foul-smelling stench overpowered her body throughout so that those women who tended her suffered more than she did" (111). In the midst of his account, the author remarks, "It is truly grievous and inhumane to speak of this process" (106). Yet speak he does, in part to stress the saint's noble endurance, in part to emphasize the transience of the flesh.

Although the body putrefies, the word might endure. For this reason, the author of the *Life of Syncletica* compared his writing to the preparation and preservation of food.

We investigated to the best of our ability the facts about her, we both heard from her contemporaries the superficial details of her early life and we gained [by observation] some enlightenment from her deeds themselves; we have come [now] to write, storing up for ourselves salvific food [τροφὰς σωτηριώδεις]. (3)

If the relationship between hearing an edifying discourse and eating it up, between text and food, would seem almost natural, for Christian authors it was leavened by the doctrine that God's Logos had become flesh, that text had become body, and that this body had been offered as food. God himself saved through rendering divine discourse good to eat.

The idea that texts were like spiritual food to be consumed by an assembled audience was a staple of early Byzantine hagiographical literature. Authors regularly presented their literary composition as an analogue for the materialization of the divine word in Jesus Christ rendered present in the eucharist. The rhetorical introduction to Leontius of Neapolis's *Life of Symeon the Fool*, a work of the 640s, describes that work as "an everlasting nourishment" that the author "unveils" for the reader. "Just as bread strengthens the body," he writes, "the word of God often awakens the soul to virtue."[23] The narratives of holy people offer instruction to the people of God; as expressions of God's Logos, they are both sacrificial bread and an extension of scripture. Such a connection between eucharist, language, revelation, and text is equally pronounced in the roughly contemporary Syriac *Life of Marutha*, where Denha, the author, rejects the notion that the "treasure" of his narrative should be hidden and announces that he "offers his effort" and "places [his work] upon the spiritual table for the soul's delectation."[24] The concept of Christian literary composition as a form of oblation underscores the materiality of texts and their assimilation to bodies.

The *Life of Syncletica* provides an excellent place to explore these themes because of its consistent interest in food, fasting, asceticism, and spiritual nutrition. Not particularly well known, even among scholars of early Christianity, the *Life of Syncletica* tells of the life and teachings of a desert mother. She was born to a prominent family in Alexandria, although her ancestors had emigrated from Macedonia; she is known to this day in the Coptic church as "the mother of nuns."[25] Her vita, composed in Greek, was once attributed to Athanasius but probably dates from the middle of the fifth century. The author derives much of his ascetical theory and the analysis of vices and virtues from the works of Evagrius of Pontus, who died in 399, especially the *Practicus*.[26] Furthermore, sayings of Syncletica derived from the *Life* appear in the sixth-century Greek and Latin collections known, in this case misleadingly, as the *Sayings of the Fathers*, or *Apophthegmata patrum* and *Verba seniorum*.

The author devoted the vast majority of the text, some 80 of its 113 paragraphs, to Syncletica's extended discourse on the practice of austerities and the cultivation of virtues. The domination of a saint's biography by a lengthy speech is by no means unprecedented, and it is worth pointing out that much of Athanasius's *Life of Anthony* is given over to a lengthy sermon on demons. The effect showcases Syncletica as speaker, directing attention to her saintly discourse, her logos. And at various points in the text, the author compares Syncletica's teachings, as well as the teachings of Christ, to a sort of food. A strong dichotomy between the physical and the spiritual pervades the text, and extends to the entire discourse on food: the ascetic avoids physical food through rigorous fasting and hungers for spiritual food in holy instruction.

The text persistently presents fasting and the regulation of diet as the key ingredient of ascetic praxis. If Syncletica ate outside of the appointed times for meals, she became instantly ill in disgust (10). She ate only bran bread and drank little water, often no water at all (17, 18). In her sermon, Syncletica stresses the importance of fasting as the most basic tool for the life of voluntary poverty, since gluttony and luxurious living were the root of the craving for property (32–34). By limiting herself to the "daily bread" sufficient to sustain life (34), the ascetic opened herself to receiving spiritual food. Within his description of the heroine's mode of life, the author terms Syncletica's fasting as a "salvific remedy" (σωτηρίου φαρμάκου) (10), as if she ingested the medicine of not eating. The author points to her long-suffered austerities as "provisions" (ἐφόδια) for the ascetic journey (13). Paradoxically, fasting itself becomes spiritual food.

Even in distinguishing between the spiritual gifts that might result from various modes of Christian practice, Syncletica's metaphors turn on

concepts of nourishment and satiety. "For the ones filled with contemplation and knowledge [θεωρία and γνῶσις] feast in one way, while those
who have a taste for asceticism and its practices feast in another, as do those
who, as they are able, act righteously in the world" (43). Contemplation,
asceticism, and lay piety figure as different regimens or diets. Asceticism, a
feasting that is not eating, participates in a eucharistic feast.

The eucharistic liturgy, presented as a wedding banquet, structures the
understanding of Syncletica's ascetic calling to a life of renunciation and
prayer. In an extended comparison with Thecla, the author explores Syncletica's symbolic union with Christ. For both women, Paul had led the
bride to the beloved. The church had served as bridal chamber. David, the
psalmist, sang the bridal hymns, and Miriam had led the dance. Moreover,
at both bridal banquets "For those partaking of the shared delicacies of the
divine banquet" the singer exclaimed, "Taste and see that the Lord is good
[χρηστός]" (Ps 34:9; LXX 33:9). The quotation from Psalm 34 underscores
access to God in consuming the sacrament. The goal of Syncletica's monastic life was union with the delectable Logos (8). In fact, Psalm 34 was already
in use as a communion hymn during the Mass of the Presanctified Gifts, a
form used primarily on weekdays during Lent. During these masses, in
keeping with the season of fasting, there was no festive eucharist; rather, the
sacrament that was distributed had already been consecrated on an earlier
occasion.[27] This reserve sacrament was a nourishment prepared in advance
and stored.

If the eucharist provides a metaphor for the ascetic life, its holy food
and drink also offer a framework for understanding Christian teaching and
texts. Since Plato's *Phaedrus*, ancient philosophers conceived of writing as
the image of speech. Writing preserved speech, capturing oral communication in a written record for the benefit of those absent. Writing constituted
a physicalization of memory. Writing was subordinate to speech because it
was material; it made speech solid. By its very nature as a tool for assisting
memory and allowing ideas to survive their authors, writing called attention
to human frailty, to forgetfulness and death. These assumptions are the
condition of possibility for Porphyry's *Life of Plotinus*. Christian philosophers baptized these truths in paradox. In Christian terms, it was humiliation and condescension indeed when the divine speech, the Logos, became
solid and material in flesh. The consequence, however, was a revaluation of
writing. Representation in text is no longer problematic for the author of
the *Life of Syncletica* in the way it had been for Porphyry.

The author of the *Life of Syncletica* employed writing as a technology for preserving holy teachings. By storing virtue, written narrative hoarded a salvific food. With regard to her teachings, the *Life of Syncletica* records Syncletica's speech, materializing in text the content of her discourse. The author understands the preservative properties of writing to extend to the whole enterprise of biographical composition, including the narration of details of her life. "We have come [now] to write, storing up for ourselves salvific food [τροφὰς σωτηριώδεις]" (3). The language of "storing up" (ἀποθησαυρίζοντες) connects the author's writing to technologies of food preservation—curing, pickling, or stockpiling in a granary.[28] The writing then keeps the salvific and nourishing text for subsequent consumption. The food of the text is described as "*sōtēriōdēs*," both "salvific" and "wholesome." This nourishment that cures the soul remains edible through the ears when it is read aloud.

To the extent that the text is salvific food, it assimilates itself to the eucharist—the salvific food at the center of Christian piety. The complex analogy, articulated in stages throughout the text, ultimately turns on the idea that all Christian teaching is Christ's, whether it be the Scriptures, the discourses of the saints, or the hagiographical writings that narrate their lives. Because they all nourish Christian souls, they are all spiritual food.

The author likens both scripture and Syncletica's teachings to milk and honey. When Syncletica is reluctant to speak, her female disciples entreat her, but in humility she demurs, answering them, "What do you imagine in this way about a sinner like me, as if I were doing or saying something worthwhile? We have a common teacher in the Lord; we draw spiritual water from the same source; we suck milk from the same breasts— the Old and the New Testaments" (21). Here the author employs concepts common in the early church about the way that Christ fed his congregation with the milk of his own breasts. The image has complex associations both with the eucharist and with Christian instruction. In the late second century, Clement of Alexandria articulated this connection in *The Pedagogue*.[29] Following common medical theory, Clement explained breast milk as a form of blood, "changed through a natural concoction after the mother has conceived; by loving affection blood degenerates and becomes white." Blood itself was understood as "a kind of liquid flesh."[30] Thus mothers, who fed their young with blood while they were fetuses in the womb continued to feed their newborns with their flesh and blood in the form of breast milk. This medical understanding stood behind Clement's exegesis of a number of scriptural passages. Clement read Israel's nourishment with milk and honey, and the Pauline passages about Christian instruction as milk (1 Cor

3:2) as types of the eucharist. "I gave you milk in Christ to drink." Teaching or doctrine figured as spiritual nourishment, "life-giving milk, flowing from breasts of tender love."³¹ Clement understood the sacrament of Christ's body and blood as a material representation of Christ's teaching. Moreover, Paul's contrast between milk and solid food defined a corresponding contrast between the teaching as it was heard and the teaching as it was incorporated as faith in the soul of the Christian believer. "It is possible to understand milk as the proclamation [κήρυγμα; that is, of the gospel], which has been broadly poured out; and solid food as the faith, which is condensed into a foundation from instruction [ἐκ κατηχήσεως], which being more substantial than hearing, is likened to solid food, given bodily existence [σωματοποιουμένη] in the soul."³²

While for Clement instruction congealed as faith, for the author of the *Life of Syncletica*, instruction solidified far more tangibly as scripture. The sacred writings were the milk of Christ's breasts solidified. It is precisely scripture's materiality, its durability and solid substance, that allow the faithful to feed on Christ's teachings. Toward the end of the vita, Syncletica declares, regarding the scriptures' use in liturgical practice, "Let incorruptible foods be brought to the table: prayer and psalms" (92). In prayer, the tongue and mouth put themselves to holy use, both consuming and producing the eucharist of sacred text. The women agree with Syncletica that they indeed have only one guide (παιδαγωγός), scripture, and one teacher (διδάσκαλος), Christ (21). But the terms *paidagogos* and *didaskalos* are interchangeable, highlighting the slippage between Christ and text.

Syncletica's response to the women's persistent call for her speech continues the discourse of lactation. The author writes that the holy woman wept "as a babe at the breast" (21). This figure is multivalent. On one level, it expresses Syncletica's humility and self-denigration in her reluctance to speak. She understands herself to be still on a diet of "milk," "a babe in Christ," in Paul's terms (1 Cor 3:1–2), a beginner.³³ On another level, however, this image points back to the idea that scripture is breast milk. Syncletica feeds on the teachings of Christ before passing this nourishment on to others.

Indeed her first words to the women are a quotation from scripture. Quoting from Proverbs 22:22 she says, "Do no violence to the poor man, for he is needy." The women gathered around her, "receiving her saying [ῥῆμα] gladly as if tasting honey and comb [κηρίου]" (21). The idea that hearing divine teachings is like eating honey and comb echoes the language of the Psalms. Psalm 19 (LXX 18:10) describes the precepts of the

Lord as "sweeter than honey and the drippings of the comb," and Psalm 119 (LXX 118:103) declares, "How sweet are thy words [λόγια] to my taste, sweeter than honey in my mouth."[34] By identifying Syncletica's first words as the honey of scripture, the author frames the whole of Syncletica's discourse as an extension of biblical wisdom literature. Her own words become like milk and honey. Furthermore, current pronunciation made the genitive *kēriou* (κηρίου; of the comb) likely a homophone for *Kyriou* (Κυρίου; of the Lord), thus connecting edible teachings with the body of Christ.[35]

Later in the text, the author deploys yet another eucharistic image to describe the nature of Syncletica's teachings. For Syncletica, Christ the teacher expresses life-giving instruction in the form of text. Christ's own textual eucharist flows in the breast milk of his Bible, Christ's transmuted blood. In an analogous communion, the author of the vita represents Syncletica's own discourse to her disciples as a "divine symposium"—that is, a holy drinking feast—in which the hearers "were made merry from the chalices of wisdom" (σοφίας κρατήρων) (30). In addition to reinforcing the connection between Syncletica's aphoristic mode and the books of Proverbs and Psalms, this figuration renders Syncletica both priest and teacher in the image of Christ. The author writes, "Syncletica was pouring out [οἰνοχοοῦσα] for them divine drink and liquid" (30). Thus Syncletica's teaching is compared to Christ's pouring out his blood: it is her true and perfect sacrifice.

This presentation of Syncletica's words as spiritual food frames the ultimate deterioration of her body. The author's description of Syncletica's dying conflates body, food, and language. At the end of her life, the devil "gnaws" at her (108), "searching for a meal" (112). In a heroic reversal, "he himself became food," bested by Syncletica's spiritual strength, "hooked by the weakness of her body" (112). With her lungs deteriorating and her mouth rotting, the Devil "afflicted her organs of speech, cutting off her spoken word," the word her women hungered for (110). In the end, malnutrition set in: the saint "could no longer partake of food, when so great an infection and stench held sway" (112). Unable to eat and unable to nourish her flock with words, Syncletica foretold her "departure from the physical body" (113). With visions of angels and martyrs' crowns, she predicted she would die in three days. And, of course, she was right.

The demise of Syncletica's body and of her ability to speak make the endurance of her words in the author's text all the more poignant. The preservation of the words in writing compensates for the corruption of the flesh. The words become edible once again in written text. As the final colophon declares, "The words issuing from the holy Syncletica . . . have been fully recorded exactly according to their proper sequence" (113). The body disintegrates, but the text reconstitutes the body of teaching in its proper order.

Teasing out a relationship between body and text, *The Life of Syncletica* relies on a complex nexus of scriptural and liturgical associations. The goal of Syncletica's ascetic practice lay in the charge to put off the bodily for the spiritual. But the gifts of this practice presented themselves as the participation in and production of Christ's own body. In fasting, Syncletica renounced physical foods for spiritual, explicitly textual, ones. The teaching of virtue, whether represented as eucharistic blood, milk, or solid food, assimilated itself to human physicality and was made spiritual body. For the author of the *Life of Syncletica*, text and discourse thus occupy a strange territory between the physical and the spiritual; identified with materiality and the body, they serve as spiritual vessels. Together the ideas that scripture is Christ's material flesh and that Syncletica's teaching was also a kind of flesh provide a model for the work of the anonymous author of the *Life of Syncletica*. He too produces a salvific food, a materialization of virtuous narrative and discourse—a logos to be consumed by subsequent readers and hearers as reserve sacrament, affording the opportunity to taste and see.

Because late antique explorations of the relationship between textuality and embodiment survive in written texts, the evidence is itself implicated in the assessment of how textual narratives were both attached to and separate from bodies. Hagiographical texts substitute for bodies. Saints' lives effect this substitution through a re-presentation of the absent. The saint reappears in stories and teachings, the material residue of a holy life. But late antiquity was also a time when philosophical ideas about the body were in flux. During the period of Christianization, the incarnation, the resurrection, and the eucharist had an impact on classical conceptions of a soul and body and thus of identity. The implications of this meditation on the body for the production of biography vary and mutate: the discourse about the relationship between textuality and materiality could be no more stable than the discourse about materiality itself.

Both Porphyry and the anonymous author of the *Life of Syncletica* use text to preserve the transient and to fix an identity that is slipping away. Solidifying the teachings now that the teacher is decayed demands more than a listing or recapitulation of instruction; in both cases, writing involves

a strategy of biographical narration. For both authors, writing is simultaneously like the body because it is material and like disembodied thought because it is perduring. Bodies are different from texts and the same as texts
at the same time. Even so, writing mediates between the two categories of
spirit and flesh with strikingly different results. For Porphyry, anxiety about
the descent of the soul into text renders his writing transgressive; his control
of the subject violates the subject as he constructs it. The contrast between
Porphyry's resistant subject and Gregory of Nyssa's cooperative subject is
instructive. Plotinus is the unwilling subject of literary composition, abhor-
ring his own representation, while Macrina offers herself willingly into text.
Within the *Life of Macrina*, Macrina leads Gregory in the act of biography,
setting up harmony between the character of Macrina and the narrative
voice that tells her story. The narrator shares her objective of thanksgiving.
If the *Life of Syncletica* demonstrates her humility by portraying her reluctance at first to speak, her teaching then flows in a steady stream until the
source dries up. In contrast to Porphyry's performance of anxiety, the author of the *Life of Syncletica* preserves her confidently in text. Textuality is
no longer an object of shame because materiality is no longer problematic
in quite the same way. Instead of generating a betraying irony about representing Syncletica's rotting body (as does the *Life of Plotinus*), the defeat of
the body depends on the victory of the body, the preservation of logos as
food. The model for subverting the body/spirit opposition is in the sancti-
fication of matter itself. This is the difference incarnation makes, not only
for its explicit revaluing of the body but also for framing the subsequent
production of the logos. For the author of the *Life of Syncletica*, as for Gregory of Nyssa, writing is no longer debased: it is a licensed, saintly mode, an
imitation of God.

Texts and Bodies in the Abgar Tradition

The theology of the incarnation afforded opportunities for the positive valuation of writing because of its emphasis on the embodiment of God. The
connection between textuality and embodiment posited in the *Life of Syncletica* tended to emphasize the endurance of writing over the transience of
the body, even while stressing the materiality of texts. Early Christian traditions regarding a written correspondence between Jesus and King Abgar of
Edessa developed a more secure connection between writing and presence,
although still retaining a relationship between writing and absence. Alone

among patristic materials, the Abgar traditions present Jesus as an author of a written text. At the culmination of this trajectory, which stretches from the late third to the early fifth centuries, is the text known as the *Teaching of Addai*. Here, the Abgar legend shifted its concern from a text produced by Jesus to an eschatological vision of the textual body.

Since the primary concern of this chapter is the relationship between body and text, consideration of this text begins with a striking revelation of the end of time. The *Teaching of Addai*, a Syriac apocryphon produced in Edessa probably soon after 414, contains one of the strangest eschatologies known from Christian antiquity.[36] The haunting image of bodies rising from graves covered in script illustrates a complex relationship between bodies and texts, between presence and memory, and between biography and critical judgment. According to this anonymous text, at the last and dreadful hour the resurrection will give answer to the incarnation as the *flesh is made word*. In the second half of the work, Addai (Thaddeus in Greek), one of the seventy-two apostles of Jesus, preaches to the people of Edessa about the coming end.

For the whole of that for which our Lord came into the world was that he might teach and show us that at the consummation of created things there will be a resurrection for all people. At that time their manner of life will be depicted in their own persons and their bodies will become parchment skins for the books of justice. There will be no one there who cannot read, because in that day everyone will read the writings of his own book. He will hold a reckoning of his deeds in the fingers of his hands. Moreover, the unlearned will know the new writing of the new languages. No one will say to his companion: "read this for me," because teaching and instruction will rule over all people.[37]

This passage reveals a markedly scribal conception of Christian life and the formation of Christian identity. Much of the rest of Addai's sermon instructs the inhabitants of Edessa how to write their bodies properly, particularly by resisting idolatry. While death separates life from the body, the resurrection returns life to the body, this time as vita. This textual tattooing renders every body a literary corpus. The vision's power lies in the regulatory effect of this promise of a biographical body; all deeds public and private will be legible. And since all will be able to read, there will be no escape from shame. Implicitly then, the faithful Christian will desire to live so as to produce a text that narrates virtuous deeds. In short, this eschatology encourages Christians to produce upon themselves the life of a saint. When living is writing, the goal is hagiography.

To make sense of this curious image and its claims about texts and bodies, it is useful to consider its literary context. The *Teaching of Addai* is a composite text that assembles documents about the origins of Christian piety in Edessa.[38] The story of Addai's visit to the city, the miracles he performed, and the sermon he delivered appears after the text recounts an earlier tradition regarding an exchange of letters between Abgar, king of Edessa, and Jesus the Messiah. Addai's preaching about graphic bodies fleshes out the tale of Jesus' own writing.

The Abgar/Jesus correspondence, generated in Syriac in the second half of the third century, mostly likely in Edessa, already engaged a discourse about writing and the body, playing on ancient tropes about the simultaneous presence and absence of writers in their letters. It was a commonplace in antiquity that letters substituted for the presence of their authors. The writer could not come in the flesh, so he sent text instead. Such literary conceits can be found, for example, in actual correspondence and in narratives involving letters. Jerome writes coyly to Rufinus, "I fancied it too bold a wish to be allowed by an exchange of letters to counterfeit to myself your presence in the flesh."[39] In Achilles Tatius's novel *Leukippe and Clitophon*, the hero, pining away in the absence of his beloved, scrutinizes each word of her missive "as if seeing her through the letters."[40] These sorts of remarks reveal an underlying epistolary theory in which writing compensates for the absence of the body.[41] In a related gesture, as the *Life of Macrina* and the *Life of Syncletica* demonstrate, texts also substitute for bodies in the hagiographical genre, here not for the bodies of authors, but for the bodies of the texts' subjects. Those separated from the saint by virtue of distance as well as those living after the saint had died might still take instruction from the holy one's deeds by hearing the exemplary life recounted in narrative. These stories become the saint's relics. Theodoret supplies the story of Maron as an alternative to his bones.[42]

The earliest appearance of the letters between Abgar and Jesus in extant Christian literature occurs in Eusebius's *Ecclesiastical History* (1.13), composed shortly before 300. By the time they had fallen into Eusebius's hands, the letters had already been placed in a narrative frame explaining their supposed provenance and consequences—if indeed the letters existed prior to the composition of their frame. It is also likely that the letters and their explanatory setting had already been translated from Syriac into Greek.[43] At the end of the first book of the *Ecclesiastical History*, Eusebius presents Greek translations of the two letters and a short *Acts of Thaddeus*, supposedly culled from the Record Office at Edessa. In the first letter, Abgar

Uchama, the Toparch of Edessa, having heard about Jesus' ability to perform curative miracles, invites Jesus to travel from Jerusalem to heal him. Abgar offers him protection from "the Jews" who are treating him with contempt and declares that Jesus is either "God come down from heaven" or God's Son. The letter models a piety of recognizable shape: Jesus restores wholeness to the bodies of the faithful.

In the second letter, Jesus replies with brevity. "Happy are you who believed in me without having seen me!" he begins, paraphrasing the reply to doubting Thomas in the Gospel of John. The final sentences of the reply make further use of Johannine vocabulary regarding the person and work of Christ, particularly the language of sending. "As to your request that I should come to you," he writes—or perhaps dictates to a certain Ananias, who carried Abgar's letter from Edessa—"I must complete all that I was *sent* to do here, and on completing it must at once be taken up to the One who *sent* me. When I have been taken up I will *send* you one of my disciples to cure your disorder and bring life to you and those with you" (1.13). The letter both explains Christ's absence from Edessa and substitutes for his presence. His logos inscribes itself in his letter: the word of the Lord sent and delivered to Abgar's court. The text is ambiguous about who actually penned the letter; it is unclear whether Eusebius regarded the "original" to have been in Jesus' hand. Ananias's role as a conduit for the transmission of the logos is nevertheless underplayed; he is merely a vessel for Jesus' communication.

In fact, both letters employ the vocabulary and inhabit the worldview of the Gospel of John.[44] Thus the forgery invites comparison with that gospel and its Christology, and with its figuration of the incarnation as the sending of the divine Logos into the world, in this context a decidedly postal image. In contrast to Jesus' letter to Abgar, where word and body are distinct, in John, the heavenly Father sent his Word into the world such that he was not absent but fully present. Jesus as God's Word not only represents him but really is him. The Father's missive is the body, the Word made flesh.

Already at this stage of the Abgar legend, Jesus' acts of sending, both missive and missionary, imitate the Father's salvific sending. While Jesus, the sender of epistle and apostle, prepares to be returned to the Father who sent him,[45] the subsequent commission of the Apostle Addai will bring healing to Abgar and good news to his people. Redacted into a composite document, the letters circulated to Eusebius with an appendix regarding Thaddeus/Addai's visit to Edessa, where he indeed cures Abgar of his disease,

preaches a version of the Apostles' Creed to Abgar's household, and prepares to speak to the people of the city. Addai brings to the king both
wholeness of body and healing logos, this time in the words of the apostle's
preaching of the faith.

The next surviving textual notice of the written correspondence between Jesus and the Edessan king Abgar dates from around 384 and demonstrates the letters' significance as relics in the possession of the royal ar-
chives in Edessa. Having completed her visit to holy sites in Palestine, the
Spanish nun Egeria decided to travel twenty-five days to Edessa. Although
her stated interest was the tomb of the Apostle Thomas, her report reveals
that it also arose from a long-standing familiarity with the letters: Egeria
already had a copy of the one from Jesus at home! While her enthusiasm
must overstate the popularity of Edessa with pilgrims, she confirms the
city's importance for Christian travelers in her travel diary.[46] "Believe me,
that there is no Christian who has come as far as the holy places of Jerusalem who does not go to Edessa to pray" (17). Moreover, Egeria's diary attests that by the last quarter of the fourth century, the correspondence between Jesus and Abgar was widely known throughout the Mediterranean
basin and had become an object of pious devotion. She writes, "Our Lord
Jesus Christ had promised in a letter, which He sent to King Abgar through
the messenger Ananias, that Saint Thomas [*sic*] would be sent to Edessa
after His ascension to heaven" (17). According to Egeria, Christ had sent
Thomas (not Thaddeus) to Abgar after ascending to heaven. Thus, upon
her own arrival in the city, some twenty-five days after leaving Jerusalem,
Egeria rushed to Thomas's shrine.

Afterwards no less than the bishop of Edessa gave her a guided tour of
other places of interest to Christian pilgrims. The palace of King Abgar was
the first stop. Here the bishop related how during a siege of the city by the
Persian army, Abgar had carried the letter of Jesus to the city gate and
prayed there with his soldiers. According to the bishop, Abgar declared that
Jesus had promised that no enemy would enter the city, and he lifted the
opened letter with hands upraised, causing a great darkness to descend
upon the Persians, who, befuddled, did not enter the city, although they
laid siege to Edessa for many months (19). The copy of the letter of Jesus
quoted in the *Teaching of Addai* is substantially the same as the version in
Eusebius, but for the addition of a final line: "As for your city may it be
blessed and may no enemy ever again rule over it."[47] Egeria herself remarks
that the version in Edessa was "certainly more extensive" than a copy she
already had at home (19). In the religious imagination of the late fourth

century, the letter of Jesus had become a miracle-working relic. Sent out from Jesus, the epistle of words substituting for the presence of the Word had become a conduit for divine power. Originally a token of Christ's absence, it had morphed into an instrument of divine presence.

The final stop on Egeria's Edessan tour confirms the letter as the focus of an urban cult. The bishop led Egeria to the city gate, saying "Let us go now to the gate, through which the messenger Ananias entered with the letter which I have been discussing" (19). Standing at the gate, after reciting a prayer, the bishop read the letter to Egeria, who received his blessing. Significantly this practice of reading a text at a holy site mirrors Egeria's experience elsewhere, where at a holy place she hears scripture read and then receives a blessing, often in the form of the eucharist, the body of Christ itself.[48] And indeed the letter of Jesus to Abgar is in some deep sense truly scriptural, the words of Christ in text. The writing itself functions as a conduit for holiness. Since the bishop read the letter to Egeria "on arriving at the gate," it seems likely that the letter of Jesus was affixed apotropaically on the city gate. (By the mid-sixth century, according to Procopius, the letter had been inscribed on the city's walls.[49]) At the end of the tour, the bishop gave Egeria copies of both letters, Abgar's and Jesus'. Surely she cherished these not merely as souvenirs of her visit but rather as relics of Christ—not unlike wood of the true cross or dirt from the site of the resurrection—potentially miraculous objects, an *eulogia* of the words of the Lord present in writing.[50]

Composed only a few decades after Egeria's journey, the *Teaching of Addai* extends the traditions about Abgar and Addai in ways that are significant to the present inquiry concerning bodies and texts. The text fills out the character and activity of Hanan (Greek: Ananias), the courier who carried the letter of Abgar to Jesus and returned with the Lord's reply. The text describes him throughout the text as "Hanan the archivist," *Hanan tabularah*, the *tabularius*. The Latin loan-word describes the court registrar, the notary, the one who keeps accounts, the one who keeps the books. This detail serves to assure the accuracy of Jesus' letter, since Hanan takes faithful dictation, accurately representing the word of the Lord. "Hanan the archivist told [Abgar] everything which he had heard from Jesus since His words had been placed by [Hanan] in written documents."[51] Here the act of inscribing the letters on the page rests solely with the professional writer and record keeper, Hanan. Jesus merely dictates his response to Abgar.

In a further elaboration of Hanan's role, Hanan also documents the appearance of Jesus' body by painting his portrait, for in addition to being the royal archivist, Hanan was the king's artist (*yiçayārā*; root *çwr*: depictor). This may even have been suggested by the Latin etymology of *tabularius*, from *tabula*, literally a panel, painting, or picture, a visual record. Thus Hanan returns to Edessa as transmitter of both the word and image of God, imitating Christ's own role as mediator between heaven and earth by mediating between Jerusalem and Edessa. Unable to persuade Jesus to return with him to Edessa, the archivist, the record keeper, enters Edessa with separate simulacra of the text and body of Jesus in the letters and the portrait. (While there is some debate over this issue, it seems quite likely that a portrait of Jesus was available for veneration in Edessa by this time, although it was not remarked upon by Egeria—perhaps because it was produced subsequent to her visit.[52]) The text also establishes textual precedence and license for Hanan's work: the Bible itself sketches the biographical portrait of Jesus. Earlier in his speech to the people of Edessa, Addai explains that the prophets "depicted" the life of the Messiah in scripture, "his birth, suffering, resurrection, ascension to this Father, and his sitting at the right hand" (39–41). Scripture itself provides a verbal portrait of the archetypal life, a life in words.

Having presented Hanan the archivist, keeper of documents and transmitter of the record of the divine body, the redactor of the *Teaching of Addai* supplied Addai with an extensive sermon about Christianity that includes the eschatological passage quoted earlier. In contrast to the two media—writing and painting—deriving from Hanan's hand, where the logos and the body are depicted separately, in Addai's vision of the end of time, text and body are fully joined. At "the separation [*purshānā*] between the sheep and the goats" (18), believer and infidel alike rise up as narratives, texts of bold and angular Syriac estrangelo script on human vellum, or perhaps in a new language, read and comprehended by all. With "their manner of life depicted [*methçiryn*; root *çwr*] in their persons, and their bodies [now] parchment skins for the books of justice," the perfection to come gathers humanity as folios of great books. All things are known at the end because they have been duly recorded and because illiteracy has vanished. The eschatological vision comments implicitly on Christ's own literacy, since in order to judge the people, he will read them like pages of a codex or so many scrolls. Here writing figures not only as an aid to recall but as the medium through which humanity acquires God's diachronic knowing. The resurrected come to know themselves as God has known them all along. Moreover, this text that celebrates the holy archivist of Edessa images God as the great archivist, a keeper of books, the librarian cataloguing biographies of vice and virtue. The general resurrection marks the opening of a great archive and images judgment as a literary-critical exercise of discerning the good texts from the bad.

Thus the *Teaching of Addai* meditates upon a tradition that already grappled with the problem of the gap between writing and presence, between the letter and the person of Jesus, between the flesh and the word of God. Looking to the last things for a resolution of that gap, the author reads the resurrection as the completion of the work of the incarnation, the joining of word and flesh, the flesh become logos. This logos-centered and logo-centric Christianity presents Christian life as scribal, scripted, and scriptural. At the end, then, a life is text, the course of life become logos. Christian life figures implicitly as a scripting in one's own flesh in preparation for judgment and redemption, a hagiographical exercise through which piety inscribes itself as writing. All Christians are now writers, and virtuous living is a practice of authorship.

*   *   *

The *Teaching of Addai* promises a consummation of textuality and embodiment. In this eschatology, people are texts; identity is perfectly enfleshed in written narrative. Textuality is no longer a problematic species of embodiment violating the upward motion of the eternal soul, as it was for Porphyry, or a durable body starkly contrasted with the blatantly more material body of corruption. Instead, the text is the body to come, the incarnate logos. In this scheme, to paraphrase Athanasius, Logos became flesh so that flesh might become Logos, fully joined to body in hypostatic union. If our biographies become our selves, this is because in the incarnation, God takes a body in order to have a biography: God humbles himself to have a story.

The joining of text and body that the *Teaching of Addai* promises at the end was already prefigured in the bodily Logos of the person of Jesus. It was also visually manifest for many early Byzantine Christians in their altar bread. Between the late fourth and the early seventh centuries, the practice of impressing bread intended for consecration with a bread stamp became widespread.[53] Among the great variety of types of bread stamps, ones bearing the sign of the cross or securing Christ's identity with his monogram (Chi-Rho) became increasingly popular.[54] A terra-cotta stamp

Figure 9. Bread stamp from Achmim (Panopolis). Sixth or seventh century. Terra-
cotta. 7.5 cm. Photo © Musée d'art et d'histoire, Ville de Genève.

found in Egypt at Achmim (Panopolis) dating from the sixth or seventh
century (Fig. 9) bears a cross with the letters "$\overline{\text{IC}}$ $\overline{\text{XC}}$ $\overline{\text{YC}}$ $\overline{\text{ΘY}}$" ("Jesus
Christ, Son of God") grouped in each of the four divisions created by a
central cross.[55] Once consecrated, this loaf-marking presented Christ as a
textual body, his signature guaranteeing the authenticity of his body. A
stone stamp of similar date, this one from Cyprus (Fig. 10), supplements
Christ's identifying name in the quadrants created by the arms of the cross
with a fragment of narrative, "$\overline{\text{IC}}$ $\overline{\text{XC}}$ NI KA" ("Jesus Christ conquers").[56]
Beyond the assertion that Christ achieves victory over sin and death, this
marking joins the essential feature of Christ's story to his flesh. The following chapter explores how this synthesis of textuality and embodiment in the
body of Christ empowered Romanos the Melodist, Byzantium's greatest
poet, to write.

Figure 10. Bread stamp from Cyprus. Sixth or seventh century. Stone. 2.9 × 2.9 cm.
Photo © Copyright The British Museum.

Chapter 8
Textuality and Redemption:
The Hymns of Romanos the Melodist

The liturgical hymns of Romanos the Melodist stand as one of the greatest achievements of Byzantine literature.[1] The works of this sophisticated sixth-century poet also recapitulate many, if not most, of the themes articulated in the course of this study. In his exploration of the place of writing in Christian narrative, Romanos ties his literary production to the Bible and engages in a mimesis of biblical authors. He writes in the context of cult and liturgy, offering scripts for worship. He inscribes his authorship as an occasion to practice humility, making writing an ascetic performance ultimately constitutive of the author's identity. In explicitly performative contexts, Romanos raises questions about textuality and materiality, about the body of the Logos and the corpus of the poet. The shift in genre from hagiography to hymnography thus allows us to consider one writer's attempt to weave related theologies of authorship together.

Through much of the age of Justinian, Romanos supplied Constantinople with dramatic verse homilies keyed to the events of the liturgical calendar. During the course of his career, Romanos rescripted the biblical narrative with two different but related techniques. First, he employed writing to expound biblical stories in the manner of midrash, reading the story by retelling the story, supplying additional detail in the process of interpretation, revealing the meaning of the narrative by supplementing it. Acknowledging that "The mystery of your plan of salvation [οἰκονομία], O our Saviour, is ineffable, incomprehensible," Romanos applied a poetic exegesis to articulate a theology of Christ's incarnation, suffering, death, and resurrection.[2] Second, and of even greater interest, Romanos frequently expanded the biblical story by inserting writing itself—that is, written documents—into the fabric of the story, so that texts appear in the sacred narrative where there were none before.[3] By this second technique, Romanos inscribed textuality into the economy of salvation; in the works of his hand, grace was sealed through the composition and dissemination of text. In this endeavor, Romanos stressed both the materiality of the written word and the physicality of the act of writing.

In the hymns considered in this chapter, Romanos explored models for understanding authorship. His different models, when considered together, are not strictly compatible; they do not present a systematic understanding of writing as a religious activity. To a great extent, the function of a particular poem within the liturgical year determined the model of authorship presented, since Romanos's ideas about writing in each case emerged as a response to and reflection on a liturgical event, marking a moment in the life of Christ as lived in the celebrations of the church. The biblical readings, or lections, appointed for a given day governed the possibilities for shaping a discourse on writing. Nevertheless, Romanos's sustained interest in interpolating writing demonstrates not only a concern to cultivate a presentation of himself as a writer but also a concern to explore authorship itself as a Christian problem, to reconcile literary creativity and the work of redemption.

Writing the Crucifixion

In the hymn "On Peter's Denial," assigned variously in the manuscript tradition to Holy Thursday and Good Friday, Romanos explored the crucifixion as a profoundly textual event.[4] In midrashic fashion, the poem fills out and meditates upon the Gospels' brief interchange between Jesus and his disciple in order to underscore the drama of divine forgiveness. At one point in the hymn, Jesus explains to Peter, whom he once helped to walk upon the water,

Look, I am now telling you that before the cock crows, you will three times disown me,
and, as if the waves of the sea were submerging and drowning your mind, you will three times deny me.
The first time you cried out, but now as you weep, you will not find me giving you my hand as before,
because, having taken in it a reed [as a pen], I am starting to write a pardon [συγχώρησις] for all Adam's descendants.
My flesh, which you see, becomes for me like paper
and my blood like ink, where I dip my pen and write [βάπτω καὶ γράφω],
as I distribute an unending gift to those who cry,
    Hasten, Holy One, save your flock. (18.7)

Dying on the cross, the body of Christ is transformed into text. His flesh like paper, his blood like ink, Christ distributes grace by writing on his body. The redemption of humanity is an act of inscription, the composition of a legal document, a συγχώρησις, such as those presented in court to mark a settlement or declare forgiveness. The body of Christ produces itself as a document of absolution. Because he will be occupied with writing, Christ's hand will be temporarily unavailable to Peter and cannot reach out to him as it had when Peter was trying to walk on the sea (18.6). Here, Christ's saving hand reaches out to undertake a more permanent and indelible task.

The writing implement is no invention but derives from a pun on the word *kalamos*, a reed. The reed figures prominently in the passion narratives of the Gospels. According to Matthew, the soldiers dressed Jesus in a scarlet robe, crowned him with thorns, and placed "a reed [κάλαμος] in his right hand" (Mt 27:29). Then they took this reed and, after spitting on Jesus, struck him on the head.[5] Later, while Christ was hanging on the cross, one of the bystanders put a vinegar-filled sponge on a reed (κάλαμος) in order to give Jesus a drink (Mt 27:48; cf. Mk 15:36). But a *kalamos* is also a stylus, a pen fashioned from a reed, a common writing implement. Playing on the reed's close association with the passion, particularly the humiliation of Christ, Romanos reads—or, perhaps, writes—a certain irony into Christ's suffering, where his torture is rendered an act of inscription. The reed that beat him becomes an instrument of redemption.[6] This pointed object Christ dips into his blood, the flowing ink that serves as the medium of his salvific writing. And perhaps Romanos has another long, thin object associated with the crucifixion in mind as well, namely the lance (λόγχη), which, according to John 19:34, the soldiers used to pierce Jesus' side, causing blood and water to flow. Thus through this compressed language, the hearer is guided to imagine Christ dipping a reed stylus into the blood flowing from the wound in his side, the gap in his breast like an inkwell.

In conceiving Christ's sacrifice as the publication of a legal pardon, Romanos presents text as an embodiment of divine grace and crucifixion as a scribal act. Golgotha becomes the scene of writing, and so does the body of Christ. In this conception of the crucifixion, the Logos made flesh renders himself again as logos, the saving word of God, now fully present in text.[7] In graphic display, the image of Christ the Logos transformed into text takes on eucharistic overtones. Playing deeply on the body (here, σάρξ) and blood of Christ, Romanos gives another dimension to the ritual of bread and wine. Echoing the words of institution, "This is my body [σῶμα] . . . this is my blood,"[8] Romanos's Christ offers himself as paper and ink. Thus, at the same time, the body is a text to be consumed by readers, and the eucharistic meal is prepared so that one might eat words.

More Textual Bodies

Part of the interest in the salvific potential of textuality resulted from the affirmation of embodiment through the incarnation. Bodies were analogous to texts, a theme already explored in the hymns of the Syriac poet Ephrem, whose poems Romanos's often resemble. Sebastian Brock has pointed to two different sorts of incarnation articulated in the works of the Syriac poet Ephrem. Born in Nisibis, probably in the first decades of the fourth century, Ephrem arrived in Edessa (modern Urfa) in the wake of the Persian conquest of Nisibis in 363, and he remained in Edessa until his death in 373.[9] Not only did God "put on the body," but in accommodating himself to human limitation, God also "put on metaphors," clothing himself in a garment of words.[10] Scripture figured as a type of divine embodiment. Scripture's linguistic description of God is an accommodation to our own boundedness in language.[11] The thirty-first of Ephrem's *Hymns on Faith* has as its refrain: "Blessed is He who has appeared to our human race under so many metaphors."[12] Ephrem explains,

We should realize that, had He not put on the names [šmh']
of such things, it would not have been possible for Him
to speak with us humans. By means of what belongs to us did He draw close to us;
He clothed Himself in language, so that he might clothe us
in His mode of life. He asked for our form and put this on,
and then, as a father with his children, He spoke with our childish state.[13]

For Ephrem, language figures not as a sign of the Fall but as a marker of human creatureliness. For this reason, in scripture, God is clothed in language, in the materiality of writing. Elsewhere, Ephrem emphasizes the bodily character of scripture. In the fifth of his *Hymns on Paradise*, Ephrem writes of his encounter with the Book of Genesis, in which "Moses described the creation of the natural world"[14]:

I read the opening of this book
and was filled with joy,

for its verses and lines
  spread out their arms to welcome me;
the first rushed out and kissed me,
  and led me on to its companion;
and when I reached that verse
  wherein is written
the story of Paradise,
  it lifted me up and transported me
from the bosom of the book
  to the very bosom of Paradise.[15]

This greeting by the community of verses ties the experience of reading scripture to the liturgical passing of the peace. With each verse as an embracing body, the reader finds himself or herself enveloped by the text. Reading is physicalized because the text is material.

Romanos's hymn "On Peter's Denial" goes a step further. As we have seen, in that hymn, Christ himself becomes text; the written sign and its physical referent are one. Since antiquity, semiotics has made much of the problematic of representation, of the system of signification in which a sign is believed to point to its referent. That relationship, dependent on the otherness between sign and signified, between text and subject, is predicated on the absence of the thing being represented.[16] While Augustine in the West and Gregory of Nyssa in the East tended to maintain this distinction, as the patristic period progressed, doctrines of the incarnation challenged the gap between between sign and signified, since in the person of Christ, God is not merely signed but present in his human body. Similarly, theological reflection on the eucharist tended to regard the collapsing of the distinction of sign and signified as the chief mystery of the eucharistic elements, which, being the body and blood of Christ, posed the same theoretical options as the incarnate God, since they were the same thing.

In the early sixth century, the author known as Dionysius the Areopagite stressed a concept of the *symbolon* to discuss the community between the sign and its referent. In the eucharist, the gifts placed on the altar were understood as "reverend symbols by which Christ is signaled and partaken," both signed and present.[17] Pseudo-Dionysius's theology of the symbol corresponds to Jean Baudrillard's conception of the simulacrum, a reality present in the supposed sign.[18] This conception of the symbol applied both to God's incarnate body and to the reproduction of this body in the eucharistic elements, which are not merely a sign, but a real presence. That God collapses the distinction between sign and signifier might have implications for the relationship between a text and its subject, between writing and the thing it points to. In the hymn "On Peter's Denial," the body of Christ functions both as signified and sign, God's physical body and material text. The distinction between sign and signifier collapses, is placed under erasure. Like his presence in the eucharist, Christ's textuality is revealed as a species of his embodiment.

For Romanos, confidence in the incarnation, the Logos made flesh, yielded this peculiar—and even ironic—revaluation of writing.[19] Written text served as an analogue of the body of Christ, the Logos inscribed in matter. Moreover, the analogy held not merely for the Son of God as narrated in the scriptures, but also for the material presence of the Logos in the eucharistic elements. In its materialization of words, writing served as a locus of Christian redemption. For Romanos, the materiality of the Logos in the incarnation and the reinscription of the Logos at the crucifixion opened opportunities for understanding the act of writing, the work of the author composing a text. Indeed, in Romanos's vision of the crucifixion, writing does more than merely imply the existence of the writer, pointing to the priority of the author or to the production of the author as a by-product of the act of composition: in the hymn "On the Denial of Peter," the writing is the author; the writer is his text; Jesus is his logos.

Signing the Cross

In the hymn "On the Denial of Peter," the inscriptional work of the passion takes its place on Christ's very body; elsewhere in Romanos's corpus, the blood shed at the crucifixion serves as ink inscribing the cross. In "On the Adoration at the Cross," the wood above Christ's head furnishes a metonym for Christ's flesh.[20] Romanos most likely composed this hymn for the feast of the Elevation of the Cross on September fourteenth.[21] Here, as the focus of liturgical celebration, the cross itself, rather than the dying and incarnate body of God, carries the text that secures the liberation of humanity from danger. But the substitution is not complete, for while Christ signs the wood rather than his flesh, his medium is still his own blood, the life-giving fluid of his material body. In addition to accounts of the crucifixion found in the canonical gospels, Romanos makes use of legends of Christ's descent into hell, preserved in the apocryphal *Gospel of Nicodemus*.[22] The poet reflects on one of the two robbers crucified at Golgotha with Christ, the one who bade Jesus to remember him in Paradise (Lk 23:39–43).[23] In this case, Romanos does not introduce writing into the story in a place where it was not, since Christ's identity is already inscribed on a plaque above his head, so much as he elaborates the narrative to have the robber transport this writing into a new place, to Eden.

The synoptic Gospels refer to the "epigraph" (ἐπιγραφή: Mk 15:26; Lk 23:38) inscribed above Christ's head, but the poet employs the term that the Gospel of John gives to the phrase "Jesus of Nazareth, King of the Jews," referring to it as his "title" (τίτλος) inscribed by Pilate himself and placed above Christ's head (Jn 19:19–22). The multiple meanings of the Latin loan-word *titulus* offer the poet possibilities for rereading an apocryphal legend. In the hymn, Jesus explains to the robber that if he were to approach paradise without "the declarations of the title-inscription" (τοῦ τίτλου τὰ θεσπίσματα), he would be consumed by the flaming sword. Here the *titulus* is both an inscription and an entitlement or warrant, granting the bearer legal access and possession. Thus Romanos translates the writing from the cross into the apocryphal narrative of the thief's approach to paradise. Jesus instructs the robber, "Taking this inscription [πρόγραμμα] here from my cross, / Robber, march up to the Cherubim, / and they will know the symbol of life."[24] Like a document securing passage into another country, the words on the cross function as a passport or letter of introduction. When the robber arrives at the gates of Eden, he presents the inscription for the Cherubim's inspection (23.10). The robber is confident because he holds the proper documentation. He speaks to the angels:

"Receive the sure seal and the divine engravings [ἐγχαράγματα—pl.],
The signature (ὑπογραφή) of [the] king, of God the All-Merciful."
. . . .
The Cherubim, receiving it, recognized the letters,
Shining out with the grace of the purple of blood.
They delighted in how beautifully it had been dictated [ὑπηγορεύθη].[25]

As in the hymn "On Peter's Denial," Christ's blood figures as ink, here the purple ink used on imperial documents.[26] The crucifixion inscribes the wood of the cross with holy blood to guarantee Christians safe passage into paradise by testifying to the crucifixion of Christ's body. Between these two poems, Christ is the inscription, epigraph, title, author, and signatory. The titular plaque, like Christ's flesh, is signed with Christ's blood to testify to his identity and authority, an authority conveyed to the bloody document itself, the text that he embodies. This correlation between text and signature, between work and author, is all the more significant because of the peculiar manner in which Romanos signed his own works, making each hymn an acrostic on his own name.

Romanos and His Production

Romanos was a highly skilled and accomplished hymnographer. Concrete historical details about Romanos's life are limited. Various middle Byzantine service books collated from the tenth through the twelfth centuries include entries for the celebration of Romanos in the calendar of the saints on October 1. According to these texts, Romanos was born in the Syrian city of Emesa and served as a deacon of the Church of the Resurrection in Beirut before arriving in Constantinople during the reign of Anastasius I (491–518).[27] It is likely that his first language was Semitic, since Syriac was the common language of Emesa and his diction contains some semiticisms. It is possible, as a later hymn composed for the feast of Saint Romanos claims, that he was of Jewish origin.[28] As a melodist, likely both cantor and composer, he served the Church of the Theotokos in the Kyrou district in the north of the capital, where he was eventually buried.[29] He continued to write numerous hymns "for the feasts of the Lord and the commemorations of various saints"[30] during most of the reign of Justinian and died sometime after 555.

His hymns, of which some sixty genuine poems survive, are chanted verse sermons, in large part celebrating the major events in the life of Christ and in the life of the Virgin, the key points of the annual liturgical cycle. Other songs responding to and expounding upon various texts from the Old Testament as well as the New Testament parables were likely tied to the lectionary as well. In this capacity, they perform a response to scripture. The thirty-four hymns on the life of Christ are most often written as dialogues between Christ and various New Testament figures. This form ultimately, and perhaps even directly, derived from Syrian models, particularly the liturgical *soghitha*. Indeed Romanos's metrics, some of his themes, and even his acrostics resemble the Syriac poems of Ephrem and his followers.[31]

Romanos's achievement as a hymnographer commenting on scripture lies in the scope of his work over the course of a lifetime. In some sense, Romanos had taken on the task of becoming Christ's hagiographer, reworking the Gospels to amplify their story and render them particularly useful to the community. As liturgical expansions on the gospel narratives, the poems serve in the construction of a Christian interiority because they ritualize the curious encounter with God. As others have noticed, the poems invite the listener to enter into the story by identifying with Christ's interlocutors—with Peter, Thomas, the sinful woman, even with Judas.[32] Thus one function of these poems is to assist in the formation of Christian subjectivity by reinforcing biblical figures as typological models.[33] This effect is heightened through the mode of performance—by the articulation of the drama of the story in dialogue. But if the hearing of these poems provides models for Christian identities, so did the writing. And at many points, Romanos reflects, both explicitly and implicitly, on the effect of writing on the creation of the author.

The liturgical function of these hymns helps to illuminate Romanos's task. During the middle Byzantine period, these texts were truncated to their preludes and first stanzas and are still performed from the pulpit sometime after the gospel reading at the monastic office of *orthros*, or morning prayer.[34] However, internal evidence strongly suggests that the original context for the performance of the works of Romanos was the night vigils for the festivals of the church calendar, popular events attended by the urban laity.[35] Romanos himself described the scene in a hymn "On the Man Possessed by Demons":

The people, faithful in their love of Christ,
   have gathered to keep a night-long vigil with psalms and odes;
   unceasingly they sing hymns to God.
So, now that [the Psalms of] David ha[ve] been sung
   and we rejoiced in the well-ordered reading of scripture,
Now let us raise a hymn to Christ and pillory the enemy.
   For this is our lyre of understanding,
   and in this understanding Christ is our leader and teacher—
he is the Master of All.[36]

The shape of the service, dedicated to the liturgy of the Word, necessarily dictated the content of the sung sermon. The gospel reading was the centerpiece, approached by the antiphonal chanting of psalms and the singing of familiar hymns, and followed by Romanos's sung homily, during which a choir, or perhaps the entire assembly, would join in the refrain. It is likely that the vigil continued with additional prayers and songs. In the passage quoted, Romanos explicitly likens his composition within the structure of the service to the psalmody that preceded the biblical lection. In his exegetical response to scripture, the poet sings like David with the lyre, in order to search and convey a deeper meaning of the biblical text. The poems are not liturgical plays, since the poet sings all of the characters himself; nevertheless, there is a dialogic quality to these hymns, as Romanos does the Gospels in different voices, dramatizing the action in often-tense scenes with plot and character development.[37] The poems thus claim a key place in the liturgical celebration, amplifying and articulating the essential content of the festival, adding to the spectacle a dramatic and probing reencounter between the characters of the biblical narrative, in this case between Jesus and the demoniac, his demons, and the people of Gerasa. At the same time, the sermon dramatizes the encounter between the crowding congregation and the holy text itself:

It is good to sing psalms and hymns to God,
  and to wound the demons with reproaches;
  they are our enemies forever.
What do we mean by this "wounding"?
  Whenever we make a comedy of [κωμῳδοῦμεν: we ridicule] their fall, rejoicing.
Truly the devil bewails whenever in our assemblies we represent in tragedy
  [τραγῳδῶμεν]
  the "triumph" of the demons.[38]

While the invocation of comedy and tragedy in this stanza are not evidence of presentation in the form of a play, the language of the theater reveals an explicit understanding of liturgy as performance, as reenactment with the power to reproduce the results of the original. By singing the fall of the devil, the devil falls once again; the service itself parries the enemy.

Romanos's poems were later known as *kontakia,* a term that first appeared some 300 years after Romanos in the ninth century. The word *kontakia* (a diminutive of κόνταξ) means "a little wooden cylinder" around which a scroll of papyrus or parchment was rolled.[39] Romanos himself entitles his *kontakia* in his acrostics variously as a "hymn," "chant," "praise," "poem," "ode," or "psalm," although the form for each of his compositions is roughly the same. The *kontakion* consists of a short prelude followed by about eighteen to twenty-four stanzas of identical meter called *oikoi,* "houses," or "units."[40] The last line of the prelude introduces a refrain that is used at the end of each of the subsequent stanzas. While a single cantor chanted the verses of each stanza, he was joined in the refrain by a choir, perhaps by the entire assembled congregation. The music composed for these chants no longer survives, but it was almost certainly strophic, with each stanza of the hymn set to the same tune. The preludes had their own tunes, but they introduced the text and melody of the refrain.[41]

Romanos did not invent this poetic type, although he surely perfected it. The form originated in the fifth century, as evidenced by the well-known anonymous "Akathistos," or "Standing," hymn, a work of the 440s. And we know the names, if not the works, of two of Romanos's predecessors: Kyriakos and Domitios. The effectiveness of Romanos's style lies in the poet's ability to communicate with and delight a large lay audience.[42] In drawing lessons dialogically from biblical stories, Romanos employs short direct sentences, extended metaphors, assonance, alliteration, and puns. He employs his refrains cleverly, slightly varying their meaning from stanza to stanza (as a modern poet might in a villanelle).[43] One must imagine a syllabic musical setting (with one note for each syllable of the text) rather than a melismatic one (with florid coloratura giving multiple notes to each syllable); Romanos surely gave primacy to conveying the words clearly to his audience.

Acrostics: BY THE HUMBLE ROMANOS

While captivated by the text and engaged in the liturgical event, what Romanos's audience might not have heard is the peculiar way in which the author placed his mark on the poems. Every one of Romanos's *kontakia* has his name embedded in it. Most *kontakia,* and all of those composed by Romanos, make use of an acrostic for the initial letters of each stanza. In Romanos's case, these acrostics always include his name. About one-quarter of Romanos's poems use the simple acrostic "ΤΟΥ ΤΑΠΕΙΝΟΥ ΡΩΜΑΝΟΥ," "BY [or OF] THE HUMBLE ROMANOS."[44] Eleven others employ the name of a poetic type, such as "hymn" or "chant," before Romanos's name, without the epithet "humble." An additional twenty-two use a combination of these forms: Romanos's name, his epithet, and the name of the poetic type. In three cases, this combination is used, but "humble" is replaced by "Kyrou," the meaning of which is unclear, although it might mean either "Mister" or "from the Kyrou district of Constantinople."[45] In a mere six poems, the title also indicates the subject: "On the Palms by Romanos"; that is, for Palm Sunday. Thus Romanos invariably represents himself as the author of the poem, and in the vast majority of cases, he also identifies himself as humble.[46]

Acrostic composition was a technique common in Semitic poetry and was also practiced occasionally in Greek verse since antiquity. Alphabetical acrostics feature in a number of the canonical Psalms, most notably Psalm

119 (LXX 118) and in the Book of Lamentations, traditionally attributed to the prophet Jeremiah.[47] Robert Taft has suggested that the chanting of Psalm 119 (LXX 118) near the beginning of occasional cathedral vigils attended by the laity was already established in late fourth-century Cappadocia.[48] Significantly, while the Septuagint (the Greek translation of the Bible) does not reproduce the four consecutive acrostics of the Book of Lamentations, the Syriac translation, which Romanos would have known in his youth, reproduces the acrostic effect of this threnodic masterpiece. Both Greek and Syriac Bibles list the letters at the beginning of each stanza of Psalm 118/119 without reproducing a progression through the letters of the alphabet in the translation itself. In the case of Lamentations, acrostics discipline the expression of overwhelming grief, imposing shape and form on the poem and on the act of composition; while the Hebrew original of Psalm 118/119, which has as its theme the blessedness of God's law, imposes the rule of beginning every one of the eight lines of each stanza with the same letter, progressing through the entirety of the Hebrew alphabet—an effect not reproduced in translations.[49] Thus, the ascetic, disciplinary potential of the acrostic form was already established in the canonical scriptures.

Both alphabetical and name acrostics were also employed by Greek poets since the classical period, becoming more common in the Hellenistic era, and are found in magical and oracular texts, funerary epigraphs, dedications of buildings, as well as in works of a more overtly literary nature.[50] Name acrostics ought to be understood against the greater background of the problem of the authenticity of literary works, a concern already present in archaic times.[51] Although the ancients' sense of intellectual property was far different from our own, "[A] poet who wished to retain the title to his poetry needed to stamp it with some mark of ownership."[52] Thus Nicander, writing either in the third or second century B.C.E., guaranteed the authenticity of his composition when he embedded his name (in the nominative case) into the initial letters of lines about one-third of the way through his lengthy hexameter account of snakes and other poisonous creatures, the *Theriaca*.[53] While the obscure placement of these letters likely means that the signing was to be secret, this technique should not be interpreted as a mark of humility. Nicander concludes the poem with the self-identifying boast, "You will treasure ever the memory of the Homeric Nicander, whom the snow-white town of Clarus nurtured."[54] Name acrostics are a technique for attaching identity to output, linking signature to authorial identity and authorial control. Romanos's use of his name in the genitive case asserts ownership as well as responsibility for composition. But acrostics could also be used to establish the "authenticity" of a forged work;[55] and indeed a significant percentage of the poems bearing the signature of our Romanos are spurious.[56]

In the early Byzantine period, Romanos's own era, acrostic composition flourished. The twenty-four stanzas of the fifth-century "Akathistos Hymn" form an alphabetical acrostic. At least two Jewish poets, Yose ben Yose and Yannai, writing in Hebrew, employed name acrostics in their liturgical *piyyutim*, probably sometime between the sixth and eighth centuries.[57] Around the same time, a number of Christian Greek poets followed Romanos's practice of signing poems with name acrostics—either with their own names or under another—such as Anastasius, Kyriakos, Domitios, Gregorius, and Stephanus. Hymns also survive with anonymous, and starkly humbling, acrostics such as "A POEM BY A SINNER."[58]

Two acrostic authors with ties to Romanos's Constantinople can be dated with some certainty to middle of the sixth century. The first is Dioscorus of Aphrodito, a Greco-Egyptian poet active from the 550s through about 585. Among his poems that survive on papyrus are six acrostics based on the names of their recipients.[59] Curiously, one of these poems, probably the earliest, is dedicated in its line-by-line acrostic to "THE LORD RO-MANOS" ("Ο ΚΥΡΙΟΣ ΡΩΜΑΝΟΣ") and "ROMANOS THE AMAZ-ING" (ΡΩΜΑΝΝΟΣ [*sic*] ΘΑΥΜΑΣΤΟΣ").[60] The recipient of the encomium was not our Romanos, but rather a young official of the imperial administration whom Dioscorus met during a visit to Constantinople in 551.[61] Nevertheless, the possibility remains that the use of a verse acrostic based on the name Romanos was suggested by a familiarity with the poems of the hymnographer. Through the use of the recipient's name—in the nominative case—in the acrostic, Dioscorus identifies the poem with his friend and dedicatee, Romanos. In some sense, he names the poem such that it is identical to his Romanos, the same Romanos who is evoked, described, and embodied in the flowery encomium of the text. Dioscorus employs the acrostic to name the subject of his portrait. Text, title, and identity are intertwined.

The second acrostic author active during the reign of Justinian used the technique to organize a prose treatise on Christian kingship instead of a poem. Romanos's contemporary, Agapetos, composed an acrostic for the Emperor Justinian advising him about how he should rule and articulating a political ideology that would become typical of Byzantium. As God's representative on earth, the emperor should exercise the virtues of philosophy, purity, piety, and love of humanity in order to enact a combination of Plato's philosopher-king and Eusebius's ideal of Christian kingship. For

Agapetos, the emperor's chief duty was to render his kingdom an imitation of heaven. The initial letters of the brief prose chapters spell out the work's address and author: "To our most divine and pious Emperor Justinian, Agapetos the least [of his] servant[s]."[62] The acrostic signals the author's own subject status with regard to the emperor, thus performing in a particularly literal fashion his role as the author-subject. The term "least" (ἐλάχιστος) echoes the biblical figuration identifying the "least" with Christ: "as you did it to the least of these my brethren, you did it to me" (Mt 25:40, compare 25:45) as well as Paul's self-denigration, "I am the least of the apostles" (1 Cor 15:9). This self-description allows Agapetos to claim authority through the articulation of humility.[63] Thus, though the acrostic device, Agapetos positions himself within the hybrid politico-religious hierarchy he outlines, exemplifying a paradox of Christian authorship; that is, while Agapetos, by his very act of composition, takes authority and exerts power in the creative process, he nevertheless enacts his own subjectivity in his subordination to the divinely ordained emperor.

To what end did Romanos use the acrostic technique? The acrostics figure as a form of *askēsis*, enacting the humility they declare. Romanos—a deacon but apparently never a monk—signs the poems, asserting his authorship and his authorial control.[64] The cultural meaning of such an act of composition is tantalizingly ambiguous. This maneuver might at first seem to be at odds with the identity "humble" that Romanos assigns to himself. But it is unlikely that such a practice would have been understood as arrogant, since Christian theories of vice and virtue condemned pride and vainglory as sinful. Chapter 5 argued that assertions of authorial humility in early Christian writings are better interpreted as performances of Christian virtue, both enacting and producing a humble subject. After all, Romanos's acrostics, while detectable by the eye looking at the hymn on the page, cannot be heard in performance.[65] By signing his name in secret, in fact, Romanos encrypts himself into the poems. Rather than acts of self-assertion, the acrostics inscribe both Romanos and his humility into the texts. And they are ascetic in another sense as well, for like the poems' complex metrics, they supply rules that must be followed. Acrostic composition predetermined which letter would begin each stanza, creating a rubric of discipline to which the poet submits. Romanos's composition thus becomes a pious performance of virtue, the production of a humble self. The humble acrostic is a mode of Christian discipline through which Romanos forms himself as a Christian author, inaugurating a sanctioned and valued Christian subjectivity.[66]

Indeed, the final stanzas of a number of his poems feature elaborate performances of the author's humility.[67] In the "Sixth Hymn on the Resurrection," Romanos responds to his own work with the words, "Yes, O Merciful, I implore you, do not abandon me / who am stained with offences, / For in iniquities and in sins my mother bore me."[68] In his hymn "On the Second Coming," assigned to the Sunday of Carnival, two weeks before Lent, and thus in the period of preparation for penitence, Romanos writes, "Raise me up, I beg, as I lie in many sins / because what I say and advise for others I do not observe. / But I implore you, give me time for repentance, / and, at the intercessions of the Ever-Virgin and Mother of God, spare me/ and do not cast me away from your presence, / Judge most just."[69] Coming at the end of his chants, these verses both enact and produce humility on the part of the singer. These performances are thus consistent with the identity that the poet inscribes in his acrostic. Moreover, this identity was assumed by the cantor during the performance of these hymns whether Romanos was the one singing or not. If another or subsequent cantor was singing, he took the part of Romanos the Melodist, voicing not only the words of the characters of the biblical narrative, for whom the poet had composed metrical speeches, but also of the character known as "the humble Romanos," the "I" of these closing stanzas, in whose name—and in whose voice—the poems are sung.

The surviving evidence for the reception of the works of Romanos suggests not only that audiences and subsequent readers understood and accepted the performed humble identity, but that they regarded it as holy. Later poets went so far as to imitate Romanos's example by writing poems in his humble name, thus conforming themselves to his humble type. Subsequent performers of the hymns, who took upon themselves the voice of the poet in singing his works, were similarly well regarded. The *Miracles of Artemios* (18), which we encountered in Chapter 4, describes a cantor who frequented all-night vigils at the Church of St. John the Baptist in the Oxeia district, in the north of the city (on the site of the present Süleymaniye Mosque), who "sang the hymns of the humble Romanos [who is] among the saints [τοῦ ἐν ἁγίοις ταπεινοῦ ῾Ρωμανοῦ]." With the dissemination of Romanos's works came familiarity with his self-adopted epithet and his self-ascribed virtue. Evidently, Romanos's humility was a thoroughly convincing performance. Early Byzantines did not question the sincerity with which the poet had signed the acrostics of his poems.

By signing "the humble Romanos" into the very body of his poems, Romanos calls attention to the works themselves as texts, as produced writings, acts of literary creation. The letters of his name and epithet order and structure the poems and work like a skeleton upon which he can affix the flesh of his composition. These writerly self-inscriptions suggest a high degree of reflection on the work of authorship and on the complex relationship between writing and the formation of the self. They betray, furthermore, a high degree of interest to understand writing as religious activity. The acrostics are signatures attaching identity to documents. Like Christ's signature upon the wood of his cross or upon his own flesh, Romanos's poems inscribe something of himself. Perhaps this is why in a number of his compositions punctuating the liturgical performance of the life of Christ throughout the Christian year, Romanos figures key moments in the gospel narrative as forms of writing, moments reflexively connected to Romanos's own practice of writing. On one level, Romanos's compositions, elaborating salvation history, participate in the publication of Christ's salvific act of inscribing pardon.

Signature, Petition, and Supplication: The Case of Leprosy

Romanos, in his humility, does not draw explicit connections between his own signed writings and Christ's saving documents, but he does attach his practice to the writing he ascribes to others in his idiosyncratic treatments of the sacred narrative. The hymn "On the Healing of the Leper," assigned to the second Wednesday after Easter, provides further perspective on the sort of written document Romanos presents himself as signing.[70] Here, writing itself becomes explicitly petitionary. In this poem, Romanos explores and expands the brief interaction between Jesus and the leper recorded in the synoptic Gospels (Mt 8:2–4; Mk 1:40–45; Lk 5:12–16). As in many of the dialogues with Jesus, Romanos invites the congregation to identify with Christ's interlocutor. The leper's physical deformity represents the spiritual deformity of all sinners, and his approach to Jesus serves as a model for all Christians. Instead of trying to conceal "the defilement of his affliction," the leper "showed his disease to the all-wise physician" (8.4).

This affliction is abhorrent and shameful to all,
and so those who are tried by this dread disease hasten to hide it.
It is the most hideous of all afflictions among mankind [ἐν ἀνθρώποις],
the flesh being cropped by it, as though it were grass [ὡς ἐπί χόρτου βοσκομένης /
τῆς σαρκὸς ὑπ' αὐτῆς].[71]

This last image deploys the language of Isaiah 40:6–8, which in the Septuagint reads, "All flesh is grass, and all the glory of man is as the flower of
grass [Πᾶσα σὰρξ χόρτος, καὶ πᾶσα δόξα ἀνθρώπου ὡς ἄνθος
χόρτου]. The grass withers and the flower *falls off* [ἐξέπεσεν], the word
[ῥῆμα] of our God remains forever."[72] In fact, by echoing the passage from
Isaiah, the poem proposes that all humanity is as grass: flesh is mortal and
falls away; all are leprous. The leper is thus a figure for all; leprosy reveals
the human condition. In this light, Romanos portrays the leper's behavior
before Jesus as that of a model penitent: "Warred on by the disease, the
leper lamented through his tears" (8.6).[73]

The gospel passages upon which this hymn expands are brief. The version in Matthew 8:2–4 reads,

A leper approached Jesus and knelt before him, saying, "Lord, if you will, you can
make me clean." And he stretched out his hand and touched him, saying, "I will;
be clean." And immediately his leprosy was cleansed. And Jesus said to him, "See
that you say nothing to any one; but go, show yourself to the priest, and offer the
gift that Moses commanded, for a proof to the people."

Where Matthew has the leper kneeling before Jesus, Luke's variant (5:12)
supplies that the leper "fell on his face and besought [ἐδεήθη; petitioned]
him." It is perhaps Luke's wording that encourages Romanos to insert writing into the narrative where it had not been before. Significantly expanding
the interchange, Romanos writes in the leper's voice:

"Strengthened by faith the woman with an issue of blood touched his hem and was
    cured.
I too will hasten to entreat the timeless Master, for [all that is] his is good."
Having said this, he runs with his petition [δέησις]
and, bending his knee to the ground, he implores Christ.
But he writes his petition in two words
and says, "If you wish, you can cleanse me completely, Lord."
For it is faith and not a mass of words that he looks for. (8.9)

The leper approaches Jesus with his *deēsis,* his petition, in writing. In his
request for healing, the leper has produced both oral entreaty and inscribed
text. The word *deēsis* itself connotes both written and oral requests and
commonly refers to intercessory prayer.[74] One model for depicting the presentation of petitions in both oral and written form also derived from the
political realm, replicating the practice of petitioning the king or emperor.
Romanos expands upon this scenario in the following stanza: the leper

brings his entreaty in writing and presents it with a short speech.[75] According to the poem, the brief written supplication consists of the simple phrase, "If you wish," two words in Greek: Ἐὰν θέλῃς.[76] In fact, this entreaty is the very type of Christian prayer, a seeking after the will of God, typified both by the Lord's Prayer ("Thy will be done" [Mt 6:10]) and Jesus' prayer at Gethsemane ("Not my will, but thine" [Mt 26:39]).

The condition of the leper's prayer—both oral and written—is analogous to Romanos's hymn itself, which at its conclusion shifts from exegesis of the gospel story to explicit entreaty:

Son of God, King before the ages and to ages
as you had mercy on the leper, driving out his affliction with a word, as you are
    powerful,
save us also, us who approach your goodness,
and grant pardon [συγχώρησις] of our faults.
.   .   .   .
Therefore we implore you: give us your aid,
at the prayers of the Mother of God and Ever-Virgin Mary[77]
through whom we all approach you and ask your help;
"Have mercy," we cry, "as Lover of mankind,
        Savior and alone without sin." (8.18)

Here the leper's approach to Christ serves as an example for Romanos and his congregation to follow. Like the afflicted man, they supplicate Christ with their petition. They too seek Christ's salvific healing. Moreover, the intercessory prayers of the Virgin were often referred to as *deēsis*.[78] Romanos's entreaty thus assimilates itself to the biblical type presented in the story of the leper. Like the leper's, Romanos's presentation to Christ is both written and sung. Indeed the hymn itself is a *deēsis,* a petition presented to "the King before the ages."

The merging of oral and written petitions, together with the merging of Romanos's petition and that of the Gospel's leper, provides a context for an extended conceit at the heart of the hymn. In the two stanzas immediately following the description of the main action, the leper's presentation of his request before Jesus, Romanos expounds the process that gives rise to petitionary composition. It is unclear whether the first of these stanzas speaks in the voice of the leper or the voice of the poet as an aside.[79] This ambiguity, however, is surely fitting, and is even emphasized by the poet's performance of these words in a liturgical context, taking on the role and voice of the leper.

When someone forced by need lacks help and words [λόγου],
and is incapable of composing a petition [δέησιν συνθεῖναι] to approach the king,
he runs straightaway to skilled people who can set down
the supplication concisely [ἱκεσίαν διαθεῖναι], not using many words.
And, as they are extremely skilled and trained in using words,
in a few phrases they set in order the untrained aim of his thoughts,
and write the words on appropriate paper [εἰς σύμμετρον χάρτην].[80]

Indeed it was common in a society of relatively few skilled literates for people to seek the service of professional writers to compose documents, including letters and legal petitions.[81] The explicit implication here is that the
leper's short written request was produced in such a fashion, through con-
sultation with a professional secretary who composed the entreaty and
committed it to a suitable sheet of papyrus. (A pleasant touch of irony lies
in the implicit contrast between the leper's letter and Romanos's own production, which is not particularly concise.)

The overlay of the leper's and the poet's voice elaborates the process
of composition:

"Now I, a simple man [ἰδιώτης], will draw up my entreaty to the Wise by faith.
For I made haste and reached most holy and discerning Faith.
I asked her help and she dictated [ὑπηγόρευσε] concisely,
on my behalf, my entreaty to King Jesus.
In two words, like a most skilled speaker,
she wrote down all the thoughts of this petition of mine.
On the paper of my soul I have my request written,
and I offer this to you, "Hasten, have mercy on me,
Benefactor of all, Lover of mankind,
        Savior and alone without sin." (8.11)

This complex passage contains, in fact, a number of elegant ambiguities.
Faith here is both an abstract concept ("by faith I will draw up my entreaty") and a personification ("I made haste and reached most holy and
discerning Faith"). Did Faith merely dictate the petition, or did she actually
write it down, inscribing the paper? By the second suggestion, she is not
only a muse but also a secretary. Moreover, her activity as scribe is further
complicated by the startling verse, "On the paper of my soul I have my
request written [ἐν χάρτῃ τῆς ψυχῆς μου γεγραμμένην τὴν αἴτησιν
ἔχω]."[82] Now Faith's inscription is spiritual rather than physical, on the
immaterial soul rather than on papyrus. This shift may underscore the degree to which grass—here both papyrus fibers and, because of the earlier

reference to Isaiah 40, the flesh—withers and dies, is impermanent and subject to decay. More lasting than paper, the faithful one's eternal soul becomes the locus of written prayer.[83] Is this inscribed soul the text that the faithful, emulating the suppliant leper, present to Jesus? By such a logic, the self is a literary corpus and the faithful one prepares this textual self as a written offering. Moreover, there may be another level of meaning embedded in the idea of inscribing the soul; for something written on the soul is something memorized and thus available to oral recall. The written provides the possibility for the subsequent reproduction of the oral. Thus, this writing on the soul emphasizes the slippage between speech and writing already present earlier in the hymn.

     The leper's visit to the professional writer has paid off. Christ is pleased by the leper's petition (8.13) and grants his request for cleansing. Having offered his petitionary text to Christ, the former leper is then commanded to offer sacrifice in accord with Mosaic law (8.15, cf. Mt 8:4). The text of Romanos's own poem supplies a model for the work of a Christian writer. Like the leper, the writer consults Faith for assistance in forming his petitionary composition, since he, like the leper, is in need of divine cleansing. Through the mechanism of his own piety, Romanos emulates his leper in crafting the poem itself. Indeed, the theme of faith-writing appears elsewhere in Romanos's works. He inserts writing guided by faith into the first of two hymns called "On the Raising of Lazarus,"[84] where Jesus learns that Lazarus is deathly ill through written correspondence, not by hearsay, as in the Gospel of John (11:6): "Arise, let us go into Judaea where we were before; / for I have received a letter, which I read with pleasure / for faith dictated it, and unshakable hope wrote it / and love sealed it" (14.3). Mary and Martha have written and sent their prayer or petition to Jesus for Lazarus's sake (14.3), thus providing a model for Christian correspondence with God.

Writing Thomas

The convergence of faith and writing is even more prominent in Romanos's reading of the apostle Thomas. In "On Doubting Thomas," assigned to Thomas Sunday, the first Sunday after Easter, Romanos probes Christ's wounds as a source of inscription, here focusing on the disciple who "with his meddling right hand [τῇ φιλοπράγμονι δεξιᾷ] . . . explored [Christ's] life-giving side."[85] The hymn links two aspects of the Divine Liturgy, the

Liturgy of the Word and the eucharistic sacrifice, by meditating on the relationship between the textual encounter with Christ, both through scriptural
reading and its expounding in homily, and the physical encounter with
Christ as God renders himself tangibly present in the bread and wine.
Thomas's encounter with "the marks of the nails and the gash of the lance"
connects the act of writing and the declaration of faith, as Thomas's hand
signs in witness to the resurrection.[86]

For the definition [ὅρος] of this faith was signed [ὑπεγράφη] surely for me
through Thomas's hand. By touching Christ
it became like a pen [κάλαμος] of a swiftly writing scribe [Ps 45:1],
writing for believers [πιστοῖς] the place from where faith springs up. (30.3)

Thus Thomas's hand underwrites (ὑπογράφω) the authenticity of the
risen body.[87] Like a notary, he testifies to the accuracy of the document.
Here the language of the reed pen (κάλαμος) quotes Psalm 45:1 (LXX 44:2),
a verse explicitly connecting writing to the oral confession of God. "My
heart blurted out [ἐξηρεύξατο] a good word [λόγος]; I speak [λέγω] my
works [ἔργα] to the king; my tongue is the pen [κάλαμος] of a swiftly
writing scribe." The psalm's comparison of speech and writing provides
Romanos with an opportunity to explore Thomas's confession, "My Lord
and my God [Jn 20:28]," as a written declaration. Here it is not Thomas's
tongue that assimilates to the scribe's pen, but rather his hand. After touching the wound, the hand can write. Thus, Romanos imagines Thomas's
hand touching Christ's wounds to be like dipping a pen into an inkwell.
But if the wound is a source of inky blood, it is also a source of water.[88] In
the verses immediately following, the poet explicates the idea of the wound
as a place "where faith springs up" in explicitly liquid form:

From there, the thief drank and came to his senses again.
From there, the disciples watered their hearts.
From there, Thomas drew the knowledge of the things he sought.
First he drinks, then gives to drink,
Having momentarily doubted, he persuaded many to say,
    "You are our Lord and our God." (30.3)

The faith that comes from contact with Christ's body figures as the potable
sacrament, the blood of Christ's wound that waters the faithful in the drinking of the eucharist. Later in the hymn, in a play on words, Romanos has

Thomas implore Jesus, "show me your wounds [πληγάς], / that like springs [πηγάς], I may draw from them and drink" (30.14).[89]

As with the reed pen in the hymn "On Peter's Denial," Romanos's treatment of Thomas's touching of Christ's body as a scribal act implicitly connects Christ's blood with ink. Here, however, it is not Christ who writes but Thomas. On yet another level, Romanos emphasizes the textuality of Thomas's confession, the words "My Lord and my God," as they appear in the written text of the Bible: "John has written the words of the Twin / clearly in the book of the Gospel" (30.4). In the Gospel of John, the words "My Lord and my God" are an reinscription of Thomas's initial inscribing of the identity of Christ.

In the final strophe of the hymn, Romanos calls attention to himself, inscribing a writerly self-consciousness onto the story of Thomas, recognizing his own work as an author in his "handling" of Christ.

Most high, by grace strengthen me in soul and flesh, and save me
so that I may touch [ἁπτόμενος; handle] your side. Receiving your grace,
your Blood and your Body, I am delivered from my evils,
so that I may find forgiveness of transgressions.
Thomas, by handling [ψηλαφῶν], has now come to know your glory,
but I am frightened, for I know your counsels,
I know my works. Conscience troubles me.
Spare me, my Savior, spare me Compassionate,
that by works and words I may unceasingly cry to you,
    "You are our Lord and our God." (30.18)[90]

Romanos the writer compares his handling of Christ in his "works and words" to Thomas's inquisitive grasp. The participle in the second line, *haptomenos,* from the verb *haptomai,* conveys both touching or grasping a physical object and touching on or handling a point or subject, thus bridging Thomas's deed with the poet's act of composition.[91]

The other word for "handling," which Romanos uses in line five of this stanza, *psēlaphōn,* from *psēlaphaō,* "to touch" or "grope," is similarly interesting. The word does not appear in the Doubting Thomas episode of the Gospel of John, but it does appear in another postresurrection account. In Luke 24:39, the risen Jesus says to his disciples, "See my hands and my feet, that it is I myself; handle me, and see [ψηλαφήσατέ με καὶ ἴδετε]; for a spirit has not flesh and bones as you see that I have." Romanos, indeed, interests himself specifically in the knowledge that Thomas derives from his groping. In the immediately previous strophe of the hymn, reworking Christ's response to Thomas in the Gospel of John—"Blessed are those who have not seen, and yet believe"—Jesus says to Thomas, "You, by handling [ψηλαφῶν] me, have come to know my glory, / while they, by reason of a sound of words [φωνῇ λόγων], worship me" (17). Through verbal echo, Romanos contrasts Thomas's "handling" with the "sound" of words—*psēlaphōn, phōnē*—in order to articulate the difference between Thomas and the other believers.[92] But in the final strophe, when Romanos again uses *psēlaphōn* ("Thomas, by handling [ψηλαφῶν], has now come to know your glory"), he uses the word to compare himself to Thomas ("but I am frightened, for I know your counsels"). Thinking now of his "works and words," *psēlaphōn*, "handling," in this instance seems to apply to his own *phōnē*. In fact, the word itself seems to pun on *psallō*, "to sing"— especially psalms, plus *phōnē*, "a voice."

The poet compares the knowledge of the Lord's glory obtained through physical contact with his own understanding and declarations: that is, with his composition of liturgical poetry. Moreover, in addition to Romanos's handling of Christ through writing, he also compares this sort of touching to his participation in the eucharist. The poet has had contact with the body of God by partaking of the sacrifice, "your Body and Blood," through which he has received grace; now he prays that, like Thomas, he may give vocal witness to the divine identity, that by his "works and words" (ἔργα and λόγοι) he may reproduce the acclamation of the once-doubtful apostle. In the language of "works and words," Romanos picks up the vocabulary of the part of Psalm 45:1 [LXX 44:2] that he left unquoted in stanza three, where he described Thomas's hand as "the pen of a swiftly writing scribe." "My heart blurted out a good word [λόγος]; I speak [λέγω] my works [ἔργα] to the king." Implicitly, then, Romanos identifies himself with the swiftly writing scribe, the poet who explored the risen Christ with his hands. Romanos calls attention to "works" in two senses, both his deeds—"I know my works. Conscience troubles me"—and his literary output, the works and words that declare Christ. Finally, Romanos presents himself as a humble sinner. Delivered from evil though contact with the body and blood of Christ, he still needs God to spare him in order to be able to write. In this move, Romanos enacts his identity as he himself has signed the poem in its acrostic, "BY THE HUMBLE ROMANOS."

Art and Representation

Other incidents in the Gospels that involve hands become for Romanos an opportunity to reflect on writing as a liturgical act. Romanos focuses on the depictive skill of the hands in his exploration of Jesus' baptism by John at the Jordan River. The hymn "On the Baptism of Christ" was written for the festival of Theophany on January 6 (Western Epiphany), celebrating the manifestation of the Trinity to humanity.[93] The theme of illumination runs through the hymn—a concept intimately related to baptism, known in Greek as *phōtismos*, or the sacrament of enlightenment.[94] The dialogue poem expands Jesus' interchange with the Baptist.[95] The hymn's prelude calls attention to themes of appearance and marking:

Today you have appeared to the inhabited world,
and your light, O Lord, has been signed [ἐσημειώθη] upon us [Ps 4:6, LXX 4:7],
who, with knowledge, sing your praise, "You have come, you have appeared,
    the unapproachable Light [1 Tim 6:16]." (5, prol.)

Romanos frames his meditation on the baptism of Jesus within the context of the baptism of all Christians. The manifestation of God in his baptism seals the community of the faithful as his own. The *sēmeion* of baptism is both a marking and signature, signaling Christ's possession and authority.[96] Once again, the imagery is drawn from the realm of the imperial bureaucracy. Like a watery ink on the parchment of a Christian's flesh, baptism indelibly effects and certifies salvation.

The passage quotes from Psalm 4:6 (LXX 4:7), "There are many who say, 'Who will show us good things? You have signed [ἐσημειώθη] upon us the light of your countenance, O Lord!'" Baptism figures as a marking of the church with light. Thus while John baptizes Jesus, Jesus is already baptizing the church "with the Holy Spirit and with fire" as John had declared in Matthew 3:11. John is hesitant to baptize Jesus, asking, with reference to Christ as the light, "Why do you bow / your head beneath my hand? For it is not used to holding fire" (5.6). Puzzled at the paradox of mixing fire and water, John raises the pressing question, "For how shall I baptize / the unapproachable Light?" In the course of the dialogue, Jesus explains to the reluctant John,

Baptist and disputant, prepare at once, not for confrontation
but for ministration [πρὸς λειτουργίαν]. For look, you will see what I am
    accomplishing.
In this way I am painting [ζωγραφῶ] for you the fair and radiant form of my
    Church,
granting to your right hand the power that after this
I shall give to the palms of my friends [Jn 15:14–15] and the priests.
I am showing you clearly the Holy Spirit,

I am making you hear the voice of the Father
as it declares me his true Son and cries, "This is
the unapproachable Light." (5.13)

Jesus thus presents the work of baptism as depiction, the making manifest of the spiritual reality of the church. The disciples, and after them the priests, have this power to paint the church through the act of baptizing, marking the identity of the church upon the faithful. This depicting is a liturgical activity, the ministration first practiced at the Jordan by both John and Jesus, who inscribe the living (*zōgrapheō*), marking them with their hands.[97] Baptism paints the "fair and radiant form" (τὴν τερπνὴν καὶ φαεινὴν μορφὴν) of the church, rendering the church itself as an illumination, like a vibrant and shining illustration in a manuscript. Moreover, the scene of the baptism of Christ not only depicts the church, but manifests the members of the Trinity as well: Christ shows John the Holy Spirit and allows him to hear the voice of the Father. And Romanos compares the Father's voice, while audible instead of visible, with the deictic action of the hand: in declaring "This is my beloved Son" (Mt 3:17), the Father "pointed out from heaven by a voice as by a finger" (5.18).

Romanos's interest in indication, signing, and depiction as the work of the ministers of the church inscribes a sacramentology that applies not only to the priestly types represented by John, whom Romanos terms "the son of the priest [i.e. Zachary] in the office of a priest" (5.15), but also implicitly to the poet himself. "Zoography" refers not merely to painting, but to vivid representation in words.[98] When in the hymn John explains his baptizing of Jesus in his own words, the humble Romanos speaks through the Forerunner's voice, accounting for his own handwork as an author: "Let no one then consider me daring. / I act, not as foolhardy, but as a servant" (5.15). When John uses his hands to participate in the work of the Lord, he is transformed and sanctified. The pattern of holiness through participation is reminiscent of the early sixth-century *Celestial Hierarchy* attributed to Dionysius the Areopagite: "Through [God's] use of deacons and priests he brings purification and light. But he himself is said to purify and to illuminate, since those orders ordained by him attribute to him the sacred activities in which they themselves engage."[99] As Romanos's John declares,

I was feeble as a mortal, but he as God of all gave me force, crying,
"Place your hand on me and I will give it strength."

For how could I have done it, had this not been what he said and what came to
    pass?
How would I have had the power to baptize the deep, I who am clay,[100]
had I not first received and accepted power from on high?
For now, with him standing by me, I sense
that I am more than I was before.
I am something else. I have been changed, I have been glorified,
for I am seeing, I am baptizing
      the unapproachable Light. (5.16)

The lowly deacon sees in John the Baptist a model for glorification through
the depiction of "the fair and radiant form" of the church, that is, of the
body of Christ. But it is likely that Romanos's connection to John the Baptist lay also in the performance of his diaconal duties. Again the works of
Pseudo-Dionysius clarify the sorts of tasks Romanos as a deacon would
have carried out while ministering at rites of baptism. According to the *Ecclesiastical Hierarchy*, it is the deacon's responsibility to "purify" candidates
for their "illumination," discerning those carrying God's likeness from
those unworthy to participate, untying their sandals and removing their
garments, turning them west for renunciation of the devil and east when
they are ready for submission to Christ.[101] Thus Romanos acted out and
identified with the work of John the Baptist even before he presented this
hymn for the feast of the Theophany, when God is manifest and the church
illumined. Composing this poem Romanos illuminates God and his works,
performing his liturgy by dipping (*baptō*) his pen and illustrating. Like
John, the poet depends on Christ to accomplish his marking. Like Christ,
he marks his sign upon his document with his acrostic signature, "BY THE
HUMBLE ROMANOS," enacting a virtue particularly fitting in a deacon,
or "servant," such as Romanos.[102]

Positioning the Author as Subject

On the cross Jesus writes; at the Jordan he paints. He inscribes salvation (in
the hymns "On Peter's Denial" and "On the Adoration at the Cross") with
bureaucratic formality and (in the hymn "On the Baptism of Christ") with
depictive flourish. He signs his works, his official documents of pardon and
safe passage, his human creations, and even his own flesh. Romanos establishes God incarnate as a progenitor of texts, both author and authority.
But Romanos the writer does not immediately identify with the model of

all-powerful *auctor*. Elsewhere in his corpus, he signs his name to poems that treat writing as an act of discipleship, as the work of the subjects of authority. Identifying with Thomas and the leper, Romanos depicts writing as an act of dependence on divine power. Like the leper, he often petitions Christ explicitly in his written works. But like Thomas, he betrays an awareness of the Christian writer's ambiguous status, for while he is the Lord's subject, he also handles the Lord as his own subject. He is both subject and author.

The poems of Romanos problematize authorship in distinctly Christian terms, situating literary composition in a space between power and humility. The sixth century, Romanos's own age, was a key moment in the integration of Byzantine imperial and religious power.[103] Recent scholarship on the cultural and military flowering of Byzantium the sixth century has sought to place the works of Romanos among other monumental productions of the reign of Justinian: the building of Hagia Sophia as well as a great number of other churches, bridges, and fortifications; the wars to reconquer territories in the West, so vividly narrated by the court historian Procopius; the Church of San Vitale in Ravenna with its stunning mosaics.[104] Averil Cameron skillfully articulates the prevailing and totalizing discourse emerging in the course of the sixth century, binding Christianity and empire inextricably to a resurgent Eastern Rome.[105] Of Romanos she has written, "The liturgical hymns of Romanos and others . . . came to serve the purpose of official communication and occupy the territory of imperial panegyric."[106] His mingling of Christian and imperial themes echoes the contemporary imperial panegyrics of Paul the Silentiary, the *Ekthesis* of Agapetos, as well as Procopius's *On the Buildings,* a work that praises in great detail the numerous architectural projects undertaken by Justinian throughout the empire.[107] But where does Romanos situate himself with respect to the monumental authority he ascribes to Christ and his imperial power? And what is the impact of this emerging notion of power on Romanos's own authority?

Although no evidence suggests that Romanos held an official appointment in Justinian's court, a connection to the imperial family may explain the degree to which the interaction in the poems between Christ and his interlocutors draws on the pageantry and patterns of the imperial court.[108] Romanos was obviously familiar with bureaucratic formalities such as the presentation of petitions, the granting of pardons, and the signing and sealing of documents.[109] He superimposes this paperwork on the life of Christ, overlapping the vocabulary of redemption and the language of imperial governance. Christ becomes the heavenly emperor meting out both justice and mercy. In these scenarios, Romanos seems not to identify with the authority itself but to assume the status of clerk or recorder. Like the biblical evangelists, whose work he expounds, Romanos employs his hand as the Lord's pen, becoming God's scribe, his tongue a mediator of God's discourse.

Romanos perhaps most identifies himself with the mechanisms of imperial power in his hymn "On Earthquakes and Fires."[110] On the basis of this work, scholars have assumed that Romanos was known to the imperial household. This poem, unique among his works for handling recent and current events, lauds the Emperor and Empress Justinian and Theodora in the wake of the Nika (that is, "victory") riots, a revolt that ravaged the capital for a week in January 532, killing as many as 30,000 people and causing a fire that severely damaged the old Hagia Sophia.[111] The poem's stark theodicy recalls at times the Book of Lamentations: "He shakes the earth, and makes the ground gnash because of our sins."[112] But, writing between 532 and the dedication of the new church in 537, Romanos depicts Justinian and Theodora as among "those who feared God." Thus while the emperor is exalted, this exaltation depends on his submission to God: he is the emperor because he is God's subject.

In the poem, Justinian prays, "Grant me victory . . . just as you made David / victorious over Goliath" (54:18), and Romanos praises the imperial couple for swiftly rebuilding the city, including "Holy Sophia, the very home of our church, / [which] is being reconstructed with such skill / that it imitates Heaven, the throne of God" (54:23). The resulting new church, an architectural wonder, contributed greatly to the prestige of the emperor and to the empire, then at a new height. It is tempting to interpret one section of the poem to mean that Romanos chanted it in front of or near the construction site:[113]

All of us who cherish Christ and strive to give him glory
beseech the Lord and Creator of the heavens
to solidify the foundation and the structure of this church.
May we be judged worthy to see this mighty building filled
and swelling with grace for those who celebrate
the liturgies and sing the odes and hymns. (54.24)

Whether Romanos ever chanted in the great church itself once it was completed is uncertain, although highly likely. In any case, in the hymn "On Earthquakes and Fires," Romanos contributes to the upbuilding and construction of heaven's image. Like an architect or engineer, he is doing foundational conceptual work. He even signs the work, mortaring himself into the substructure, with the acrostic "A PSALM OF THE HUMBLE ROMANOS." Solidifying the foundations, he creates space to "celebrate the liturgies and sing the odes and hymns." In the edifice, he has created for himself a literary space in which to perform his composition.

In the following century, Romanos's hymns were sung regularly elsewhere in the capital; the poet himself was regarded as a saint.[114] But his status as holy, like Justinian's positioning as pious emperor, depended on a proper relationship with superior authority. The grace Romanos hopes will come to the celebrants and cantors of the liturgy depends on their subjectivity within the scheme of the divine regime. Consistently, Romanos the deacon identifies himself as a subject of that divine regime.

Despite the variety of Romanos's models for writing in the poems considered in this chapter, his literary practice is remarkably consistent. The great hymnographer opens up the biblical narrative and inserts text: both his text, a complex exegesis of the readings appointed by the lectionary, and text itself, ink on paper. Incarnation, atonement, judgment, and redemption become textual events, the entire history of salvation an archive of parchment and papyrus. The doctrine of the Word made flesh offered possibilities to see the materialization of words in writing as an image of God's work, to see literary composition as a liturgical imitation of Christ. And Romanos was first and foremost a liturgist, a writer in and for the service of God, presenting his poems as liturgical offerings. To the extent that he recites confession over his compositions in his final stanzas, the hymns are in themselves sin offerings, types of the great sin offering for the life of the world. Writing for the popular vigil, he donates himself to the service of God. In Christ crucified he finds his model, a sacrificial rendering of oneself in text. In humility and obedience on the cross, Jesus revealed himself the subject-author of salvation. Like the body on the cross that becomes both scribe and script, Romanos's poems merge identity and text. Evidence of the creator lies hidden in the creation. Through his use of acrostics, Romanos weaves himself into the body of his work, to become both writer and poem, fully identified with and embodied in his creation. Like Christ in the altar bread, Romanos's literary oblations render him truly present in text, while through his own material textuality, he hopes to inscribe himself on the body of God.

Romanos's literary corpus plays with the wide range of conceptions of Christian authorship available in late antiquity. His poems employ writing to extend and inhabit the world of the Bible, implicitly fashioning himself a latter-day gospeler. His deeds of authorship integrate writing with prayer, petition, supplication, and worship. Authoring hymns affords him opportunities to enact humility. The texts that he produces ultimately produce him as "the humble Romanos," conforming to Christian patterns of virtue and self-discipline. Exploring the salvific materiality of texts, Romanos's authorship imitates the incarnation itself, the enfleshment of logos. The resulting author participates fully in the piety and practice of early Byzantine Christianity.

Chapter 9
Hagiographical Practice
and the Formation of Identity:
Genre and Discipline

The making of Romanos the Melodist did not end with the composition of his hymns. Indeed the formation of his identity had only begun. Subsequent centuries saw the production of legends furnishing a more elaborate portrait of the author. The *Menologium of Basil II*, a service book richly illustrated around the year 1000, included the following entry for October 1, the feast of Saint Romanos:

The venerable Romanos was from Syria and became a deacon of the holy church of Beirut. Arriving in Constantinople in the reign of the emperor Anastasius, Romanos went and settled in the Church of the Most Holy Theotokos in the Kyrou district, where he received the gift [χάρισμα] of the *kontakia*. In piety he would celebrate and pass the night, praying during the vigil at the [Church of the Theotokos] of Blachernae, before returning to the Kyrou. Then on one of these nights, the most holy Theotokos appeared to him while he was asleep and gave him a paper scroll and said, "Take this paper and eat it." It seems that the saint opened his mouth and swallowed the paper. Now it was the festival of Christ's Nativity [that is, Christmas Eve]. And immediately awakening from his sleep he was astonished and glorified God. Thereupon he mounted the ambo and began to chant, "Today the Virgin gives birth to him who is above all being." He also composed nearly one thousand *kontakia* for other festivals before departing for the Lord.[1]

The accompanying image (Fig. 11) depicts the key event described in the text. In the illumination, the poet sleeps just outside the church as he receives the scroll from the Virgin Mary. Significantly, both the verbal and the visual account have deemphasized the labor of writing, replacing the scene of literary composition with the miracle of inspiration. This version of the story in which Romanos delivers his first and most famous hymn assimilates Romanos to the model of the prophet Ezekiel, receiving and consuming the heavenly scroll that nourishes the author with the license to

ο ϲ ἰ ο ϲ ρ ω μ ᾳ ν ό ϲ , Ν ω λ ἰ ρ χ ϑ μ ὁ ν ᾳ π ω ο ο υ ρ ί ᾳ ο δ ι ᾳ ι ω ρ ο ο ‑ τ υ χ ᾳ μ ω
τ λ ω δ μ ᾳ λ ἰ ρ υ τ ω ᾳ ί ᾳ ο ἰ Ϯ λ ι ϕ λ ο ί ᾳ ο · κ ᾳ τ ᾳ λ ᾳ ὢ ω ρ δ Ϯ τ λ ω κ ω μ
ϛ ᾳ ν Τ ι ν ο υ ‑ ω ο λ ι μ δ ω ί τ ω μ χ ε ρ μ ω ρ ᾳ μ ω ϛ ᾳ ο τ ο υ τ ο υ μ ᾳ ο ϊ λ δ ω ϲ
λ ω λ ι λ δ Ϯ λ ᾳ ι κ ᾳ τ δ μ ὁ ν δ μ ὁ ρ τ ω ρ μ ᾳ ω τ λ ω ‑ ω δ ρ ᾳ ί ᾳ ο Θ Κ ο υ .
ϛ ο τ ᾳ λ ω ρ ο υ ό ω ο υ κ ᾳ ι τ ο χ ᾳ ρ ι ο μ ᾳ τ ω ρ μ κ ο ρ τ ᾳ κ ί ω ρ ὁ δ ζ ω
τ ο δ ρ ᾳ ι λ ᾳ μ ζ ω ᾳ ρ ό δ ι ᾳ ω ρ κ ᾳ ι δ ι ω ρ υ κ τ ε ρ δ ι ω υ κ ᾳ ι λ ι τ ᾳ
μ ᾳ ω ρ δ ρ τ ι ν ω ᾳ μ μ υ ϧ δ ι τ ω ρ υ μ ᾳ ρ ϛ ρ μ ω μ . ‑ ω ᾳ ρ δ ϕ ε ‑ ω δ λ μ
ϛ ο τ ᾳ κ υ ρ ρ υ ὁ μ μ ᾳ δ Ϯ τ ω ρ μ υ κ τ ω μ · κ ο ι μ ω μ δ μ ᾳ ο ᾳ ι τ ο · ὁ ϕ λ
Ν λ ι κ ᾳ τ ι ν ω ρ ο ι ο λ ι ‑ ω δ ρ ᾳ ί ᾳ ι δ Κ ο ο · κ ᾳ ι δ Ϯ δ ᾳ ο κ ε τ ο μ ο ρ χ ᾳ ρ
τ ο υ . λ ᾳ ι ε ί ω δ · ι ᾳ μ δ τ ο ρ χ ᾳ ρ τ η ρ κ ᾳ ι λ ᾳ τ ᾳ ν ϕ υ ϛ ᾳ μ τ ο ρ · ὁ μ ο
μ ι ο δ ρ ό ι ω ν ὁ ϛ ρ ο ο ᾳ ρ ό ι ϛ ᾳ ι τ ο ϛ ο μ ᾳ λ ᾳ ι λ ᾳ τ ᾳ ν ω ἰ ε ι ρ τ ο ρ χ ᾳ ρ Τ η ρ ·
λ ω δ Ϯ λ ι δ ο ρ τ ι ν ω ρ ᾳ ι ω ρ χ ε ι ϛ ο υ ϛ ρ μ ω ρ · Κ ᾳ ι δ λ δ ϛ ω ο ϛ δ ϛ ρ
Θ ϛ ο δ κ τ ο υ ι ω ρ ο υ · δ ᾳ ω μ ᾳ ζ ε κ ᾳ ι δ ὁ ο ζ ᾳ ϑ δ ᾳ ω ρ Θ μ ϛ ρ τ ᾳ ᾳ ι
μ ᾳ ι ᾳ ο ϛ ο τ ο ρ ᾳ μ μ ω ρ ᾳ ι . λ ι ρ ϛ ᾳ ρ τ ο τ ο υ ϕ ᾳ χ λ ε ι ρ λ ι ‑ ω ᾳ ρ δ ϛ ρ ο ο
ο λ ι μ δ ρ ρ η τ ο ρ ι ‑ ω δ ρ ο υ ο ι ο ρ τ ι κ τ ϛ Π ο ι λ ο ᾳ ο δ Ϯ λ ᾳ ι ϛ δ ρ ω ρ υ ε
ο ρ τ ω ρ μ κ ο ρ τ ᾳ κ ι ω ω ϛ ε Π δ ρ ί ω χ λ ι ᾳ ‑ ω ρ ο ο κ υ ό ζ δ λ ἰ μ λ ω δ τ ι ·

Figure 11. Miniature and brief narrative biography of Romanos the Melodist from the *Menologion of Basil II*, circa 1000. Vaticanus graecus 1613, p. 78. Photo © Bibloteca Apostolica Vaticana (Vatican).

speak. Unlike the fifth-century author of the *Life and Miracles of Thecla*, Romanos did not claim such an image for himself. But its ascription to the poet nevertheless underscores the degree to which Byzantine conceptions of Christian authorship called on biblical precedents.

Like John the Evangelist in the *Acts of John by Prochoros* and the *Memorial of Saint John*, later tradition retrofitted Romanos as a charismatic prophet. As in the case of the evangelists, later generations continued to elaborate the authorial identities of more recently canonical writers. While Romanos had made himself humble, the church made him a saint. As the tenth-century *Synaxarium of Constantinople* states, "Many [of his poems] are preserved in the church in the district of Kyros, set down in his own hand. He attained perfection in peace and was buried in the same church, in which his synaxis [commemorative liturgy] is also celebrated." After the death of the author, the hagiographical practice continued, forming the author through narrative and liturgy.

What, then, was a Christian author? Focusing on the first particularly Christian literary genres has uncovered emergent conceptions of Christian authorship. Rhetorical performances embedded in texts situated literary production in a variety of Christian contexts. Textual strategies both simple and complex effected the integration of literary composition into emergent devotional roles. Authors represented their writing as part of their identities as disciple, monk, priest, deacon, devotee, pilgrim, prophet and evangelist, and even sinner. The emergence of such a range of writerly subjectivities coincided with the emergence of new styles of the Christian self. Constraints placed on the production of identity by an emerging Christian ethic of obedience and humility, in particular, regulated strategies for claiming and exercising authority. This new aesthetic of authorship resulted both in and through efforts to portray the author as a pious Christian. Engaging in literary composition, a writer both displayed and produced authorial piety.

A number of important issues will merit further study. Recent work on masculinity in late antiquity has sharpened an understanding of how Christianity transformed the cultural performance of gender. Indeed, hagiographical narratives in particular display shifting categories of male and female under the influence of asceticism.[2] In antiquity, literary authorship itself was a masculine discourse, the result of years of rhetorical training.[3] While the texts considered here produced both male and female saints as objects of veneration, all were written by men. To what extent was the early Christian practice of authorship gendered male? The Christianization of the Roman literate classes in the fourth century brought new constraints to male identity and the exercise of authorial power. Some authors, such as Gregory of Nyssa, destabilized their masculinity in the process of writing.[4] Such performances conformed to emerging theologies of gender. Indeed the new styles of literary composition were an integral part of these authors' performances of a newly qualified masculinity. Some women, of course, did write, just as some worked as scribes.[5] But hagiographical texts did not attach themselves securely to female identities. The near-exclusive transmission of men's texts in subsequent centuries seems to confirm that writerly authority was widely invested as male. The process of copying clearly favored the reinscription of texts written (or believed to be written) by men. Masculinity shifted, and authorship shifted with it.

The reorientation of gender coincided with a revaluation of power. In fact, the widely used rhetoric of humility was always already a discourse about power and of power. The authors examined here were never merely "the author as expressed in the text" but were rather participants in broad networks of interaction in which texts were instruments of power and authority. Many of the authors considered here wrote to establish, enhance, or shore up their positions in local and regional hierarchies, both monastic and diocesan. The most obviously political performance examined here may be that of the author of the *Life and Miracles of Thecla*. At the end of his text, he prayed to the exalted saint to grant him to "persuade [his] hearers," to gain their "respect." He hoped that he would, thanks to Thecla, have "applause and honor, and a solid reputation among the orators."[6] To be politically successful, perhaps an author's agenda would need to be more subtle. Theodoret's writing, for example, affirmed his standing throughout the church.[7] In renegotiating the relationship between authorship and authority, Christianity nevertheless maintained the power of skilled literacy to mark and maintain a cultural elite.

Rather more can also be said about the birth of the hagiographical genre and about its place in late antique and early Byzantine historiography. The genre hagiography emerged in late antiquity both to describe and to prescribe patterns of monastic life. From its origins with Athanasius's *Life of Antony*, Christian monastic biography asserted a normative power, calling its audience to the imitation of narrated models. The Antony to be emulated was the textual persona of his vita. Athanasius used writing to create a monastic type, "a sufficient picture for monastic practice."[8] Cuing his readers to the suasion of his own text, Athanasius explained of Antony that "simply by seeing his conduct many aspired to become imitators of his way of life" (47). The text replaced vision because now, "seeing" Antony's conduct could occur only through report: Antony could be seen only in representation. The narrative of Antony's life effected the production of monks and monastic institutions, setting the patterns of piety and practice.

Seeing monks in texts, as textual subjects, also featured in the *Life of Antony*'s regulatory instructions, where textuality functioned as a critical tool. In Athanasius's account, Antony encourages his disciples, "Now daily let each one recount to himself his actions of the day and night. . . . Let each one of us note and write down [σημειώμεθα καὶ γράφωμεν] our actions and the stirrings of our souls as though we were going to give an account to each other. . . . Let this writing [γράμμα] replace the eyes of our fellow ascetics, so that, blushing as much to write as to be seen, we might never be absorbed by evil things" (55).[9] Displacing onto Antony's lips, through hagiographical ventriloquy, his own normative rule that monks should keep diaries of the movements of their soul, Athanasius imposes writing as an exercise of monastic witness, a mode in which monks see and are seen, even if only by themselves. Writing is prescribed as a mode of discipline, as a form of chastising vision. The slippage between the literary and the visual rests on the idea that reading is a form of seeing and that writing is analogous to arts such as painting. The bishop, overseeing his flock, institutes writing as the instrument of survey and surveillance, an epistemological tool both for knowing the self and for forming the self. The faithful monk would rewrite himself until he read properly. In writing as he did, Athanasius granted monks the mandate to author themselves. Or, more precisely, Athanasius called on monks to compose and govern themselves in conformity with his story of Antony, who was himself "governed by the Logos" of God (14). Athanasius set textual boundaries on either side of the monk, one of shame and one of desire. Monastic life took place in the territory between the dreadful honesty of a written diary and Antony's textualized ideal. Within this space, the monk faced the dazzling narrative of the holy exemplar with fervent longing. Asceticism navigated between textual possibilities.[10]

In the Athanasian ideal, monastic identity was formed in and by text—and disciplined in and by text. The impact of such a link between writing and monasticism ought not be underestimated. Because of the wide dissemination and popularity of the *Life of Antony*, subsequent hagiographers inevitably wrote in the tradition of Athanasius, following his model. Generations of monks strove to emulate the holy identities materially present, especially in narrative. Early Byzantine monasticism is in large part a product of texts and textuality. To the extent that this monasticism can be the object of modern study, the writings, together with archeological remains and surviving art, are subject to our own carefully guided acts of interpretation. No diaries of the sort that Athanasius's Antony prescribes survive among the papyrus discovered in the Egyptian desert, but a significant number of biographies of monastic heroes do from ancient and medieval libraries. The disciplined historian no longer engages in the romantic notion that the surviving texts provide unmediated access to monastic persons. Hagiography did, and does, offer images of holiness embodied, textual identities invested with cultural value. The texts provided an instrument in the formation of monks and, even when consumed by lay audiences, provided an instrument in the formation of the idea of monasticism. Hagiography served to set boundaries, establish patterns, and inflame desire.[11]

Asceticism pervaded early Byzantine Christianity. Through a piety of self-restriction, monks and laity alike fashioned themselves to conform to the body of Christ. In the *Life of Antony,* Athanasius called distant monks to imitate Antony; but in his festal letters, he called all the Christians of Egypt to a temporary monasticism of fasting and prayer during Lent.[12] As a cultural performance, ascetic practice deployed power over the subject to produce identities conforming to established ideals.[13] Preaching exhorted Christians to emulate the virtues of biblical exemplars; ascetic theorists called on Christians not only to train the movements of their bodies but to edit the movements of their souls.[14] Performances of fasting, vigilant prayer, and resistance of demonic temptation presented a visible spectacle, directed toward the laity, toward other ascetics, toward the ascetic self, or even God, but always depending on an audience for meaning. Ascetic achievement was a text to be read.[15] The rise of local holy men and women, together with the rise of holy narratives recounting successful efforts, presented a great number of spectacles upon which Christians might gaze and that they might subsequently emulate.

The formation of the Christian subject took place at the convergence of narrative and matter. Preachers and hagiographers exhorted Christians to conform themselves to biblical exemplars and the lives of the saints, to resemble sacred narrative in themselves. Much more than a call to reproduce static portraits of holiness, written texts set forth narrative models, modes of life enshrined in writing. To the extent that they emulated Christ himself, holy men and women made Christ legible in their bodies, became representations of the Logos enfleshed—textual bodies. This complex interplay between textuality and embodiment was embedded in the deep structure of Christian praxis. Text bounded, defined, disciplined, and produced the Christian body. While the Neoplatonist Porphyry rendered his subject Plotinus resistant to representation, textual and otherwise, Gregory of Nyssa's sister Macrina willingly offered herself in narrative. The author of the *Life of Syncletica* further explored the relationship between text and body whereby texts served to preserve words for further consumption, much as the eucharist preserved the embodied Logos. The practices of Christianity reproduced corporeal text.

Ascetic practice and the making of texts were parallel enterprises. Both involved the manipulation of raw material to produce holy identities. Hagiography employed the technology of literary composition to render these ascetic performances acutely visible and present. But the production of collective biography by the second and third generation of hagiographers, in the *History of the Monks of Egypt*, in Palladius's *Lausiac History*, and in Theodoret of Cyrrhus's *Religious History* belies a movement toward holy individuals. Instead, collective biography demonstrates a movement toward the generic (that is, toward genre), a variety of people moving toward and sharing in a similar ideal.[16] The placement of Symeon the Stylite's story (twenty-sixth out of thirty) within Theodoret's extended travelogue of northern Syrian day trips shows one bishop's attempt to blend a particularly prominent ascetic into a broadly holy geography where so many of the local mountaintops were theaters for ascetic achievement. Time and space, calendar and landscape, were quickly filled with broadly similar options for visits, veneration, and devotion. Ascetic practice and hagiographical narrative strove toward imitation and pattern, and thus toward genre.

What then of the relationship between the lives of the saints and the *Lives of the Saints?* Is the distinction merely typographic? I have treated hagiographic writings as textual performances of early Byzantine monasticism. This hermeneutic bracketed demands to distinguish between what monks did and what texts meant. With the positivist questions temporarily withdrawn, however, other questions come to the fore. Is the text a simulacrum of monastic practice, or is monastic practice a simulacrum of the text? Hagiography presented ascetics as conforming to models established by other ascetics, rendering asceticism an ultimately generic activity. The hagiographer's task included asserting or demonstrating that the saint was just like and, sometimes, even better than biblical types or previous monks, that he or she was conforming to high ideals. The biblicizing aesthetic in particular blurred the boundaries between saint's life and scripture, positing a continuum of sacred writing.

The genre hagiography itself arose through imitation, through authors' emulation of earlier texts. On the one hand, hagiography began with the biblical texts that the hagiographers imitated. On the other hand, and perhaps in a more proper sense, hagiography as a practice began not with the first saints' lives but with the subsequent generation of texts imitating the first. Both of these realizations decenter the supposed origin of the genre in Athanasius's *Life of Antony*.[17] Significantly Athanasius's *Life of Antony* and Gregory of Nyssa's *Life of Macrina,* two of the earliest saint's lives, both remark their own generic instability, a mix of oration and letter.[18] Only later could the genre emerge, iterative and mimetic. By the sixth century, the Palestinian lives of Cyril of Scythopolis not only present monks excelling in established modes of life, they also present these ideals according to established patterns of generic composition. Cyril's extensive quotation and borrowing from earlier hagiographic texts exhibits not only the rich contents of the library at Mar Saba, but also Cyril's sense of genre through which he consciously produces a text of the same type, something belonging on the same shelf. The parallel moves toward regularity and conformity of ascetic practice and its textual representation depended, in the final analysis, on the creation of hagiography as a genre of authorial conduct.

This study has engaged the history of Christian ideas about authorship by observing writers engaged in acts of simultaneous representation, producing at once both saint and self. Authors inscribed themselves into texts, rendering themselves present in the narrative persona or voice. These authorial identities were more than accidental by-products of literary activity. Acts of self-inscription were acts of self-production governed by reference to religious norms. In this process, a new kind of authorship was born. The introductions and conclusions of saints' lives quickly became places where authors presented textualized performances of their own devotional and ascetic virtues, particularly humility and obedience.[19] Christian authors emerged as materialized subjects of their own writerly activity, woven into the fabric of their texts, offered humbly and willingly to readers and listeners.

When Theodoret set out in the *Religious History* to "honor the celebrated life" of the saints in writing (prol. 2), he understood the preservation of their memory to demand both a new genre and a new kind of author. In accord with ancient divisions among literary forms, he regarded the work of poets and historians as appropriate to record "bravery in acts of war." With less admiration, he explained that tragedians "makes conspicuous . . . misfortunes that had rightly been hidden away"; "certain others expend their words on comedy and laughter" (prol. 2). The new Christian genre had for Theodoret no name. Terming it neither "eulogy" (prol. 8) nor "panegyric," his "narrative form, . . . a plain tale of some few facts" (prol. 9), emerged as a new literary discipline that befitted the new achievements of those "lovers of the beauty of God," who "bore nobly the revolt of the passions and were steadfast in shaking off the showers of the devil's darts" (prol. 5).

Theodoret was not merely advocating a new genre, what he would later call "the lives of the saints"; he was proposing a new style of author.[20] Significantly, Theodoret speaks initially in his prologue not of genres but of their agents—of poets, historians, tragedians, and comics—identities that arise through the production of specific kinds of literature. If his new narrative genre had no name, neither did its production afford him an established identity. The production of saints' lives made Theodoret a writer of saints' lives, a specifically Christian identity that was relatively new and not yet entirely fixed. Like his saints based on biblical precedents, Theodoret was already molding himself in continuity both with Christian devotees of the saints and with past authors. He too was tending toward sameness and conformity to prior models.

The ascetic revolution of late antiquity was a potent generative matrix. While hagiography provides a window onto the newness of early Christian monasticism, intensive study of the texts as texts has yielded the conclusion that in hagiography *two* new things are emerging: a new system of practice and a new method of representing this practice in literature. These two developments, asceticism and saints' lives, are mutually bound, and not merely because modern scholars' access to late antique monasticism must proceed through the surviving literary texts. Genre also was discipline. Asceticism produced new *literary* disciplines, new practices of authorship. The birth of hagiography marked an evolution in the concept of the author. In prescribing complex and demanding rules for the representation of the self, hagiography reshaped the habits of literary composition.

Abbreviations

ACW	Ancient Christian Writers
AnBoll	*Analecta Bollandiana*
ANF	Ante-Nicene Fathers
BMGS	*Byzantine and Modern Greek Studies*
CSCO	Corpus Scriptorum Christianorum Orientalium
DOP	*Dumbarton Oaks Papers*
Ep., Epp.	Letter, Letters
FOTC	Fathers of the Church
GCS	Die griechischen christlichen Schriftsteller der ersten drei Jahrhunderte
GRBS	*Greek, Roman, and Byzantine Studies*
HME	*History of the Monks of Egypt (Historia monachorum in Aegypto)*
JAAR	*Journal of the American Academy of Religion*
JAC	*Jahrbuch für Antike und Christentum*
JECS	*Journal of Early Christian Studies*
JRS	*Journal of Roman Studies*
JThS	*Journal of Theological Studies*
Lampe	*A Patristic Greek Lexicon*, edited by G. W. H. Lampe (Oxford: Oxford University Press, 1961)
LCL	Loeb Classical Library
LSJ	*A Greek-English Lexicon*, compiled by Henry George Liddell and Robert Scott, revised and augmented throughout by Sir Henry Stuart Jones, 9th ed., with supplement (Oxford: Oxford University Press, 1968)
LXX	Septuagint
NPNF	Nicene and Post-Nicene Fathers
ODB	*Oxford Dictionary of Byzantium*
PG	Patrologia Graeca, ed. J. P. Migne
PL	Patrologia Latina, ed. J. P. Migne
PO	*Patrologia Orientalis*

prol.	prologue
SC	Sources chrétiennes
Sub.	Subsidia
VC	*Vigiliae Christianae*

Notes

Chapter 1

1. Greek text and translation in Gregory of Nazianzus, *Autobiographical Poems*, ed. Carolinne White (Cambridge: Cambridge University Press, 1996), 165–81.

2. Frank D. Gilliard, "More Silent Reading in Antiquity: Non omne verbum sonabat," *Journal of Biblical Literature* 112 (1993): 689–94; Paul Saenger, *Space between Words: The Origins of Silent Reading* (Stanford: Stanford University Press, 1997).

3. Οὕτω πεδῆσαι τὴν ἐμὴν ἀμετρίαν. The poem is titled "Εἰς τὰ ἔμμετρα." Gregory of Nazianzus, *Poems* 2.1.39 (PG 37:1329–36), line 35; text in *Autobiographical Poems*, ed. White, 2–9; translation in Peter Gilbert, *On God and Man: The Theological Poetry of Gregory of Nazianzus* (Crestwood, N.Y.: St. Vladimir's Seminary Press, 2001), 153–56; see also 13–14.

4. Athanasius, *Life of Antony* 55; edition: *Vie d'Antoine*, ed. G. J. M. Bartelink, SC 400 (Paris: Cerf, 1994). See also David Brakke, *Athanasius and the Politics of Asceticism* (Oxford: Clarendon, 1995), 260.

5. John Chrysostom, *Homilies on Matthew* 41.6 (PG 57.540).

6. On attempts to estimate population and the extent of literacy among Christians, see Keith Hopkins, "Christian Number and Its Implications," *JECS* 6 (1998): 185–226; Robert Browning, "Literacy in the Byzantine World," *BMGS* 4 (1978): 39–54; Robin Lane Fox, "Literacy and Power in Early Christianity," in *Literacy and Power in the Ancient World*, ed. Alan K. Bowman and Greg Woolf (Cambridge: Cambridge University Press, 1994), 126–48.

7. On modesty and authority, see Virginia Burrus, *"Begotten, Not Made": Conceiving Manhood in Late Antiquity* (Stanford: Stanford University Press, 2000), 167–79; Carlin A. Barton, *Roman Honor: The Fire in the Bones* (Berkeley: University of California Press, 2001); Peter Brown, *Authority and the Sacred: Aspects of the Christianization of the Roman World* (Cambridge: Cambridge University Press, 1995). On asceticism and the formation of identity, see Richard Valantasis, "Constructions of Power in Asceticism," *JAAR* 63 (1995): 775–821.

8. For an introduction to the period, see Averil Cameron, *The Mediterranean World in Late Antiquity, AD 395–600* (London: Routledge, 1993).

9. Michel Foucault, "What Is an Author?" in *Language, Counter-Memory, Practice*, trans. Sherry Simon and ed. Donald F. Bouchard (Ithaca: Cornell University Press, 1977). For a survey of the problem, see Donald E. Pease, "Author," in

Critical Terms for Literary Study, ed. Frank Lentricchia and Thomas McLaughlin (Chicago: University of Chicago Press, 1995), 105–17. For later medieval Western perspectives, see A. J. Minnis, *Medieval Theory of Authorship: Scholastic Literary Attitudes in the Later Middle Ages,* 2nd ed. (Philadelphia: University of Pennsylvania Press, 1988).

10. For criticism of positivist approaches, see Thomas J. Heffernan, *Sacred Biography: Saints and Their Biographers in the Middle Ages* (New York: Oxford University Press, 1988), 38–71; and Evelyne Patlagean, "Ancient Byzantine Hagiography and Social History," in *Saints and Their Cults: Studies in Religious Sociology, Folklore and History,* ed. Stephen Wilson (Cambridge: Cambridge University Press, 1983), 101–21 (originally published as "À Byzance: Ancienne hagiographie et histoire sociale," *Annales* 23 [1968]: 106–26).

11. Peter Brown (*The Cult of the Saints: Its Rise and Function in Latin Christianity* [Chicago: University of Chicago Press, 1981], 12–22) offers some perspective on the two-tiered model of popular and elite religion.

12. Émile Durkheim, *The Elementary Forms of Religious Life,* trans. Karen E. Fields (New York: Free Press, 1995), 44 (original French edition, 1912); Catherine Bell, *Ritual Theory, Ritual Practice* (New York: Oxford University Press, 1992), 13, 19–29. William Scott Green ("The Difference Religion Makes," *JAAR* 62 [1994]: 1197) bemoans the separation of theology from religion in contemporary religious studies, seeing the former as the intellectual elaboration of the latter.

13. Gregory of Nyssa, *Life of Moses* 1.7, 46; 2.24–26, 81, 152–61.

14. Harry Y. Gamble, *Books and Readers in the Early Church: A History of Early Christian Texts* (New Haven: Yale University Press, 1995); Claudia Rapp, "Christians and Their Manuscripts in the Greek East in the Fourth Century," in *Scritture, libri e testi nelle aree provinciali di Bisanzio,* ed. Guglielmo Cavallo, Guiseppe de Gregorio, and Marilena Maniaci (Spoleto: Centro Italiano di Studi Sull'Alto Medioevo, 1991), 127–48; Claudia Rapp, "Holy Texts, Holy Men and Holy Scribes," in *The Early Christian Book,* ed. William Klingshirn and Linda Safran (Washington, D.C.: Catholic University of America Press, forthcoming 2004); Kim Haines-Eitzen, *Guardians of Letters: Literacy, Power, and the Transmitters of Early Christian Literature* (New York: Oxford University Press, 2000); Elizabeth A. Clark, *Reading Renunciation: Asceticism and Scripture in Early Christianity* (Princeton: Princeton University Press, 1999); Paul Griffiths, *Religious Reading: The Place of Reading in the Practice of Religion* (New York: Oxford University Press, 1999). Habits are ultimately regulatory: see Pierre Bourdieu, *The Logic of Practice,* trans. Richard Nice (Stanford: Stanford University Press, 1990), 52–65.

15. Robert Browning, "The 'Low Level' Saint's Life in the Early Byzantine World," in *The Byzantine Saint,* ed. Sergei Hackel (San Bernardino, Calif.: Borgo, 1983), 117–27; reprinted in Browning, *History, Language, and Literacy in the Byzantine World* (London: Variorum, 1989), VIII; Derek Krueger, *Symeon the Holy Fool: Leontius's Life and the Late Antique City* (Berkeley: University of California Press, 1996), 37–38n5. For perspective on divergence between style and audience, see also Claudia Rapp, "Byzantine Hagiographers as Antiquarians, Seventh to Tenth Centuries," *Byzantinische Forschungen* 21 (1995): 31–44.

16. See Marc van Uytfanghe, "L'Hagiographie: un 'genre' chrétien ou antique

tardif?" *AnBoll* 111 (1993): 135–88. On genre analysis and its limitations, see Alastair Fowler, *Kinds of Literature: An Introduction to the Theory of Genres and Modes* (Oxford: Clarendon, 1982); and Hans Robert Jauss, "Theory of Genres and Medieval Literature," in *Modern Genre Theory*, ed. David Duff, trans. Timothy Bahti (Harlow: Pearson, 2000), 127–47 (originally published in French in 1970). In *Generic Composition in Greek and Roman Poetry* (Edinburgh: Edinburgh University Press, 1972) Francis Cairns provides a classic study of genre in antiquity.

17. Richard A. Burridge, *What Are the Gospels? A Comparison with Graeco-Roman Biography* (Cambridge: Cambridge University Press, 1995).

18. Patricia Cox Miller, *Biography in Late Antiquity: A Quest for the Holy Man*, Transformation of the Classical Heritage 5 (Berkeley: University of California Press, 1983); Averil Cameron, "Eusebius's *Vita Constantini* and the Construction of Constantine," in *Portraits: Biographical Representation in the Greek and Latin Literature of the Roman Empire*, ed. M. J. Edwards and S. C. R. Swain (Oxford: Clarendon, 1997), 145–74; Averil Cameron, "Form and Meaning: The *Vita Constantini* and the *Vita Antonii*," in *Greek Biography and Panegyric in Late Antiquity*, ed. Tomas Hägg and Philip Rousseau (Berkeley: University of California Press, 2000), 72–88.

19. Tomas Hägg and Philip Rousseau, "Biography and Panegyric," in *Greek Biography*, ed. Hägg and Rousseau, 1–28. I have left it to others to undertake a study of Greco-Roman religious polytheist performances of authorship. For some perspective, see John J. Winkler, *Auctor and Actor: A Narratological Reading of Apuleius' Golden Ass* (Berkeley: University of California Press, 1985).

20. See also Virginia Burrus, *The Sex Lives of Saints: An Erotics of Ancient Hagiography* (Philadelphia: University of Pennsylvania Press, 2003), 19–52. Claudia Rapp, " 'For Next to God, You Are My Salvation': Reflections on the Rise of the Holy Man in Late Antiquity," in *The Cult of the Saints in Late Antiquity and the Middle Ages: Essays on the Contribution of Peter Brown*, ed. James Howard-Johnston and Paul Antony Hayward (Oxford: Oxford University Press, 1999), 63–81.

21. Pseudo-Dionysius, *Ecclesiastical Hierarchy* 1.1.4 (376c); 3.2.1 (425c); 3.3.4 (429c); edition: *Corpus Dionysiacum*, ed. Beate Suchla et al., 2 vols. (Berlin: De-Gruyter, 1990–91). Paul Rorem, *Biblical and Liturgical Symbols Within the Pseudo-Dionysian Synthesis*, Studies and Texts 71 (Toronto: Pontifical Institute of Medieval Studies, 1978), 21.

22. See Chapter 6.

23. See Averil Cameron, *Christianity and the Rhetoric of Empire: The Development of Christian Discourse* (Berkeley: University of California Press, 1991), 189; Brian Stock, *Augustine the Reader: Meditation, Self-Knowledge, and the Ethics of Interpretation* (Cambridge, Mass.: Harvard University Press, 1996), 7–9; Robert Markus, "St. Augustine on Signs," *Phronesis* 2 (1957) 60–83, reprinted in Markus, *Signs and Meanings: World and Text in Ancient Christianity* (Liverpool: Liverpool University Press, 1996), 71–104.

24. Verna E. F. Harrison, "Word as Icon in Greek Patristic Theology," *Sobornost* 10 (1988): 38–49.

25. Moshe Barasch, *Icon: Studies in the History of an Idea* (New York: New York University Press, 1992); Eric D. Perl, " '. . . That Man Might Become God': Central Themes in Byzantine Theology," in *Heaven on Earth: Art and the Church in*

Byzantium, ed. Linda Safran (University Park, Pa.: Pennsylvania State University Press, 1998), 39–57.

26. G. W. Bowersock, "The Syriac Life of Rabbula and Syrian Hellenism," in *Greek Biography*, ed. Hägg and Rousseau, 257–59; Patricia Cox Miller, "'Hagio-poiesis': Hagiography and Theological Aesthetics in Late Ancient Christianity," unpublished paper. On visuality as a goal of narrative representation, see Ann Vasaly, *Representations: Images of the World in Ciceronian Oratory* (Berkeley: University of California Press, 1993).

27. *Life of Chariton* 1. Edition: G. Garitte, "La Vie prémétaphrastique de s. Chariton," *Bulletin de l'Institut Historique Belge de Rome* 21 (1941): 5–46; trans. Leah Di Segni, in *Ascetic Behavior in Greco-Roman Antiquity: A Sourcebook*, ed. Vincent Wimbush (Minneapolis: Fortress, 1990), 393–421.

28. Roger S. Bagnall, "Jesus Reads a Book," *JThS* 51 (2000): 577–88; Raymond E. Brown, *The Gospel According to John*, Anchor Bible 29 (Garden City, N.Y.: Doubleday, 1966), 1:335–6.

29. *Gospel of Truth* 20:24–25; *L'Évangile de vérité*, ed. J. E. Ménard, Nag Hammadi Studies 2 (Leiden: Brill, 1972).

30. Evagrius of Pontus, *Letter to Melania* 2; trans. M. Parmentier, "Evagrius of Pontus' "Letter to Melania I," *Bijdragen, tijdschrift vor filosofie en theologie* 46 (1985): 2–38.

31. R. C. Hill, "St. John Chrysostom and the Incarnation of the Word in Scripture," *Compass Theology Review* 14 (1980): 34–38; Hill, "On Looking Again at *Sunkatabasis*," *Prudentia* 13 (1981): 3–11.

32. See also Hebrews 8:10; compare Jeremiah 17:1, 31:33; Ezekiel 11:19. See also Irenaeus, *Against the Heresies* 3.4.2.

33. Romanos the Melodist, *Hymns* 56.9. Edition: *Sancti Romani Melodi Cantica: Cantica Genuina*, ed. P. Maas and C. A. Trypanis (Oxford: Clarendon, 1963), 485.

34. Roland Barthes, "Authors and Writers," in *Critical Essays*, trans. Richard Howard (Evanston: Northwestern University Press, 1972), 143–50, originally published as "Écrivains et écrivants," in *Essais critique* (Paris: Seuil, 1964), 147–54; see also Barthes, "The Death of the Author," in *Image, Music, Text*, trans. Stephen Heath (New York: Hill and Wang, 1977), 142–48 (originally published in French in 1968); David Glenn Kropf, *Authorship as Alchemy: Subversive Writing in Pushkin, Scott, and Hoffmann* (Stanford: Stanford University Press, 1994). Roland Barthes's distinction between the author and the writer applies appropriately to modern European literary culture since the nineteenth century, when the rise of biographical criticism introduced a split between the authorial voice in a text and the writer's life as available to the student of literature. It is not clear how early Byzantine Greeks would have made such a distinction. Nevertheless, the interplay between the author's textual performance and his identity outside the text are a constant concern in this study.

35. Zachary Leader, *Writer's Block* (Baltimore: Johns Hopkins University Press, 1991).

36. Common terms for "author" include "συγγραφεύς" and "ποιήτης" (also in compounds). "Authority" was most commonly expressed as "ἡγεμονία,"

"ἐξουσία," "αὐθεντία," and "δύναμις" (also "power"). See also Minnis, *Medieval Theory of Authorship*, 10–15; and Pease, "Author," 106, although neither handles the Greek evidence.

37. On the prologues and epilogues of later Byzantine saints' lives, see Thomas Pratsch, *Topos Hagiographikos: Untersuchungen zur byzantinischen hagiographischen Literatur des 7.-11. Jahrhunderts* (forthcoming). For a modern example of how a book's front matter performs authorial identity, see Mark Bauerline, "A Thanking Task: What Acknowledgements Pages Say about Academic Life," *Times Literary Supplement*, November 9, 2001.

38. For a survey of the problem of determining literary intention, see Annabel Patterson, "Intention," in *Critical Terms for Literary Study*, ed. Lentricchia and McLaughlin, 135–46; Jeffrey Stout, "What Is the Meaning of a Text?" *New Literary History* 1 (1982): 1–12. Regarding the problem in the analysis of religious rituals, see Catherine Bell, "Performance," in *Critical Terms for Religious Studies*, ed. Mark C. Taylor (Chicago: University of Chicago Press, 1998), 205–24.

39. Cameron, *Christianity and the Rhetoric of Empire*, 5. On discourse and the formation of subjectivity, see Paul Bové, "Discourse," in *Critical Terms for Literary Study*, ed. Lentricchia and McLaughlin, 53–62; and Pease, "Author," 106.

40. Citations of ancient texts refer to section numbers, except for those works where the convention is to cite the page numbers of the critical edition. These are designated with a comma between the title and the page number.

Chapter 2

1. Marc van Uytfanghe, "L'Hagiographie: Un 'genre' chrétien ou antique tardif?" *AnBoll* 111 (1993): 170–79.

2. Text: Théodoret de Cyr, *Histoire des moines de Syrie*, ed. Pierre Canivet and Alice Leroy-Molinghen, 2 vols., SC 234 and 257 (Paris: Cerf, 1977–79). With occasional modification, I employ here the fine English translation of R. M. Price: Theodoret of Cyrrhus, *A History of the Monks of Syria*, trans. R. M. Price, Cistercian Studies 88 (Kalamazoo, Mich.: Cistercian, 1985). Translations of other texts are my own, except as noted.

3. For the titles of the work, see Theodoret, *Religious History*, prologue (hereafter prol.) 10. For the date, see Price, *A History of the Monks of Syria*, xiii–xv. Canivet (*Le monachisme syrien selon Théodoret de Cyr*, Théologie historique 42 [Paris: Beauchesne, 1977], 31–35) argued for dating the text to 444, as did Leroy-Molinghen, "A propos de la Vie de Syméon Stylite," *Byzantion* 34 (1964): 375–84.

4. Theodoret of Cyrrhus, *Ep.* 82; edition: Théodoret de Cyr, *Correspondance*, ed. Yvan Azéma, SC 98 (Paris: Cerf, 1964), 2:202.

5. Through a comparison of phrases beginning and ending each vignette, Paul Devos ("La structure de l'Histoire Philothée de Théodoret de Cyr: Le nombre de chapitres," *AnBoll* 97 [1979]: 319–35) has shown that Theodoret organized the work in twenty-eight sections.

6. The work's organizational scheme is charted by Price, *A History of the Monks of Syria*, xvi–xvii; compare Canivet, *Le monachisme syrien*, 85–86.

7. Regarding the account of James of Cyrrhestica, one of the longest and more rhetorically elevated in the collection, Theodoret writes, "We have composed this as a narrative [διηγηματικῶς] not as a panegyric" (*Religious History*, 21.35). Photius (*Bibliotheca* 203) admired Theodoret's style. On Theodoret's erudition, see Canivet, *Le monachisme syrien*, 51–54. See also Canivet in Théodoret de Cyr, *Thérapeutique des maladies helléniques*, 2 vols., SC 57 (Paris: Cerf, 1958), 1:60–67; Price, *A History of the Monks of Syria*, xv; M. M. Wagner "A Chapter in Byzantine Epistolography: The Letters of Theodoret of Cyrus," *DOP* 4 (1948): 119–81; Theresa Urbainczyk, *Theodoret of Cyrrhus: The Bishop and the Holy Man* (Ann Arbor: University of Michigan Press, 2002), 14–21. The monumental *Cure of Pagan Maladies* (*Graecarum affectionum curatio*) demonstrates the full range of Theodoret's knowledge of classical texts, although Canivet (in Théodoret de Cyr, *Thérapeutique*, 1:55–59) has shown that some of this familiarity came second-hand through works of Clement of Alexandria and Eusebius of Caesarea.

8. On the pervasiveness of Syriac language and culture among Syrian monastics, see Canivet, *Le monachisme syrien*, 235–53. Writing in 374 from Chalcis, Jerome (*Ep.* 7.1–2; trans. Freemantle) bemoaned that "in that part of the desert which forms a broad boundary between the Syrians and the Arabs . . . an old man must either learn a barbarous language or remain silent." Theodoret himself appears to have been bilingual from childhood. Canivet (*Le monachisme syrien*, 39) believes that Theodoret's first language was Syriac. See also the remarks of Paul Peeters, "Grecs hybrides et orientaux hellénisants," in *Orient et Byzance: Le tréfonds oriental de l'hagiographie byzantine* (Brussels: Société des Bollandistes, 1950), 89.

9. Susan Ashbrook Harvey ("The Sense of a Stylite: Perspectives on Symeon the Elder," *VC* 42 [1988]: 378) remarks, "His audience . . . and thus his chosen literary form, is that of the hellenized world." Theodoret traveled regularly to Antioch to lecture and teach; see Theodoret, *Ep.* 125 (ed. Azéma, 3:96), compare *Epp.* 81, 83, and C. Thomas McCollough, "A Christianity for an Age of Crisis: Theodoret of Cyrus' *Commentary on Daniel*," in *Religious Writings and Religious Systems: Systemic Analysis of Holy Books in Christianity, Islam, Buddhism, Greco-Roman Religions, Ancient Israel, and Judaism*, ed. Jacob Neusner, Ernest S. Frerichs, and A. J. Levine (Atlanta: Scholars Press, 1989–), 2:160. Theodoret reports (*Religious History* 2.21) that Cyrrhus was two days' (δύο σταθμούς) journey from Antioch. For a brief assessment of Cyrrhus's history, topography, and provincial character, see Canivet, *Thérapeutique*, 1:17–19.

10. Theodoret, *Ecclesiastical History* 4.27.2. Text: *Kirchengeschichte*, ed. L. Parmentier and F. Scheidweiler, GCS (Berlin: Akademie-Verlag, 1954), 267. Theodoret refers his reader to the *Religious History* by name also at *Ecclesiastical History* 1.7.4, 2.30.3, 3.24.1, and 4.25.5. Theodoret intended his *Ecclesiastical History* as a continuation of Eusebius's (Theodoret, *Ecclesiastical History*, prol.).

11. On Theodoret's life, see Canivet, *Le monachisme syrien*, 37–63; Price, *A History of the Monks of Syria*, ix–xiii; and especially Frances Young, *From Nicaea to Chalcedon: A Guide to the Literature and Its Background* (Philadelphia: Fortress, 1983), 265–89. For Theodoret's mother in particular, compare Theodoret, *Religious*

History 6.14, 9.4–9, 13.16–18. On his dedication from birth, see Theodoret, *Religious History* 13.17 and Theodoret, *Ep.* 81, ed. Azéma, 2:196.

12. Theodoret, *Religious History* 12.4.

13. On the monastery at Nicerte, see Canivet, *Le monachisme syrien,* 59–61, 187–93.

14. At the time of his deposition in 449, Theodoret wrote to Pope Leo, "All the people of the East know that during the whole time I have been bishop I have acquired neither a house, nor a field, neither an obol, nor a tomb, but have embraced a voluntary poverty, and that I distributed immediately after the death of my parents everything which I inherited from them" (Theodoret, *Ep.* 113, ed. Azéma, 3:66). Compare Canivet, *Le monachisme syrien,* 62.

15. Compare Theodoret, *Religious History* 1.7, 2.9, 5.8, 10.9, 17.5. Of James of Nisibis, Theodoret (*Religious History* 1.7) writes, "To fasting, sleeping on the ground and wearing sackcloth was now added the whole range of care for the needy—I mean looking after widows and tending orphans, reproving the perpetrators of injustice and justly assisting their victims."

16. Theodoret, *Ep.* 119.

17. Ernst Honigmann, "Theodoret of Cyrrhus and Basil of Seleucia: The Time of Their Death," in *Patristic Studies,* Studi e testi 173 (Rome: Biblioteca apostolica vaticana, 1953), 174–84. Yvan Azéma ("Sur la date de la mort de Théodoret de Cyr," *Pallas* 31 [1984]: 137–55) prefers to date Theodoret's death to 460.

18. On Symeon the Stylite, see Robert Doran, *The Lives of Symeon Stylites,* Cistercian Studies 112 (Kalamazoo, Mich.: Cistercian, 1992), 15–66; Harvey, "The Sense of a Stylite," 376–94; and David T. M. Frankfurter, "Stylites and *Phallobates*: Pillar Religions in Late Antique Syria," *VC* 44 (1990): 168–98. For the *Religious History* as a source for the history of Syrian monasticism, see Arthur Vööbus, *History of Asceticism in the Syrian Orient: A Contribution to the History of Culture in the Near East,* vol. 2, CSCO 197/Sub. 17 (Louvain: Secrétariat de CSCO, 1960); and Canivet, *Le monachisme syrien.* For its use as a source for the history of Syrian village life, see Peter Brown, "The Rise and Function of the Holy Man in Late Antiquity," in *Society and the Holy in Late Antiquity* (Berkeley: University of California Press, 1982), 103–52; and Brown, "Town, Village and Holy Man: The Case of Syria," in *Society and the Holy,* 153–65. For a useful corrective to Brown's holy-man model, see Philip Rousseau, "Eccentrics and Coenobites in the Late Roman East," *Byzantinische Forschungen* 24 (1997): 35–50.

19. Price employs this phrase in *A History of the Monks of Syria,* xi. A different view of historicity is advanced by Vööbus (*History of Asceticism,* 2:12), who proves hostile to other aims of the text: "To be sure, there is much worthless stuff of legends, but it also is certain that amid fictions and exaggerations, we may here discover the grain of true history."

20. For some of the specifically hellenizing philosophical and theological biases of the text, see Harvey, "The Sense of a Stylite."

21. I have found most useful the work of Marc van Uytfanghe, *Stylisation biblique et condition humaine dans l'hagiographie mérovingienne (600–750)* (Brussels: Paleis der Academiën, 1987); and van Uytfanghe, "L'Empreinte biblique sur la plus ancienne hagiographie occidentale," in *Le monde latin antique et la Bible,* ed. Jac-

ques Fontaine et Charles Pietri, *Bible de tous les temps* 2 (Paris: Beauchesne, 1985), 565–611. See also Réginald Grégoire, *Manuale di agiologia: Introduzione alla letteratura agiographica* (Fabriano: Monastero San Silvestro Abate, 1987), 249–303; Henri Crouzel, "L'Imitation et la 'suite' de Dieu et du Christ dans les premiers siècles chrétiens ainsi que leurs sources gréco-romaines et hébraïques," *JAC* 21 (1978): 7–41; James W. Earl, "Typology and Iconographic Style in Early Medieval Hagiography," *Studies in the Literary Imagination* 8 (1975): 15–46; D. M. Deliyannis, "A Biblical Model for Serial Biography: The Book of Kings and the Roman *Liber Pontificalis*," *Revue Bénédictine* 107 (1997): 15–23; and the brief discussion in Derek Krueger, *Symeon the Holy Fool: Leontius's Life and the Late Antique City* (Berkeley: University of California Press, 1996), 108–10.

22. For a detailed treatment, see Victor Saxer, *Bible et hagiographie: Textes et thèmes bibliques dans les Actes des martyrs authentiques des premiers siècles* (Berne: Lang, 1986).

23. Defining the hagiographical genre has proved difficult. The best discussion of the problem is van Uytfanghe, "L'Hagiographie: un 'genre' chrétien ou antique tardif?"

24. E.g. Theodoret, *Religious History* 1.6, 8; 3.8; 11.2; 17.3; 26.17.

25. For ascetics imitating the Savior and becoming "new prophets," see *HME [Historia Monachorum in Aegypto]*, prol. 5; ed. A.-J. Festugière, Sub. Hag. 53 (Brussels: Société des Bollandistes, 1971), 7. Van Uytfanghe (*Stylisation biblique*, 18) distinguishes three modes of hagiographical typology: 1) *adnominatio*, where the name of a biblical figure is transposed to the subject of the hagiography (such as when the Christ is called a "new Adam"); 2) *assimilatio*, which stresses that a saint resembles a biblical figure; and 3) *comparatio*, which draws comparison between an event in the life of the saint and an event in the Bible. Van Uytfanghe regards the first form as the rarest and suggests that it might have been regarded as too direct (18n4). Each of these is found in the *Religious History*. Young, "Panegyric and the Bible," *Studia Patristica* 25 (1991): 194–208, affords further perspective on biblical typology as a compositional mode.

26. For the rejection of family, see Theodoret, *Religious History* 3.14–15, where Theodoret paraphrases Matthew 10:37 and Luke 14:26; and *Religious History* 15.6, where Theodoret quotes Matthew 19:29. Publius (*Religious History* 5.1–2) distributes his possessions "according to divine law." Symeon the Stylite's conversion to the ascetic life is presented as a response to the Beatitudes (*Religious History* 26.2). Symeon (*Religious History* 26.7; compare. 29.7) longs to fast for forty days like Moses and Elijah. But Marcianus (*Religious History* 3.12) presents fasting as dependent on human authority rather than divine law. Still useful on the components of ascetic praxis is Vööbus, *History of Asceticism*, 2:256–91.

27. Compare *Religious History* 1.6, 8; 3.8; 6.14; 8.8, 14; 17.3; 26.17. The wide semantic range of *mimēsis* encompasses the concepts of imitation, copy, and representation, including both literary and visual portraiture; compare LSJ and Lampe, s.v. "μίμησις" and *ODB* s.v. "imitation."

28. On Elijah as a model ascetic, see also Theodoret, *Religious History* 4.4; 17.6.

29. For example: Athanasius, *Life of Antony* 7; *Apophthegmata Patrum: Alphabetical Collection*, Nisterius 2 (PG 65.305); *Life of Pachomius* (*Vita prima Graeca*) 2,

ed. F. Halkin, Subsidia Hagiographica 19 (Brussels: Société des Bollandistes, 1932); John Cassian, *Conferences* 14.4, 18.6 (where Hebrews 11:37–38 is taken to apply to Elijah and Elisha); Ephrem, *Hymns on the Nativity* 14.16–17, ed. Edmund Beck, CSCO 186 (Louvain: CSCO, 1959), 80; Gregory of Nyssa, *Commentary on the Song of Songs* 7, ed. Werner Jaeger and Hermann Langerbeck (Leiden: Brill, 1960), 6:222–23; Ambrose, *Ep.* 63.75–8 (Elijah and John the Baptist). On Elijah and John the Baptist in Egyptian monasticism, see David T. M. Frankfurter, *Elijah in Upper Egypt: The Apocalypse of Elijah and Early Egyptian Christianity* (Minneapolis: Fortress, 1993), 65–74. On biblical precedents in Athanasius's *Life of Antony* in particular, see Antoine Guillaumont, "La conception du désert chez les moines d'Egypte," *Revue de l'histoire des religions* 188 (1975): 3–21.

30. Theodoret does not include Ephrem in the *Religious History*, most likely because he was not a monk—this despite Palladius's attempts in the *Lausiac History* (40), to recast Ephrem in the mold of an Evagrian monastic, a trend followed in later Syriac lives of Ephrem; see Joseph P. Amar, "Byzantine Ascetic Monachism and Greek Bias in the *Vita* Tradition of Ephrem the Syrian," *Orientalia Christiana Periodica* 58 (1992): 123–56. Theodoret was, however, familiar with that poet's life and output. In his *Ecclesiastical History* (4.29.3), Theodoret explains that Ephrem's songs were still performed on the festivals of the martyrs, and in a letter to monks at Constantinople, Theodoret (*Ep.* 146 [PG ed. #145], ed. Azéma, 3:190) describes Ephrem as the "harp of the Spirit, who each day waters the people of Syria with the streams of his grace." See also Theodoret, *Ecclesiastical History* 2.30.11.

31. Ephrem, *Hymns on the Nativity* 14.16–19, ed. Beck, 80; trans. Kathleen McVey, *Ephrem the Syrian: Hymns* (New York: Paulist, 1989), 144.

32. On the remaking of the Bible as an ascetic prooftext, see Elizabeth A. Clark, *Reading Renunciation: Asceticism and Scripture in Early Christianity* (Princeton: Princeton University Press, 1999).

33. Similar typological figuration appears throughout the later Syriac *Life of Symeon Stylites*, composed in 473. See Doran, *The Lives of Symeon Stylites*, 51–52.

34. Han J. W. Drijvers, "Spätantike Parallelen zur altchristlichen Heiligenverehrung unter besonderer Berücksichtigung des syrischen Stylitenkultus," *Göttingen Orientforschungen* 1, Reihe: Syrica 17 (1978): 77–113. But see the cautionary remarks of Frankfurter in "Stylites and *Phallobates*," 186–87. Harvey ("Sense of a Stylite," 384) explores allusions in the Syriac *Life of Symeon* to the transfiguration.

35. See, for example, Susan Ashbrook Harvey, *Asceticism and Society in Crisis: John of Ephesus and* The Lives of the Eastern Saints (Berkeley: University of California Press, 1990), 16; Doran, *The Lives of Symeon Stylites*, 40; and Canivet and Leroy-Molinghen, in Théodoret, *Histoire des moines de Syrie*, 2:185n3.

36. See Doran, *The Lives of Symeon Stylites*, 55–59. Doran (58) observes Theodoret's "knowledge of scripture" in accounting for the differences between the prophetic deeds mentioned in the *Religious History* and in the Syriac *Life of Symeon* (trans. in Doran).

37. Canivet and Leroy-Molinghen (*Histoire des moines de Syrie*, 1:20–21) and Harvey ("Sense of a Stylite," 378) advance a different view of the relationship of the chapter on Symeon the Stylite to the rest of the *Religious History*. While the same level of rhetoric is not maintained throughout the work, I believe the narrative tech-

nique Theodoret employs in narrating James of Nisibis and Symeon the Stylite are closely related.

38. For other exorcisms, see Theodoret, *Religious History* 6.6; 9.4, 9, 10; 13.10; 16.2.

39. Compare *HME,* prol. 9.

40. Bernard Flusin (*Miracle et histoire dans l'oeuvre de Cyrille de Scythopolis* [Paris: Études augustiniennes, 1983], 157): "Il n'y a pas de miracle sans un précédent biblique," and, with specific reference to Theodoret's *Religious History,* "Cette référence à la Bible, directe ou indirecte, explicite ou tue, est la loi du miracle: ce que Dieu a accompli, il l'accomplit encore."

41. *HME* 14.16, ed. Festugière, 107; Athanasius, *Life of Antony* 60 (compare Palladius, *Lausiac History* 8.6). Athanasius explains that walking on water is "for the Lord alone."

42. Doran (*The Lives of Symeon Stylites,* 52) has observed that John 14:12 is commonly quoted by biblical exegetes to explain miracles performed after Jesus (with reference to Theodore of Mopsuestia, Cyril of Alexandria, and John Chrysostom). This text is quoted three times in the Syriac *Life of Symeon Stylites,* in sections 12, 65, and 78. In section 65, the quotation appears in tandem with Acts 5:15, as it does here.

43. For a similar view of ascetics' miracles, see *HME,* prol. 9, 13.

44. Julian: Theodoret, *Ecclesiastical History* 3.24.1–4, on Julian's prescience of the death of the emperor Julian the Apostate retells Theodoret, *Religious History* 2.14; *Ecclesiastical History* 4.27.1–4 refers the reader to the *Religious History* for an account of Julian's miracles during a trip to Antioch (*Religious History* 2.17–19). Aphrahat: *Ecclesiastical History* 4.26 narrates a story not in *Religious History* 8 about Aphrahat and the emperor Julian in which the apostate's pagan followers are said to have "hardened their hearts like Pharaoh." Macedonius: *Ecclesiastical History* 5.20.5–10 narrates an account of Macedonius's intervention in the Riot of the Statues of 387 that is similar to the account in the *Religious History* 13.7. Many other holy men of the *Religious History* are mentioned in a list of ascetics active during the reign of Julian the Apostate in *Ecclesiastical History* 4.28.

45. See Urbainczyk, *Theodoret of Cyrrhus,* 23–27. Marcel Richard ("Théodoret, Jean d'Antioche et les moines d'Orient," *Mélanges de Science Religieuse* 3 [1946]: 147–56) convincingly refuted the argument of Peeters ("S. Syméon Stylite et ses premiers biographes," *AnBoll* 61 [1943]: 29–71; reprinted with corrections as "Un saint hellénisé par annexion: Syméon Stylite," in *Orient et Byzance,* 93–136) that the *Religious History* was composed in order to shore up support for Theodoret's theology among Syrian monks and to provide a contrast to Cyril of Alexandria's own base among the monks of the Egyptian desert; compare Young, *From Nicaea to Chalcedon,* 51–2. Theodoret did however cite the *Religious History,* calling it the "Lives of the Saints" in a 448 letter to Eusebius, bishop of Ancyra, in a list of his works that could be examined to prove his orthodoxy (Theodoret, *Ep.* 82; ed. Azéma, 2:202, line 19); Canivet, *Le monachisme syrien,* 29.

46. Giovan Domenico Mansi, *Sacrorum conciliorum nova et amplissima collectio* (Graz: Akademische Druck-und Verlagsanstalt, 1960), 7:189; Young, *From Ni-*

caea to Chalcedon, 224–29, 271–75. Theodoret's works defending Nestorius against Cyril were condemned a century later at the Fifth Ecumenical Council of 553.

47. Harvey ("Sense of a Stylite," 380) however observes: "surely his Simeon represents a mirrored image of his Christological position. Salvation for him is an achievement of union between humanity and God in which the integrity of each nature, human and divine, remains intact but truly full." On the role of James, Symeon, and Baradatus in the reconciliation with John of Antioch, see Canivet, *Le monachisme syrien,* 179, 196; A.-J. Festugière, *Antioche païenne et chrétienne: Libanius, Chrysostome et les moines de Syrie,* Bibliothèque des écoles françaises d'Athènes et de Rome 194 (Paris: Boccard, 1959), 420–21.

48. Young wisely observes regarding the theological controversy, "Cyril and Theodoret had long episcopates and were by no means monopolized by this issue" (*From Nicaea to Chalcedon,* 229).

49. Theodoret explained in the preface to his *Commentary on the Psalms* (PG 80.860), "I have read various commentaries and have found that some descended insatiably into allegory, while others adapted the prophesies to the historical past, such that their interpretation applies more to Jews than to those nourished by the faith [i.e., Christians]. I have made it my duty to avoid both extremes." On the significance of these remarks, see Young, *From Nicaea to Chalcedon,* 285; and Manlio Simonetti, "La tecnica esegetica di Teodoreto nel *Commento ai Salmi,*" *Vetera Christianorum* 23 (1986): 81–116. Other recent studies of Theodoret's exegesis include Silke-Petra Bergjan, "Die dogmatische Funktionalisierung der Exegese nach Theodoret von Cyrus," in *Christliche Exegese zwischen Nicaea und Chalcedon,* ed. J. van Oort and U. Wickert (Kampen, The Netherlands: Pharos, 1992), 32–48; F. Cocchini, "L'esegesi paolina di Teodoreto di Cirro," *Annali di storia dell'esegesi* 11 (1994): 511–32; and Jean-Noel Guinot, *L'Exégèse de Théodoret de Cyr,* Théologie historique 100 (Paris: Beauchesne, 1995).

50. Young, *From Nicaea to Chalcedon,* 285.

51. See the remarks of Rowan Greer, in *Theodore of Mopsuestia: Exegete and Theologian* (London: Faith Press, 1961), 94. The following studies remain useful classics: Jean Daniélou, *From Shadows to Reality: Studies in the Biblical Typology of the Fathers,* trans. Wulstan Hibberd (London: Burns and Oates, 1960); and Daniélou, *The Bible and the Liturgy,* Liturgical Studies 3 (Notre Dame, Ind.: University of Notre Dame Press, 1956; French ed. 1951).

52. See Theodoret, *Commentary on Zechariah* 9.23 (PG 81.1917); Theodoret, *Commentary on the Psalms,* 28.1 (PG 80.1063). On typology in Theodoret's biblical exegesis, see Thomas McCollough, "Theodoret of Cyrus as Biblical Interpreter and the Presence of Judaism in Later Roman Syria" (Ph.D. diss., Notre Dame University, 1984), 192–96.

53. See McCollough, "Theodoret of Cyrus as Biblical Interpreter," 25–29. McCollough (82–99) reviews the evidence for Jewish life at Antioch, Aleppo/Beroea, Apamea, and Caesarea. For Antioch, see Robert Wilken, *John Chrysostom and the Jews: Rhetoric and Reality in the Late Fourth Century* (Berkeley: University of California Press, 1983).

54. Theodoret, *Religious History* 21.15–18. On Theodoret's efforts against Mar-

cionites in Cyrrhestica, compare Theodoret, *Religious History* 22.1; Theodoret, *Ecclesiastical History* 5.31.3; and Theodoret, *Epp.* 81, 113.

55. Theodoret would later turn his attention to a commentary on Isaiah, perhaps his most important exegetical work. Modern edition: Théodoret de Cyr, *Commentaire sur Isaïe*, ed. J. N. Guinot, 3 vols., SC 276, 295, 315 (Paris: Cerf, 1981–84).

56. For ascetics as models for emulation and mimesis, see also *HME*, prol. 2. See 1 Thessalonians 1:6–7 for imitators of the Lord becoming examples for others.

57. For another perspective on Theodoret's treatment of James of Nisibis, see the brief discussion by Han J. W. Drijvers, "Hellenistic and Oriental Origins," in *The Byzantine Saint: University of Birmingham Fourteenth Spring Symposium of Byzantine Studies*, ed. Sergei Hackel (San Bernardino, Calif.: Borgo, 1983), 28–30.

58. Theodoret (*Religious History* 1.10) reemphasizes this point in an apocryphal account of the Council of Nicaea, where James's deeds in protection of the orthodox faith against the teachings of Arius resembled those of Aaron's grandson Phinehas, who slew the apostate Zimri in the inner room of the tabernacle (Num 25:1–15; compare Ps 106:30–31). James called on the council's participants to fast so that God's will with regard to Arius might be manifest. When they gathered for the divine liturgy, many thought that Arius's blasphemy would be pardoned, but instead, according to Theodoret at least, a miracle occurred. Instead of receiving reconciliation, Arius defecated himself to death in the holy assembly. Whereas Phinehas had used a spear, Theodoret remarks, "James's tongue had sufficed" to destroy the impious one (1.10). Canivet and Leroy-Molinghen (*Histoire des moines de Syrie*, 1:179n6) regarded this episode as an interpolation, largely because it is a fiction. Moreover, it contradicts Theodoret's account of the death of Arius in the *Ecclesiastical History* (1.14). But Price (*A History of the Monks of Syria*, 21–22) defends the passage's authenticity on stylistic grounds. Obviously Theodoret does not adhere to positivist historical principles in selecting what to narrate. To the case for authenticity, I might add that the episode is consistent with Theodoret's efforts to link the saint to biblical precedents. David Brakke (*Athanasius and the Politics of Asceticism* [Oxford: Clarendon, 1995], 132–33) offers more examples of varying accounts of Arius's death that distort history to reveal a biblical lesson.

59. Some years later, Theodoret appended to the *Religious History* a treatise *On Divine Love* in which he illustrated this virtue through appeals to various biblical characters. The text is included in Théodoret, *Histoire des moines de Syrie*, ed. Canivet and Leroy-Molinghen, 2:245–315.

60. Van Uytfanghe ("L'empreinte biblique," 568–73) offers a similar assessment of the potential of typological composition in saints' lives. This view, however, contrasts with Augustine's sharp distinction between the biblical and the postbiblical world, of which Robert Markus (*Saeculum: History and Society in the Theology of Saint Augustine* [Cambridge: Cambridge University Press, 1970], 43) has written, "All history [outside the Scriptural canon] is starkly secular, that is to say, it is incapable of being treated in terms of its place in the history of salvation." It would be of interest to determine whether Theodoret's tendency to highlight continuity between the biblical world and his late ancient present represents a distinctly "hagiographical" view of history.

61. *HME,* epilogue 2; ed. Festugière, 135; trans. Norman Russell, *The Lives of the Desert Fathers* (London: Mowbray, 1980), 118.

62. These attributions, of course, also make claims for the holy men. Theodoret implicitly places Julian in a class with Sarah's divine visitors, while Maësymas thus resembles Elijah and Elisha. In a gesture with somewhat different implications, Theodoret (*Religious History* 1.10) dubs the emperor Constantine "the Zerubbabel of our flock."

63. In this aspect, the *Religious History* resembles developments in two forms of contemporary religious practice: namely, pilgrimage and the performance of the divine liturgy. On pilgrimage and the divine liturgy as reenactment or mimesis, see Jonathan Z. Smith, *To Take Place: Toward Theory in Ritual* (Chicago: University of Chicago Press, 1987), 88–95; and Gary Vikan, "Pilgrims in Magi's Clothing: The Impact of Mimesis on Early Byzantine Pilgrimage Art," in *The Blessings of Pilgrimage,* ed. Robert Ousterhout, Illinois Byzantine Studies 1 (Urbana: University of Illinois Press, 1990), 97–107. We must leave a full exploration of these parallels for another study.

64. Basil of Caesarea, *Ep.* 2; ed. Roy J. Deferrari, LCL (London: Heinemann, 1926), 1:14–16. *Apophthegmata Patrum: Alphabetical Series* John the Persian 4 (PG 65.237) and Nisterius 2 (PG 65.305). Compare Douglas Burton-Christie, *The Word in the Desert: Scripture and the Quest for Holiness in Early Christian Monasticism* (New York: Oxford University Press, 1993), esp. 168–69; and David Brakke, *Athanasius and the Politics of Asceticism* (Oxford: Clarendon, 1995), 163–70.

65. On this point, Theodoret (prol. 8) cites Paul's advice to the Corinthians regarding differing gifts of the Spirit (1 Cor 12:8–11).

66. It is interesting to note that Theodoret omits mention of the genre of the Greek *bios,* such as in the work of Plutarch.

67. The notion that different ascetics offer examples of different virtues stands behind Athanasius's description of Antony's ascetic formation: "[Antony] observed the graciousness of one, the earnestness at prayer in another; studied the even temper of one and the kindheartedness of another" (Athanasius, *Life of Antony* 4; trans. Robert T. Meyer [New York: Newman, 1950], 21.) For a general view, see Peter Brown, "The Saint as Exemplar in Late Antiquity," in *Saints and Virtues,* ed. Jack Stratton Hawley (Berkeley: University of California Press, 1987), 3–14, first published in *Representations* 1 (1983): 1–25.

68. For the emphatic force of this prepositive particle, see Herbert Weir Smyth, *Greek Grammar* (Cambridge: Harvard University Press, 1920), 669.

69. The belief that the Gospels of Matthew and John were eyewitness accounts, while Luke and Mark were second-hand accounts by followers, respectively, of Paul and Peter, was widespread. Canivet and Leroy-Molinghen (*Histoire des moines de Syrie,* 1:159) cite as examples John Chrysostom, *Homilies on Matthew* 1.2–3 (PG 57.16); Augustine, *On the Consensus of the Evangelists* 1.3 and 8; and Cyril of Alexandria, *Commentary on John* 1, prol. (PG 73.20–21).

70. On Theodoret's oral sources, see Canivet and Leroy-Molinghen, *Histoire des moines de Syrie,* 18–22.

71. Compare Theodoret, *Religious History,* prol. 6, where Theodoret invites the reader to hear what God is "saying through the prophet" Jeremiah.

72. For example: Theodoret, *Religious History*, prol. 2–3, 5.6, 9.6, 12.6; compare Theodoret, *Ecclesiastical History*, prol. Georgia Frank (*The Memory of the Eyes: Pilgrimage to Living Saints in Christian Late Antiquity* [Berkeley: University of California Press, 2000]) explores themes of visual piety in the *Religious History* and in late antique hagiography more generally. On the relationship between verbal and visual portraits, see also Averil Cameron, *Christianity and the Rhetoric of Empire: The Development of Christian Discourse* (Berkeley: University of California Press, 1991), 54–61.

73. Basil, *Ep.* 2; ed. Deferrari, 1:14. This trope, of course, is widespread; see Canivet and Leroy-Molinghen, *Histoire des moines de Syrie*, 1:149–50.

Chapter 3

1. Text and translation: James Drescher, *Apa Mena: A Selection of Coptic Texts Relating to St. Menas* (Cairo: Publications de la Société d'Archéologie Copte, 1946). See also Peter Grossman, "The Pilgrimage Center of Abû Mînâ," in *Pilgrimage and Holy Space in Late Antique Egypt*, ed. David Frankfurter (Leiden: Brill, 1998), 281–302; Martin Krause, "Menas the Miracle Maker, Saint," in *The Coptic Encyclopedia* 5:1589–90; Krause, "Karm Abu Mena," *Reallexikon zur byzantinischer Kunst* 3:1116–58. The encomium is attributed only to "John, Patriarch of Alexandria," so it is possibly the work of the earlier John III (681–89) as C. Detlef and G. Müller ("John III, The Merciful," *The Coptic Encyclopedia* 4:1337–38) speculate.

2. Drescher, *Apa Mena*, text: 35–36; translation (modified): 128–29.

3. Drescher, *Apa Mena*, 36, 129.

4. Drescher, *Apa Mena*, 36–37, 129.

5. Text: *Historia Monachorum in Aegypto*, ed. A.-J. Festugière, Subsidia Hagiographica 34 (Brussels: Société des Bollandistes, 1961); translation: Norman Russell, *The Lives of the Desert Fathers* (Cistercian Publications, 1980). On the authorship and date, see Benedicta Ward in the introduction to Russell, *Lives of the Desert Fathers*, 6–7. For a discussion of the text and analysis of its relationship to travel writing, see Georgia Frank, *The Memory of the Eyes: Pilgrims to Living Saints in Christian Late Antiquity* (Berkeley: University of California Press, 2000), 35–61.

6. *HME* 26. See also Frank, *Memory of the Eyes*, 59 and 29–34. On pilgrimage as a biblical quest, see also Blake Leyerle, "Landscape as Cartography in Early Christian Pilgrimage Narratives," *JAAR* 64 (1996): 119–43.

7. Frank (*Memory of the Eyes*, 53) is right to hear the echo of Herodotus, *Histories* 1.1. But the phrase μεγάλα καὶ θαυμαστά was also a commonplace for Septuagint translators; see Tobit 12:22, Job 42:3. Within the canon of the Christian Bible, the phrase is most familiar at Revelation 15:3 ("Great and wonderful are Your deeds"). For "θαυμαστός" and "τέρας" as synonyms, see Exodus 15:11 ("wonderful in glory, doing marvels"). See also Jeremiah 32:20–21 (LXX 39:20–21), where the prophet, praising God in a list of his deeds, identifies him as the one "who did signs and marvels in the land of Egypt [σημεῖα καὶ τέρατα ἐν γῇ Αἰγύπτῳ] and to this day both in Israel and among the people of the earth . . . and You brought your

people Israel out of the land of Egypt with signs and marvels [καὶ ἐξήγαγες τὸν λαόν σου Ισραηλ ἐκ γῆς Αἰγύπτου ἐν σημείοις καὶ ἐν τέρασιν], with a strong hand and a raised arm." Acts 7:36 (here of Moses): "He led them out [ἐξήγαγεν], having done marvels and signs in the land of Egypt [τέρατα καὶ σημεῖα ἐν γῇ Αἰγύπτῳ]."

8. Jacob of Serug, *Homily on Ephrem*, ed. and trans. Joseph P. Amar, *A Metrical Homily on Holy Mar Ephrem*, PO 47.1 (Turnhout: Brepols, 1995).

9. Another interesting exception of sorts are the so-called "Lives of the Prophets." See David Satran, *Biblical Prophets in Byzantine Palestine: Reassessing the Lives of the Prophets*, Studia in Veteris Testamenti Pseudepigrapha 11 (Leiden: Brill, 1995).

10. Investigation of the genesis and evolution of these traditions continues. For a compilation of these legends, see W. Bauer, "The Picture of the Apostle in Early Christian Tradition," in Edgar Hennecke and Wilhelm Schneemelcher, eds., *New Testament Apocrypha*, 3rd ed., trans. R. McL. Wilson (Philadelphia: Westminster, 1965), 2:35–74 (the essay is omitted from later editions). See R. Alan Culpepper, *John, the Son of Zebedee: The Life of a Legend* (Columbia: University of South Carolina Press, 1994); C. Clifton Black, *Mark: Images of an Apostolic Interpreter* (Columbia: University of South Carolina Press, 1994); and Wolfgang A. Bienert, "The Picture of the Apostles in Early Christian Tradition," in Edgar Hennecke and Wilhelm Schneemelcher, eds., *New Testament Apocrypha*, 5th ed., trans. R. McL. Wilson (Cambridge: Clark, 1992), 22–23. Relevant sections of Eusebius's *Ecclesiastical History* include 2.15; 3.4, 39; 5.8; 6.13; text: Eusebius of Caesarea, *Historia Ecclesiastica*, 2 vols., Greek text with English translation by Kirsopp Lake and J. E. L. Oulton, LCL (London: Heinemann, 1926–32). For discussion of Papias's ideas about the evangelists, see Robert M. Grant, *The Earliest Lives of Jesus* (New York: Harper, 1961). Irenaeus, *Against the Heresies* 3.1.1; Latin text with fragment of Greek original (preserved in Eusebius, *Ecclesiastical History* 5.8.2–4): Irénée de Lyon, *Contre les hérésies*, ed. Adelin Rousseau and Louis Doutreleau, SC 11, 3.2.33; translation: Robert M. Grant, *Irenaeus of Lyons* (London: Routledge, 1997), 124.

11. For the various *Acts of John*, see Éric Junod and Jean-Daniel Kaestli, eds., *Acta Johannis*, 2 vols., Corpus Christianorum Series Apocryphorum (Turnhout: Brepols, 1983); Aurelio de Santos Otero, "Later Acts of the Apostles," in Edgar Hennecke and Wilhelm Schneemelcher, eds., *New Testament Apocrypha*, rev. ed., trans. R. McL. Wilson (Cambridge: Clark, 1992), 2:426–482; Culpepper, *John, the Son of Zebedee*, 187–232; and Yuko Taniguchi, François Bovon, and Athanasios Antonopoulos, "The *Memorial of Saint John the Theologian* (*BHG* 919fb)," in *The Apocryphal Acts of the Apostles: Harvard Divinity School Studies*, ed. François Bovon, Ann Graham Brock, and Christopher R. Matthews (Cambridge: Harvard University Press, 1999), 333–53.

12. Text: Éric Junod and Jean-Daniel Kaestli, eds., *Acta Johannis;* English translation in Hennecke and Schneemelcher, eds., *New Testament Apocrypha*, 5th ed., trans. R. McL. Wilson, 2:172–209. Another English translation is available in James K. Elliott, ed., *The Apocryphal New Testament: A Collection of Apocryphal Christian Literature in an English Translation* (Oxford: Clarendon, 1993). For discussions regarding the date, Gnostic elements, and history of the text, see Éric Junod

and Jean-Daniel Kaestli, *L'Histoire des actes apocryphes des apôtres du IIIe au IXe siè-cle: Le cas des Actes de Jean* (Geneva: Revue de théologie et de philosophie, 1982); Knut Schäferdiek, "The Acts of John," in Hennecke and Schneemelcher, eds., *New Testament Apocrypha*, 5th ed., 2:152–71; Culpepper, *John, the Son of Zebedee*, 187–90.

13. The Gnostic character of the text is reconsidered, albeit inconclusively, by Gerard Luttikhuizen in "A Gnostic Reading of the Acts of John," in *The Apocryphal Acts of John*, ed. Jan N. Bremmer, Studies on the Apocryphal Acts of the Apostles 1 (Kampen: Pharos, 1995), 119–52.

14. See also Junod and Kaestli, *L'Histoire des actes apocryphes*, passim; Schäfer-diek, "The Acts of John," 152–56; François Bovon, "Byzantine Witnesses for the Apocryphal Acts of the Apostles," in *The Apocryphal Acts of the Apostles*, ed. Bovon, Brock, and Matthews, 87–98.

15. Text: *Acta Joannis*, ed. Theodor Zahn (Erlangen: Deichert, 1880; reprint Hildesheim, 1975), 3–165. Although there is no published English translation of the Greek text, a thorough synopsis is included in Culpepper, *John, the Son of Zebedee*, 206–22. Nancy Ševčenko, "The Cave of the Apocalypse," in *Hiera Monē Hagiou Iōannou tou Theologou—900 Chronia historikēs martyrias* (Athens: Hē Hetaireia, 1989), 169–78, provides an English translation of some of the pages (154–56) relevant to the present discussion. Italian translation of the complete Greek text: M. Erbetta, *Gli apocrifi del Nuovo Testamento* (Turin: Marietti, 1971), 2:68–110. The text was enormously popular later in Byzantium and was translated into Coptic, Arabic, Ethiopic, and Armenian; see Elliott, ed., *Apocryphal New Testament*, 348. While the Armenian version contains roughly the same text as the Greek, the Arabic and Ethi-opic (possibly dependent on the same Coptic version?) include only the early epi-sodes in Ephesus, not the scene of composition on Patmos. English translation of the Arabic version: Agnes Smith Lewis, *The Mythological Acts of the Apostles* (Lon-don: Clay, 1904), 37–53. English translation of the Ethiopic version: E. A. Wallis Budge, *The Contendings of the Apostles* (Amsterdam: Apa-Philo, 1976; originally published 1902), 2:186–220. French translation of the Armenian version: Louis Lel-oir, *Écrits apocryphes sur les apôtres: Traduction de l'édition arménienne de Venise* (Brepols: Turnhout, 1986), 1:289–407. See also Otero, "Later Acts of Apostles," 429–35; Junod and Kaestli, *Acta Johannis*, 2:718–49. The text was apparently avail-able to the compiler of the *Chronicon Paschale* in 630.

16. *Acts of John by Prochoros*, 154–55. See also Culpepper, *John, the Son of Zeb-edee*, 220–21. I have employed Ševčenko's translation ("The Cave of the Apoca-lypse," 169–70) where possible, and with slight modification.

17. *Acts of John by Prochoros*, 157–58. For subsequent Byzantine and post-Byz-antine traditions about the supposed autograph copies, see Ševčenko, "The Cave of the Apocalypse."

18. On the production of books both generally and in early Christian con-texts, see Harry Y. Gamble, *Books and Readers in the Early Church* (New Haven: Yale University Press, 1995), 66–81, 83–94; Kim Haines-Eitzen, *Guardians of Letters: Literacy, Power, and the Transmitters of Early Christian Literature* (New York: Ox-ford University Press, 2000).

19. See the section on pencraft below. The gospel prologue known as the *Me-morial of Saint John*, which bases its account on the narrative in the Prochoros *Acts*,

appears to be late. The *Memorial* is sufficiently different in its treatment of John's act of composition to raise doubts about whether the relationship is one of direct literary dependence. Taniguchi, Bovon, and Antonopoulos ("The *Memorial of Saint John the Theologian*") have not speculated on the text's date, although it must be later than the mid-sixth century, since it is also dependent on the Pseudo-Dionysian corpus. It is likely a product of a period when portraits of John and Prochoros were becoming standard in illustrated Byzantine gospel books. At present I am inclined to date it no earlier than the ninth century.

20. Ševčenko, "The Cave of the Apocalypse," 169; Hugo Buchthal, "A Byzantine Miniature of the Fourth Evangelist and Its Relatives," *DOP* 15 (1961): 127–39; Herbert Hunger, "Evangelisten," *Reallexikon zur byzantinischen Kunst* 2:466–67.

21. Ševčenko, "The Cave of the Apocalypse," 172–74.

22. Junod and Kaestli, *Acta Johannis*, 2:741. Otero, "Later Acts of Apostles," 430.

23. Ševčenko, "The Cave of the Apocalypse," 173; Taniguchi, Bovon, and Antonopoulos, "The *Memorial of Saint John the Theologian*," 339–40. These scenes may also recall the transfiguration of Jesus: Mark 9:2–8; Matthew 17:1–8; Luke 9:28–36.

24. John Chrysostom, *Homilies on Philemon*, prol. (PG 62:701); trans. NPNF, first series, 13:545. For Chrysostom's interest in Paul, see Margaret Mary Mitchell, *The Heavenly Trumpet : John Chrysostom and the Art of Pauline Interpretation* (Tübingen: Mohr Siebeck, 2000); Mitchell, "The Archetypal Image: John Chrysostom's Portraits of Paul," *Journal of Religion* 75 (1995): 15–43.

25. On the date of these sermons and their place in John's preaching on biblical texts, see J. N. D. Kelly, *Golden Mouth: The Story of John Chrysostom—Ascetic, Preacher, Bishop* (Ithaca: Cornell University Press, 1995), 90. Questions of the dating and provenance of Chrysostom's sermons, however, have been reopened, with particular attention to those on the Pauline letters; see Pauline Allen, "The Homilist and the Congregation: A Case Study of Chrysostom's Homilies on Hebrews," *Augustinianum* 36 (1996): 404–7; Wendy Mayer, "John Chrysostom and his Audiences: Distinguishing Different Congregations at Antioch and Constantinople," *Studia Patristica* 31 (1997): 70–75; and Pauline Allen and Wendy Mayer, "Traditions of Constantinopolitan Preaching: Towards a New Assessment of Where Chrysostom Preached What," *Byzantinishe Forschungen* 24 (1997): 93–114.

26. This sermon was most likely preached in the lavish Golden Church, the cathedral of Antioch built by Constantine the Great. While the testimony of Eusebius and John Chrysostom attest to the rich adornment of gold, silver, precious stones, and statues, whether the church contained images—and more particularly images of the evangelists—cannot be known. Yet is tempting to imagine Chrysostom gesturing toward a mosaic of Matthew when prompting his audience to consider the "image" of this gospeler. Eusebius, *Life of Constantine* 3.50; Eusebius, *Tricennial Oration* 9.15; John Chrysostom, *Homilies on Ephesians* 10.2. For a composite description of the great church, see Glanville Downey, *A History of Antioch in Syria: From Seleucus to the Arab Conquest* (Princeton: Princeton University Press, 1961), 342–46. On Chrysostom's preaching in this church, see Kelly, *Goldenmouth*, 57; and Wendy Mayer, "John Chrysostom: Extraordinary Preacher, Ordinary Audi-

ence," in *Preacher and Audience: Studies in Early Christian and Byzantine Homiletics,* ed. Mary B. Cunningham and Pauline Allen (Leiden: Brill, 1998), 126.

27. John Chrysostom, *Homilies on Matthew* 47.4 (PG 58:485–86); my translation, but compare NPNF first series, 10:295 (there *Homilies on Matthew* 47.5).

28. John Chrysostom, *Homilies on Matthew* 1.1 (PG 57:15). See also John Chrysostom, *Homilies on Matthew* 30.1.

29. Jerome, *Against Jovinian* 1.28. John's celibacy is a major theme as early as the late second-century apocryphal *Acts of John* (113). See also Tertullian, *On Monogamy [De monagamia]* 17.1; Methodius of Olympus, *On the Resurrection* 1.59.6. Bauer, "The Picture of the Apostle," 51.

30. See Henry Chadwick, *Priscillian of Avila: The Occult and the Charismatic in the Early Church* (Oxford: Clarendon, 1976), 105; text in Hans Lietzmann, *Das Muratorische Fragment und die monarchianischen Prologe zu den Evangelien,* 2nd ed. (Berlin: De Gruyter, 1933), 13.

31. Eusebius, *Ecclesiastical History* 3.23, compare Clement of Alexandria, *The Rich Man Who Finds Salvation* 42.

32. Epiphanius, *Panarion* 58.4.5–6. Translation: Philip R. Amedon, *The Panarion of St. Epiphanius, Bishop of Salamis: Selected Passages* (New York: Oxford University Press, 1990).

33. Epiphanius, *Panarion* 78.13.3–4.

34. For text and translation, see R. G. Heard, "The Old Gospel Prologues," *JThS* 6 (1955): 7. For further discussion of the Greek prologue to the Gospel of Luke, see Jürgen Regul, *Die antimarcionitischen Evangelienprologe* (Freiburg: Herder, 1969), 197–242. This prologue probably introduced an independently bound copy of Luke.

35. Clement, *The Paedagogue* 2.1.16. Bauer ("The Picture of the Apostle," 60, 65) believed that Clement's assertion of Matthew's vegetarianism based itself in a confusion with traditions about Matthias; see also Clement, *Stromateis* 3.26.3. The image also recalls John the Baptist.

36. *Acts of John at Rome* 5, 6; text: *Acta Johannis,* ed. Junod and Kaestli, 2:835–86. See Culpepper, *John, the Son of Zebedee,* 205–206. Observers marveled at the sparse diets of the Egyptian monks; see Frank, *Memory of the Eyes,* 58.

37. *Acts of John by Prochoros,* 154. On the lack of ascetic themes, see Otero, "Later Acts," 430; Junod and Kaestli, *Acta Johannis,* 744–46.

38. Basil of Caesarea, *Longer Rules* 16.2 (PG 31.959); translation: M. Monica Wagner, *Saint Basil: Ascetical Works,* FOTC 9 (Washington, D.C.: Catholic University of America Press, 1950), 269.

39. John of Damascus, *The Fount of Knowledge: Dialectics* (PG 94.521).

40. On the ascetic exegesis of scripture and the recreation of the Bible as an ascetic text, see Elizabeth A. Clark, *Reading Renunciation: Asceticism and Scripture in Early Christianity* (Princeton: Princeton University Press, 1999).

41. Black (*Mark,* 156–70) reviews these Palestinian traditions regarding Mark, but misses the ascetic aspect of the connection of Mark to the founding of Alexandrian Christianity. See also Robert M. Grant, *Eusebius as Church Historian* (Oxford: Clarendon, 1980), 72–76.

42. Jerome, *On Illustrious Men* 8, see also 11; edition: W. Herding, ed. (Leipzig:

Teubner, 1924). For a looser connection between Mark and the Therapeutics, see Epiphanius of Salamis, *Panarion* 29.5.1–4. For a comparison of Eusebius's and Jerome's treatment of Mark, see Black, *Mark*, 167–70.

43. Origen, *Against Celsus [Contra Celsum]* 1.64.

44. Origen, *Homilies on Genesis* 1.13; Origen also portrays James and Paul as converted to the image of God. See also Origen, *Against Celsus* 1.63.

45. John Chrysostom, *Homilies on Matthew* 30.1 (PG 57:363).

46. John Chrysostom, *Homilies on the Acts of the Apostles* 1.3.

47. John Chrysostom, *Homilies on John* 33.3 (PG 59:191); compare translation in NPNF, first series, 14:117.

48. John Chrysostom, *Homilies on John* 33.3 (PG 59:192).

49. John Chrysostom, *Homilies on John* 72.2 (PG 59:391).

50. John Chrysostom, *Homilies on John* 85.2 (PG 59:461).

51. John Chrysostom, *Homilies on Romans* 1.1 (PG 60:395).

52. Eusebius, *Ecclesiastical History* 2.15; trans. Williamson, 88; Eusebius elaborates the account of Clement of Alexandria, whom he cites at *Ecclesiastical History* 6.14.

53. John Chrysostom, *Homilies on Matthew* 1.3 (PG 57:17).

54. Epiphanius of Salamis, *Panarion* 51.12.2. In the mid-sixth century, the Alexandrian Cosmas Indicopleustes (*Christian Topography* 5.190, 196, 198, and 202; edition: Wanda Wolska-Conus, SC 159 [Paris: Cerf, 1970]) presented Matthew, Mark, and John writing in response to requests. His understanding of Luke's motivation derived from the Gospel's own claim (Lk 1:1–4) to be a corrective to other writings in circulation.

55. Lietzmann, *Das Muratorishe Fragment*, 4–5. For discussion of the date of the fragment, see Geoffrey Mark Hahneman, *The Muratorian Fragment and the Development of the Canon* (Oxford: Clarendon, 1992), 215–18. A translation is available in F. F. Bruce, *The Canon of Scripture* (Downers Grove, Ill.: Intervarsity Press, 1988), 159.

56. *The Syriac History of John*, text and translation in William Wright, ed., *Apocryphal Acts of the Apostles: Edited from Syriac Manuscripts in the British Museum and Other Libraries* (Amsterdam: Philo, 1968; originally published 1871), relevant text at 57–59. See Junod and Kaestli, *Acta Johannis*, 2:705–17; Otero, "Later Acts of Apostles," 435–36; Culpepper, *John, the Son of Zebedee*, 223–30.

57. John Chrysostom, *Homilies on Matthew* 1.5 (PG 57:20).

58. Eusebius, *Ecclesiastical History* 3.24. See also Clement, *Stromateis* 4.133.3, where apostles are portrayed as recipients of divine grace.

59. John Chrysostom, *Homilies on John* 2.1 (PG 59:29).

60. John Chrysostom, *Homilies on John* 2.1, quoting Acts 4:13.

61. John Chrysostom, *Homilies on John* 2.2 (PG 59:31).

62. John Chrysostom, *Homilies on John* 2.3 (PG 59:32).

63. Romanos, *Hymns* 33.18; edition: *Sancti Romani Melodi Cantica: Cantica Genuina*, ed. Paul Maas and C. A. Trypanis (Oxford: Clarendon, 1963); translation: Ephrem Lash, in Romanos the Melodist *On the Life of Christ: Kontakia* (San Francisco: HarperCollins, 1995), 216 (modified).

64. Heard, "Old Gospel Prologues," 7.

65. John Chrysostom, *Homilies on John* 88.2 (PG 59:481).

66. Basil Studer, "The Bible as Read in the Church," in *History of Theology: The Patristic Period,* ed. Angelo Di Bernardino and Basil Studer, trans. Matthew J. O'Connell (Collegeville, Minn.: Michael Glazier, 1997), 1:357. On the theology of inspiration, see also Henri de Lubac, *Histoire et esprit: L'Intelligence de l'Écriture d'après Origène* (Paris: Aubier, 1950), 295–304.

67. Paul Zanker (*The Mask of Socrates: The Image of the Intellectual in Antiquity,* trans. Alan Shapiro [Berkeley: University of California Press, 1995], 330) uses the portrait of Mark inspired by a dictating Sophia in the Rossano Gospels Codex to argue that Christian theological claims about authority and the transmission of knowledge rendered the writer a mere stenographer. I would prefer to interpret the image as a guarantor of the authority of the text without erasing Mark's agency. Even beyond the problems with Zanker's interpretation, the folio has been demonstrated to be a ninth-century addition to the sixth-century manuscript. See O. Kresten and G. Prato, "Die Miniatur des Evangelisten Markus im Codex Purpureus Rossanensis: Eine spätere Einfügung," *Römische Historische Mitteilungen* 27 (1985): 381–403; John Lowden, "The Beginnings of Biblical Illustration," in *Imaging the Early Medieval Bible,* ed. John Williams (University Park: Pennsylvania State University Press, 1999), 21n29. Beyond the claims to divine inspiration, the church fathers seem to have been little interested to understand the mechanism of the Holy Spirit's work upon the biblical authors, although Theodore of Mopsuestia believed that the Spirit had acted differently upon different writers. See J. N. D. Kelly, *Early Christian Doctrines* (London: Black, 1958), 62–64; see also Theodore of Mopsuestia, *On Job* (PG 66:697).

68. Irenaeus, *Against the Heresies* 3.1.1 (SC 211:20–24). The text is quoted by Eusebius, *Ecclesiastical History* 5.8.

69. Edition: *Origène: Traité des principes,* vol. 3 (books 3 and 4), ed. Henri Crouzel and Manlio Simonetti, SC 268 (Paris: Cerf, 1980). Translation: Karlfried Froehlich in *Biblical Interpretation in the Early Church* (Philadelphia: Fortress, 1984), 48–78. On Origen's hermeneutics, see Henri Crouzel, "The School of Alexandria and Its Fortunes," in *History of Theology,* ed. Di Bernardino and Studer, 1:164–69; Ronald Heine, "Reading the Bible with Origen," in *The Bible in Greek Christian Antiquity,* ed. Paul M. Blowers (Notre Dame, Ind.: University of Notre Dame Press, 1997), 131–48; and Patricia Cox Miller, "Poetic Words, Abysmal Words: Reflections on Origen's Hermeneutics," in *The Poetry of Thought in Late Antiquity: Essays in Imagination and Religion* (Aldershot: Ashgate, 2001), 211–19. Basil of Caesarea and Gregory of Nazianzus excerpted much of this book in their anthology, the *Philocalia,* compiled around 358 and intended as a handbook for Christian monks. See Philip Rousseau, *Basil of Caesarea* (Berkeley: University of California Press, 1994), 11–14, 82–84. Despite the condemnation of much of the rest of Origen's work, these guidelines for the interpretation of the Bible continued to circulate widely in the early Byzantine period and framed the understanding of inspired writing.

70. Origen, *On First Principles* 4.1, 6.

71. See Paul Rorem, *Biblical and Liturgical Symbols within the Pseudo-Dionysian Synthesis,* Studies and Texts 71 (Toronto: Pontifical Institute of Mediaeval Studies, 1984), 19–21.

72. See F. E. Brightman, *Liturgies Eastern and Western* (Oxford: Clarendon, 1895), 1:531n5. For formulae introducing the gospel reading in later liturgies, see Juan Mateos, *Le Typicon de la Grande Église*, Orientalia Christiana Analecta 165 (Rome: Pontifical Institute, 1962), 1:46 (tenth century); and Brightman, *Liturgies*, 156 (Coptic Jacobite), 372 (modern "Liturgy of St. John Chrysostom"), 426 (Armenian). Also useful is Juan Mateos, *La Célébration de la parole dans la liturgie Byzantine*, Orientalia Christiana Analecta 191 (Rome: Pontifical Institute, 1971), 144.

73. John Chrysostom, *Homilies on the Acts of the Apostles* 19.4 (PG 60:156).

74. John Chrysostom, *Homilies on Hebrews* 8.4 (PG 63:75–76).

75. John Chrysostom, *Homilies on John* 2.1 (PG 59:29).

76. The question of the history of evangelist portraits was first raised systematically by A. M. Friend in "The Portraits of the Evangelists in Greek and Latin Manuscripts," Parts 1 and 2, *Art Studies: Medieval, Renaissance and Modern* 5 (1927): 115–50; and 7 (1929): 3–46. See also Robert S. Nelson, *The Iconography of Preface and Miniature in the Byzantine Gospel Book* (New York: New York University Press, 1980); Joyce Kubiski, "The Medieval 'Home Office': Evangelist Portraits in the Mount Athos Gospel Book, Stavronikita Monastery, MS 43," *Studies in Iconography* 22 (2001): 21–53 (see 46n2 for additional bibliography).

77. Maggie Duncan-Flowers, "A Pilgrim's Ampulla from the Shrine of St. John the Evangelist at Ephesus," in *The Blessings of Pilgrimage*, Illinois Byzantine Studies 1, ed. Robert Ousterhout (Urbana: University of Illinois Press, 1990), 125–39, with bibliography.

78. On such ampullae more generally, see Gary Vikan, *Byzantine Pilgrimage Art* (Washington, D.C.: Dumbarton Oaks, 1982); André Grabar, *Les ampoules de Terre Sainte (Monza, Bobbio)* (Paris: Klincksieck, 1958).

79. Slobodan Ćurčić and Archer St. Clair, *Byzantium at Princeton* (Princeton: Princeton University Press, 1986), 120–21; Princeton University Art Museum inventory number: Antioch 3581-P346 24-L. See also Duncan-Flowers, "A Pilgrim's Ampulla." For similar flasks, see also Catherine Metzger, *Les ampoules à eulogie du Musée du Louvre*, (Paris: Éditions de la Réunion des musées nationaux, 1981), 22; Sheila D. Campbell, "Armchair Pilgrims: Ampullae from Aphrodisias in Caria," *Mediaeval Studies* 50 (1988): 539–45 and figs., esp. 12.

80. For discussion and examples, see Stephen J. Davis, *The Cult of Saint Thecla: A Tradition of Women's Piety in Late Antiquity* (Oxford: Oxford University Press, 2001), 115–24, 215–20.

81. Duncan-Flowers ("A Pilgrim's Ampulla," 127 and fig. 44) provides an important comparandum in the image of John in the canon tables of the Rabbula Gospels. Note that in the Rabbula Gospels, John sits beside a lampstand.

82. Standing and seated evangelists also appear together in canon tables of the Rabbula Gospels executed in 586, although the seated figures of John and Matthew appear to be reading from their texts rather than writing. See Friend, "The Portraits of the Evangelist," 115–30; Duncan-Flowers, "An Ampulla from the Shrine of St. John," 127.

83. See Clive Foss, *Ephesus After Antiquity* (Cambridge: Cambridge University Press, 1979), 43, 87–94; Duncan-Flowers, "A Pilgrim's Ampulla," 136–37n14. On confusion about two possible tombs of John, see Culpepper, *John, the Son of Zeb-*

edee, 147–50. Although most sources claimed that John wrote at Ephesus, a fragment of an Armenian translation of Ephrem the Syrian's *Commentary on the Diatessaron* assigned the composition to Antioch; *Acts of John by Prochoros* (154–58) assigns the composition to Patmos (although the topography of the island as described in the Prochoros *Acts* is pure fantasy); see Culpepper, *John, the Son of Zebedee,* 157, 220. The *Memorial of Saint John the Theologian,* dependent on the traditions of the *Acts of John by Prochoros,* also assigns the composition of the Gospel to Patmos; see Taniguchi, Bovon, and Antonopoulos, "The *Memorial of Saint John,*" 338–39, 359.

84. On visualization at pilgrim's shrines, see Frank, *The Memory of the Eyes,* 102–14. For pilgrim's souvenirs representing events said to have taken place at the locations pilgrims visited, see Gary Vikan, *Byzantine Pilgrimage Art* (Washington, D.C.: Dumbarton Oaks, 1982), esp. 18–23.

85. The scholarly literature on San Vitale is enormous. I cite here some of the works helpful in my own efforts. Jaś Elsner, *Art and the Roman Viewer: The Transformation of Art from the Pagan World to Christianity* (Cambridge: Cambridge University Press, 1995), 177–89; and Otto G. von Simson, *Sacred Fortress: Byzantine Art and Statecraft in Ravenna* (Princeton: Princeton University Press, 1987, originally published 1948), 23–39. On the political history related to the decoration of the church, see Irina Andreescu-Treadgold and Warren Treadgold, "Procopius and the Imperial Panels of S. Vitale," *Art Bulletin* 79 (1997): 708–23. On the history and technique of the execution of the mosaics, with particular attention to the evangelist portraits, see Irina Andreescu-Treadgold, "The Two Original Mosaic Decorations of San Vitale," *Quaderni di soprintendenze (Ravenna)* 3 (1997): 16–22.

86. Friedrich Wilhelm Deichmann, *Ravenna: Geschichte und Monumente* (Wiesbaden: Steiner, 1969), 1:234–43; von Simson, *Sacred Fortress,* 29–33.

87. *Apocalypse of Paul;* Martha Himmelfarb, *Ascent to Heaven in Jewish and Christian Apocalypses* (New York: Oxford University Press, 1993); Kirsti Barrett Copeland, "Mapping the Apocalypse of Paul: Geography, Genre and History" (Ph.D. diss., Princeton University, 2001). See also Anân Ishô, *The Paradise of the Fathers,* in *Book of Paradise, Being the histories and Sayings of the Monks and Ascetics of the Egyptian Desert by Palladius, Heironymous and Others: The Syriac Texts, According to the Recension of Anân Ishô of Bêth Abhê,* ed. and trans. E. A. Wallis Budge, 2 vols., Lady Meux Manuscript 6 (London, 1904); translation republished as Anân Ishô, *The Paradise or Garden of the Holy Fathers.* 2 vols. (London: Chatto and Windus, 1907).

88. On Matthew, see Friedrich Wilhelm Deichmann, *Ravenna: Geschichte und Monumente* (Weisbaden: Steiner, 1969), 1:240, 246, 332; Patrizia Angiolini Martinelli, ed., *La Basilica di San Vitale a Ravenna,* Mirabilia italiae 6 (Modena: Panini, 1997), 1:224. On the technique and history of the execution of the image, see Irina Andreescu-Treadgold, "The Mosaic Workshop at San Vitale," in *Mosaici a S. Vitale e altri restauri: Il restauro in situ di mosaici parietali,* ed. Anna Maria Iannucci, Cesare Fiori, and Cetty Muscolino (Ravenna: Longo, 1992), 31–41 (with interleaved corrected version 1–8, esp. 6).

89. Irenaeus, *Against the Heresies* 3.11.8; ed. Rousseau and Doutreleau, 3.2.160–66, with Greek fragment preserved in Anastasius of Sinai (late seventh century), *Question and Responses* 144; trans., Grant, *Irenaeus,* 131.

90. Robert S. Nelson, *The Iconography of Preface and Miniature in the Byzantine Gospel Book* (New York: New York University Press, 1980), 5–10, 15–57; von Simson, *Sacred Fortress*, 26.

91. *ODB* s.vv.

92. Friend, "Portraits of the Evangelists" 1:142–44; and Friend, "Portraits of the Evangelists," 2:7–9.

93. Thomas Mathews, *The Early Churches of Constantinople: Architecture and Liturgy* (University Park: Pennsylvania State University Press, 1971), 146–47; Mathews, *The Clash of Gods: A Reinterpretation of Early Christian Art* (Princeton: Princeton University Press, 1993), 171; Elsner, *Art and the Roman Viewer*, 187; Robert Taft, *The Great Entrance: A History of the Transfer of Gifts and Other Preanaphoral Rites of the Liturgy of St. John Chrysostom*, Orientalia Christiana Analecta 200 (Rome: Pontifical Institute, 1975), 30–31.

94. On dictation and the use of secretaries in Greco-Roman antiquity, see E. Randolph Richards, *The Secretary in the Letters of Paul* (Tübingen: Mohr, 1991), 14–67.

95. Romans 16:22, "I, Tertius, the one writing this letter, greet you all in the Lord." Richards, *The Secretary*, 57; Harry Y. Gamble, *Books and Readers in the Early Church: A History of Early Christian Texts* (New Haven: Yale University Press, 1995), 95–96. Haines-Eitzen, *Guardians of Letters*, 35–36.

96. Haines-Eitzen, *Guardians of Letters*, 36. See 2 Thessalonians 3:17; 1 Corinthians 16:21; Philemon 19; Galatians 6:11.

97. Eusebius, *Ecclesiastical History* 6.23. Haines-Eitzen, *Guardians of Letters*, 5; on female scribes, see 41–52.

98. Gerontius, *Life of Melania* 26; text and translation Elizabeth A. Clark, *The Life of Melania the Younger* (New York: Mellen, 1984), 12, 46; see Haines-Eitzen, *Guardians of Letters*, 48–49.

99. Claudia Rapp, "Christians and Their Manuscripts in the Greek East in the Fourth Century," in *Scritture, libri e testi nelle aree provinciali de Bisanzio*, ed. Guglielmo Cavallo, Giuseppe de Gregorio, and Marilena Maniaci (Spoleto: Centro italiano di studi sull'alto medioevo, 1991), 127–48; Haines-Eitzen, *Guardians of Letters*, 49; Gamble, *Books and Readers*, 170–74. For the earliest portrait of a monk as writer, see the Cassiodorus image in the Codex Amiantinus; Lawrence Nees, "Problems of Form and Function in Early Medieval Illustrated Bibles from Northwest Europe," in *Imaging the Early Medieval Bible*, ed. Williams, 148–58 and color plate 10.

100. Friend, "Portraits of the Evangelists," 1:146–47; Buchthal, "A Byzantine Miniature of the Fourth Evangelist," 127–39; J. Weitzmann-Fiedler, "Ein Evangelientyp mit Aposteln als Begleitfiguren," *Adolph Goldschmidt zu seinem seibenzigsten Geburtstag* (Berlin: Würfel, 1935), 30–34; Nelson, *Iconography of Preface and Miniature*, 86–87. In time, likely under the influence of the iconography of John and Prochoros and traditions regarding their associations with apostles who were eyewitnesses, Mark would be represented with Peter, and Luke would be represented with Paul; see Nelson, *Iconography of Preface and Miniature*, 75ff.

101. Friend, "Portraits of the Evangelists," 1:123–33; Robert P. Bergman, "Portraits of the Evangelists in Greek Manuscripts," in *Illuminated Greek Manuscripts*

from American Collections, ed. Gary Vikan (Princeton: Princeton University Press, 1973), 44–49; Kubiski, "The Medieval 'Home Office,'" 43.

102. William Loerke, "Incipits and Author Portraits in Greek Gospel Books: Some Observations," in *Byzantine East, Latin West: Art-Historical Studies in Honor of Kurt Weitzmann,* ed. Christopher Moss and Katherine Kiefer (Princeton: Department of Art and Archeology, 1995), 378. Loerke, however, goes on to defend a sixth-century date for the image of Mark in the Rossano Gospels. See also P. Pettimengin and B. Flusin, "Le livre antique et la dictée," in *Mémorial Andre-Jean Festugière: Antiquité paienne et chrétienne,* ed. E. Lucchesi and H. D. Saffrey (Geneva: Cramer, 1984), 247–62.

103. Friend, "Portraits of the Evangelists"; Nelson, *Iconography of Preface and Miniature,* 1–14, 75–92. Kubiski ("The Medieval 'Home Office,'") makes a very strong case, based especially on stylistic analysis of their architectural elements, that the seated evangelist portraits in the tenth-century Stavronikita Gospels derive from late antique examples.

104. See Philippians 2:7.

Chapter 4

1. *Miracles of Artemios* 21. Text, translation, and studies are in Virgil S. Crisafulli and John W. Nesbitt, *The Miracles of St. Artemios: A Collection of Miracle Stories by an Anonymous Author of Seventh-Century Byzantium,* trans. Virgil S. Crisafulli, with an introduction and commentary by Virgil S. Crisafulli and John W. Nesbitt, supplemented by a reprinted Greek text and an essay by John F. Haldon (Leiden: Brill, 1997). This edition reprints the Greek text of A. Papadopoulos-Kerameus in *Varia Graeca Sacra: sbornik greceskich neizdannych bogoslovskich tekstov IV-XV vekov,* Zapiski Istoriko-filologicheskago fakul'teta Imperatorskago S.-Peterburgskago universiteta [Records of the Historical-Philological faculty of the University of St. Petersburg] 95 (St. Petersburg: Krishbaum, 1909): 1–75 (reprint with new preface by Jürgen Dummer [Leipzig: Zentralantiquariat der Deutschen Demokratischen Republik, 1975]). I have employed Crisafulli's translation with occasional modification. On this text within the genre of miracle collections, see Vincent Déroche, "Tensions et contradictions dans les recueils de miracles de la première époque byzantine," in *Miracle et karāma: Hagiographies médiévales comparées,* ed. Denise Aigle (Turnhout: Brepols: 2000), 145–66; and Vincent Déroche, "Pourquoi écrivait-on des recueils de miracles? L'exemple des miracles de Saint Artémios," in *Les saints et leur sanctuaire: textes, images et monuments,* ed. Catherine Jolivet-Lévy, Michel Kaplan, and Jean-Pierre Sodini, Byzantina sorbonensia 11 (Paris: Publications de la Sorbonne, 1993), 95–116. See also Lennart Rydén, "Gaza, Emesa and Constantinople: Late Ancient Cities in the Light of Hagiography," in *Aspects of Late Antiquity and Early Byzantium,* ed. Lennart Rydén and Jan Olof Rosenqvist, Swedish Research Institute in Istanbul Transactions 4 (Stockholm: Almqvist and Wiksell, 1993), 133–44.

2. Supplicants visited other shrines in Constantinople for different ailments.

The *Miracles of Artemios* itself (18) relates that the Church of Saint Pantelemon specialized in exorcizing the possessed. Saint Therapon was more of a generalist, as was the Theotokos, especially at her shrine in the Kyrou district where the poet Romanos himself had served. See Haldon in *Miracles of St. Artemios*, ed. Crisafulli and Nesbitt, 38–40.

3. *Miracles of Artemios* 24. For the legend of Saint Artemios, see Nesbitt in *Miracles of St. Artemios*, ed. Crisafulli and Nesbitt, 1–7.

4. *Miracles of Artemios* 24. On the translation of this passage, see the comments of Crisafulli and Nesbitt, *Miracles of St. Artemios*, 266.

5. For the church plan, see Cyril Mango, "History of the Templon and the Martyrion of St. Artemios at Constantinople," *Zograf* 10 (1979): 40–43; Crisafulli and Nesbitt, *Miracles of Saint Artemios*, 9–19. See also Jean-Pierre Sodini, "Les cryptes d'autel paléochrétiennes: classification," *Travaux et mémoires* 8 (1981): 440–43. A chapel dedicated to Saint Febronia was in the south aisle.

6. Crisafulli and Nesbitt (*Miracles of St. Artemios*, 22–25) reconstruct the activities at the shrine. For preparation of the lamp, see *Miracles of Artemios* 4, 23; for drinking the oil, see *Miracles of Artemios* 15; for application of the wax salve to the exterior of the body, see *Miracles of Artemios* 19, 37.

7. Crisafulli and Nesbitt, *Miracles of St. Artemios*, 18.

8. For this trope (with some variation) in the text see *Miracles of Artemios* 2, 3, 5, 7, 8, 10, 11, 14, 17, 20, 21, 22, 30, 33, 34, 35, 37, 39, 42. Compare Luke 5:26. Crisafulli and Nesbitt, *Miracles of St. Artemios*, 233. For God, and not the saint, as the agent of the miraculous, see Déroche, "Pourquoi écrivait-on des recueils de miracles?" 164–65.

9. For a similar relationship between text and cult, see the *Miracles of Cosmas and Damian*.

10. Haldon, in *Miracles of St. Artemios*, ed. Crisafulli and Nesbitt, 35. José Grosdidier de Matons ("Les *Miracula Sancti Artemii*: Note sur quelques questions de vocabulaire," in *Mémorial André-Jean Festugière: Antiquité, Païenne et Chrétienne*, ed. E. Lucchesi and H. D. Saffrey [Geneva: Cramer, 1984], 263–66) suggests on the basis of his medical knowledge that the author was an attendant at the nearby hospital of Christodotē. It seems just as likely that some members of the church staff could have possessed such information.

11. Crisafulli and Nesbitt, *Miracles of St. Artemios*, 27.

12. Crisafulli and Nesbitt, *Miracles of St. Artemios*, 7.

13. Crisafulli and Nesbitt, *Miracles of St. Artemios*, 25.

14. For the debate over the dating and stages of composition, compare Crisafulli and Nesbitt (*The Miracles of St. Artemios*, xii, 7–8), who see the hand of a single author, with John Haldon (in *Miracles of St. Artemios*, ed. Crisafulli and Nesbitt, 33–35), who concludes that Miracles 18–45 are the work of a later writer. The text underwent some sort of redaction after the condemnation of the patriarch Sergius (610–38) in 680 (see *Miracles of Artemios* 39).

15. Crisafulli and Nesbitt, *Miracles of St. Artemios*, 27.

16. For another example of first-person narrative, see the story of Theognis in *Miracles of Artemios* 33.

17. *Miracles of Artemios*, introduction.

18. "Since therefore we have set forth this goal [σκοπός], at this point we must somehow begin what was promised" (*Miracles of Artemios*, introduction, line 7).

19. Theodoret of Cyrrhus, *Religious History:* text: Théodoret de Cyr, *Histoire des Moines de Syrie*, ed. Pierre Canivet and Alice Leroy-Molinghen, 2 vols., SC 234 and 259 (Paris: Cerf, 1977–79). The translation employed here with occasional modification is Theodoret of Cyrrhus, *A History of the Monks of Syria*, trans. R. M. Price, Cistercian Studies 88 (Kalamazoo: Cistercian, 1985). In addition to Chapter 2, see Pierre Canivet, *Le monachisme syrien selon Théodoret de Cyr*, Théologie historique 42 (Paris: Beauchesne, 1977). For the date, see Price, *History of the Monks of Syria*, xiii–xv.

20. For the work's twenty-eight (not thirty) chapters, see Paul Devos, "La structure de l'Histoire Philothée de Théodoret de Cyr: Le nombres de chapitres," *AnBoll* 97 (1979): 319–35.

21. Studies of Symeon the Stylite include Susan Ashbrook Harvey, "The Sense of a Stylite: Perspective on Symeon the Elder," *VC* 42 (1988): 376–94; David T. M. Frankfurter, "Stylites and *Phallobates*: Pillar Religions in Late Antique Syria," *VC* (1990): 168–98; and Robert Doran, *The Lives of Symeon Stylites*, Cistercian Studies 12 (Kalamazoo: Cistercian, 1992).

22. On the varieties of ascetic practice described in the text, see Arthur Vöö-bus, *History of Asceticism in the Syrian Orient: A Contribution to the History of Culture in the Near East*, vol. 2, CSCO 197/Sub. 17 (Louvain: Secrétariat du CSCO, 1960), 256–315; and Canivet, *Le monachisme syrien*, 255–73. On the biblical grounding of these modes of life, see Chapter 2.

23. Peter Brown, "The Rise and Function of the Holy Man in Late Antiquity," in *Society and the Holy in Late Antiquity* (Berkeley: University of California Press, 1982), 120–30 (first published in *JRS* 61 [1971]: 80–101).

24. See also Theresa Urbainczyk, *Theodoret of Cyrrhus: The Bishop and the Holy Man* (Ann Arbor: University of Michigan Press, 2002), 130–42. For Theodoret's biography see Canivet, *Le monachisme syrien*, 37–63; Canivet and Leroy-Molinghen, *Histoire des moines*, 1:13–18; Price, *History of the Monks*, xi–xiii.

25. Peter was something of a spiritual director to Theodoret's mother, having once cured her of an eye disease and prompted her interest in spare and modest living (*Religious History* 9.5–8). Peter also exorcized the family cook (9.9).

26. Price (*History of the Monks*, 80n15) and Canivet and Leroy-Molinghen (*Histoire des moines*, 403) date this visit to 407.

27. Price (*History of the Monks*, 57n8) dates this visit to the early 410s.

28. On Theodoret's learning and output, see Canivet, *Le monachisme syrien*, 51–54; Canivet, *Théodoret de Cyr: Thérapeutique des maladies hellénique*, SC 57 (Paris: Cerf, 1958), 1:55–67; Price, *History of the Monks of Syria*, xv; and Jean-Noël Guinot, *L'Exégèse de Théodoret de Cyr*, Théologie historique 100 (Paris: Beauchesne, 1995), 35–76.

29. Sarah: Genesis 17:17–19; Hannah: 1 Samuel 1:11; Elizabeth: Luke 1:5–17.

30. On the development of the concept of *eulogia* in early Byzantine Christianity, see Gary Vikan, *Byzantine Pilgrimage Art* (Washington, D.C.: Dumbarton Oaks, 1982), 10–14; compare Lampe, s.v. "Εὐλογία." The index to the critical edi-

tion (Canivet and Leroy-Molinghen, eds., 2:391) lists the forty-six occurrences of the term in the *Religious History*.

31. For examples of the saints' *eulogia* conferred by water, see *Religious History* 2.17; 13.9, 13, 16–17; 21.14; by oil: 8.11; 21.16; 26.20.

32. Vikan, *Byzantine Pilgrimage Art*, 13.

33. For the *eulogia* of the corpse, see *Religious History* 10.8, 17.10; of garments: 26.12, compare 9.15. Biblical precedents for healing garments include Mark 5:25–34 and Acts 19:11–12. Even simply seeing Symeon the Stylite or his image might convey benefit to the devoted (*Religious History* 26.11). On visual pieties, see Georgia Frank, *The Memory of the Eyes: Pilgrimage to Living Saints in Christian Late Antiquity* (Berkeley: University of California Press, 2000), 102–33.

34. Peter Brown ("Rise and Function of the Holy Man," 120) writes that the work "was written to validate and publicize the local traditions surrounding the holy men of Syria."

35. εὐλογία: *Religious History* 1.14, 4.13, 9.16, 10.9, 11.5, 16.4, 17.11, 19.3, 23.2, 25.2, 29.7; πρεσβεία: 2.22, 6.14, 8.15, 12.7, 18.4; ἐπικουρία: 3.23, 7.4, 20.4; μνήμη: 5.10; ῥοπή: 13.18.

36. *Religious History* 13.19: Ἡμεῖς δε τέλος ἐπιθέντες τῷ διηγήματι τὴν ἀπὸ τῆς διηγήσεως εὐωδίαν ἐκαρπωσάμεθα.

37. Theodoret quotes 2 Corinthians 15 in the epilogue, "On Divine Love," which he later appended to the *Religious History*. See *Religious History* 31.19. See also Susan Ashbrook Harvey, *Scenting Salvation: Ancient Christianity and the Olfactory Imagination* (Berkeley: University of California Press, forthcoming).

38. Texts: Cyril of Scythopolis, *Life of Euthymius*, in *Kyrillos von Skythopolis*, ed. Eduard Schwartz, *Texte und Untersuchungen* 49, no. 2 (1939): 3–85; Cyril of Scythopolis, *Life of Sabas*, in *Kyrillos*, ed. Schwartz, 85–200. Citations are to pagination in this edition. The translation employed here with slight modification is Cyril of Scythopolis, *The Lives of the Monks of Palestine*, trans. R. M. Price and John Binns, Cistercian Studies 114 (Kalamazoo: Cistercian Publications, 1991). Principal recent studies include John Binns, *Ascetics and Ambassadors of Christ: The Monasteries of Palestine 314–631* (Oxford: Clarendon, 1994); Cynthia Jean Stallman-Pacitti, *Cyril of Scythopolis: A Study of Hagiography as Apology* (Brookline: Hellenic College Press, 1991); Bernard Flusin, *Miracle et histoire dans l'œuvre de Cyrille de Scythopolis* (Paris: Études Augustiniennes, 1983).

39. Studies of Palestinian monasticism include Yizhar Hirschfeld, *The Judean Desert Monasteries in the Byzantine Period* (New Haven: Yale University Press, 1992), 69–78; Madeleine Joly, "Les fondations d'Euthyme et de Sabas: texte et archéologie," in *Les saints et leur sanctuaire*, ed. Jolivet-Lévy, Kaplan, and Sodini, 49–64; Binns, *Ascetics and Ambassadors*, 99–120; Derwas Chitty, *The Desert a City: An Introduction to the Study of Egyptian and Palestinian Monasticism under the Christian Empire* (Oxford: Blackwell, 1966), 82–86, 105–18; and Joseph Patrich, *Sabas, Leader of Palestinian Monasticism: A Comparative Study in Eastern Monasticism, Fourth to Seventh Centuries* (Washington, D.C.: Dumbarton Oaks, 1995).

40. Cyril, *Life of Euthymius*, 61, 69–85; Cyril, *Life of Sabas*, 184–87; Flusin, *Miracle et histoire*, 191–92; Hirschfeld, *Judean Desert Monasteries*, 130–43.

41. Stallman-Pacitti, *Cyril of Scythopolis*, 67–105; Binns, *Ascetics and Ambassadors*, 183–217.

42. For Cyril's life, see Binns, *Ascetics and Ambassadors*, 23–40; Schwartz, *Kyrillos*, 408–15; Flusin, *Miracle et histoire*, 11–17, 29–32.

43. Cyril, *Life of Sabas*, 180. Binns (*Ascetics and Ambassadors*, 25–27) argues convincingly that Cyril's description of Euthymius's father (*Life of Euthymius*, 10) as a λογιώτατος and σχολαστικός retrojects the experience of Cyril's own father.

44. Cyril, *Life of Euthymius*, 5, 71; compare Binns, *Ascetics and Ambassadors*, 29. G. M. Fitzgerald (*A Sixth-Century Monastery in Beth-shan [Scythopolis]* [Philadelphia: University of Pennsylvania Press, 1939], 13) identified the monastery of Beella with a monastic foundation on the outskirts of Beit She'an with a sixth-century inscription mentioning a certain "George, priest, superior, and prior."

45. Binns, *Ascetics and Ambassadors*, 57–66. On the formation of monastic libraries in general, see Harry Y. Gamble, *Books and Readers in the Early Church: A History of Early Christian Texts* (New Haven: Yale University Press, 1995), 170–74.

46. Flusin, *Miracle et histoire*, 41–86; Binns, *Ascetics and Ambassadors*, 57–66 (57n3 lists bibliography of earlier studies); Binns, in Cyril of Scythopolis, *Lives of the Monks of Palestine*, l–li. About a decade after composing the *Religious History*, Theodoret described it as "easily accessible to those to wish to become acquainted with [its contents]" (Theodoret, *Ecclesiastical History* 4.27.1). For Cyril's dependence on Theodoret, see Flusin, *Miracle et histoire*, 67–70. Cyril's literary afterlife is well documented in middle-Byzantine collections of monks' lives and menologia; see Schwartz, *Kyrillos*, 317.

47. Binns (*Ascetics and Ambassadors*, 28) observes that Cyril "showed himself capable of the elegant ekphrasis on the beauties of the site of Euthymius' monastery." Compare Cyril, *Life of Euthymius*, 64–65. See also Nikos Kalogeras, "The Role of the Audience in the Construction of Narrative: A Note on Cyril of Scythopolis," *Jahrbuch der österreichischen Byzantinistik* 52 (2002): 149–159; and Kalogeras, "Rhetoric and Emulation in the Work of Cyril of Scythopolis and the *Vita Abraamii,*" *Byzantinoslavica* 61 (2003): 1–16.

48. Cyril, *Life of Euthymius*, 6; Binns, *Ascetics and Ambassadors*, 28; A.-J. Festugière, *Les moines d'Orient* (Paris: Cerf, 1962), 3.1:42–44.

49. Dorotheus of Gaza, *Discourses* 2.33; edition: Dorothée de Gaza, *Œuvres spirituelles*, ed. L. Regnault and J. de Préville (Paris: Cerf, 1963), 196; trans.: Dorotheus of Gaza, *Discourses and Sayings*, trans. Eric P. Wheeler, Cistercian Studies 33 (Kalamazoo: Cistercian, 1977), 98.

50. Binns, *Ascetics and Ambassadors*, 218–44, especially the comparative chart on 224; Flusin, *Miracle et histoire*, 155–214.

51. On women and weaving in early Byzantium, see Nicholas P. Constas, "Weaving the Body of God: Proclus of Constantinople, the Theotokos, and the Loom of the Flesh," *JECS* 3 (1995): 169–94.

52. LSJ s.v. ὑφαίνω; compare Latin *texo*.

53. For the copying and ownership of books as forms of devotion, see Claudia Rapp, "Christians and Their Manuscripts in the Greek East in the Fourth Century," in *Scritture, libri e testi nelle aree provinciali de Bisanzio*, ed. Guglielmo Cavallo, Giu-

seppe de Gregorio, and Marilena Maniaci (Spoleto: Centro italiano di studi sull'alto medioevo, 1991), 127–48.

54. *Life of Thecla* and *Miracles of Thecla*: text: Gilbert Dagron, ed., *Vie et miracles de Sainte Thècle: Texte grec, traduction et commentaire* (Brussels: Société des Bollandistes, 1978). See also Gilbert Dagron, "L'Auteur des 'Actes' et des 'Miracles' de Sainte Thècle," *AnBoll* 92 (1974): 5–11. Translations are my own. For an excellent study of the phenomenon of Thecla piety, see Stephen J. Davis, *The Cult of Saint Thecla: A Tradition of Women's Piety in Late Antiquity* (Oxford: Oxford University Press, 2001).

55. Dagron, *Vie et miracles*, 15.

56. The translation follows the text of the Septuagint.

57. The *Acts of Paul and Thecla* has received significant scholarly attention. I cite only a few important studies: Stevan L. Davies, *The Revolt of the Widows: The Social World of the Apocryphal Acts* (Carbondale, Ill.: Southern Illinois University Press, 1980); Dennis Ronald MacDonald, *The Legend and the Apostle: The Battle for Paul in Story and Canon* (Philadelphia: Westminster, 1983); Virginia Burrus, *Chastity as Autonomy: Women in the Stories of the Apocryphal Acts*, Studies in Women and Religion 23 (Lewiston: Edwin Mellen, 1987); Ross Shepard Kraemer, *Her Share of the Blessings: Women's Religion among Pagans, Jews, and Christians in the Greco-Roman World* (New York: Oxford University Press, 1992), 151–54; Kate Cooper, *The Virgin and the Bride: Idealized Womanhood in Late Antiquity* (Cambridge, Mass.: Harvard University Press, 1996), 50–56.

58. Egeria, *Travels* 23; text: *Égérie, journal de voyage*, ed. Pierre Maraval, SC 296 (Paris: Cerf, 1982); trans.: John Wilkinson, *Egeria's Travels*, 3rd ed. (Warminster: Aris and Phillips, 1999). See Davis, *Cult of Saint Thecla*, 37–39; Dagron, *Vie et miracles*, 55–79. On the buildings at the shrine, see Stephen Hill, *The Early Byzantine Churches of Cilicia and Isauria*, Birmingham Byzantine and Ottoman Monographs 1 (Aldershot: Variorum, 1996), 208–34.

59. Egeria, *Travels* 23. Davis (*Cult of Saint Thecla*, 40) is confident in identifying the second-century *Acts of Paul and Thecla* as the work read.

60. *Life of Thecla* 28.7–8. Scott Johnson ("Cult and Competition: Textual Appropriation in the Fifth-Century *Life and Miracles of Thecla*," an unpublished paper delivered to the Byzantine Studies Conference, Columbus, Ohio, October, 4, 2002) has convincingly argued that the *Life and Miracles* systematically deemphasizes the ascetic character of the earlier traditions.

61. On the fourth-century church standing at the time that the *Life and Miracles* was composed, see Hill, *Early Byzantine Churches*, 217–20. This structure was replaced with a much larger church in the second half of the fifth century during the reign of the emperor Zeno.

62. Davis, *Cult of Saint Thecla*, 48–64; Dagron, *Vie et miracles*, 131.

63. For Thecla as a patron of rhetoric, see Methodius of Olympus, *Symposium* 8 and 11.

64. *Life of Thecla*, prol., also *Life of Thecla* 28. See Dagron, *Vie et miracles*, 21.

65. *Life of Thecla*, prol., 7–9.

66. *Miracles of Thecla*, prol., 105–10.

67. Homer: *Life of Thecla* 27.58; *Miracles of Thecla* 10.15, 26; 16.15; 27.19; 35.15; 38.16. Plato: *Miracles of Thecla* 39.5; 40.17. See Dagron, *Vie et miracles*, 19, 76, 157.

68. For a similar assessment, see Dagron, *Vie et miracles*, 19.

69. *Miracles of Thecla* 37–41.

70. *Miracles of Thecla* 37. Dagron (*Vie et miracles*, 391) translates "οἱ λόγοι" as "les Lettres" and "ἐλλογίμους" as "personnalités littérairs," thus capturing the echoing in the Greek.

71. On grammarians and rhetoricians generally, see Robert A. Kaster, *Guardians of Language: The Grammarian and Society in Late Antiquity* (Berkeley: University of California Press, 1988).

72. On the paganism of teachers of rhetoric, see Dagron, *Vie et miracles*, 91–92, 129–30.

73. Davis, *Cult of Saint Thecla*, 74–77, Dagron, *Vie et miracles*, 81–90.

74. See LSJ s.v. for references in the Hippocratic corpus and in Galen. This dictionary tentatively suggests "small-pox."

75. Holy water figured prominently in the cult of Saint Thecla. Her image appears on numerous small clay flasks surviving from late antiquity used for the collection and transport of holy water and oil. Vikan, *Byzantine Pilgrimage Art*, has a visual example; see also Davis, *Cult of Saint Thecla*, 114–20.

76. On Thecla's varied wardrobe, see Dagron, *Vie et miracles*, 98.

77. The Vulgate (Latin) translation of the Book of Ezekiel, chapters 9 and 10, says that the man assigned first to mark the elect of city (Ez 9:4) and later to "fill [his] hands with burning coals from between the cherubim, and scatter them over the city (Ez 10:2)" is "a man clothed in linen, with a writing case at his side" (Ez 9:2, compare 9:3, 11). This reads the Hebrew "*qst hspr*" as "*qeset hasefer*," perhaps "writing case." Not only is the proper translation of "*qst*" in doubt, but the Greek Septuagint and the Syriac Peshitta read "*hspr*" as "sapphire" and translate that as the man has a "sapphire [lapis lazuli?] belt." Thus while the Vulgate associates coal with a scribe (reasonably so, since his first job is to mark the righteous of Jerusalem), it is uncertain whether a Greek speaker would have regarded this coal-bearing figure as a writer.

78. Aelian, *Historical Miscellany [Varia Historia]* 10.21; text edited and translated by N. G. Wilson, LCL (Cambridge, Mass.: Harvard University Press, 1997). For a Christian parallel, see Paulinus's Latin *Life of Ambrose* 3.

79. Alice Swift Riginos, *Platonica: The Anecdotes Concerning the Life and Writings of Plato* (Leiden: Brill, 1976), 17–21. L. G. Westerink, *Anonymous Prolegomena to Platonic Philosophy: Introduction, Text, Translation, and Indices* (Amsterdam: North-Holland, 1962), 5–7. See Riginos, *Platonica*, 17, for full citations of this tradition, including Cicero, *De div.* 1.36.78, 2.31.66; Pliny, *Natural History* 11.17.55.

80. Aelian, *Historical Miscellany* 12.45.

81. *Life of Pindar* 2. Text: A. B. Drachmann, *Scholia vetera in Pindari carmina* (Leipzig: Teubner, 1903; reprint, Amsterdam: Hakkart, 1969), 1:1–11. Translation: Mary R. Lefkowitz, *The Lives of the Greek Poets* (Baltimore: Johns Hopkins, 1981), 155–57, see also 59. For the date, see Johannes Irmscher, "Pindar in Byzanz," in *Aischylos und Pindar: Studien zu Werk und Nachwirking*, ed. Ernst Günther Schmidt (Berlin: Akademie-Verlag, 1981), 296–302, esp. 297.

82. Ilona Opelt, "Die christliche Spätantike und Pindar," *Byzantinische Forschungen* 2 (1967): 284–98.

83. See Riginos, *Platonica*, 19; Lefkowitz, *Lives of the Greek Poets*, 24.

84. Artemidorus of Daldis, *The Interpretation of Dreams* 2.20. Text: *Artemidori Daldiani Onirocriticon Libri V*, ed. Roger A. Pack (Leipzig: Teubner, 1963). Translation: Artemidorus, *The Interpretation of Dreams: Oneirocritica*, trans. Robert J. White (Park Ridge, N.J.: Noyes, 1975) (translation modified; text at 2.22).

85. Dagron, *Vie et miracles*, 17–18. Two additional miracles (45–46) and a new epilogue were added in a third revision of the text after 468. See Dagron, *Vie et miracles*, 18–19.

86. On late antique invective, see Jacqueline Long, *Claudian's In Eutropium: Or, How, When, and Why to Slander a Eunuch* (Chapel Hill: University of North Carolina Press, 1996), esp. 78–96. Long highlights the use and teaching of invective, particularly in and around the city of Antioch in the second half of the fourth century, in the works of Libanius, Julian, and Aphthonius, and offers Gregory of Nazianzus's *Orations against Julian* as a Christian example. Seleucia was in the larger cultural sphere of Antioch and is mentioned frequently in the *Life and Miracles of Thecla;* see, for example *Miracles of Thecla* 17.

87. For Basil's works, see Johannes Quasten, *Patrology* (Utrecht: Spectrum, 1953–1986), 3:526–7; *Clavis Patrum Graecorum*, 3:278–83. Photius, *Bibliotheca* 168, ed. R. Henry (Paris: Belles Lettres, 1959).

88. On the possibility of generational conflict, see Dagron, *Vie et miracles*, 319n8.

89. On the conflict and the invective vocabulary, see Dagron, *Vie et miracles*, 15–16, 319.

90. David Brakke, "Ethiopian Demons: Male Sexuality, the Black-Skinned Other, and the Monastic Self," *Journal of the History of Sexuality* 10 (2001): 501–35.

91. In another example of a saint showing the author's literary license through hands, Martin appears to Sulpicius holding the *Life of Martin* that Sulpicius had composed. See Sulpicius Severus, *Ep.* 2.3; Virginia Burrus, *The Sex Lives of Saints: An Erotics of Ancient Hagiography* (Philadelphia: University of Pennsylvania Press, 2003), 105–7.

92. Dagron, *Vie et miracles*, 17.

93. On Xenarchis and women's literacy, see Davis, *Cult of Saint Thecla*, 146–47.

94. *Miracles of Thecla* 41.

95. For a sixth-century discussion of earaches, see Alexander of Tralles, *On Fevers* 3.2.

96. He uses and then glosses the word δεικτήριον, "place of declamation." This continues his interweaving of formal rhetorical vocabulary.

97. Dagron, *Vie et miracles*, 399n6, regards this as a "comparaison passablement sacrilège."

98. The passage in the *Miracles of Thecla* (41.26–27) reads: θαῦμα πλεῖστον ἐπὶ μηδενὶ θαυμαστῷ τῶν ἐμῶν ἀπενέγκασθαι λόγων. Luke 4:22 reads: Καὶ πάντες ἐμαρτύρουν αὐτῷ καὶ ἐθαύμαζον ἐπὶ τοῖς λόγοις τῆς χάριτος τοῖς ἐκπορευομένοις ἐκ τοῦ στόματος αὐτοῦ. Compare the reaction to the report of

the shepherds in Luke 2:18, "And all who heard it wondered at what the shepherd told them [καὶ πάντες οἱ ἀκούσαντες ἐθαύμασαν περὶ τῶν λαληθέντων ὑπὸ τῶν ποιμένων πρὸς αὐτούς]."

99. Matthew 13:57: "A prophet is not without honor except in his own country." Compare Mark 6:4, Luke 4:24.

100. On the manuscripts and their history, see Dagron, *Vie et miracles*, 13–15, 140–51.

101. Dagron, *Vie et miracles*, 14. Dagron argues that one twelfth-century manuscript (Atheniensis 2095) may provide evidence that a copyist was aware that the attribution was problematic. Its titling describes the text with the sentence "συνεγράφη δὲ παρὰ Βασιλείου ἐπισκόπου ᾿Ισαυρίας Σελευκείας" (Dagron, *Vie et miracles*, 14, 144), possibly to be translated, "It is ascribed to Basil bishop of Seleucia in Isauria."

102. According to Photius (*Bibliotheca* 168), Basil did compose a versified version of the *Acts of Thecla*, but that text, which does not survive, cannot be the *Life and Miracles of Thecla* in question. See Dagron, *Vie et miracles*, 14.

103. I thank Bill North for suggesting this point.

Chapter 5

1. Text: *The Life of Daniel the Stylite*, in *Les saints stylites*, ed. H. Delehaye, Subsidia hagiographica 14 (Brussels: Société des Bollandistes, 1923), 1–94. Translation: Elizabeth Dawes and Norman H. Baynes, *Three Byzantine Saints* (Crestwood, N.Y.: St. Vladimir's Seminary Press, 1977), 1–71. See Robin Lane Fox, "The *Life of Daniel*," in *Portraits: Biographical Representation in the Greek and Latin Literature of the Roman Empire*, ed. M. J. Edwards and Simon Swain (Oxford: Clarendon, 1997), 175–226.

2. For a broadly accessible account of asceticism in late antiquity, see Peter Brown, *The Body and Society: Men, Women, and Sexual Renunciation in Early Christianity* (New York: Columbia University Press, 1988).

3. See *Dictionnaire de Spiritualité*, s.v. "humilité"; and Klaus Wengst, *Humility: Solidarity of the Humiliated*, trans. John Bowden (London: SCM, 1988) (originally published as *Demut: Solidarität der Gedemütigen*, 1987). Valuation of humility is lacking in both Plato and Aristotle. For a classic Christian treatment of vices and virtues, see Evagrius of Pontus, *Practicus*, in *Traité pratique, ou, le moine*, ed. A. and C. Guillaumont, 2 vols., SC 170, 171 (Paris: Cerf, 1971); translation: John Eudes Bamberger, *Evagrius: The Praktikos and Chapters on Prayer* (Spencer, Mass.: Cistercian, 1970).

4. Averil Cameron, "Ascetic Closure and the End of Antiquity," in *Asceticism*, ed. Vincent Wimbush and Richard Valantasis (New York: Oxford University Press, 1995), 153.

5. Peter Brown, "The Saint as Exemplar in Late Antiquity," in *Saints and Virtues*, ed. John Stratton Hawley (Berkeley: University of California Press, 1987), 1–14; Susan Ashbrook Harvey, *Asceticism and Society in Crisis: John of Ephesus and the*

Lives of the Eastern Saints (Berkeley: University of California Press, 1990), xiii, 5; Elizabeth A. Clark, "The Ascetic Impulse in the Religious Life," in *Asceticism*, ed. Wimbush and Valantasis, 508.

6. For example, Basil of Caesarea, *Ep.* 2; Antoine Guillaumont, "La conception du désert chez les moines d'Egypte," *Revue de l'histoire des religions* 188 (1975): 3–21; David Brakke, *Athanasius and the Politics of Asceticism* (Oxford: Clarendon, 1995), 161–170. See also Chapter 2.

7. For example: Evagrius, *Practicus* (see n3) and Dorotheus of Gaza, *Discourses*; edition: Dorotheus of Gaza, *Œuvres spirituelles*, ed. L. Regnault and J. de Préville (Paris: Cerf, 1963); translation: Dorotheus of Gaza, *Discourses and Sayings*, trans. Eric P. Wheeler, Cistercian Studies 33 (Kalamazoo, Mich.: Cistercian, 1977).

8. Claudia Rapp, "Christians and Their Manuscripts in the Greek East in the Fourth Century," in *Scritture, libri e testi nelle aree provinciali di Bisanzio*, ed. Guglielmo Cavallo, Giuseppe de Gregorio, and Marilena Maniaci (Spoleto: Centro italiano di studi sull'alto medioevo, 1991), 127–48; Claudia Rapp, "Holy Texts, Holy Men and Holy Scribes," in *The Early Christian Book*, ed. William Klingshirn and Linda Safran (Washington, D. C.: Catholic University Press, forthcoming 2004); Douglas Burton-Christie, *The Word in the Desert: Scripture and the Quest for Holiness in Early Christian Monasticism* (New York: Oxford University Press, 1993), 43–48, 108–14. On reading and exegesis as a form of asceticism with reference to Augustine, see also Geoffrey Galt Harpham, *The Ascetic Imperative in Culture and Criticism* (Chicago: University of Chicago Press, 1987), 134.

9. Athanasius, *Life of Antony* 55; text: G. J. M. Bartelink, *Athanasius: Vie d'Antoine*, SC 400 (Paris: Cerf, 1994); translation: Robert T. Meyer, *St. Athanasius: The Life of Saint Antony* (New York: Newman, 1950). See also Brakke, *Athanasius and the Politics of Asceticism*, 260. Athanasius (*Life of Antony* 67) also suggests the holy man's face is a text to be read and interpreted.

10. Patricia Cox Miller, "Desert Asceticism and 'The Body from Nowhere,'" *JECS* 2 (1994): 144. See also Brakke, *Athanasius and the Politics of Asceticism*, 246; Harpham, *Ascetic Imperative*, 67–88; and Richard Valantasis, "Constructions of Power in Asceticism," *JAAR* 63 (1995): 798–99.

11. John Moschus, *Spiritual Meadow [Pratum spirituale]*, prol. (*PG* 87:2851); translation: John Wortley, *John Moschus: The Spiritual Meadow* (Kalamazoo, Mich.: Cistercian, 1992), 3.

12. Leontius of Neapolis, *Life of Symeon the Fool*. Greek text edited by Lennart Rydén in *Léontios de Néapolis: Vie de Syméon le Fou et Vie de Jean de Chypre*, edited by A.-J. Festugière, Bibliothèque archéologique et historique 95 (Paris: Geuthner, 1974), 1–222. Translation: Derek Krueger, *Symeon the Holy Fool: Leontius's Life and the Late Antique City*, Transformation of the Classical Heritage 25 (Berkeley: University of California Press, 1996), 131–71.

13. See Georgia Frank, *The Memory of the Eyes: Pilgrims to Living Saints in Christian Late Antiquity* (Berkeley: University of California Press, 2000), 35–49.

14. Text: *History of the Monks of Egypt [Historia monachorum in Aegypto]*, ed. A.-J. Festugière, Subsidia hagiographica 53 (Brussels: Société des Bollandistes, 1961). Translation: Norman Russell, *The Lives of the Desert Fathers* (London: Cistercian, 1980). For the spiritual benefit accruing to the author of this composition, see also

Claudia Rapp, "Storytelling as Spiritual Communication in Early Greek Hagiography: The Use of *Diegesis*," *JECS* 6 (1998): 441. On the genre of collective biography, see Patricia Cox Miller, "Strategies of Representation in Collective Biography: Constructing the Subject as Holy," in *Greek Biography and Panegyric in Late Antiquity*, ed. Tomas Hägg and Philip Rousseau (Berkeley: University of California Press, 2000), 209–54.

15. Texts: Cyril of Scythopolis, *Life of Euthymius*, in *Kyrillos von Skythopolis*, ed. Eduard Schwartz, *Texte und Untersuchungen* 49, no. 2 (1939): 3–85; Cyril of Scythopolis, *Life of Sabas*, in *Kyrillos*, ed. Schwartz, 85–200. Translation: *Cyril of Scythopolis: The Lives of the Monks of Palestine*, ed. R. M. Price and John Binns, Cistercian Studies 114 (Kalamazoo, Mich.: Cistercian, 1991).

16. A.-J. Festugière, "Lieux communs littéraires et thèmes de folk-lore dans l'hagiographie primitive," *Wiener Studien* 73 (1960): 130. For this topos from the tenth to the fourteenth centuries, see C. Wendel, "Die ΤΑΠΕΙΝΟΤΗΣ des griechischen Schreibermönches," *Byzantinische Zeitschrift* 43 (1950): 259–66.

17. Bernard Flusin, *Miracle et histoire dans l'oeuvre de Cyrille de Scythopolis* (Paris: Études augustiniennes, 1983), 41–86; John Binns, *Ascetics and Ambassadors of Christ: The Monasteries of Palestine 314–631* (Oxford: Clarendon, 1994), 57–66 (57n3 lists bibliography of earlier studies); Binns, introduction to *Lives of the Monks of Palestine*, l–li. See also Chapter 4.

18. Valantasis, "Constructions of Power," 797–800.

19. Compare Binns, *Ascetics and Ambassadors*, 31–32.

20. Compare Flusin, *Miracle et histoire*, 107–8.

21. See Tom Driver, *The Magic of Ritual: Our Need for Liberating Rites that Transform Our Lives and Our Communities* (San Francisco: HarperCollins, 1991), 88; Catherine Bell, *Ritual Theory, Ritual Practice* (New York: Oxford University Press, 1992), 88–93.

22. Evagrius of Pontus, *Practicus* 57–58.

23. Pseudo-Macarius, *Homilies* 15.37; text: *Die 50 geistlichen Homilien des Makarios*, ed. H. Dörries, E. Klostermann, and M. Kroeger, Patristische Texte und Studien 4 (Berlin: de Gruyter, 1964); translation: George Maloney, *Pseudo-Macarius: The Fifty Spiritual Homilies; and, The Great Letter* (New York: Paulist, 1992).

24. On levels of style and language in the *Life of Symeon*, see Krueger, *Symeon the Holy Fool*, 19–20.

25. Antony of Choziba, *Life of George of Choziba*; text: C. House, ed., "Vita sancti Georgii Chozibitae auctore Antonio Chozibita," *AnBoll* 7 (1888): 95–144; and House, "Nota in Vitam Sancti Georgii Chozibitae," *AnBoll* 8 (1889): 209–10. Translation by Tim Vivian and Apostolos N. Athanassakis in *Journeying into God: Seven Early Monastic Lives*, ed. Tim Vivian (Minneapolis: Fortress, 1996), 71–105.

26. On the interpolation see Vivian, *Journeying into God*, 63–65.

27. Antony, *Life of George* 35, 37; see Vivian, *Journeying into God*, 65.

28. Valantasis, "Constructions of Power in Asceticism," 797–98; Miller, "Desert Asceticism," 137–39.

29. Dorotheus of Gaza, *Discourses* 2.33 (ed. Regnault and de Préville, 196; translation Wheeler, 98).

30. Dorotheus, *Discourses* 2.33.

31. *Man of God of Edessa*, in *La légende syriaque de saint Alexis, l'homme de Dieu*, ed. Arthur Amiaud, Bibliothèque de l'Ecole des Hautes Etudes 79 (Paris, 1889). This edition contains the Syriac text and a French translation.

32. My reading of the *Life of Antony* has been greatly influenced by Brakke, *Athanasius and the Politics of Asceticism*, 216–65. Athanasius (*Life of Antony* 78, 82, 91) also displaces his teachings against the Arians onto Antony. By announcing that he received Antony's cloak, Athanasius claims to be Antony's legitimate successor (91).

33. For a parallel elision of agency in icon painting, see Gilbert Dagron, "Holy Images and Likeness," *DOP* 45 (1991): 23–33.

34. Brakke, *Athanasius and the Politics of Asceticism*, 262.

35. See Chapter 4.

36. Jerome, *Life of Hilarion* 1; text: PL 23:29–54; translation: Marie Ligouri Ewald, in *Early Christian Biographies*, ed. Roy J. Deferrari (Washington, D.C.: Catholic University Press, 1952), 245.

37. Theodoret, *Religious History* 1.1. Text: *Théodoret de Cyr, Histoire des moines de Syrie*, ed. Pierre Canivet and Alice Leroy-Molinghen, 2 vols., SC 234 and 257 (Paris: Cerf, 1977–79). Translation: Theodoret of Cyrrhus, *A History of the Monks of Syria*, trans. R. M. Price, Cistercian Studies 88 (Kalamazoo, Mich.: Cistercian, 1985).

38. For the classic treatment, see Ihor Ševčenko, "Levels of Style in Byzantine Prose," *Jahrbuch der österreichischen Byzantinistik* 31 (1981): 289–312. See also Claudia Rapp, "Byzantine Hagiographers as Antiquarians, Seventh to Tenth Centuries," *Byzantinische Forschungen* 21 (1995): 31–44.

39. Krueger, *Symeon the Holy Fool*, 5.

40. Leontius, *Life of John the Almsgiver*, prol. in *Léontios de Néapolis: Vie de Syméon le Fou et Vie de Jean de Chypre*, ed. A.-J. Festugière, Bibliothèque archéologique et historique 95 (Paris: Geuthner, 1974), 334 (my translation). See Ševčenko, "Levels of Style," 295–96.

41. It is useful to remember that Papias, Clement, and Origen had remarked that various Gospels and even Paul failed to meet the literary critical standards for good rhetoric taught in Greek schools. Origen (*Contra Celsum* 1.62) wrote of the apostles, "In them there was no power of speaking or of giving an ordered narrative by the standards of Greek dialectical or rhetorical arts which convinced their hearers" (trans. Henry Chadwick, 57). See Robert M. Grant, *The Earliest Lives of Jesus* (New York: Harper and Bros., 1961), 17–18, 36–37, 53–56. Writing more elegantly than the apostles could be worrisome.

42. Palladius, *Lausiac History*. Text: G. J. M. Bartelink, ed., *Palladio: La storia lausiaca*, Vite dei Santi 2 (Milan: Mondadori, 1974), which emends Cuthbert Butler, ed., *Palladius: Lausiac History*, 2 vols., Text and Studies: Contributions to Biblical and Patristic Literature 6 (Cambridge: Cambridge University Press, 1898–1904). Translation: Palladius, *The Lausiac History*, trans. Robert T. Meyer, ACW 34 (New York: Newman, 1964).

43. Antony, *Life of George* 58. For Christological use of "ἀσθένεια," see Lampe, s.v.

44. Thus also Bartelink, *Palladio*, 402; Meyer, *Lausiac History*, 219–20, nn. 570,

572. For speaking about one's achievements in the third person as an ascetic ideal, see *HME* 2.9–10.

45. For the receipt of miraculous powers as a result of ascetic practice, see Theodoret, *Religious History,* prol. 8, 10.

Chapter 6

1. Text: Grégoire de Nysse, *Vie de Sainte Macrine,* ed. Pierre Maraval, SC 178 (Paris: Cerf, 1971). Quotations are based on the translation of Virginia Woods Callahan, *Gregory of Nyssa: Ascetical Works,* FOTC 58 (Washington, D.C.: Catholic University Press, 1967), 159–91, although modification was frequently necessary to present a richer sense of the Greek. Another translation is Kevin Corrigan, *The Life of Saint Macrina by Gregory Bishop of Nyssa* (Toronto: Peregrina, 1998).

2. Gregory of Nyssa, *Life of Gregory the Wonderworker,* in *Gregorii Nysseni Sermones,* ed. Gunther Heil (Leiden: Brill, 1990) 2:96. Translation: Michael Slusser, *St. Gregory Thaumaturgus: Life and Works,* FOTC 98 (Washington, D.C.: Catholic University Press, 1998), 83.

3. See Chapter 5.

4. Anthony Meredith, *The Cappadocians* (Crestwood, N.Y.: St. Vladimir's Seminary Press, 1995), provides a useful introduction to the lives and theology of these three most influential churchmen.

5. On Gregory's theology of language, see Frances M. Young, "The God of the Greeks and the Nature of Religious Language," in *Early Christian Literature and the Classical Intellectual Tradition: In Honorem Robert M. Grant,* ed. William R. Schoedel and Robert L. Wilken (Paris: Beauchesne, 1979), 59, 67–71; and Alden A. Mosshamer, "Disclosing but Not Disclosed: Gregory of Nyssa as Deconstructionist," in *Studien zu Gregor von Nyssa und der christlichen Spätantike,* ed. Hubertus R. Drobner and Christoph Klock, Supplements to *Vigiliae Christianae* 12 (Leiden: Brill, 1990), 99–123.

6. For a discussion of the text's genre, see also Pierre Maraval, "La *Vie de Sainte Macrine* de Grégoire de Nysse: continuité et nouveauté d'un genre littéraire," in *Du héros païen au saint chrétien,* ed. Gérard Freyburger and Laurent Pernot (Paris: Études Augustiniennes, 1997), 133–38.

7. His treatise *On the Soul and Resurrection* (1) used the same grief to establish a scene for the composition of philosophical dialogue. Text: PG 46: 11–160; translation: Catherine P. Roth, *St. Gregory of Nyssa: The Soul and Resurrection* (St. Vladimir's Seminary Press, 1993).

8. Maraval, *Vie de Sainte Macrine,* 57–67.

9. Gregory of Nyssa, *Ep.* 19, contains a brief description of Macrina. G. Pasquali, ed., *Gregorii Nysseni Epistulae* (Leiden: Brill 1959), 64–65.

10. On the number of children, see Maraval, *Vie de Sainte Macrine,* 159n3, 186n1.

11. On the family, see Philip Rousseau, *Basil of Caesarea* (Berkeley: University

of California Press, 1994), 1–26; Susanna Elm, *"Virgins of God": The Making of Asceticism in Late Antiquity* (Oxford: Clarendon, 1994), 78–91.

12. It is likely that they manumitted their slaves; see Elm, *Virgins of God,* 84–86.

13. Elm, *Virgins of God,* 39–47, 92–102. See also Arnaldo Momigliano, "The Life of St. Macrina by Gregory of Nyssa," in *On Pagans, Jews, and Christians* (Middletown, Conn.: Wesleyan University Press, 1987), 206–21.

14. Compare Gregory of Nyssa, *Ep.* 19.7. On Macrina's asceticism, see also Elizabeth Castelli, "Virginity and Its Meaning for Women's Sexuality in Early Christianity," *Journal of Feminist Studies in Religion* 2 (1986): 67, 74.

15. See Maraval, *Vie de Sainte Macrine,* 158–159n2; Corrigan, *The Life of Saint Macrina,* 61.

16. See Maraval, *La Vie de Sainte Macrine,* 68–71.

17. Basil of Caesarea, *Ep.* 2; Basil, *On the Holy Spirit* 73; Basil, *Longer Rules* 37.2–5. Robert Taft, *The Liturgy of the Hours in East and West: The Origins of the Divine Office and Its Meaning for Today* (Collegeville, Minn.: Liturgical Press, 1986), 36–41, 84–87. See also Gregory of Nyssa, *Ep.* 19.8.

18. Susan Ashbrook Harvey ("The Stylite's Liturgy: Ritual and Religious Identity in Late Antiquity," *JECS* 6 [1998]: 523–539) offers an important study linking hagiographical composition and the liturgy.

19. Susan Ashbrook Harvey, "Women in Early Byzantine Hagiography: Reversing the Story," in *That Gentle Strength: Historical Perspectives on Women in Christianity,* ed. Lynda L. Coon, Katherine J. Haldane, and Elizabeth W. Sommer (Charlottesville: University Press of Virginia, 1990), 37–38.

20. Compare Gregory of Nyssa, *Life of Macrina* 22.

21. Momigliano, "The Life of St. Macrina," 208; and Charalambos Apostolopoulos, *Phaedo Christianus: Studien zur Verbindung und Abwägung des Verhältnisses zwischen dem platonishen "Phaidon" und dem Dialog Gregors von Nyssa "Über die Seele und die Auferstehung"* (Frankfurt am Main: Peter Lang, 1986). The classic study of Gregory's Platonism remains Jean Daniélou, *Platonisme et théologie mystique: Doctrine spirituelle de Saint Grégoire de Nysse* (Paris: Aubier, 1944, reprinted 1953). See also Anthony Meredith, "Gregory of Nyssa and Plotinus," *Studia Patristica* 17, no. 3 (1982): 1120–26; and Rowan Williams, "Macrina's Deathbed Revisited: Gregory of Nyssa on Mind and Passion," in *Christian Faith and Greek Philosophy in Late Antiquity: Essays in Tribute to George Christopher Stead,* ed. Lionel R. Wickham and Caroline P. Bammel (Leiden: Brill, 1993), 227–46.

22. See Elizabeth A. Clark, "Holy Women, Holy Words: Early Christian Women, Social History, and the 'Linguistic Turn,'" *JECS* 6 (1998): 423–30; Virginia Burrus, "Is Macrina a Woman? Gregory of Nyssa's *Dialogue on the Soul and Resurrection,*" in *The Blackwell Companion to Postmodern Theology,* ed. Graham Ward (Oxford: Blackwell, 2001), 249–64 (revised and refocused in Virginia Burrus, *Begotten, not Made: Conceiving Manhood in Late Antiquity* [Stanford: Stanford University Press, 2000], 112–122); compare Roth, *St. Gregory of Nyssa,* 11, 15.

23. Gregory of Nazianzus, *Ep.* 238.1, ed. Paul Gallay, *Saint Grégoire de Nazianze: Lettres* (Paris: Les Belles Lettres, 1967), 2:128.

24. For the importance of self-control in grief and the occasional inability of

male authors to maintain composure, see also Jerome, *Ep.* 38.2 (on the death of Blesilla); and Augustine, *Confessions* 9.11–12 (on the death of his mother). For gendered aspects of lament with reference to Gregory of Nyssa, see Margaret Alexiou, *The Ritual Lament in Greek Tradition* (Cambridge: Cambridge University Press, 1974), 27–31; and Burrus, *Begotten Not Made*, 121–22.

25. Mary Carruthers (*The Craft of Thought: Meditation, Rhetoric, and the Making of Images, 400–1200*, Cambridge Studies in Medieval Literature 34 [Cambridge: Cambridge University Press, 1998], 9) explains, "The arts of memory are among the arts of thinking, especially involved with fostering the qualities we now revere as 'imagination' and 'creativity.'"

26. Gregory states (*Life of Macrina* 15) that Basil died about nine months before the synod in Antioch, after which Gregory returned to Annisa. But the date of Basil's death is uncertain. See Pierre Maraval, "La Date de la mort de Basile de Césarée," *Études Augustiniennes* 34 (1988): 25–38; and Rousseau, *Basil of Caesarea*, 360–63.

27. On the inspiration of the Holy Spirit for hagiographical composition, see Gregory of Nyssa, *Life of Gregory the Wonderworker* 3, (ed. Heil). On Gregory's ideas about the inspiration of scripture, see Mariette Canévet, *Grégoire de Nysse et l'herméneutique biblique: Étude des rapports entre le langage et la connaissance de Dieu* (Paris: Études augustiniennes, 1983), 66–67.

28. On the materiality of memory, see also Carruthers, *The Craft of Thought*, 99.

29. Athanasius, *Life of Antony*, prol.

30. For examples, see the works collected in *Funeral Orations by Saint Gregory Nazianzen and Saint Ambrose*, trans. Leo P. McCauley et al., FOTC 22 (Washington, D.C.: Catholic University Press, 1953). On orality in Christian narrative traditions in late antiquity, see Douglas Burton-Christie, *The Word in the Desert: Scripture and the Quest for Holiness in Early Christian Monasticism* (New York: Oxford University Press, 1993), 76–103; and Claudia Rapp, "Storytelling as Spiritual Communication in Early Greek Hagiography: The Use of *Diegesis*," *JECS* 6 (1998): 431–48.

31. For this commonplace, see Gregory of Nyssa, *Against Eunomius* 2.208; Jerome, *Ep.* 3.1; Evagrius of Pontus, *Letter to Melania* 2 (ed. M. Parmentier, *Bijdragen, tijdschrift voor filosofie en theologie* 46 [1985] 2–38); Achilles Tatius, *Leukippe and Clitophon* 5.19. See also Margaret M. Mitchell, "The Archetypal Image: John Chrysostom's Portraits of Paul," *Journal of Religion* 75 (1995): 24–25; and H. Koskenniemi, *Studien zur Idee und Phraseologie des griechischen Briefes bis 400 n. Chr.*, Suomalaisen Tiedeakatemian Toimituksia/Annales Academiae Scientiarum Fennicae 102.2 (Helsinki: Suomalainen Tiedeakatemia, 1956), 40–41, 179–80.

32. See Maraval, *Vie de Sainte Macrine*, 137n2, 263n1.

33. LSJ, s.v. "μακρηγορία" cites the pejorative use of the term in classical writers. But the term is neutral in late antiquity; compare Palladius, *Dialogue on the Life of John Chrysostom* 89.18 and Hesychius, *Lexicon* 129.1.

34. Plato, *Phaedrus* 257b–279b. For the influence of and familiarity with the *Phaedrus* more generally, including among Christians, see M. B. Trapp, "Plato's

Phaedrus in Second-Century Greek Literature," in *Antonine Literature*, ed. D. A. Russell (Oxford: Clarendon, 1990), 141–73. On speech and writing in the *Phaedrus*, see also Jacques Derrida, "Plato's Pharmacy," in *Dissemination*, trans. Barbara Johnson (Chicago: University of Chicago Press, 1981), 61–171; and Derrida, *Of Grammatology*, trans. Gayatri Spivak (Baltimore: Johns Hopkins University Press, 1976). Derrida's reading of the *Phaedrus* reveals that the traditional speech/writing oppositional hierarchy is among the things undermined by the dialogue's own textuality. The "meaning" of the dialogue may well be the opposite of its content. Gregory's view of the speech/writing distinction is similarly deconstructive, as we see below.

35. Gregory of Nyssa, *Against Eunomius* 2.208 (text: *Gregorii Nysseni Opera*, ed. Werner Jaeger, 2nd edition [Leiden: Brill, 1960], 1:285; translation: NPNF 2.5:271).

36. Gregory of Nyssa, *Against Eunomius* 3:50 (text: ed. Jaeger, 2:179). See also Mosshamer, "Disclosing but Not Disclosed," 103.

37. Within the *Life of Macrina*, Gregory uses the word "διάστημα" to refer twice to intervals of time (15.11, 37.14) and once to an interval of space (33.25). On the concept of *diastēma* in Gregory's theology, see T. Paul Verghese, "ΔΙΑΣΤΗΜΑ and ΔΙΑΣΤΑΣΙΣ in Gregory of Nyssa: Introduction to a Concept and the Posing of a Problem," in *Gregor von Nyssa und die Philosophie*, ed. Heinrich Dörrie, Margarete Altenburger, and Uta Schramm (Leiden: Brill, 1976), 243–58; L. G. Patterson, "The Conversion of *Diastēma* in the Patristic View of Time," in *Lux in Lumine: Essays to Honor W. Norman Pittenger*, ed. R. A. Norris (New York: Seabury, 1966), 93–111; and Hans Urs von Balthasar, *Presence and Thought: An Essay on the Religious Philosophy of Gregory of Nyssa*, trans. Mark Sebanc (San Francisco: Ignatius Press, 1988; originally published as *Présence et pensée*, 1942), 27–35. On *diastēma* and language, see Mosshammer, "Disclosing but Not Disclosed," 103–12. Mosshamer argues convincingly that Gregory's concept of *diastēma* anticipates discussions of difference in postmodern critical theory.

38. For a parallel appreciation of the deconstructive (and reconstructive) power of the eucharist with regard to language and signification, see Catherine Pickstock, *After Writing: On the Liturgical Consummation of Philosophy* (Oxford: Blackwell, 1998).

39. Georg Luck, "Notes on the *Vita Macrinae* by Gregory of Nyssa," in *The Biographical Works of Gregory of Nyssa*, ed. Andreas Spira (Cambridge, Mass.: Philadelphia Patristic Foundation, 1984), 28–30; Anthony Meredith, "A Comparison between the *Vita Sanctae Macrinae* of Gregory of Nyssa and the *Vita Plotini* of Porphyry and the *De vita Pythagorica* of Iamblichus," in *The Biographical Works of Gregory of Nyssa*, ed. Spira, 188.

40. See Chapter 5.

41. On *skopos* as an aim or destination of thought, see M. Harl, "Le guetteur et la cible: les deux sens de *skopos* dans la langue religieuse des chrétiens," *Revue des études grecques* 74 (1961): 450–68; Carruthers, *The Craft of Thought*, 79–82, 262.

42. This last sentence, secure in the manuscript tradition of the *Life of Macrina* (compare the edition of V. Woods Callahan, in *Gregorii Nysseni: Opera Ascet-*

ica [Leiden: Brill, 1952], 394, ll. 5–6), is lacking in the translation of Corrigan (*The Life of Saint Macrina*, 38).

43. On evening prayer in fourth-century Cappadocia, see Taft, *Liturgy of the Hours*, 36–39.

44. For another example of how liturgical activity can structure hagiographical narrative, see Harvey, "The Stylite's Liturgy," 537–39.

45. On *historia* and *theōria*, see Gregory of Nyssa, *Life of Moses* 1.15. For Macrina's own practice of *theōria*, see Gregory of Nyssa, *Life of Macrina* 18.11. See also Mosshammer, "Disclosing but Not Disclosed," 121.

46. Georg Luck notes that at this point in the text, Gregory shifts from an "elegant, cultivated Greek" to a colloquial style; "Notes on the *Vita Macrinae*," 26.

47. Although Gregory does not say so, it is tempting to read the text to mean that the girl was healed while her mother was narrating about Macrina.

48. Gregory of Nyssa, *On the Inscriptions of the Psalms* 2.3, ed. J. McDonough, *Gregorii Nysseni Opera*, ed. Werner Jaeger (Leiden: Brill, 1962), 5:75–76; trans. Ronald E. Heine, *Gregory of Nyssa: Treatise on the Inscriptions of the Psalms* (Oxford: Clarendon, 1995), 130. On the date, see Heine, *Gregory of Nyssa: On the Inscriptions of the Psalms*, 8–11.

49. For the chanting of psalms forming Christian identity, see also Athanasius, *Letter to Marcellinus on the Interpretation of the Psalms*.

50. Gregory of Nyssa, *Life of Gregory the Wonderworker* 3 (trans. Slusser, 41).

51. Gregory's description seems to echo Plato, *Phaedrus* 246b–c. Compare Meredith, "A Comparison between the *Vita Sanctae Macrinae* of Gregory of Nyssa," 190.

52. Patricia Cox Miller, *Dreams in Late Antiquity: Studies in the Imagination of a Culture* (Princeton: Princeton University Press, 1994), 236–40.

53. In the presence of Macrina's corpse, dressed for burial, Gregory remarks: "Even in the dark, the body glowed, the divine power adding such grace to her body that, as in the vision in my dream, rays seemed to be shining forth from her loveliness" (32).

54. Georgia Frank ("Macrina's Scar: Homeric Allusion and Heroic Identity in Gregory of Nyssa's *Life of Macrina*," *JECS* 8 [2000]: 511–30) articulates further implications of the scar episode for understanding Gregory's narrative practice.

55. On the relationship between memory and authority more generally, see Mary Carruthers, *The Book of Memory: A Study of Memory in Medieval Culture* (Cambridge: Cambridge University Press, 1990), 189–220.

56. See also Eugenio Marotta, "La basa biblica della *Vita s. Macrinae* di Gregorio di Nissa," *Vetera Christianorum* 5 (1968): 73–88.

57. See Taft, *Liturgy of the Hours*, 39, 42–43, 47, 51. This passage in the *Life of Macrina* provides possible early evidence for the use of incense at evening prayer, a practice that became established by the time Theodoret wrote his *Questions on Exodus*, around 453; see Taft, *Liturgy of the Hours*, 47–48; Susan Ashbrook Harvey, *Scenting Salvation: Ancient Christianity and the Olfactory Imagination* (Berkeley: University of California Press, forthcoming).

58. See Lampe, s.v. "εὐχαριστία." Gregory of Nyssa, *Life of Macrina* 22.4; 25.9, 13. Robert Taft (*Liturgy of the Hours*, 37–39) observes that Macrina's deathbed

hymn of "thanksgiving for the light" must have been the already ancient "Phōs hilaron" ("O Gracious Light"), quoted by her brother, Basil of Caesarea, in *On the Holy Spirit* 29 (73).

59. On the development and contents of the anaphora, often called in English the "prayer of consecration," see W. Jardine Grisbrooke, "Anaphora," in *The Westminster Dictionary of Worship*, ed. J. G. Davies (Philadelphia: Westminster, 1972), 10–17; and E. J. Yarnold, "The Liturgy of the Faithful in the Fourth and Early Fifth Centuries," in *The Study of Liturgy*, ed. Cheslyn Jones, Geoffrey Wainwright, and Edward Yarnold (New York: Oxford University Press, 1978), 189–201. See also John H. McKenna, *Eucharist and Holy Spirit: The Eucharistic Epiclesis in Twentieth Century Theology (1900–1960)* (Great Wakering, U.K.: Mayhew-McCrimmon, 1975), 69–71. For patristic use of "εὐχαριστία" to denote the liturgical sacrifice, see also John Chrysostom, *Homilies on First Corinthians* 27.4 (NPNF 1.12:161).

60. See, however, the nuanced discussion in Taft, *Liturgy of the Hours*, 331–65.

61. Taft, *Liturgy of the Hours*, 336, 344–45.

62. These elements are neatly articulated in R. J. Halliburton, "The Patristic Theology of the Eucharist," in *The Study of the Liturgy*, ed. Jones et al., 201–208; Gregory Dix, *The Shape of the Liturgy*, 2nd ed. (London: Dacre, 1945), 238–47. For an early (third-century) example of an anaphoral liturgy, see Hippolytus of Rome, *On the Apostolic Tradition*, ed. Gregory Dix, 2nd ed. (London: S.P.C.K., 1968), 7–9. See also Theodore of Mopsuestia's catechetical homily, *On Eucharist and Liturgy*, ed. A. Mingana, Woodbrooke Studies 6 (Cambridge: Heffer and Sons, 1933), esp. 89, 99–100.

63. Hippolytus, *On the Apostolic Tradition* 4. See also Peter Cobb, "The Apostolic Tradition of Hippolytus," in *The Study of the Liturgy*, ed. Jones et al., 173–76.

64. Hippolytus, *On the Apostolic Tradition* 10.3–5.

65. F. E. Brightman, *Liturgies Eastern and Western* (Oxford: Clarendon, 1896), 402–405. See Hugh Wybrew, "The Byzantine Liturgy from the *Apostolic Constitutions* to the Present Day," in *Study of the Liturgy*, ed. Jones et al., 209–10.

66. Brightman, *Liturgies Eastern and Western*, 321–28.

67. Wybrew, "The Byzantine Liturgy," 209. The *Apostolic Constitutions* (7.25; 8.12) gives two examples of thanksgiving prayers that are essentially renarrations of aspects of salvation history; edition: *Les Constitutions apostoliques*, ed. Marcel Metzger, 3 vols., SC 320, 329, and 336 (Paris: Cerf, 1985–87); English trans.: ANF 7.

68. John Chrysostom, *Homilies on Matthew* 25.3 (PG 57:331; NPNF 1.10:174).

69. John Chrysostom, *Homilies on Matthew* 25.3.

70. John Chrysostom, *Homilies on First Corinthians* 24.1 (PG 57:212; NPNF 1.12:139). Brightman (*Liturgies Eastern and Western*, 474, 479n19) believed that Chrysostom was paraphrasing an anaphoral prayer in use at Antioch.

71. On the prayer as a literary creation, see Maraval, *La Vie de Sainte Macrine*, 74–77.

72. Marotta, "La basa biblica della *Vita s. Macrinae*," 78–81; and Maraval, *La Vie de Sainte Macrine*, 74.

73. Maraval, *La Vie de Sainte Macrine*, 75. For extensive attention to biblical citations, see the notes to *Life of Macrina* 24, in *The Life of Saint Macrina by Gregory, Bishop of Nyssa*, trans. Kevin Corrigan (Toronto: Peregrina, 1987), 67–68.

74. Maraval, *La Vie de Sainte Macrine*, 75–77.

75. On prayer and incense, with reference to Psalm 141:2 (LXX 140:2), see also Gregory of Nyssa, *Life of Moses* 2.185.

76. See John T. Cummings, "The Holy Death-Bed Saint and Penitent: Variation of a Theme," in *The Biographical Works of Gregory of Nyssa*, ed. Spira, 246. For Gregory's conception of the good death in his *Homilies on Ecclesiastes* with reference to the *Life of Macrina*, see Lucas F. Mateo Seco, "'Ο εὔκαιρος θάνατος: Consideraciones en torno a la muerte en las *Homilias al Eclesiastes de Gregorio de Nisa*," in *Gregory of Nyssa: Homilies on Ecclesiastes: An English Version with Supporting Studies*, ed. Stuart George Hall (Berlin: de Gruyter, 1993), 277–97.

Chapter 7

1. Incarnational theology yielded an especially positive valuation of the body and therefore of materiality, perhaps most forcefully among Syrian Christians. This appreciation of matter manifested itself not only in consideration of the human body conformed through praxis to the Christian ideal but to the eucharistic sacrament as well. In the *Hymns against Heresies* (47.2; trans. Sebastian Brock, *The Luminous Eye: The Spiritual World Vision of Saint Ephrem the Syrian*, rev. ed. [Kalamazoo: Cistercian, 1992], 37), the poet Ephrem wrote,

If our Lord had despised the body
as something unclean or hateful or foul,
then the Bread and the cup of Salvation
should also be something hateful and unclean to those heretics;
for how could Christ have despised the body
yet clothed himself in the Bread?

See Susan Ashbrook Harvey, "Embodiment in Time and Eternity: A Syriac Perspective," *St. Vladimir's Seminary Quarterly* 43 (1999): 105–30. For another example of the textual body, see Patricia Cox Miller, "The Blazing Body: Ascetic Desire in Jerome's *Letter to Eustochium*," *JECS* 1 (1993): 23.

2. Text and translation: Porphyry, *Life of Plotinus*, in *Plotinus: Enneads*, vol. 1, translated by A. H. Armstrong, LCL (Cambridge: Harvard University Press, 1966), 2–85. Studies include Patricia Cox Miller, *Biography in Late Antiquity: A Quest for the Holy Man* (Berkeley: University of California Press, 1983), 102–33; Richard Valantasis, *Spiritual Guides of the Third Century: A Semiotic Study of the Guide-Disciple Relationship in Christianity, Neoplatonism, Hermetism, and Gnosticism*, Harvard Dissertations in Religion 27 (Minneapolis: Fortress, 1991); Luc Brisson et al., *Porphyre: La vie de Plotin*, 2 vols. (Paris: Vrin, 1982–92). Perhaps the best introduction to Plotinus's philosophy is Pierre Hadot, *Plotinus, or The Simplicity of Vision*, trans. Michael Chase (Chicago: University of Chicago Press, 1993; originally published as *Plotin ou la simplicité du regard*, 3rd ed., 1989).

3. On Plotinus's objections to the portrait, see Jean Pépin, "L'Épisode du portrait de Plotin," in Brisson et al., *Porphyre*, 2:301–30. See also Danny Praet, "Hagiog-

raphy and Biography as Prescriptive Sources for Late Antique Sexual Morals," *Litterae Hagiologicae* 5 (1999): 2–13. On the materiality of paintings more generally, see Liz James, "Color and Meaning in Byzantium," *JECS* 11 (2003): 223–33.

4. Miller (*Biography in Late Antiquity*, 108) also stresses the humor in the relating of this anecdote.

5. Plotinus also objects to subjecting himself (ἀνασχέσθαι) to a painter or a sculptor. The only positive use of this verb in the text describes Plotinus's enduring the task of keeping track of the accounts for the estates of the children over whom he was guardian (9.12).

6. For a chronology of Plotinus's life, see Hadot, *Plotinus,* 117–19. On Plotinus's classroom, see Gillian Clark, "Philosophic Lives and the Philosophic Life," in *Greek Biography and Panegyric in Late Antiquity,* ed. Tomas Hägg and Philip Rousseau (Berkeley: University of California Press, 2000), 38–41.

7. Denis O'Brien ("Comment écrivait Plotin?" in Brisson et al., *Porphyre,* 1:346–60) argues for a different construal of "ἠνέσχετο" in this passage and would translate, "For, when he had written anything, he could never *manage* to copy out a second time what he had written; no indeed, he could not manage to read it, even once." While this reading makes slightly better sense of Porphyry's remark about Plotinus's eyesight, O'Brien does not consider the other uses of the verb within the text. Consistent translation suggests that Porphyry means to convey that Plotinus had an aversion to rereading his text, as most other translators, including Armstrong, have rendered the text. However, it is possible that O'Brien is right about the other verbs in the sentence, in which case, Plotinus's aversion is both to reading and to recopying his output.

8. See also Pépin, "L'Épisode du portrait de Plotin," 302–22.

9. Plotinus, *Enneads* 1.2.2; 1.2.7; see Frederic M. Schroeder, "Plotinus and Language," in *The Cambridge Companion to Plotinus,* ed. Lloyd P. Gerson (Cambridge: Cambridge University Press, 1996), 338.

10. Plotinus, *Enneads* 2.9.16.

11. Plotinus, *Enneads* 6.9.4; see also Dominic J. O'Meara, *Plotinus: An Introduction of the* Enneads (Oxford: Clarendon, 1993), 105.

12. Stephen R. L. Clark, "Plotinus: Body and Soul," in *The Cambridge Companion to Plotinus,* ed. Lloyd P. Gerson (Cambridge: Cambridge University Press, 1996), 275–95; Margaret Miles, "Image," in *Critical Terms for Religious Studies,* ed. Mark C. Taylor (Chicago: University of Chicago Press, 1998), 160–72.

13. Hadot, *Plotinus,* 31; Clark, "Plotinus," 288–90.

14. Plotinus, *Enneads* 1.6.4.

15. Porphyry, *To Marcella* 8; text and translation: *Porphyry the Philosopher: To Marcella,* ed. Kathleen O'Brien Wicker (Atlanta: Scholars Press, 1987).

16. Porphyry, *To Marcella* 10; note the echo of Plato, *Republic* 532c, in the treatment of "shadow" and "visible form [image]."

17. Porphyry, *To Marcella* 10.

18. Porphyry, *To Marcella* 32.

19. Porphyry, *To Marcella* 33.

20. Miller (*Biography in Late Antiquity*, 109) gains leverage on Porphyry's ideas about representation from two passages in Macarius of Magnesia's *Apocriticus*

that Adolf von Harnack (Porphyrius, *"Gegen die Christen"*, 15 *Bücher: Zeugnisse, Fragmente und Referate,* Abhandlung der königlich preussischen Akademie der Wissenschaften, Phil. Hist. Klasse 1, [Berlin: Verlag der königl. Akademie der Wiss., 1916], 92–93 [frags. 76 and 77]) attributed to Porphyry's *Against the Christians.* However, T. D. Barnes ("Porphyry *Against the Christians:* Date and the Attribution of Fragments," *JThS* n.s. 24 [1973]: 424–42) argued convincingly that because Macarius never mentions Porphyry, much less attributes statements to him, the material attributed to Porphyry by Harnack should be disregarded when trying to attain information about Porphyry's thought. Therefore I have chosen not to consider these fragments in the present investigation. See also Anthony Meredith, "Porphyry and Julian against the Christians," *Aufstieg und Niedergang der römischen Welt,* 2.23.2, ed. Wolfgang Haase (Berlin: De Gruyter, 1980), 1126–27. For an attempt to read Porphyry as an imitator of the gospels, see M. J. Edwards, "Birth, Death, and Divinity in Porphyry's *Life of Plotinus,*" in *Greek Biography,* ed. Hägg and Rousseau, 29–51.

21. Athanasius, *On the Incarnation of the Word* 8.

22. Text: Pseudo-Athanasius, *The Life of Syncletica,* PG 28:1487–1558. Translations: Pseudo-Athanasius, *The Life of Blessed Syncletica,* trans. Elizabeth Bryson Bongie (Toronto: Peregrina, 1996); and Elizabeth A. Castelli, "Pseudo-Athanasius: The Life and Activity of the Holy and Blessed Teacher Syncletica," in *Ascetic Behavior in Greco-Roman Antiquity: A Sourcebook,* ed. Vincent L. Winbush (Minneapolis: Fortress, 1990), 265–311. I have based my translations on Bongie's with frequent modification. See also Castelli, "Mortifying the Body, Curing the Soul: Beyond Ascetic Dualism in *The Life of Saint Syncletica,*" *Differences: A Journal of Feminist Cultural Studies* 4 (1992): 134–53.

23. Leontius of Neapolis, *Life of Symeon the Fool,* 121; Greek text edited by Lennart Rydén in *Vie de Syméon le Fou et Vie de Jean de Chypre,* edited by A.-J. Festugière, Bibliothèque archéologique et historique 95 (Paris: Geuthner, 1974), 1–222; translation in Derek Krueger, *Symeon the Holy Fool: Leontius's* Life and the Late Antique City, Transformation of the Classical Heritage 25 (Berkeley: University of California Press, 1996), 132.

24. Denha, *Life of Maroutha* 1; ed. and trans. F. Nau, *PO* 3.1.53–96. On reading as food, see Mary Carruthers, *The Craft of Thought: Meditation, Rhetoric, and the Making of Images, 400–1200* (Cambridge: Cambridge University Press, 1998), 90–91, 108–09, 124; and Carruthers, *The Book of Memory* (Cambridge: Cambridge University Press, 1990), 165–73.

25. Castelli, "Mortifying the Body," 138.

26. A. S. E. Parker, "The *Vita Syncleticae:* Its Manuscripts, Ascetical Teachings and Its Use in Monastic Sources," *Studia Patristica* 30 (1997): 231–34.

27. M. Arranz, "La Liturge des Présanctifiés de l'ancien Euchologe byzantin," *Orientalia Christiana Periodica* 47 (1981): 332–88; Thomas H. Schattauer, "The Koinonicon of the Byzantine Liturgy: An Historical Study," *Orientalia Christiana Periodica* 49 (1983): 96–98, 114–18; Robert F. Taft, *A History of the Liturgy of St. John Chrysostom, vol. 5: The Precommunion Rites* (Rome: Pontifical Oriental Institute, 2000), 275–77; Georgia Frank, "'Taste and See': The Eucharist and the Eyes of Faith in the Fourth Century," *Church History* 70 (2001): 619–643.

28. LSJ, s.vv. "ἀποθησαυρίζω" and "θησαυρίζω."

29. Clement of Alexandria, *Le Pédagogue*, Book 1, ed. Henri-Irénée Marrou, trans. Marguerite Harl, SC 70 (Paris: Cerf, 1960). See Denise Kimber Buell, *Making Christians: Clement of Alexandria and the Rhetoric of Legitimacy* (Princeton: Princeton University Press, 1999), 136–79; Edward Engelbrecht, "God's Milk: An Orthodox Confession of the Eucharist," *JECS* 7 (1999): 509–26.

30. Clement, *The Pedagogue* 1.39.2; trans. Buell, *Making Christians,* 154–56.

31. Clement, *The Pedagogue* 1.35.2–3; trans. Buell, *Making Christians,* 137–38. On eucharists of milk and honey, see Andrew McGowan, *Ascetic Eucharists: Food and Drink in Early Christian Ritual Meals* (Oxford: Clarendon, 1999), 107–15; Engelbrecht, "God's Milk," 519–22.

32. Clement, *The Pedagogue* 1.38.1; trans. Buell, *Making Christians* 142–43, modified.

33. See also Hebrews 5:12, "For though by this time you ought to be teachers, you need someone to teach you again the first principles of God's word. You need milk, not solid food." Compare 1 Peter 2:2. For later use of this topos, see Carolyn Walker Bynum, *Jesus as Mother: Studies in the Spirituality of the High Middle Ages* (Berkeley: University of California Press, 1982), 125–28.

34. Compare Proverbs 16:24 ("Pleasant words are like a honeycomb, sweetness to the soul and health to the body"), Proverbs 24:13 (where wisdom is honey), and Proverbs 27:7. A very common variant of Luke 24:42 states that after the resurrection, the disciples fed Jesus both fish and honey from the comb; Nestle-Aland, *Novum Testamentum Graece*, 26th ed., ad loc.; Andrew McGowan, *Ascetic Eucharists: Food and Drink in Early Christian Ritual Meals* (Oxford: Clarendon, 1999), 127–28.

35. See Geoffrey Horrocks, *Greek: A History of the Language and Its Speakers* (London: Longman, 1997), 109–11.

36. *The Teaching of Addai,* trans. George Howard, Texts and Translations 16 (Chico: Scholars Press, 1981) reproduces the Syriac text of George Phillips, *The Doctrine of Addai, The Apostle, Now First Edition in a Complete Form in the Original Syriac* (London: Trübner, 1876). I have employed Howard's translation, occasionally modified. For a definitive study sorting out the history of the Abgar tradition, see Sebastian Brock, "Eusebius and Syriac Christianity," in *Eusebius, Christianity, and Judaism,* ed. H. W. Attridge and G. Hata (Detroit: Wayne State University Press, 1992), 212–34, reprinted in Sebastian Brock, *From Ephrem to Romanos: Interactions between Syriac and Greek in Late Antiquity,* Variorum Collected Studies Series 664 (Aldershot: Ashgate, 1999), II. See also J. W. Drijvers, "The Protonike Legend, the *Doctrina Addai,* and Bishop Rabbula of Edessa," *VC* 51 (1997): 298–315; J. K. Elliott, *The Apocryphal New Testament: A Collection of Apocryphal Christian Literature in an English Translation* (Oxford: Clarendon, 1993), 538–42.

37. *The Teaching of Addai,* ed. Howard, 46–47. For more examples of bodily inscription, see Susanna Elm, "Marking the Self in Late Antiquity: Inscriptions, Baptism and the Conversion of Mimes," in *Stigmata-Körperinschriften,* ed. Bettina Menke and Barbara Vinken (Paderborn: Fink, 2004), 47–68.

38. Brock, "Eusebius and Syriac Christianity," 214–15.

39. Jerome, *Ep.* 3.1; trans. NPNF 2.6:4.

40. Achilles Tatius, *Leukippe and Clitophon* 5.19, in *Collected Ancient Greek*

Novels, edited by B. P. Reardon, trans. John J. Winkler (Berkeley: University of California Press, 1989), 243.

41. H. Koskenniemi, *Studien zur Idee und Phraseologie des greichischen Briefes bis 400 n. Chr.,* Suomalaisen Tiedeakatemian Toimituksia/Annales Academiae Scientiarum Fennicae 102.2 (Helsinki: Suomalainen Tiedeakatemia, 1956), 40–41, 179–80.

42. Theodoret, *Religious History* 16.4.

43. Brock, "Eusebius and Syriac Christianity," 213, 221, 226–29. Eusebius, *Ecclesiastical History:* text: E. Schwartz, *Eusebius Werke 2.1–3: Die Kirchengeschichte,* GCS 9.1–3 (Leipzig, 1903–1909); translation: Eusebius, *The History of the Church from Christ to Constantine,* trans. G. A. Williamson (Hammondsworth: Penguin, 1965). Timothy Barnes (*Constantine and Eusebius* [Cambridge, Mass.: Harvard University Press, 1981], 129–30, 347n15) suggests that the section of Book I dealing with Edessa may not have occurred in Eusebius's first edition.

44. Williamson in Eusebius, *The History of the Church from Christ to Constantine,* 67n2.

45. Williamson in Eusebius, *History of the Church,* 67n2.

46. Égérie, *Journal de voyage,* ed. and trans. Pierre Maraval, SC 296 (Paris: Cerf, 1982). Translation: Egeria, *Diary of a Pilgrimage,* trans. George E. Gingras, ACW 38 (New York: Paulist, 1970). See also *Egeria's Travels,* trans. John Wilkinson, 3rd ed. (Warminster: Aris and Phillips, 1999); Blake Leyerly, "Landscape as Cartography in Early Christian Pilgrimage Narratives," *JAAR* 64 (1996): 119–43.

47. *Teaching of Addai,* 8–9; compare Eusebius, *Ecclesiastical History* 1.13, trans. Williamson, 67. See also P. Devos, "Egérie à Edesse. S. Thomas l'Apôtre. Le Roi Abgar," *AnBoll* 85 (1967): 381–400.

48. On the relationship between text and travel for Egeria and other pilgrims, see Georgia Frank, *The Memory of the Eyes: Pilgrims to Living Saints in Christian Late Antiquity* (Berkeley: University of California Press, 2000), 102–18; Leyerle, "Landscape as Cartography," 126–29.

49. Procopius, *Wars* 2.12.26.

50. Compare Egeria, *Travels* 3.6–7; 11.1; 15.6; 21.3. See Gary Vikan, *Byzantine Pilgrimage Art* (Washington, D.C.: Dumbarton Oaks, 1982); Vikan, "Early Byzantine Pilgrimage *Devotionalia* as Evidence of the Appearance of Pilgrimage Shrines," *Jahrbuch für Antike und Christentum, Ergänzungsband* 20 (1995): 1.377–88; and Cynthia Hahn, "Loca Sancta Souvenirs: Sealing the Pilgrim's Experience," in *The Blessings of Pilgrimage,* ed. Robert Ousterhout, Illinois Byzantine Studies 1 (Urbana: University of Illinois Press, 1990), 85–96.

51. *Teaching of Addai,* 10–11.

52. See Averil Cameron, "The History of the Image of Edessa: The Telling of a Story," in *Okeanos: Essays Presented to Ihor Ševčenko on His Sixtieth Birthday,* ed. Cyril Mango and O. Prisak, *Harvard Ukrainian Studies* 7 (1984): 80–94; John of Damascus, *On the Orthodox Faith* 4.16.

53. The most comprehensive study is George Galavaris, *Bread and the Liturgy: The Symbolism of Early Christian and Byzantine Bread Stamps* (Madison: University of Wisconsin Press, 1970).

54. For examples, see Galavaris, *Bread and the Liturgy,* 53–69.

55. Galavaris, *Bread and the Liturgy*, 73–74. This object is now in the Musée d'Art et d'Histoire, Geneva.

56. Galavaris, *Bread and the Liturgy*, 74–75. This piece is now in the British Museum.

Chapter 8

1. The Greek text of Romanos used here is *Sancti Romani Melodi Cantica: Cantica Genuina*, ed. Paul Maas and C. A. Trypanis (Oxford: Clarendon, 1963) (hereafter, Romanos, *Hymns*). The poems are cited by the numbers assigned in this edition, followed by stanza numbers and occasionally by lines. The English titles of the hymns are those given by Maas and Trypanis. A second excellent edition of the hymns with commentary and French translation was published by José Grosdidier de Matons, *Romanos le Mélode: Hymnes*, 5 vols., SC 99, 110, 114, 128, 283 (Paris: Cerf, 1965–81). Because the numbering in that edition differs from the Oxford edition, I have supplied the SC hymn number in parentheses at the first citation of each hymn. Elsewhere, references to the edition of Grosdidier de Matons are noted by volume number within that edition (not the volume within the SC series) and page. Where possible, I have employed the fine translations of Ephrem Lash (Saint Romanos the Melodist, *On the Life of Christ: Kontakia*, trans. Ephrem Lash [San Francisco: Harper Collins, 1995]), occasionally modified. Translations of other hymns are my own except as noted. Worthy of mention are the translations of R. J. Schork (*Sacred Song from the Byzantine Pulpit: Romanos the Melodist* [Gainesville: University of Florida Press, 1995]), which are richly poetic and very good at conveying the spirit of the original, although in many cases they are not strictly literal. The entire corpus of Romanos was also translated by Marjorie Carpenter, *Kontakia of Romanos, Byzantine Melodist*, 2 vols. (Columbia: University of Missouri Press, 1970–73), about which there was much controversy.

2. Romanos, "On the Resurrection V" (*Hymns* 28.1 [SC #43]). The language closely resembles Justinian's 551 *Confession of Faith* (*Chronicon Pascale* 1.662). The term *"oikonomia"* in the sense of "the divine plan of salvation history" was widespread in Greek theological and ecclesiastical discourse. G. Blum, "Oikonomia und Theologia: Der Hintergrund einer konfessionellen Differenz zwischen östlichen and westlichen Christentum," *Ostkirchliche Studien* 33 (1984): 281–301; Robert Markus, "Trinitarian Theology and the Economy," *JThS* n.s. 9 (1958): 89–102; H. Thurn, *Oikonomia von der frühbyzantinischen Zeit bis zum Bilderstreit. Semasiologische Untersuchungen einer Wortfamilie* (Munich: Steinbauer und Rau, 1961).

3. Romanos's interest in written documentation and bureaucracy was first noted by Herbert Hunger, "Romanos Melodos, Dichter, Prediger, Rhetor—und sein Publikum," *Jahrbuch der österreichischen Byzantinistik* 34 (1984): 39–42.

4. Romanos, *Hymns* 18 (SC #24); translation: Lash, *On the Life of Christ*, 129–38. On the liturgical occasion, see Grosdidier de Matons, *Romanos le Mélode: Hymnes*, 4:100; Lash, *On the Life of Christ*, 128.

5. Matthew 27:29; cf. Mark 15:19.

6. See also Romanos, "On the Passion of Christ" (*Hymns* 20.22 [SC #36]): "Beaten on the head with a reed, he signed the exile of his enemies."

7. Elsewhere in the works of Romanos, in "On the Multiplication of Loaves" (*Hymns* 13.9 [SC #24]) the poet reflects on Christ "nourishing the people with words of truth."

8. Cf. 1 Corinthians 11:24–25; Matthew 26:26–29; "Liturgy of St. Basil" in *Liturgies Eastern and Western* ed. F. E. Brightman (Oxford: Clarendon, 1895), 328.

9. According to Jerome (*On Illustrious Men* 115), Ephrem served as a deacon of the church in Edessa, composing hymns to be performed after the scriptural lections. On Ephrem's biography, see Sebastian Brock, *Saint Ephrem the Syrian: Hymns on Paradise* (Crestwood, N.Y.: St. Vladimir's Seminary Press, 1990), 8–25. For Ephrem's ideas about the body of Christ, see also Robert Murray, *Symbols of the Church and Kingdom: A Study in Early Syriac Tradition* (Cambridge: Cambridge University Press, 1975), 69–94; and Susan Harvey, "Embodiment in Time and Eternity: A Syriac Perspective," *St. Vladimir's Theological Quarterly* 43 (1999): 105–30.

10. See also Brock, *St. Ephrem: Hymns on Paradise*, 45–49; Sebastian Brock, *The Luminous Eye: The Spiritual World Vision of St. Ephrem the Syrian* (Kalamazoo: Cistercian, 1992), 36–43, 53–66; see also Murray, *Symbols*, 69–94.

11. Compare R. C. Hill, "St. John Chrysostom and the Incarnation of the Word in Scripture," *Compass Theology Review* 14 (1980): 34–38.

12. Ephrem, *Hymns on Faith* 31; text: Edmund Beck, ed., *Des heiligen Ephraem des Syrers: Hymnen De Fide* CSCO 154 (Louvain: Durbecq, 1955), 105–108; translation: Brock, *Ephrem: Hymns on Paradise*, 45–46.

13. Ephrem, *Hymns on Faith* 31:2. "It is our metaphors that He put on— though He did not literally do so / He then took them off—without actually doing so; when wearing them, He was at the same time stripped of them" (Ephrem, *Hymns on Faith* 31:3; trans. Brock, *Ephrem: Hymns on Paradise*, 46).

14. Ephrem, *Hymns on Paradise* 5.2; text: Edmund Beck, *Des heiligen Ephraem des Syrers: Hymnen De Paradiso und Contra Julianum*, CSCO 174 (Louvain: CSCO, 1957), 15–19; translation: Brock, *Ephrem: Hymns on Paradise*, 102.

15. Ephrem, *Hymns on Paradise* 5.3; trans. Brock, 103.

16. The classic Christian version of this theoretical tradition in the West is represented by Augustine's *On Christian Doctrine [De doctrina christiana]*. See B. D. Jackson, "The Theory of Signs in Saint Augustine's *De Doctrina Christiana*," *Revue des Études Augustiniennes* 15 (1969): 9–49; M. D. Jordan, "Words and Word: Incarnation and Signification in Augustine's *De doctrina christiana*," *Augustinian Studies* 11 (1980): 177–96. In the East, Gregory of Nyssa articulated a less-systematic approach in his treatises *Against Eunomius;* these ideas are well summarized by Alden A. Mosshammer, "Disclosing but Not Disclosed: Gregory of Nyssa as Deconstructionist," in *Studien zu Gregor von Nyssa und der christlichen Spätantike,* ed. Hubertus R. Drobner and Christoph Klock (Leiden: Brill, 1990), 108–12.

17. Pseudo-Dionysius the Areopagite, *The Ecclesiastical Hierarchy* 3.3.9; trans. Colm Luibheid in Pseudo-Dionysius, *The Complete Works* (New York: Paulist, 1987), 219. See also Moshe Barasch, *Icon: Studies in the History of an Idea* (New York: New York University Press, 1992), 168–72.

18. Jean Baudrillard, *Simulacra and Simulation*, trans. Sheila Faria Glaser (Ann Arbor: University of Michigan Press, 1991; French edition 1981), 1–7.

19. Poststructuralist philosophical and literary theory has contributed to contemporary discourse the concept of logocentrism, the idea that the Western tradition (if such a thing exists) has favored speech over writing in its yearning for presence. Yet, as Derrida has shown, the written discourse about the primacy of speech reflects an often-unacknowledged graphocentrism, an investing of authority (and ultimately divine authority) in the written. See particularly Jacques Derrida, *Of Grammatology*, trans. Gayatri Spivak (Baltimore: Johns Hopkins University Press, 1978), originally published as *De la grammatologie* (Paris: Seuil, 1967); and Derrida, *Writing and Difference*, trans. Alan Bass (Chicago: University of Chicago Press, 1978), originally published as *L'écriture et la différence* (Paris: Seuil, 1967). See also, and perhaps especially, the cogent discussion by Barbara Johnson, "Writing," in *Critical Terms for Literary Study*, ed. Frank Lentricchia and Thomas McLaughlin, 2nd ed. (Chicago: University of Chicago Press, 1995), 39–49.

20. Romanos, *Hymns* 23 (SC #39).

21. Maas and Trypanis (*Sancti Romani Melodi Cantica Genuina*, 172) assign the hymn to "Friday in Lent," that is, Good Friday. However, Grosdidier de Matons (*Romanos le Mélode: Hymnes*, 4.312–19) makes a convincing case that the themes of the poem fit the liturgy for the Elevation of the Cross on September fourteenth, which was already celebrated in Constantinople in the mid-sixth century.

22. *Gospel of Nicodemus* 2.10.

23. The positive valuation of the thief within the context of the liturgy gained currency during the course of the sixth century. According to the *Historiarum Compendium* of Cedrenus (PG 121:748), Justin II introduced the troparion "Cenae tuae mysticae" into the celebrations of Holy Thursday in 573/74. The text of this hymn translates, "At your mystical supper, Son of God, receive me today as a partaker, for I will not betray the sacrament to your enemies, nor give you a kiss like Judas, but like the thief I confess you: remember me Lord in your kingdom." See Robert F. Taft, *The Great Entrance: A History of the Transfer of Gifts and Other Preanaphoral Rites of the Liturgy of St. John Chrysostom*, 2nd ed., Orientalia Christiana Analecta 200 (Rome: Pont. Institutum Studiorum Orientalium, 1978), 68–70, 487–88 (text and translation of this hymn appear on 54); and Thomas H. Schattauer, "The Koinonicon of the Byzantine Liturgy: An Historical Study," *Orientalia Christiana Periodica* 49 (1983): 109–10. I thank Patrick Viscuso for assisting me with these references. The hymn is now an integral part of the "Liturgy of St. John Chrysostom," in *Liturgies Eastern and Western*, ed. Brightman, 394. Jacob of Serug (c. 450–521) also composed a hymn in which the thief bears a letter written in Christ's blood to the cherubim in paradise. See Johannes B. Glenthøj, "The Cross and Paradise: The Robber and the Cherub in Dialogue," in *In the Last Days: On Jewish and Christian Apocalyptic and Its Period*, ed. Knud Jeppesen, Kirsten Nielsen, and Bent Rosendal (Aarhus: Aarhus University Press, 1994), 60–77; Sebastian Brock, "Some Aspects of Greek Words in Syriac," *Synkretismus im syrisch-persischen Kulturgebiet*, ed. A. Dietrich (Göttingen: Vandenhoek und Ruprecht, 1975), 104–106, reprinted in Sebastian Brock, *Syriac Perspectives on Late Antiquity* (London: Variorum, 1984), IV.

24. Romanos, *Hymns* 23.5; my translation.

25. Romanos, *Hymns* 23.11; my translation. See the notes to this stanza in Grosdidier de Matons, *Romanos le Mélode: Hymnes*, 4:339.

26. See also Grosdidier de Matons, *Romanos le Mélode: Hymnes*, 4:339n1.

27. For discussion of the sources for Romanos's biography, see José Grosdidier de Matons, *Romanos le Mélode et les origines de la poésie religieuse à Byzance* (Paris: Beauchesne, 1977), 159–98. The closely related citations of Romanos in menologia, menaia, and synaxaria may derive from a no longer extant source, possibly as early as the eighth century. See also Schork, *Sacred Song*, 3–6; and Lash, *On the Life of Christ*, xxvi–xviii.

28. The anonymous hymn acclaims him as "from the race of Hebrews." The text appears in Grosdidier de Matons, *Romanos le Mélode et les origines*, 167–70, and its implications receive balanced treatment on 180–81; see also the discussions in Schork, *Sacred Song*, 5; and Maas and Trypanis, *Sancti Romani Melodi Cantica Genuina*, xvin1.

29. Later traditions also associate him with the Church of the Virgin at Blachernae; see Grosdidier de Matons, *Romanos le Mélode et les origines*, 164–65. On Romanos as the singer of his own hymns, see also Hunger, "Romanos Melodos," 16.

30. Grosdidier de Matons, *Romanos le Mélode et les origines*, 161–62; English translations of accounts from the menologia are available in Schork, *Sacred Song*, 4; and Lash, *On the Life of Christ*, xxvii.

31. The Syriac origins of the *kontakion* have been convincingly demonstrated by Sebastian Brock in "From Ephrem to Romanos," *Studia Patristica* 20 (1989): 139–51; reprinted in Brock, *From Ephrem to Romanos: Interactions between Syriac and Greek in Late Antiquity* (Aldershot: Ashgate, 1999), IV. See also André de Halleux, "Héllenisme et syrianité de Romanos le Mélode," *Revue d'Histoire Ecclésiastique* 73 (1978): 632–41; William L. Petersen, *The Diatessaron and Ephrem Syrus as Sources of Romanos the Melodist*, CSCO 475 (Louvain: Peters, 1985); and the excellent essay by Lucas Van Rompay, "Romanos le Mélode: Un poète syrien à Constantinople," in *Early Christian Poetry: A Collection of Essays*, ed. J. den Boeft and A. Hilhorst, Supplements to *Vigiliae Christianae* 22 (Leiden: Brill, 1993), 283–96. For additional perspective on dialogue hymns, see Brock, "Dialogue Hymns of the Syriac Churches," *Sobornost: Eastern Churches Review* 5, no. 2 (1983): 35–45; and Brock, "Syriac Dispute Poems: The Various Types," in *Dispute Poems and Dialogues in the Ancient and Mediaeval Near East: Forms and Types of Literary Debates in Semitic and Related Literatures*, ed. G. J. Reinink and H. L. J. Vanstiphout, Orientalia Lovaniensia Analecta 42 (Leuven: Department Oriëntalistiek, 1991), 109–19; reprinted in Brock, *From Ephrem to Romanos*, VII. On the implications of the performance of these hymns for the formation of piety, see Susan Ashbrook Harvey, "Spoken Words, Voiced Silence: Biblical Women in Syriac Tradition," *JECS* 9 (2001): 105–131.

32. Andrew Louth (in Lash, *On the Life of Christ*, xvi), points to Romanos's "liturgical story-telling": "In each case, an event, as related in the Scriptures and celebrated in the Liturgy, is retold in such a way as to enable those who hear it to enter into it." On the dialogic qualities of the hymn "Mary at the Cross" (*Hymns* 19 [SC #35]), see Gregory W. Dubrov, "A Dialogue with Death: Ritual Lament and the *Threnos Theotokou* of Romanos Melodos," *GRBS* 35 (1994): 385–405.

33. For this mechanism, see the penitential "Prayer" of Romanos (*Hymns* 56,

prelude and strophe 1; SC #55), in which the poet desires to conform himself to the models provided by the repentant tax collector and harlot. For this as a liturgical mode, consider the precommunion "Cenae tuae" prayer (see note 23).

34. Alexander Lingas (personal correspondence, December 19, 2000) explains current usage: "The prologue and the first oikos of the kontakion for the day are recited after the Gospel of orthros . . . but not directly after. They occur after ode 6 of the kanon (which itself follows Psalm 50 and the litany)." Furthermore, "The usual manner of performance is that one of the cantors will recite the kontakion (prologue) and the oikos from the choir stalls or cantor's stand (psalterion). In many places it is customary that he intones the refrain, which is repeated by the other cantors." See also Grosdidier de Matons, *Romanos le Mélode et les origines,* 98–108; Louth, in Lash, *On the Life of Christ,* xvi; Schork, *Sacred Song,* 6. On larger questions of Byzantine liturgical chant forms, see Irenée-Henri Dalmais, "Tropaire, Kontakion, Canon: Les éléments constitutifs de l'hymnographie byzantine," in *Liturgie und Dichtung: Ein interdisziplinäres Kompendium I: Historische Präsentation,* ed. H. Becker and R. Kaczynski (St. Ottilien: EOS-Verlag, 1983), 421–34.

35. Alexander Lingas, "The Liturgical Place of the Kontakion in Constantinople," in *Liturgy, Architecture, and Art in the Byzantine World: Papers of the XVIII International Byzantine Congress (Moscow, 8–15 August 1991) and Other Essays Dedicated to the Memory of Fr. John Meyendorff,* ed. Constantine C. Akentiev (St. Petersburg: Publications of the St. Petersburg Society for Byzantine and Slavic Studies, 1995), 50–57 (with relevant additional bibliography); José Grosdidier de Matons, "Liturgie et Hymnographie: Kontakion et Canon," *Dumbarton Oaks Papers* 34/35 (1980–1981): 31–43; Grosdidier de Matons *Romanos le Mélode: Hymnes,* 3:45–46; Grosdidier de Matons, "Aux origines de l'hymnographie byzantine: Romanos le Mélode et le Kontakion," in *Liturgie und Dichtung,* ed. Becker and Kaczynski, 443. So also Schork, *Sacred Song,* 86. For the place of the hymns of Romanos in the urban vigils in the mid-seventh century, see *Miracles of Artemios* 18. On the so-called cathedral vigil, see also the excellent overview in Robert Taft, *The Liturgy of the Hours in East and West: The Origins of the Divine Office and Its Meaning for Today,* 2nd ed. (Collegeville, Minn.: Liturgical Press, 1993), 165–90.

36. Romanos, *Hymns* 11.1 (SC #22); my translation.

37. See also Hunger, "Romanos Melodos," 17–22, on the dramatic aspects of these works, including the use of irony; and Harvey, "Spoken Words."

38. Romanos, *Hymns* 11.2. On the language of comedy and tragedy, see Grosdidier de Matons, *Romanos le Mélode: Hymnes,* 3:57.

39. Maas and Trypanis, *Sancti Romani Melodi Cantica: Cantica Genuina,* xiii; Margaret Alexiou, *After Antiquity: Greek Language, Myth, and Metaphor* (Ithaca: Cornell University Press, 2002), 52–53.

40. On the form and meter of the *kontakia,* see Grosdidier de Matons, *Romanos le Mélode et les origines,* 3–47; Lash, *On the Life of Christ,* xxviii–xxxi; Schork, *Sacred Song,* 6–8.

41. See Christian Thodberg, "Kontakion," *The New Grove Dictionary of Music.* See also Jørgen Raasted, "Zum Melodie des Kontakions Ἡ παϱθένος σήμεϱον," *Cahiers de l'Institut du Moyen-Age Grec et Latin* 59 (1989): 233–46; Raasted, "Kontakion Melodies in Oral and Written Tradition," in *The Study of Medieval*

Chant: Paths and Bridges, East and West: In Honor of Kenneth Levy, ed. Peter Jeffery (Woodbridge, England and Rochester, N.Y.: Boydell, 2001), 273–81.

42. On the lay audience, see Grosdidier de Matons, *Romanos le Mélode et les origines,* 286, 303; Hunger, "Romanos Melodos," 36.

43. For appreciation of Romanos's language and style, see Hunger, "Romanos Melodos," 30–36.

44. Romanos sometimes spells "ΤΑΠΕΙΝΟΥ" as the homophone "ΤΑΠΙ-ΝΟΥ." See K. Krumbacher, "Die Akrostichis in der griechischen Kirchenpoesie," *Sitzungsberichte der philos.-philol. und der histor. Klasse der K. Bayer. Akad. d. Wiss.* 2 (1903): 551–692.

45. See Schork, *Sacred Song,* 198n2; and Grosdidier de Matons, *Romanos le Mélode et les origines,* 188–89.

46. Grosdidier de Matons, *Romanos le Mélode et les origines,* 42–45; Schork, *Sacred Song,* 8; Lash, *On the Life of Christ,* 29.

47. See also Psalms 9–10, 25, 34, 37, 111, 112, and 145.

48. Taft, *Liturgy of the Hours,* 41, 177, 280; based on Basil, *Ep.* 207.3. It is not clear at what point Lamentations became a fixture of vigils during Holy Week.

49. On the acrostics in Lamentations as ascetic, see Norman K. Gottwald, *Studies in the Book of Lamentations,* rev. ed. (London: SCM, 1962), 23–32; and Roland Boer, *Knockin' on Heaven's Door: The Bible and Popular Culture* (London: Routledge, 1999), 124–25.

50. See D. E. Graf, "Akrostichis," in *Realencyclopädie der classischen Altertumswissenschaft,* ed. A. Pauly and G. Wissowa; Hans Arnim Gärtner, "Akrostichon," *Der Neue Pauly: Enzyklopädie der Antike,* ed. Hubert Cancik and Helmuth Schneider; Edward Courtney, "Greek and Latin Acrostichs," *Philologus* 134 (1990): 3–13.

51. See Theognis (sixth century B.C.E. Elegies, ed. Douglas Young (Leipzig: Teubner, 1961), lines 19–30. For discussion, see Andrew L. Ford, "The Seal of Theognis: The Politics of Authorship in Archaic Greece," in *Theognis of Megara: Poetry and the Polis,* ed. Thomas J. Figueira and Gregory Nagy (Baltimore: Johns Hopkins University Press, 1985), 82–95.

52. Edward Courtney, "Greek and Latin Acrostichs," 8.

53. Nicander, *Theriaca* 345–53; (ed. A. S. F. Gow and A. F. Scholfield [Cambridge: Cambridge University Press, 1953]; the poem has 958 lines. See also Nicander, *Alexipharmaca* 266–74, where there may be another attempt at an acrostic. Courtney, "Greek and Latin Acrostichs," 12.

54. Nicander, *Theriaca* 957–98; see also *Alexipharmaca* 629–30.

55. Courtney, "Greek and Latin Acrostichs," 9.

56. The spurious works attributed in their acrostics to Romanos were published by Paul Maas and C. A. Trypanis in *Sancti Romani Melodi Cantica: Cantica Dubia* (Berlin: De Gruyter, 1970).

57. See E. Fleischer, "Piyyut," *Encyclopaedia Judaica* 13:573–602, and "Acrostics: Post-Biblical," *Encyclopaedia Judaica* 2.230–31. The terms "פיוט" (*piyyut*), "liturgical poem," and "פייטן" (*paytan*), "liturgical poet," are derived from the Greek "ποιήτης," and thus from the same root as the English words "poet" and "poem." See J. Yalahom, "*Piyyût* as Poetry," in *The Synagogue in Late Antiquity,* ed. Lee I. Levine (Philadelphia: American Schools of Oriental Research, 1987), 111–26. *Piyyu-*

tim were composed in a context of Jewish and Christian interaction; see W. J. van Bekkum, "Anti-Christian Polemics in Hebrew Liturgical Poetry (*Piyyut*) of the Sixth and Seventh Centuries," in *Early Christian Poetry*, ed. Boeft and Hilhorst, 297–308.

58. Grosdidier de Matons, *Romanos le Mélode et les origines*, 43. These early Byzantine works are difficult to date; some may be earlier than or contemporary with Romanos, but the consensus is that most are later.

59. For editions and translations of these poems, see Leslie S. B. MacCoull, *Dioscorus of Aphrodito: His Work and His World* (Berkeley: University of California Press, 1988), 68, 81, 103, 105, 107, 111.

60. *Papyrus grecs et démotiques recueillis en Égypte*, ed. Théodore Reinach (Paris: Leroux, 1905), II 82 and *Catalogue of the Literary Papyri in the British Museum*, ed. H. J. M. Milne, 98; MacCoull, *Dioscorus*, 68–72; see also Jean-Luc Fournet, *Hellénisme dans l'Égypte du VIe siècle: La bibliothèque de l'œuvre de Dioscore d'Aphrodité* (Cairo: Institut français d'archéologie orientale, 1999), 1:378–80 (text and translation), 2:475–486 (commentary).

61. This has been decisively resolved by Fournet, *Hellénisme*, 2:475–77; against Clement A. Kuehn, "Dioskoros of Aphrodito and Romanos the Melodist," *Bulletin of the American Society of Papyrologists* 27 (1990): 103–107, which attempted to identify the recipient of Dioscorus's poem with Romanos the Melodist. (R. J. Schork also proposed this identification in a paper presented at the Sixteenth Annual Byzantine Studies Conference, Baltimore, October 26–28, 1990.) I thank Leslie Mac-Coull for helping me sort this problem out and for directing me to the work of Fournet.

62. Or: "his lowliest servant." ΤΩ ΘΕΙΟΤΑΤΩ ΚΑΙ ΕΥΣΕΒΕΣΤΑΤΩ ΒΑΣΙΛΕΙ ΗΜΩΝ ΙΟΥΣΤΙΝΙΑΝΩ ΑΓΑΠΗΤΟΣ Ο ΕΛΑΧΙΣΤΟΣ ΔΙΑ-ΚΟΝΟΣ. Agapetos, *Ekthesis*, PG 86.1:1163–83. A partial English translation appears in Ernest Barker, *Social and Poltical Thought in Byzantium* (Oxford: Clarendon, 1957), 54–63. See also Averil Cameron, *Procopius and the Sixth Century* (Berkeley: University of California Press, 1985), 252–53; Patrick Henry, "A Mirror for Justinian: The *Ekthesis* of Agapetus Diaconus," *GRBS* 8 (1967): 281–308.

63. The epithet ἐλαχείστου [*sic*] appears in the hymn "On Symeon the Stylite," spuriously attributed and ascribed to Romanos. See Maas and Trypanis, eds., *Sancti Romani Melodi Cantica: Cantica Dubia*, 71–78, and the editors' comments, xi, 197.

64. That Romanos was not a monk is inferred from his hymn "On Life in the Monastery" (Oxford edition #55), which views the monastery from the outside looking in.

65. See Grosdidier de Matons, *Romanos le Mélode et les origines*, 44.

66. Compare Richard Valantasis, "Constructions of Power in Asceticism," *JAAR* 63 (1995): 797. The case of the many poems attributed in their acrostics to Romanos, but composed by others, underlines the possibility for using the acrostics to enact humility. The issue is not so much that these later authors forged Romanos's signature, but rather that in their copying of his meters and probably also his tunes, they submitted to the same discipline, modeling themselves, and not merely their works, on the saintly poet. On the forgers' reuse of Romanos's meters, see

Maas and Trypanis, *Sancti Romani Melodi Cantica: Cantica Dubia,* xii. Explicitly attributing works to another enacted the very essence of humility: not claiming agency in one's good actions.

67. For other aspects of Romanos's final stanzas, see J. H. Barkhuizen, "Romanos Melodos and the Composition of his Hymns: Prooimion and Final Strophe," *Hellenika* 40 (1989): 62–77.

68. Romanos, *Hymns* 29.24 (SC #40).

69. Romanos, *Hymns* 34.24 (SC #50).

70. Romanos, *Hymns* 8 (SC #20); translation, Lash, *On the Life of Christ,* 51–58.

71. Romanos, *Hymns* 8.5; translation Lash, modified.

72. The wording also recalls Psalm 103:15 (LXX 102:15): "As for man his days are like grass [ἄνθρωπος, ὡσεὶ χόρτος αἱ ἡμέραι αὐτοῦ]."

73. In this and other aspects, the hymn "On the Leper" is closely related to the hymn "On the Woman with the Issue of Blood," Romanos, *Hymns* 12 (SC #23). See the remarks introducing that hymn in Grosdidier de Matons, *Romanos le Mélode: Hymnes,* 3:79–83.

74. See Lampe and LSJ, s.v. "δέησις."

75. See also Lash, *On the Life of Christ,* 54n14. The relevant stanza is quoted below.

76. Compare Grosdidier de Matons, *Romanos le Mélode: Hymnes,* 2:373n2. Schork's English translation (*Sacred Song,* 73) alters the "two words" to "three" in order to convey this sense: "He framed the gist of his prayer in three words: / "*If you wish,* you can completely cure me, Lord." Emphasis in original.

77. The wording of this line disrupts the meter and is insecure. See the apparatus in Maas and Trypanis, *Sancti Romani Melodi Cantica: Cantica Genuina,* 63. Grosdidier de Matons suggests that the invocation of the Virgin is a later insertion (*Romanos le Mélode: Hymnes,* 2:379n9).

78. See *ODB* s.v. "deesis."

79. See Schork, *Sacred Song,* 70; also Grosdidier de Matons, *Romanos le Mélode: Hymnes,* 2:371n1.

80. Romanos, *Hymns* 8.10; translation Lash, slightly modified.

81. See the essays collected in *The Uses of Literacy in Early Medieval Europe,* ed. Rosamund McKitterick (Cambridge: Cambridge University Press, 1990).

82. Thus read both the Maas and Trypanis and the Grosdidier de Matons editions, meaning that the speaker has the request written on his soul, presumably by faith. But the reading is uncertain, and the text survives only in one manuscript with a number of textual problems; could Romanos have written "γεγραμμένος," rendering the line, "*I have written* the request on the paper of my soul," reading ἔχω as an auxiliary verb with the perfect middle participle? Even more curious: Does Romanos hear a pun in the words "paper" (χάρτης; 8.10.8) and "grass" (χόρτος; 8.5.4)?

83. For interesting comparisons in the West, see Mary Carruthers's remarks on "compunction" in Latin monastic texts, *The Craft of Thought: Meditation, Rhetoric, and the Making of Images, 400–1200* (Cambridge: Cambridge University Press, 1998), 96, 101, 198. In the twelfth century, Bernard of Clairvaux compared the work

of *compunctio*, with its overtones of puncturing and wounding, to the indelible marking of parchment; *Ad clericos* 15.28; quoted in Carruthers, *Craft of Thought*, 96.

84. Romanos, *Hymns* 14 (SC #26).

85. Romanos, *Hymns* 30, prelude 1 (SC #46); translation Lash, *On the Life of Christ*, 183–191.

86. Romanos, *Hymns* 30, prelude 2. Romanos also compares Thomas's hand to Moses' hand at the burning bush, matter that has contacted the divine presence, yet not been consumed; *Hymns* 30.2.

87. "ὑπογράφω" and "ὑπογραφή" became, in late antiquity, standard terms for "I sign" and "signature"; see Lampe s.vv.

88. Romanos's typological exploration of the connection between the wound in Christ's side, which flowed with life-giving water, and the side of the first Adam, out of which came Eve, have been discussed by Roland Joseph Reichmuth in "Typology in the Genuine Kontakia of Romanos the Melodist" (Ph.D. diss., University of Minnesota, 1975), 38–41.

89. Compare Lash, *On the Life of Christ*, 256–57.

90. On the textual problems with this strophe, see Maas and Trypanis, *Sancti Romani Melodi Cantica: Cantica Genuina*, 241, and Grosdidier de Matons, *Romanos le Mélode: Hymnes*, 5:60–61.

91. See LSJ, s.v. "ἅπτω." For another example of a Christian poet punning on these two senses of ἁπτόμενος, see Gregory of Nazianzus, "On Silence at the Time of Fasting," *Poems* 2.1.34, lines 99–104. Here Gregory compares his own "impure touching upon [ἁπτόμενος] the pure Trinity" in literary composition to two biblical instances of impure touching: the sons of Aaron who died after handling the sacrifice (Lev 10:1–2) and Uzzah's fatal touching of the holy ark (2 Sam 6:6–7). For text and translation, see Gregory of Nazianzus, *Autobiographical Poems*, trans. and ed. by Carolinne While (Cambridge: Cambridge University Press, 1996), 173.

92. Romanos also puns on ψηλαφῶν and φωνή in his hymn "On Jacob and Esau" (*Hymns* 42.9.3–4, [SC #4]), although here he contrasts the different information conveyed by touch and sound: Isaac thinks he is touching Esau, but he hears the voice of Jacob (compare Gen 27:22).

93. Romanos, *Hymns* 5 (SC #16); translated by Lash, *Kontakia*, 39–47.

94. For baptism as illumination, see Gregory of Nazianzus, *Oration* 40, a discourse on baptism preached in Constantinople on January 6, 381.

95. For interpretations of this hymn, see Louth's introduction to Lash, *On the Life of Christ*, xvii–xx; and Grosdidier de Matons, *Romanos le Mélode: Hymnes*, 2:229–32.

96. See Lampe, s.v. "σημείωσις."

97. Also, "Do not hesitate, baptize me. Just lend me your right hand. / I dwell in your spirit and I possess you wholly. / Why then do you not stretch out your palm to me? / I am within you and outside you. Why do you flee from me? [Ps 139:6–16] / Stand your ground and grasp / the unapproachable Light" (Romanos, *Hymns* 5.9).

98. See Lampe, s.vv. "ζωγραφέω" (2d) and "ζωγράφος."

99. Pseudo-Dionysius, *Celestial Hierarchy* 13.4; trans. Luibheid, 180.

100. On the textual problems with this and the preceding line, see Grosdidier de Matons, *Romanos le Mélode: Hymnes,* 2:256–57.

101. Pseudo-Dionysius, *Ecclesiastical Hierarchy* 2.2.6, 5.1.6.

102. On deacons' humility, see Pseudo-Dionysius, *Ecclesiastical Hierarchy* 5.3.7–8.

103. See Sabine MacCormack, *Art and Ceremony in Late Antiquity* (Berkeley: University of California Press, 1981), 67–78, 150–58, 240–66; Peter Brown, *Power and Persuasion in Late Antiquity: Towards a Christian Empire* (Madison: University of Wisconsin Press, 1992), 154–57.

104. Michael Maas, *John Lydus and the Roman Past: Antiquarianism and Politics in the Age of Justinian* (London: Routledge, 1992), 16. Averil Cameron, *Christianity and the Rhetoric of Empire: The Development of Christian Discourse* (Berkeley: University of California Press, 1991), 194, 204; Averil Cameron, *Procopius and the Sixth Century* (Berkeley: University of California Press 1985), 254 (although Romanos was *not* a deacon of Hagia Sophia).

105. For a complex portrait of power and culture in the reign of Justinian, see Averil Cameron, *Christianity and the Rhetoric of Empire,* 189–221.

106. Cameron, *Christianity and the Rhetoric of Empire,* 19. See with caution G. Downey, "Julian and Justinian and the Unity of Faith and Culture," *Church History* 28 (1959): 339–49.

107. Cameron, *Christianity and the Rhetoric of Empire,* 198–99.

108. Schork (*Sacred Song,* 6) is rightly cautious regarding Romanos's possible connection to the imperial family. Nevertheless the poet's familiarity with court ceremony is obvious. See, for example, his hymn "On the Entry into Jerusalem" (*Hymns* 16; SC #32); and Eva Catafygiotu Topping, "Romanos, On the Entry into Jerusalem: A *Basilikos Logos,*" *Byzantion* 47 (1977): 65–91, who sees this poem as dating from the early part of Romanos's career. For a catalogue of Romanos's use of imperial vocabulary, including images of kingship, see J. H. Barkhuizen, "Christ as Metaphor in the Hymns of Romanos the Melodist (Part 1)," *Acta Patristica et Byzantina* 2 (1991): 1–15. For a catalogue of medical language, itself a discourse of power and subjection, see Barkhuizen, "Christ as Metaphor in the Hymns of Romanos the Melodist (Part 2)," *Acta Patristica et Byzantina* 3 (1992): 1–14.

109. Hunger, "Romanos Melodos," 39–42.

110. Romanos, *Hymns* 54 (SC #54); translated by Schork, *Sacred Song,* 184–95.

111. On the Nika riots, see Alan Cameron, *Circus Factions: Blues and Greens at Rome and Byzantium* (Oxford: Oxford University Press, 1976), esp. 277–80; and J. B. Bury, "The Nika Riot," *Journal of Hellenic Studies* 17 (1897): 92–119. Precisely which earthquakes Romanos had in mind is unclear; see Grosdidier de Matons, *Romanos le Mélode: Hymnes,* 5:462–464. See also Eva Catafygiotu Topping, "On Earthquakes and Fires: Romanos' Encomium to Justinian," *Byzantinische Zeitschrift* 71 (1978): 22–35.

112. Romanos, *Hymns* 54:13; trans., Schork, *Sacred Song,* 190.

113. Maas and Trypanis (*Sancti Romani Melodi Cantica: Cantica Genuina,* xix) proposed that the poem was composed for the dedication of the new church on December 27, 537, but see Grosdidier de Matons, *Romanos le Mélode: Hymnes,* 5:457–59.

114. *The Miracles of Saint Artemios* 18. Grosdidier de Matons ("Aux origines de l'hymnographie byzantine," in *Liturgie und Dichtung*, ed. Becker and Kaczynski, 447) posited that the legends of Romanos preserved in middle Byzantine service books derived from an eighth-century source.

Chapter 9

1. Text in José Grosdidier de Matons, *Romanos le Mélode et les origines de la poésie religieuse à Byzance* (Paris: Beauchesne, 1977), 161–62 (my translation). The parallel text in the *Synaxarium of Constantinople* (also known as the *Synaxarium of Sirmond*) reads, "In this church [the Church of the Theotokos in the Kyros district of Constantinople] Romanos received the gift of composing kontakia when the holy Mother of God appeared to him in a dream during the evening of Christ's Nativity [that is, Christmas Eve] and gave him a scroll and ordered him to swallow it. After he had swallowed it he at once awoke from his trance and having mounted the ambo, he began to declaim and chant most melodiously, 'Today the Virgin gives birth to him who is above all being.'" In Romanos the Melodist, *On the Life of Christ: Kontakia*, trans. Ephrem Lash (San Francisco: HarperCollins, 1995), xxvii.

2. Virginia Burrus, *"Begotten, Not Made": Conceiving Manhood in Late Antiquity* (Stanford: Stanford University Press, 2000); Mathew Kuefler, *The Manly Eunuch: Masculinity, Gender Ambiguity and Christian Ideology in Late Antiquity* (Chicago: University of Chicago Press, 2001); Virginia Burrus, *The Sex Lives of Saints: An Erotics of Ancient Hagiography* (Philadelphia: University of Pennsylvania Press, 2003); David Brakke, "The Problematization of Noctural Emissions in Early Christian Syria, Egypt, and Gaul," *JECS* 3 (1995): 419–60; David Brakke, "Ethiopian Demons: Male Sexuality, the Black-Skinned Other, and the Monastic Self," *Journal of the History of Sexuality* 10 (2001): 501–35.

3. Maud W. Gleason, *Making Men: Sophists and Self-Presentation in Ancient Rome* (Princeton: Princeton University Press, 1995).

4. Burrus, *"Begotten, Not Made,"* 80–133.

5. Kim Haines-Eitzen, "'Girls Trained in Beautiful Writing': Female Scribes in Roman Antiquity and Early Christianity," *JECS* 6 (1998): 629–46.

6. *Miracles of Thecla* 46; ed. Gilbert Dagron, *Vie et miracles de Sainte Thècle: Texte grec, traduction et commentaire* (Brussels: Société des Bollandistes, 1978).

7. Theresa Urbainczyk, *Theodoret of Cyrrhus: The Bishop and the Holy Man* (Ann Arbor: University of Michigan Press, 2002). For an example of the role of text in reinforcing relations between author and patron, see Claudia Rapp, "Palladius, Lausus and the *Historia Lausiaca*." in *Novum Millenium: Studies on Byzantine History and Culture Dedicated to Paul Speck*, ed. Claudia Sode and Sarolta Takács (Aldershot: Ashgate, 1999), 279–89.

8. Athanasius, *Life of Antony*, introduction, ed. G. J. M. Bartelink, *Athanasius: Vie d'Antoine* (Paris: Cerf, 1994); trans. Robert Gregg, *Athanasius: The Life of Antony and the Letter to Marcellinus* (New York: Paulist 1980). On the normative power of hagiography, see Peter Brown, "The Saint as Exemplar in Late Antiquity," in *Saints*

and Virtues, ed. Jack Stratton Hawley, (Berkeley: University of California Press, 1987), 1–14; Susan Ashbrook Harvey, *Asceticism and Society in Crisis: John of Ephesus and the Lives of the Eastern Saints* (Berkeley: University of California Press, 1990), xiii, 5; Elizabeth A. Clark, "The Ascetic Impulse in the Religious Life," in *Asceticism,* ed. Vincent Wimbush and Richard Valantasis (New York: Oxford University Press, 1995), 503.

9. David Brakke, *Athanasius and the Politics of Asceticism* (Oxford: Clarendon, 1995), 260.

10. See also Averil Cameron, "Ascetic Closure and the End of Antiquity," in *Asceticism,* ed. Wimbush and Valantasis, 153.

11. On the erotics of hagiography, see Virginia Burrus, "Queer Lives of Saints: Jerome's Hagiography," *Journal of the History of Sexuality* 10 (2001): 442–79.

12. Brakke, *Athanasius,* 182–98.

13. Richard Valantasis, "Constructions of Power in Asceticism," *JAAR* 63 (1995): 775–821.

14. Evagrius, *Practicus,* ed. A. and C. Guillaumont, *Évagre le Pontique: Traité pratique, ou, le moine,* 2 vols. (Paris: Cerf, 1971). Dorotheus of Gaza, *Discourses* [Didaskalia], ed. L. Regnault and J. de Preville, *Dorothée de Gaza: Œuvres spirituelles* (Paris: Cerf, 1963).

15. Athanasius, *Life of Antony* 67. See also Georgia Frank, *The Memory of the Eyes: Pilgrims to Living Saints in Christian Late Antiquity* (Berkeley: University of California Press, 2000), 13–16.

16. Patricia Cox Miller, "Strategies of Representation in Collective Biography: Constructing the Subject as Holy," in *Greek Biography and Panegyric in Late Antiquity,* ed. Tomas Hägg and Philip Rousseau (Berkeley: University of California Press, 2000), 209–54.

17. Already in the fourth century, Jerome's *Life of Paul the First Hermit* attempted to displace the primacy of the *Life of Antony.* Burrus, "Queer Lives of Saints," 447.

18. Athanasius, *Life of Antony,* prol.; Gregory of Nyssa, *Life of Macrina,* prol. See also, Claudia Rapp, "'For Next to God, You Are My Salvation': Reflections on the Rise of the Holy Man in Late Antiquity," in *The Cult of the Saints in Late Antiquity and the Middle Ages: Essays on the Contribution of Peter Brown,* ed. James Howard-Johnston and Paul Antony Hayward (Oxford: Oxford University Press, 1999), 63–65.

19. See Chapter 5.

20. Theodoret, *Ep.* 82.

Bibliography

Primary Sources

Translations are cited below text editions. Preferred editions and translations are cited first.

Achilles Tatius. *Leukippe and Clitophon*. Ed. and trans. S. Gaselee. Rev. ed. LCL. Cambridge: Harvard University Press, 1969.
———. *Leukippe and Clitophon*. In *Collected Ancient Greek Novels*, ed. B. P. Reardon, trans. John J. Winkler. Berkeley: University of California Press, 1989.
Acts of John. In *Acta Johannis*, ed. Éric Junod and Jean-Daniel Kaestli. 2 vols. Corpus Christianorum Series Apocryphorum. Turnhout: Brepols, 1983.
Acts of John. Trans. in *New Testament Apocrypha*, ed. Edgar Hennecke and Wilhelm Schneemelcher, rev. ed., trans. R. McL. Wilson, 2:172–209. Cambridge: Clark, 1992.
Acts of John. Trans. in *The Apocryphal New Testament: A Collection of Apocryphal Christian Literature in an English Translation*, ed. James K. Elliott. Oxford: Clarendon, 1993.
Acts of John at Rome. In *Acta Johannis*, ed. Éric Junod and Jean-Daniel Kaestli, 2:835–86. Corpus Christianorum Series Apocryphorum. Turnhout: Brepols, 1983.
Acts of John by Prochoros. In *Acta Joannis*, ed. Theodor Zahn, 3–165. Erlangen: Deichert, 1880; reprint Hildesheim, 1975.
Acts of John by Prochoros. Italian trans. and Greek text in *Gli apocrifi del Nuovo Testamento*, ed. M. Erbetta, 2:68–110. Turin: Marietti, 1971.
Acts of John by Prochoros. English trans. of Arabic version in *The Mythological Acts of the Apostles*, trans. Agnes Smith Lewis, 37–53. London: Clay, 1904.
Acts of John by Prochoros. English trans. of Ethiopic version in *The Contendings of the Apostles*, trans. E. A. Wallis Budge, 2:186–220. Amsterdam: Apa-Philo, 1976. Originally published 1902.
Acts of John by Prochoros. French trans. of Armenian version in *Écrits apocryphes sur les apôtres: Traduction de l'édition arménienne de Venise*, trans. Louis Leloir, 1:289–407. Brepols: Turnhout, 1986.
Acts of Paul and Thecla. In *Acta Apostolorum Apocrypha*, ed. R. A. Lipsius and M. Bonnet, 1:235–72. Leipzig: Mendelssohn, 1891. Reprinted Hildesheim: Georg Olms, 1959.
Aelian. *Historical Miscellany [Varia Historia]*. Ed. and trans. N. G. Wilson. LCL. Cambridge, Mass.: Harvard University Press, 1997.

Agapetos. *Ekthesis.* PG 86.1:1163–83.

Alexander of Tralles. *Oeuvres médicales d'Alexandre de Tralles.* Ed. Félix Brunet. Paris: Geuthner, 1933–37.

Ambrose. *Selected Works and Letters.* Trans. H. De Romestin. NPNF, 2nd series, vol. 10. 1896. Repr. Peabody, Mass.: Hendrickson, 1994.

Anân Ishô. *The Paradise of the Fathers.* In *Book of Paradise, being the histories and sayings of the monks and ascetics of the Egyptian desert by Palladius, Heironymous and others: The Syriac texts, according to the recension of Anân Ishô of Bêth Abhê,* ed. and trans. E. A. Wallis Budge. 2 vols. Lady Meux Manuscript 6. London, 1904. Translation republished as Anân Ishô, *The Paradise or Garden of the Holy Fathers,* 2 vols. London: Chatto and Windus, 1907.

Anastasius of Sinai. *Questions and Responses.* "Le texte grec des récit utile à l'âme d'Anastase (le Sinaïte)." Ed. F. Nau. *Oriens Christianus* 3 (1903): 56–90.

Antony of Choziba. *Life of George of Choziba.* "Vita sancti Georgii Chozibitae auctore Antonio Chozibita." Ed. C. House. *Analecta Bollandiana* 7 (1888): 95–144; and C. House, "Nota in Vitam Sancti Georgii Chozibitae." *Analecta Bollandiana* 8 (1889): 209–10.

———. *Life of George of Choziba.* In *Journeying into God: Seven Early Monastic Lives,* ed. Tim Vivian, trans. Tim Vivian and Apostolos N. Athanassakis, 71–105. Minneapolis: Fortress, 1996.

Apocalypse of Paul. In *Eschatologie et au-delà: Recherches sur* L'apocalypse de Paul, ed. Claude Carozzi. Aix-en-Provence: Publications de l'Université de Provence, 1994.

Apophthegmata patrum: Alphabetical Collection. PG 65.71–440.

Apostolic Constitutions. Les Constitutions apostoliques. Ed. Marcel Metzger. 3 vols. SC 320, 329, 336. Paris: Cerf, 1985–87. English trans. ANF 7.387–505.

Artemidorus of Daldis. *The Interpretation of Dreams. Artemidori Daldiani Onirocriticon Libri V.* Ed. Roger A. Pack. Leipzig: Teubner, 1963.

———. *The Interpretation of Dreams: Oneirocritica.* Trans. Robert J. White. Park Ridge, N.J.: Noyes, 1975.

Athanasius. *Letter to Marcellinus on the Interpretation of the Psalms.* Trans. Robert C. Gregg. New York: Paulist, 1980.

———. *Life of Antony. Vie d'Antoine.* Ed. G. J. M. Bartelink. SC 400. Paris: Cerf, 1994.

———. *Life of Antony.* Trans. Robert T. Meyer. New York: Newman, 1950.

———. *On the Incarnation of the Word.* In *Contra gentiles and De incarnatione,* ed. and trans. Robert W. Thomson. Oxford: Clarendon 1971.

[Athanasius, Pseudo-]. *The Life of Syncletica.* PG 28:1487–1558.

———. *The Life of the Blessed Syncletica.* Trans. Elizabeth Bryson Bongie. Toronto: Peregrina, 1996.

———. "Pseudo-Athanasius: The Life and Activity of the Holy and Blessed Teacher Syncletica." Trans. Elizabeth A. Castelli. In *Ascetic Behavior in Greco-Roman Antiquity: A Sourcebook,* ed. Vincent L. Winbush, 256–311. Minneapolis: Fortress, 1990.

Augustine. *Confessions.* Trans. R. S. Pine-Coffin. Harmondsworth: Penguin, 1961.

———. *On Christian Doctrine. De doctrina Christiana.* Ed. and trans. R. P. H. Green. Oxford: Clarendon, 1995.

———. *On the Consensus of the Evangelists [De consensu evangelistarum].* PL 34: 1041–1230. Trans. NPNF 1.6:77–236.

Basil of Caesarea. *Letters.* Ed. Roy J. Deferrari. and Martin R. P. McGuire. 4 vols. LCL. London: Heinemann, 1961–62.

———. *Longer Rules.* PG 31:901–1305.

———. *Longer Rules.* In *Ascetical Works,* trans. M. Monica Wagner. FOTC 9. Washington, D.C.: Catholic University of America Press, 1950.

———. *On the Holy Spirit.* PG 32:68–217.

Catalogue of the Literary Papyri in the British Museum. Ed. H. J. M. Milne. London: The Trustees, 1927.

Cedrenus, George. *Historiarum Compendium.* PG 121:23–1166.

Chronicon Paschale (284–628). Trans. Michael Whitby and Mary Whitby. Translated Texts for Historians 7. Liverpool: Liverpool University Press, 1989.

Cicero. *De divinatione.* Ed. William Armstead Falconer. LCL. Cambridge: Harvard University Press, 1938.

Clement of Alexandria. *Opera.* Ed. O. Stählin. GCS 12, 15, 17, 39. Leipzig: Hinrichs, 1905–1909.

———. *The Pedagogue. Le Pédagogue.* Ed. Henri-Irénée Marrou, French trans. Marguerite Harl. 3 vols. SC 70, 108, 158. Paris: Cerf, 1960–70.

———. *The Rich Man Who Finds Salvation.* In *Clement of Alexandria: Selections,* ed. G. W. Butterworth. LCL. London: Heinemann, 1919.

———. *Stromateis.* In *Opera,* ed. O. Stählin, GCS 15, 17. Leipzig: Hinrichs, 1909.

Cosmas Indicopleustes. *Christian Topography.* Ed. Wanda Wolska-Conus. SC 159. Paris: Cerf, 1970.

Cyril of Alexandria. *Commentary on John.* PG 73:9–1056; 74:9–756.

Cyril of Scythopolis. *Life of Euthymius.* In *Kyrillos von Skythopolis,* ed. Eduard Schwartz. *Texte und Untersuchungen* 49.2 (1939): 3–85.

———. *Life of Sabas.* In *Kyrillos von Skythopolis,* ed. Eduard Schwartz. *Texte und Untersuchungen* 49.2 (1939): 85–200.

———. *The Lives of the Monks of Palestine.* Trans. R. M. Price and John Binns. Cistercian Studies 114. Kalamazoo: Cistercian Publications, 1991.

Denha. *Life of Maroutha.* PO 3.1.53–96.

Dionysius, Pseudo-. *Corpus Dionysiacum.* Ed. Beate Suchla et al. 2 vols. Berlin: De Gruyter, 1990–91.

———. *The Complete Works.* Trans. Colm Luibheid with forward and notes by Paul Rorem. New York: Paulist Press, 1987.

Dorotheus of Gaza. *Œuvres spirituelles.* Ed. L. Regnault and J. de Préville. Paris: Cerf, 1963.

———. *Discourses and Sayings.* Trans. Eric P. Wheeler. Cistercian Studies 33. Kalamazoo: Cistercian, 1977.

Egeria. *Travels. Journal de voyage.* Ed. Pierre Maraval. SC 296. Paris: Cerf, 1982.

———. *Egeria's Travels.* Trans. John Wilkinson. 3rd. ed. Warminster: Aris and Phillips, 1999.

————. *Diary of a Pilgrimage.* Trans. George E. Gingras. ACW 38. New York: Paulist, 1970.

Ephrem the Syrian. *Hymns against Heresies. Hymnen contra haereses.* Ed. Edmund Beck. 2 vols. CSCO 169, 170. Louvain: Durbecq, 1957.

————. *Hymns on Faith. Des heiligen Ephraem des Syrers: Hymnen De Fide.* Ed. Edmund Beck. CSCO 154. Louvain: Durbecq, 1955.

————. *Hymns on Paradise. Des heiligen Ephraem des Syrers: Hymnen De Paradiso und Contra Julianum.* Ed. Edmund Beck. CSCO 174. Louvain: CSCO, 1957.

————. *Hymns on Paradise.* Trans. Sebastian Brock. Crestwood, N.Y.: St. Vladimir's Seminary Press, 1990.

————. *Hymns on the Nativity.* Ed. Edmund Beck. CSCO 186. Louvain: CSCO, 1959.

————. *Hymns.* Trans. Kathleen McVey. New York: Paulist, 1989.

Epiphanius of Salamis. *Panarion.* Ed. K. Holl and J. Dummer. 3 vols. GCS 25, 31^2, 37^2. Leipzig: Hinrichs, 1915, 1980, 1985.

————. *The Panarion of St. Epiphanius, Bishop of Salamis: Selected Passages.* Trans. Philip R. Amedon. New York: Oxford University Press, 1990.

Eusebius of Caesarea. *Ecclesiastical History. Historia Ecclesiastica.* Greek text with English trans. by Kirsopp Lake and J. E. L. Oulton. 2 vols. LCL. London: Heinemann, 1926–32.

————. *Ecclestiastical History. Eusebius Werke 2.1–3: Die Kirchengeschichte.* Ed. E. Schwartz. GCS 9.1–3. Leipzig: Hinrichs, 1903–1909.

————. *The History of the Church from Christ to Constantine.* Trans. G. A. Williamson. Hammondsworth: Penguin, 1965.

————. *Life of Constantine.* Trans. Averil Cameron and Stuart G. Hall. Oxford: Clarendon, 1999.

———— *Tricennial Oration.* In *In Praise of Constantine: A Historical Study and New Translation of Eusebius's Tricennial Orations,* trans. Harold Allen Drake. Berkeley: University of California Press, 1976.

Evagrius of Pontus. *Letter to Melania.* Trans. M. Parmentier. *Bijdragen, tijdschrift voor filosofie en theologie* 46 (1985): 2–38.

————. *Practicus. Traité pratique, ou, le moine.* Ed. A. and C. Guillaumont. 2 vols. SC 170, 171. Paris: Cerf, 1971.

————. *The Praktikos and Chapters on Prayer.* Trans. John Eudes Bamberger. Spencer, Mass.: Cistercian, 1970.

Gerontius. *The Life of Melania the Younger.* Ed. and trans. Elizabeth A. Clark. New York: Mellen, 1984.

Gospel of Nicodemus. In *Evangelia apocrypha,* ed. C. Tischendorf, 210–486. 2nd ed. Leipzig, 1876.

Gospel of Nicodemus. ANF 8:416–467.

Gospel of Truth. L'Évangile de vérité. Ed. J. E. Ménard. Nag Hammadi Studies 2. Leiden: Brill, 1972.

Gregory of Nazianzus. *Autobiographical Poems.* Ed. and trans. Caroline White. Cambridge: Cambridge University Press, 1996.

————. *Funeral Orations.* In *Funeral Orations by Saint Gregory Nazianzen and Saint*

Ambrose, trans. Leo P. McCauley et al. FOTC 22. Washington, D.C.: Catholic University Press, 1953.

———. *Letters. Lettres*. Ed. Paul Gallay. Paris: Les Belles Lettres, 1967.

———. "On Baptism" (Oration 40). In *Grégoire de Nazianze: Discours 38–41*, ed. C. Moreschini and P. Gallay. SC 358. Paris: Cerf, 1990.

———. *On God and Man: The Theological Poetry of Gregory of Nazianzus*. Trans. Peter Gilbert. Crestwood, N.Y.: St. Vladimir's Seminary Press, 2001.

———. *Orations*. PG 35 and 36.

———. *Poems*. PG 37:397–1600.

Gregory of Nyssa. *Against Eunomius*. In *Gregorii Nysseni Opera: Vols. 1 and 2*, ed. Werner Jaeger. 2nd ed. Leiden: Brill, 1960.

———. *Against Eunomius*. Trans. NPNF 2.5:35–100, 250–314, 135–248 (in that order).

———. *Commentary on the Song of Songs*. In *Gregorii Nysseni Opera: Vol. 6*, ed. Werner Jaeger and Hermann Langerbeck. Leiden: Brill, 1960.

———. *Homilies on Ecclesiastes*. In *Gregory of Nyssa: Homelies on Ecclesiastes: An English Version with Supporting Studies*, ed. Stuart George Hall. Berlin: de Gruyter, 1993.

———. *Letters. Gregorii Nysseni Epistulae*. Ed. G. Pasquali. Leiden: Brill, 1959.

———. *Life of Gregory the Wonderworker*. In *Gregorii Nysseni Sermones*, ed. Gunther Heil. 3 vols. Leiden: Brill, 1990.

———. *Life of Gregory the Wonderworker*. In *St. Gregory Thaumaturgus: Life and Works*, trans. Michael Slusser. FOTC 98. Washington, D.C.: Catholic University Press, 1998.

———. *Life of Macrina. Grégoire de Nysse, Vie de Sainte Macrine*. Ed. Pierre Maraval. SC 178. Paris: Cerf, 1971.

———. *Life of Macrina*. In *Gregorii Nysseni: Opera Ascetica*, ed. V. Woods Callahan. 370–414. Leiden: Brill, 1952.

———. *Life of Macrina*. In *Gregory of Nyssa: Ascetical Works*, trans. Virginia Woods Callahan, 159–91. FOTC 58. Washington, D.C.: Catholic University Press, 1967.

———. *The Life of Saint Macrina by Gregory Bishop of Nyssa*. Trans. Kevin Corrigan. Toronto: Peregrina, 1998.

———. *Life of Moses*. Trans. Abraham J. Malherbe and Everett Ferguson. New York: Paulist, 1978.

———. *On the Inscriptions of the Psalms*. In *Gregorii Nysseni Opera: Vol. 5*, ed. Werner Jaeger and J. McDonough. Leiden: Brill, 1962.

———. *Gregory of Nyssa's Treatise on the Inscriptions of the Psalms*. Trans. Ronald E. Heine. Oxford: Clarendon, 1995.

———. *On the Soul and Resurrection*. PG 46: 11–160.

———. *St. Gregory of Nyssa: The Soul and Resurrection*. Trans. Catherine P. Roth. Crestwood, N.Y.: St. Vladimir's Seminary Press, 1993.

Herodotus. *Histories*. Ed. Alfred D. Godley. 4 vols. LCL. London: Heinemann, 1930–38.

Hesychius of Alexandria. *Lexicon*. Ed. Kurt Latte. 2 vols. Copenhagen: Munksgaard, 1953.

Hippolytus of Rome. *On the Apostolic Tradition.* Ed. Gregory Dix. 2nd ed. London: S.P.C.K., 1968.

History of the Monks of Egypt. Historia Monachorum in Aegypto. Ed. A.-J. Festugière. Subsidia Hagiographica 53. Brussels: Société des Bollandistes, 1971.

History of the Monks of Egypt. The Lives of the Desert Fathers. Trans. Norman Russell. London: Mowbray, 1980.

Irenaeus. *Against the Heresies. Contre les hérésies.* Ed. Adelin Rousseau and Louis Doutreleau et al. 5 vols. SC 34, etc. Paris: Cerf, 1952–.

———. *Against the Heresies.* In *Irenaeus of Lyons,* trans. Robert M. Grant. London: Routledge, 1997.

Jacob of Serug. *A Metrical Homily on Holy Mar Ephrem.* Ed. and trans. Joseph P. Amar. *PO* 47.1. Turnhout: Brepols, 1995.

Jerome. *Against Jovinian.* PL 23:211–338

———. *Letters. Jérôme: Correspondance.* Ed. J. Labourt. 8 vols. Paris: Budé, 1949–1963.

———. *Letters.* Trans. W. H. Freemantle. NPNF 2.6:1–295.

———. *Life of Hilarion.* PL 23:29–54.

———. *Life of Hilarion.* In *Early Christian Biographies,* ed. Roy J. Deferrari, trans. Marie Ligouri Ewald. Washington, D.C.: Catholic University Press, 1952.

———. *Life of Paul the First Hermit.* PL 23:17–28.

———. *On Illustrious Men. De viris illustribus.* Ed. W. Herding. Leipzig: Teubner, 1924.

———. *On Illustrious Men.* Trans. Thomas P. Halton. FOTC 100. Washington: Catholic University of America Press, 1999.

John Cassian. *Conferences.* Trans. Colm Luibheid. New York: Paulist, 1985.

John Chrysostom. *Homilies on Ephesians.* PG 62:9–176. NPNF 1.13:46–172

———. *Homilies on First Corinthians.* PG 61:9–382. NPNF 1.12.

———. *Homilies on Hebrews.* PG 63:9–236. NPNF 1.14:335–524.

———. *Homilies on John.* PG 59:23–482. NPNF 1.14:1–334.

———. *Homilies on Matthew.* PG 57:13–58:794. NPNF 1.10:1–334.

———. *Homilies on Philemon.* PG 62:701–720. NPNF 1.13:545–557.

———. *Homilies on Romans.* PG 60:391–682. NPNF 1.11:329–564.

———. *Homilies on the Acts of the Apostles.* PG 60:13–384. NPNF 1.11:1–328

John Moschus. *Spiritual Meadow (Pratum Spirituale).* PG 87.3.2851–3112.

———. *The Spiritual Meadow.* Trans. John Wortley. Kalamazoo, Mich.: Cistercian, 1992.

John of Alexandria. *Encomium on Apa Mena.* In *Apa Mena: A Selection of Coptic Texts Relating to St. Menas,* ed. James Drescher. Cairo: Publications de la Société d'Archéologie Copte, 1946.

John of Damascus. *The Fount of Knowledge: Dialectics.* PG 94:521–676.

———. *On the Orthodox Faith.* PG 94:789–1228.

———. *Writings.* Trans. Frederic H. Chase, Jr. Washington: Catholic University of America Press, 1970.

Leontius of Neapolis. *Life of John the Almsgiver.* In *Vie de Syméon le Fou et Vie de Jean de Chypre,* ed. A.-J. Festugière, 257–637. Bibliothèque archéologique et historique 95. Paris: Geuthner, 1974.

————. *Life of Symeon the Fool.* In *Vie de Syméon le Fou et Vie de Jean de Chypre,* ed. A.-J. Festugière, text ed. Lennart Rydén, 1–222. Bibliothèque archéologique et historique 95. Paris: Geuthner, 1974.

————. *Life of Symeon the Fool.* In *Symeon the Holy Fool: Leontius's Life and the Late Antique City,* trans. Derek Krueger, 131–71. Transformation of the Classical Heritage 25. Berkeley: University of California Press, 1996.

Life of Chariton. "La Vie prémétaphrastique de s. Chariton." Ed. G. Garitte. *Bulletin de l'Institut Historique Belge de Rome* 21 (1941): 5–46.

Life of Chariton. In *Ascetic Behavior in Greco-Roman Antiquity: A Sourcebook,* ed. Vincent Wimbush, trans. Leah Di Segni, 393–421. Minneapolis: Fortress, 1990.

Life of Daniel the Stylite. In *Les saints stylites,* ed. H. Delehaye, 1–94. Subsidia hagiographica 14. Brussels: Société des Bollandistes, 1923.

Life of Daniel the Stylite. In *Three Byzantine Saints,* trans. Elizabeth Dawes and Norman H. Baynes, 1–71. Crestwood, N.Y.: St. Vladimir's Seminary Press, 1977.

Life and Miracles of Thecla. Vie et miracles de Sainte Thècle: Texte grec, traduction et commentaire. Ed. and French trans. Gilbert Dagron. Brussels: Société des Bollandistes, 1978.

Life of Pachomius (Vita prima Graeca). Ed. F. Halkin. Subsidia Hagiographica 19. Brussels: Société des Bollandistes, 1932.

Life of Pindar. In *Scholia vetera in Pindari carmina,* ed. A. B. Drachmann, 1:1–11. Leipzig: Teubner, 1903; repr. Amsterdam: Hakkart, 1969.

Life of Pindar. Trans. in Mary R. Lefkowitz. *The Lives of the Greek Poets,* 155–57. Baltimore: Johns Hopkins, 1981.

Macarius, Pseudo-. *Homilies. Die 50 geistlichen Homilien des Makarios.* Ed. H. Dörries, E. Klostermann, and M. Kroeger. Patristische Texte und Studien 4. Berlin: de Gruyter, 1964.

————. *The Fifty Spiritual Homilies; and, The Great Letter.* Trans. George Maloney. New York: Paulist, 1992.

Man of God of Edessa. La légende syriaque de saint Alexis, l'homme de Dieu. Ed. Arthur Amiaud. Bibliothèque de l'Ecole des Hautes Etudes 79. Paris, 1889.

Menologio di Basilio II [Cod. Vaticano greco 1613]. 2 vols. Turin: Bocca, 1907 (facsimile).

Menologium of Basil II. PG 117.9–614 (text).

Methodius of Olympus. *On the Resurrection.* PG 18:265–329.

————. *Symposium.* Trans. Hebert Musurillo. ACW 27. Westminster, Md.: Newman, 1958.

Miracles of Artemios. In *The Miracles of St. Artemios: A Collection of Miracle Stories by an Anonymous Author of Seventh-Century Byzantium,* trans. with an introduction and commentary by Virgil S. Crisafulli and John W. Nesbitt, with an essay by John F. Haldon. Leiden: Brill, 1997.

Miracles of Artemios. In *Varia Graeca Sacra: sbornik greceskich neizdannych bogoslovskich tekstov IV-XV vekov,* ed. A. Papadopoulos-Kerameus, 1–75. Zapiski Istoriko-filologicheskago fakul'teta Imperatorskago S.-Peterburgskago universiteta (Records of the Historical-Philological faculty of the University of St. Petersburg) 95. St. Petersburg: Krishbaum, 1909. Repr. with new preface by Jürgen

Dummer. Leipzig: Zentralantiquariat der Deutschen Demokratischen Republik, 1975.

Miracles of Cosmas and Damian. Kosmas und Damian: Texte und Einleitung. Ed. Ludwig Deubner. Leipzig: Teubner, 1907.

Miracles of Cosmas and Damian. In *Sainte Thècle, Saints Côme et Damien, Saints Cyr et Jean (Extraits), et Saint Georges,* trans. A.-J. Festugière, 83–213. Paris: Picard, 1971.

Miracles of Thecla. In *Vie et miracles de Sainte Thècle: Texte grec, traduction et commentaire,* ed. Gilbert Dagron. Brussels: Société des Bollandistes, 1978.

Novum testamentum Graece. Ed. Eberhard and Erwin Nestle, revised by Barbara and Kurt Aland. 26th ed. Stuttgart: Deutsche Bibelgesellschaft, 1985.

Nicander of Colophon. *Poems and Poetical Fragments.* Ed. A. S. F. Gow and A. F. Scholfield. Cambridge: Cambridge University Press, 1953.

Origen. *Against Celsus. Contra Celsum.* Trans. Henry Chadwick. Cambridge: Cambridge University Press, 1965.

———. *Homilies on Genesis and Exodus.* Trans. Ronald E. Heine. FOTC 71. Washington: Catholic University of America Press, 1982.

———. *On First Principles. Traité des principes.* Ed. Henri Crouzel and Manlio Simonetti. Vol. 3 (books 3 and 4). SC 268. Paris: Cerf, 1980.

———. *On First Principles.* Book 4. In *Biblical Interpretation in the Early Church,* trans. Karlfried Froehlich. 48–78. Philadelphia: Fortress, 1984.

Palladius. *Dialogue on the Life of John Chrysostom.* Trans. R. T. Meyer. ACW 45. New York: Newman, 1985.

———. *Lausiac History. La storia lausiaca.* Ed. G. J. M. Bartelink. Vite dei Santi 2. Milan: Mondadori, 1974.

———. *Lausiac History.* Ed. Cuthbert Butler. 2 vols. Texts and Studies: Contributions to Biblical and Patristic Literature 6. Cambridge: Cambridge University Press, 1898–1904.

———. *The Lausiac History.* Trans. Robert T. Meyer. Ancient Christian Writers 34. New York: Newman, 1964.

Papyrus grecs et démotiques recueillis en Égypte. Ed. Théodore Reinach. Paris: Leroux, 1905.

Paulinus. *The Life of Ambrose.* In *Early Christian Biographies,* trans. John A. Lacy, ed. Roy J. Deferrari, 27–66. FOTC 15. Washington, D.C.: Catholic University Press, 1952.

Photius. *Bibliotheca.* Ed. R. Henry. 8 vols. Paris: Belles Lettres, 1959–77.

Plato. *Dialogues.* Ed. Harold North Fowler et al. 10 vols. LCL. London: Heinemann, 1926–1961.

———. *Phaedrus.* Trans. Robin Waterfield. Oxford: Oxford University Press, 2002.

Pliny the Elder. *Natural History.* Ed. H. Rackham and W. H. S. Jones. 9 vols. LCL. London: Heinemann, 1938–63.

Plotinus. *Enneads.* Ed. and trans. A. H. Armstrong. 7 vols. LCL. Cambridge: Harvard University Press, 1966–1988.

Porphyry. *Against the Christians. "Gegen die Christen," 15 Bücher: Zeugnisse, Fragmente und Referate.* Ed. Adolf von Harnack. Abhandlung der königlich preussischen Akademie der Wissenschaften, Phil. Hist. Klasse 1. Berlin: Verlag der königl. Akademie der Wiss., 1916.

———. *Life of Plotinus.* In *Plotinus: Enneads,* ed. and trans. A. H. Armstrong, 1: 2–85. LCL. Cambridge: Harvard University Press, 1966.

———. *To Marcella. Porphyry the Philosopher: To Marcella.* Ed. and trans. Kathleen O'Brien Wicker. Atlanta: Scholars Press, 1987.

Procopius. *Wars.* Ed. and trans. H. B. Dewing. 7 vols. LCL. London: Heinemann, 1914–1940.

Romanos the Melodist. *Hymns. Sancti Romani Melodi Cantica Genuina.* Ed. Paul Maas and C. A. Trypanis. Oxford: Clarendon, 1963.

———. *Romanos le Mélode: Hymnes.* Ed. and French trans. José Grosdidier de Matons. 5 vols. SC 99, 110, 114, 128, 283. Paris: Cerf, 1965–1981.

———. *On the Life of Christ: Kontakia.* Trans. Ephrem Lash. San Francisco: HarperCollins, 1995.

———. *Sacred Song from the Byzantine Pulpit: Romanos the Melodist.* Trans. R. J. Schork. Gainesville: University of Florida Press, 1995.

———. *Kontakia of Romanos, Byzantine Melodist.* Trans. Marjorie Carpenter. 2 vols. Columbia: University of Missouri Press, 1970–73.

Romanos the Melodist, Pseudo-. *Sancti Romani Melodi Cantica: Cantica Dubia.* Ed. Paul Maas and C. A. Trypanis. Berlin: De Gruyter, 1970.

Sacrorum conciliorum nova et amplissima collectio. Ed. G. D. Mansi. 53 vols. Paris: Weller, 1901–27; repr. Graz: Akademische Druck-und Verlagsanstalt, 1960.

Sulpicius Severus. *Letters.* Ed. C. Hahn. Corpus scriptorum ecclesiasticorum Latinorum 1:138–51. NPNF 2.11.18–23.

Syriac History of John. Apocryphal Acts of the Apostles: Edited from Syriac Manuscripts in the British Museum and Other Libraries, ed. and trans. William Wright. Amsterdam: Philo, 1968; originally published 1871.

The Teaching of Addai. Ed. and trans. George Howard. Texts and Translations 16. Chico: Scholars Press, 1981.

———. *The Doctrine of Addai, the Apostle, Now First Edited in a Complete Form in the Original Syriac.* Ed. George Phillips. London: Trübner, 1876.

Tertullian. *De monogamia.* ANF 4:59–72.

Theodore of Mopsuestia. *On Eucharist and Liturgy.* Ed. A. Mingana. Woodbrooke Studies 6. Cambridge: Heffer and Sons, 1933.

———. *On Job [fragment].* PG 66:697–98.

Theodoret of Cyrrhus. *Religious History. Histoire des moines de Syrie.* Ed. Pierre Canivet and Alice Leroy-Molinghen. 2 vols. SC 234 and 257. Paris: Cerf, 1977–79.

———. *A History of the Monks of Syria [Religious History].* Trans. R. M. Price. Cistercian Studies 88. Kalamazoo, Mich.: Cistercian, 1985.

———. *Commentary on the Psalms.* PG 80.857–1997.

———. *Commentary on the Psalms.* Trans. Robert C. Hill. 2 vols. FOTC. Washington, D.C.: Catholic University of America Press, 2000–2001.

———. *Commentary on Isaiah. Commentaire sur Isaie.* Ed. J. N. Guinot. 3 vols. SC 276, 295, 315. Paris: Cerf, 1981–84.

———. *Commentary on Zechariah.* PG 81.1873–1960.

———. *Ecclesiastical History. Kirchengeschichte.* Ed. L. Parmentier and F. Scheid-weiler. GCS. Berlin: Akademie-Verlag, 1954.

———. *Letters. Correspondance.* Ed. Yvan Azéma. 4 vols. SC 40, 98, 111, 429. Paris: Cerf, 1955–98.

———. *The Cure for Pagan Maladies. Thérapeutique des maladies helléniques.* Ed. Pierre Canivet. 2 vols. SC 57. Paris: Cerf, 1958.

———. *On Divine Love.* In *Histoire des moines de Syrie,* ed. Pierre Canivet and Alice Leroy-Molinghen, 2:245–315. Paris: Cerf, 1977–79.

———. *Questions on Exodus.* PG 80:225–98.

Theognis. *Elegies.* Ed. Douglas Young. Leipzig: Teubner, 1961.

Secondary Sources

Alexiou, Margaret. *After Antiquity: Greek Language, Myth and Metaphor.* Ithaca: Cornell University Press, 2002.

———. *Ritual Lament in Greek Tradition.* Cambridge: Cambridge University Press, 1974.

Allen, Pauline. "The Homilist and the Congregation: A Case Study of Chrysostom's Homilies on Hebrews." *Augustinianum* 36 (1996): 387–421.

Allen, Pauline, and Wendy Mayer. "Traditions of Constantinopolitan Preaching: Towards a New Assessment of Where Chrysostom Preached What." *Byzantin-ishe Forschungen* 24 (1997): 93–114.

Amar, Joseph P. "Byzantine Ascetic Monachism and Greek Bias in the *Vita* Tradi-tion of Ephrem the Syrian." *Orientalia Christiana Periodica* 58 (1992): 123–56.

Andreescu-Treadgold, Irina. "The Mosaic Workshop at San Vitale." In *Mosaici a S. Vitale e altri restauri: Il restauro in situ di mosaici parietali,* ed. Anna Maria Iannucci, Cesare Fiori, and Cetty Muscolino, 31–41 (with interleaved corrected version, 1–8). Ravenna: Longo, 1992.

———. "The Two Original Mosaic Decorations of San Vitale." *Quaderni di soprin-tendenze (Ravenna)* 3 (1997): 16–22.

Andreescu-Treadgold, Irina, and Warren Treadgold. "Procopius and the Imperial Panels of S. Vitale." *Art Bulletin* 79 (1997): 708–23.

Apostolopoulos, Charalambos. *Phaedo Christianus: Studien zur Verbindung und Ab-wägung des Verhältnisses zwischen dem platonishen "Phaidon" und dem Dialog Gregors von Nyssa "Über die Seele und die Auferstehung."* Frankfurt am Main: Peter Lang, 1986.

Arranz, M. "La Liturge des Présanctifiés de l'ancien Euchologe byzantin." *Orien-talia Christiana Periodica* 47 (1981): 332–88.

Azéma, Yvan. "Sur la date de la mort de Théodoret de Cyr." *Pallas* 31 (1984): 137–55.

Bagnall, Roger S. "Jesus Reads a Book." *JThS* 51 (2000): 577–88.

Bandy, Anastasius C. "Addenda et Corrigenda to Carpenter, M. *Kontakia of Ro-manos, Byzantine Melodist, Vol. 2: On the Christian Life,* Part 1." *Byzantine Studies* 7 (1980): 78–113.

————. "Addenda et Corrigenda to Carpenter, M. *Kontakia of Romanos, Byzantine Melodist, Vol. 2: On the Christian Life,* Part 2." *Byzantine Studies* 7 (1980): 221–60.

Barasch, Moshe. *Icon: Studies in the History of an Idea.* New York: New York University Press, 1992.

Barker, Ernest. *Social and Poltical Thought in Byzantium from Justinian I to the Last Palaeologos.* Oxford: Clarendon, 1957.

Barkhuizen, J. H. "Christ as Metaphor in the Hymns of Romanos the Melodist." Parts 1 and 2. *Acta Patristica et Byzantina* 2 (1991): 1–15; 3 (1992): 1–14.

————. "Romanos Melodos and the Composition of his Hymns: Prooimion and Final Strophe." *Hellenika* 40 (1989): 62–77.

Barnes, T[imothy] D. "Porphyry *Against the Christians*: Date and the Attribution of Fragments." *JThS* n.s. 24 (1973): 424–42.

Barnes, Timothy. *Constantine and Eusebius.* Cambridge, Mass.: Harvard University Press, 1981.

Barthes, Roland. "Authors and Writers." In *Critical Essays,* trans. Richard Howard, 143–50. Evanston: Northwestern University Press, 1972. Originially published as "Écrivains et écrivants," in *Essais critique* (Paris: Seuil, 1964), 147–54.

————. "The Death of the Author." In *Image, Music, Text,* trans. Stephen Heath, 142–48. New York: Hill and Wang, 1977. Originally published as "La mort de l'auteur" in 1968, reprt. in *Le bruissement de la langue* (Paris: Seuil, 1984), 61–67.

Barton, Carlin A. *Roman Honor: The Fire in the Bones.* Berkeley: University of California Press, 2001.

Baudrillard, Jean. *Simulacra and Simulation.* Trans. Sheila Faria Glaser. Ann Arbor: University of Michigan Press, 1991.

Bauer, W. "The Picture of the Apostle in Early Christian Tradition." In *New Testament Apocrypha,* ed. Edgar Hennecke and Wilhelm Schneemelcher, 3rd ed., trans. R. McL. Wilson, 2:35–74. Philadelphia: Westminster, 1965.

Bauerline, Mark. "A Thanking Task: What Acknowledgements Pages Say about Academic Life." *Times Literary Supplement,* November 9, 2001.

Bell, Catherine. "Performance." In *Critical Terms for Religious Studies,* ed. Mark C. Taylor, 205–24. Chicago: University of Chicago Press, 1998.

————. *Ritual Theory, Ritual Practice.* New York: Oxford University Press, 1992.

Bergjan, Silke-Petra. "Die dogmatische Funktionalisierung der Exegese nach Theodoret von Cyrus." In *Christliche Exegese zwischen Nicaea und Chalcedon,* ed. J. van Oort and U. Wickert, 32–48. Kampen, The Netherlands: Pharos, 1992.

Bergman, Robert P. "Portraits of the Evangelists in Greek Manuscripts." In *Illuminated Greek Manuscripts from American Collections,* ed. Gary Vikan, 44–49. Princeton: Princeton University Press, 1973.

Bienert, Wolfgang A. "The Picture of the Apostles in Early Christian Tradition." In *New Testament Apocrypha,* ed. Edgar Hennecke and Wilhelm Schneemelcher, 5th ed., trans. R. McL. Wilson, 2:5–27. Cambridge: Clark, 1992.

Binns, John. *Ascetics and Ambassadors of Christ: The Monasteries of Palestine 314–631.* Oxford: Clarendon, 1994.

Black, C. Clifton. *Mark: Images of an Apostolic Interpreter.* Columbia: University of South Carolina Press, 1994.

Blum, G. "Oikonomia und Theologia: Der Hintergrund einer konfessionellen Differenz zwischen östlichen and westlichen Christentum." *Ostkirchliche Studien* 33 (1984): 281–301.

Boer, Roland. *Knockin' on Heaven's Door: The Bible and Popular Culture.* London: Routledge, 1999.

Bourdieu, Pierre. *The Logic of Practice.* Trans. Richard Nice. Stanford: Stanford University Press, 1990. Originally published as *Le sens pratique,* 1980.

Bové, Paul. "Discourse." In *Critical Terms for Literary Study,* ed. Frank Lentricchia and Thomas McLaughlin, 2nd ed., 50–65. Chicago: Chicago University Press, 1995.

Bovon, François. "Byzantine Witnesses for the Apocryphal Acts of the Apostles." In *The Apocryphal Acts of the Apostles: Harvard Divinity School Studies,* ed. François Bovon, Ann Graham Brock, and Christopher R. Matthew, 87–98. Cambridge: Harvard University Press, 1999.

Bowersock, G. W. "The Syriac Life of Rabbula and Syrian Hellenism." In *Greek Biography and Panegyric in Late Antiquity,* ed. Tomas Hägg and Philip Rousseau, 255–71. Berkeley: University of California Press, 2000.

Brakke, David. *Athanasius and the Politics of Asceticism.* Oxford: Clarendon, 1995.

———. "Ethiopian Demons: Male Sexuality, the Black-Skinned Other, and the Monastic Self." *Journal of the History of Sexuality* 10 (2001): 501–35.

———. "The Problematization of Noctural Emissions in Early Christian Syria, Egypt, and Gaul." *JECS* 3 (1995): 419–60.

Brightman, F. E., ed. *Liturgies Eastern and Western.* Oxford: Clarendon, 1895.

Brisson, Luc, et al. *Porphyre: La vie de Plotin.* 2 vols. Paris: Vrin, 1982–1992.

Brock, Sebastian. "Dialogue Hymns of the Syriac Churches." *Sobornost: Eastern Churches Review* 5:2 (1983): 35–45.

———. "Eusebius and Syriac Christianity." In *Eusebius, Christianity, and Judaism,* ed. H. W. Attridge and G. Hata, 212–34. Detroit: Wayne State University Press, 1992. Repr. in Sebastian Brock, *From Ephrem to Romanos: Interactions between Syriac and Greek in Late Antiquity,* Variorum Collected Studies Series 664 (Aldershot: Ashgate, 1999), II.

———. "From Ephrem to Romanos." *Studia Patristica* 20 (1989): 139–51. Repr. in Sebastian Brock, *From Ephrem to Romanos: Interactions between Syriac and Greek in Late Antiquity* (Aldershot: Ashgate, 1999), IV.

———. *From Ephrem to Romanos: Interactions between Syriac and Greek in Late Antiquity.* Aldershot: Ashgate, 1999.

———. *The Luminous Eye: The Spiritual World Vision of Saint Ephrem the Syrian.* Rev. ed. Kalamazoo: Cistercian, 1992.

———. *Saint Ephrem the Syrian: Hymns on Paradise.* Crestwood, N.Y.: St. Vladimir's Seminary Press, 1990.

———. "Some Aspects of Greek Words in Syriac." In *Synkretismus im syrisch-persischen Kulturgebiet,* ed. A. Dietrich, 80–108. Göttingen: Vandenhoek und Ruprecht, 1975. Repr. in Sebastian Brock, *Syriac Perspectives on Late Antiquity* (London: Variorum, 1984), IV.

―――. "Syriac Dispute Poems: The Various Types." In *Dispute Poems and Dialogues in the Ancient and Mediaeval Near East: Forms and Types of Literary Debates in Semitic and Related Literatures,* ed. G. J. Reinink and H. L. J. Vanstiphout, 109–19. Orientalia Lovaniensia Analecta 42. Leuven: Department Oriëntalistiek, 1991. Repr. in Sebastian Brock, *From Ephrem to Romanos: Interactions between Syriac and Greek in Late Antiquity* (Aldershot: Ashgate, 1999), VII.

Brown, Peter. *Authority and the Sacred: Aspects of the Christianization of the Roman World.* Cambridge: Cambridge University Press, 1995.

―――. *The Body and Society: Men, Women, and Sexual Renunciation in Early Christianity.* New York: Columbia University Press, 1988.

―――. *The Cult of the Saints: Its Rise and Function in Latin Christianity.* Chicago: University of Chicago Press, 1981.

―――. *Power and Persuasion in Late Antiquity: Towards a Christian Empire.* Madison: University of Wisconsin Press, 1992.

―――. "The Rise and Function of the Holy Man in Late Antiquity." In *Society and the Holy in Late Antiquity,* 103–52. Berkeley: University of California Press, 1982. First published in *Journal of Roman Studies* 61 (1971): 80–101.

―――. "The Saint as Exemplar in Late Antiquity." In *Saints and Virtues,* ed. Jack Stratton Hawley, 3–14. Berkeley: University of California Press, 1987. First published in *Representations* 1 (1983): 1–25.

―――. *Society and the Holy in Late Antiquity,* Berkeley: University of California Press, 1982.

―――. "Town, Village and Holy Man: The Case of Syria." In *Society and the Holy in Late Antiquity,* 153–65. Berkeley: University of California Press, 1982.

Brown, Raymond E. *The Gospel According to John.* 2 vols. Anchor Bible 29. Garden City, N.Y.: Doubleday, 1966.

Browning, Robert. "Literacy in the Byzantine World." *BMGS* 4 (1978): 39–54.

―――. "The 'Low Level' Saint's Life in the Early Byzantine World." In *The Byzantine Saint,* ed. Sergei Hackel, 117–27. Studies Supplementary to *Sobornost* 5. San Bernardino, Calif.: Borgo, 1983. Repr. in Robert Browning, *History, Language, and Literacy in the Byzantine World* (London: Variorum, 1989), VIII.

Bruce, F. F. *The Canon of Scripture.* Downers Grove, Ill.: Intervarsity Press, 1988.

Buchthal, Hugo. "A Byzantine Miniature of the Fourth Evangelist and Its Relatives." *DOP* 15 (1961): 127–39.

Buell, Denise Kimber. *Making Christians: Clement of Alexandria and the Rhetoric of Legitimacy.* Princeton: Princeton University Press, 1999.

Burridge, Richard A. *What Are the Gospels? A Comparison with Graeco-Roman Biography.* Cambridge: Cambridge University Press, 1995.

Burrus, Virginia. *"Begotten, Not Made": Conceiving Manhood in Late Antiquity.* Stanford: Stanford University Press, 2000.

―――. *Chastity as Autonomy: Women in the Stories of the Apocryphal Acts.* Studies in Women and Religion 23. Lewiston: Edwin Mellen, 1987.

―――. "Is Macrina a Woman? Gregory of Nyssa's *Dialogue on the Soul and Resurrection.*" In *The Blackwell Companion to Postmodern Theology,* ed. Graham Ward, 249–64. Oxford: Blackwell, 2001.

——. "Queer Lives of Saints: Jerome's Hagiography." *Journal of the History of Sexuality* 10 (2001): 442–79.

——. *The Sex Lives of Saints: An Erotics of Ancient Hagiography.* Philadelphia: University of Pennsylvania Press, 2003.

Burton-Christie, Douglas. *The Word in the Desert: Scripture and the Quest for Holiness in Early Christian Monasticism.* New York: Oxford University Press, 1993.

Bury, J. B. "The Nika Riot." *Journal of Hellenic Studies* 17 (1897): 92–119.

Bynum, Carolyn Walker. *Jesus as Mother: Studies in the Spirituality of the High Middle Ages.* Berkeley: University of California Press, 1982.

Cairns, Francis. *Generic Composition in Greek and Roman Poetry.* Edinburgh: Edinburgh University Press, 1972.

Cameron, Alan. *Circus Factions: Blues and Greens at Rome and Byzantium.* Oxford: Oxford University Press, 1976.

Cameron, Averil. "Ascetic Closure and the End of Antiquity." In *Asceticism,* ed. Vincent Wimbush and Richard Valantasis, 147–61. New York: Oxford University Press, 1995.

——. *Christianity and the Rhetoric of Empire: The Development of Christian Discourse.* Berkeley: University of California Press, 1991.

——. "Eusebius's *Vita Constantini* and the Construction of Constantine." In *Portraits: Biographical Representation in the Greek and Latin Literature of the Roman Empire,* ed. M. J. Edwards and S. C. R. Swain, 145–74. Oxford: Clarendon, 1997.

——. "Form and Meaning: The *Vita Constantini* and the *Vita Antonii.*" In *Greek Biography and Panegyric in Late Antiquity,* ed. Tomas Hägg and Philip Rousseau, 72–88. Berkeley: University of California Press, 2000.

——. "The History of the Image of Edessa: The Telling of a Story." In *Okeanos: Essays Presented to Ihor Ševčenko on His Sixtieth Birthday,* ed. Cyril Mango and O. Prisak. *Harvard Ukrainian Studies* 7 (1984): 80–94.

——. *The Mediterranean World in Late Antiquity, AD 395–600.* London: Routledge, 1993.

——. *Procopius and the Sixth Century.* Berkeley: University of California Press, 1985.

Campbell, Sheila D. "Armchair Pilgrims: Ampullae from Aphrodisias in Caria." *Mediaeval Studies* 50 (1988): 539–45.

Canévet, Mariette. *Grégoire de Nysse et l'herméneutique biblique: Étude des rapports entre le langage et la connaissance de Dieu.* Paris: Études augustiniennes, 1983.

Canivet, Pierre. *Le monachisme syrien selon Théodoret de Cyr.* Théologie historique 42. Paris: Beauchesne, 1977.

Carruthers, Mary. *The Book of Memory: A Study of Memory in Medieval Culture.* Cambridge: Cambridge University Press, 1990.

——. *The Craft of Thought: Meditation, Rhetoric, and the Making of Images, 400–1200.* Cambridge Studies in Medieval Literature 34. Cambridge: Cambridge University Press, 1998.

Castelli, Elizabeth. "Mortifying the Body, Curing the Soul: Beyond Ascetic Dualism in *The Life of Saint Syncletica.*" *Differences: A Journal of Feminist Cultural Studies* 4 (1992): 134–53.

———. "Virginity and Its Meaning for Women's Sexuality in Early Christianity." *Journal of Feminist Studies in Religion* 2 (1986): 61–88.

Chadwick, Henry. *Priscillian of Avila: The Occult and the Charismatic in the Early Church.* Oxford: Clarendon, 1976.

Chitty, Derwas. *The Desert a City: An Introduction to the Study of Egyptian and Palestinian Monasticism under the Christian Empire.* Oxford: Blackwell, 1966.

Clark, Elizabeth A. "The Ascetic Impulse in the Religious Life." In *Asceticism,* ed. Vincent Wimbush and Richard Valantasis, 505–10. New York: Oxford University Press, 1995.

———. "Holy Women, Holy Words: Early Christian Women, Social History, and the 'Linguistic Turn.'" *JECS* 6 (1998): 413–30.

———. *Reading Renunciation: Asceticism and Scripture in Early Christianity.* Princeton: Princeton University Press, 1999.

Clark, Gillian. "Philosophic Lives and the Philosophic Life." In *Greek Biography and Panegyric in Late Antiquity,* ed. Tomas Hägg and Philip Rousseau, 29–51. Berkeley: University of California Press, 2000.

Clark, Stephen R. L. "Plotinus: Body and Soul." In *The Cambridge Companion to Plotinus,* ed. Lloyd P. Gerson, 275–95. Cambridge: Cambridge University Press, 1996.

Clavis Patrum Graecorum. Ed. Mauritius Geerard. Turnhout: Brepols, 1974–87.

Cocchini, F. "L'esegesi paolina di Teodoreto di Cirro." *Annali di storia dell'esegesi* 11 (1994): 511–32.

Constas, Nicholas P. "Weaving the Body of God: Proclus of Constantinople, the Theotokos, and the Loom of the Flesh." *JECS* 3 (1995): 169–94.

Cooper, Kate. *The Virgin and the Bride: Idealized Womanhood in Late Antiquity.* Cambridge, Mass.: Harvard University Press, 1996.

Copeland, Kirsti Barrett. *Mapping the Apocalypse of Paul: Geography, Genre and History.* Ph.D. diss., Princeton University, 2001.

Courtney, Edward. "Greek and Latin Acrostichs." *Philologus* 134 (1990): 3–13.

Crisafulli, Virgil S., and John W. Nesbitt. *The Miracles of St. Artemios: A Collection of Miracle Stories by an Anonymous Author of Seventh-Century Byzantium.* Leiden: Brill, 1997.

Crouzel, Henri. "L'Imitation et la 'suite' de Dieu et du Christ dans les premiers siècles chrétiens ainsi que leurs sources gréco-romaines et hébraïques." *JAC* 21 (1978): 7–41.

———. "The School of Alexandria and Its Fortunes." In *History of Theology: The Patristic Period,* ed. Angelo Di Bernardino and Basil Studer, trans. Matthew J. O'Connell, 1:145–84. Collegeville, Minn.: Michael Glazier, 1997.

Culpepper, R. Alan. *John, the Son of Zebedee: The Life of a Legend.* Columbia: University of South Carolina Press, 1994.

Cummings, John T. "The Holy Death-Bed Saint and Penitent: Variation of a Theme." In *The Biographical Works of Gregory of Nyssa,* ed. Andreas Spira, 241–63. Cambridge, Mass.: Philadelphia Patristic Foundation, 1984.

Ćurčić, Slobodan, and Archer St. Clair. *Byzantium at Princeton.* Princeton: Princeton University Press, 1986.

Dagron, Gilbert. "L'Auteur des 'Actes' et des 'Miracles' de Sainte Thècle." *AnBoll* 92 (1974): 5–11.

———. "Holy Images and Likeness." *DOP* 45 (1991): 23–33.

Dalmais, Irenée-Henri. "Tropaire, Kontakion, Canon: Les élélements constitutifs de l'hymnographie byzantine." In *Liturgie und Dichtung: Ein interdisziplinäres Kompendium I: Historische Präsentation,* ed. H. Becker and R. Kaczynski, 421–34. St. Ottilien: EOS-Verlag, 1983.

Daniélou, Jean. *The Bible and the Liturgy.* Liturgical Studies 3. Notre Dame, Ind.: University of Notre Dame Press, 1956; French ed. 1951.

———. *From Shadows to Reality: Studies in the Biblical Typology of the Fathers.* Trans. Wulstan Hibberd. London: Burns and Oates, 1960.

———. *Platonisme et théologie mystique: Doctrine spirituelle de Saint Grégoire de Nysse.* Paris: Aubier, 1944, repr. 1953.

Davies, Stevan L. *The Revolt of the Widows: The Social World of the Apocryphal Acts.* Carbondale, Ill.: Southern Illinois University Press, 1980.

Davis, Stephen J. *The Cult of Saint Thecla: A Tradition of Women's Piety in Late Antiquity.* Oxford: Oxford University Press, 2001.

Deichmann, Friedrich Wilhelm. *Ravenna: Geschichte und Monumente.* Wiesbaden: Steiner, 1969.

Deliyannis, D. M. "A Biblical Model for Serial Biography: The Book of Kings and the Roman *Liber Pontificalis.*" *Revue Bénédictine* 107 (1997): 15–23.

De Lubac, Henri. *Histoire et esprit: L'Intelligence de l'Écriture d'après Origène.* Paris: Aubier, 1950.

den Boeft, J., and A. Hilhorst ed. *Early Christian Poetry: A Collection of Essays.* Supplements to *Vigiliae Christianae* 22. Leiden: Brill, 1993.

Déroche, Vincent. "Pourquoi écrivait-on des recueils de miracles? L'exemple des miracles de Saint Artémios." In *Les saints et leur sanctuaire: textes, images et monuments,* ed. Catherine Jolivet-Lévy, Michel Kaplan, and Jean-Pierre Sodini, 95–116. Byzantina sorbonensia 11. Paris: Publications de la Sorbonne, 1993.

———. "Tensions et contradictions dans les recueils de miracles de la première époque byzantine." In *Miracle et karāma: Hagiographies médiévales comparées,* ed. Denise Aigle, 145–66. Turnhout: Brepols, 2000.

Derrida, Jacques. *Dissemination.* Trans. Barbara Johnson. Chicago: University of Chicago Press, 1981.

———. *Of Grammatology.* Trans. Gayatri Spivak. Baltimore: Johns Hopkins University Press, 1976. Originally published as *De la grammatologie* (Paris: Seuil, 1967).

———. *Writing and Difference.* Trans. Alan Bass. Chicago: University of Chicago Press, 1978. Originally published as *L'écriture et la différence* (Paris: Seuil, 1967).

Detlef, C., and G. Müller. "John III, The Merciful." *The Coptic Encyclopedia* 4:1337–38.

Devos, P. "Egérie à Edesse. S. Thomas l'Apôtre. Le Roi Abgar." *Analecta Bollandiana* 85 (1967): 381–400.

Devos, Paul. "La structure de l'Histoire Philothée de Théodoret de Cyr: Le nombre de chapitres." *AnBoll* 97 (1979): 319–35.

Dictionnaire de Spiritualité. Paris: Beauchesne, 1937–95.

Dix, Gregory. *The Shape of the Liturgy.* 2nd ed. London: Dacre, 1945.

Downey, G. "Julian and Justinian and the Unity of Faith and Culture." *Church History* 28 (1959): 339–49.

Downey, Glanville. *A History of Antioch in Syria: From Seleucus to the Arab Conquest.* Princeton: Princeton University Press, 1961.

Doran, Robert. *The Lives of Symeon Stylites.* Cistercian Studies 112. Kalamazoo, Mich.: Cistercian, 1992.

Drescher, James. *Apa Mena: A Selection of Coptic Texts Relating to St. Menas.* Cairo: Publications de la Société d'Archéologie Copte, 1946.

Drijvers, Han J. W. "Hellenistic and Oriental Origins." In *The Byzantine Saint: University of Birmingham Fourteenth Spring Symposium of Byzantine Studies,* ed. Sergei Hackel, 25–30. San Bernardino, Calif.: Borgo, 1983.

———. "Spätantike Parallelen zur altchristlichen Heiligenverehrung unter besonderer Berücksichtigung des syrischen Stylitenkultus." *Göttingen Orientforschungen* 1, Syrica 17 (1978): 77–113.

Drijvers, J. W. "The Protonike Legend, the *Doctrina Addai,* and Bishop Rabbula of Edessa." *Vigiliae Christianae* 51 (1997): 298–315.

Driver, Tom. *The Magic of Ritual: Our Need for Liberating Rites that Transform Our Lives and Our Communities.* San Francisco: HarperCollins, 1991.

Dubrov, Gregory W. "A Dialogue with Death: Ritual Lament and the *Threnos Theotokou* of Romanos Melodos." *GRBS* 35 (1994): 385–405.

Duncan-Flowers, Maggie. "A Pilgrim's Ampulla from the Shrine of St. John the Evangelist at Ephesus." In *The Blessings of Pilgrimage,* ed. Robert Ousterhout, 125–39. Illinois Byzantine Studies 1. Urbana: University of Illinois Press, 1990.

Durkheim, Émile. *The Elementary Forms of Religious Life.* Trans. Karen E. Fields. New York: Free Press, 1995; original French ed. 1912.

Earl, James W. "Typology and Iconographic Style in Early Medieval Hagiography." *Studies in the Literary Imagination* 8 (1975): 15–46.

Edwards, M. J. "Birth, Death, and Divinity in Porphyry's *Life of Plotinus.*" In *Greek Biography and Panegyric in Late Antiquity,* ed. Tomas Hägg and Philip Rousseau, 52–71. Berkeley: University of California Press, 2000.

Edwards, M. J., and S. C. R. Swain, eds. *Portraits: Biographical Representation in the Greek and Latin Literature of the Roman Empire.* Oxford: Clarendon, 1997.

Elliott, James K., ed. *The Apocryphal New Testament: A Collection of Apocryphal Christian Literature in an English Translation.* Oxford: Clarendon, 1993.

Elm, Susanna. "Marking the Self in Late Antiquity: Inscriptions, Baptism and the Conversion of Mimes." In *Stigmata-Körperinschriften,* ed. Bettine Menke and Barbara Vinken, 47–68. Paderborn: Fink, 2004.

———. *'Virgins of God': The Making of Asceticism in Late Antiquity.* Oxford: Clarendon, 1994.

Elsner, Jaś. *Art and the Roman Viewer: The Transformation of Art from the Pagan World to Christianity.* Cambridge: Cambridge University Press, 1995.

Engelbrecht, Edward. "God's Milk: An Orthodox Confession of the Eucharist." *JECS* 7 (1999): 509–26.

Festugière, André-Jean. *Antioche païenne et chrétienne: Libanius, Chrysostome et les moines de Syrie.* Bibliothèque des écoles françaises d'Athènes et de Rome 194. Paris: Boccard, 1959.

———. "Lieux communs littéraires et thèmes de folk-lore dans l'hagiographie primitive." *Wiener Studien* 73 (1960): 123–52.

———. *Les moines d'Orient.* 4 vols. Paris: Cerf, 1961–65.

FitzGerald, G. M. *A Sixth Century Monastery in Beth-shan (Scythopolis).* Philadelphia: University of Pennsylvania Press, 1939.

Fleischer, E. "Acrostics: Post-Biblical." *Encyclopaedia Judaica* 2:230–31.

———. "Piyyut." *Encyclopaedia Judaica* 13:573–602.

Flusin, Bernard. *Miracle et histoire dans l'oeuvre de Cyrille de Scythopolis.* Paris: Études augustiniennes, 1983.

Ford, Andrew L. "The Seal of Theognis: The Politics of Authorship in Archaic Greece." In *Theognis of Megara: Poetry and the Polis,* ed. Thomas J. Figueira and Gregory Nagy, 82–95. Baltimore: Johns Hopkins University Press, 1985.

Foss, Clive. *Ephesus After Antiquity.* Cambridge: Cambridge University Press, 1979.

Foucault, Michel. "What Is an Author?" In *Language, Counter-Memory, Practice,* trans. Sherry Simon and ed. Donald F. Bouchard. Ithaca: Cornell University Press, 1977.

Fournet, Jean-Luc. *Hellénisme dans l'Égypte du VIe siècle: La bibliothèque et l'œuvre de Dioscore d'Aphrodité.* 2 vols. Cairo: Institut français d'archéologie orientale, 1999.

Fowler, Alastair. *Kinds of Literature: An Introduction to the Theory of Genres and Modes.* Oxford: Clarendon, 1982.

Fox, Robin Lane. "Literacy and Power in Early Christianity." In *Literacy and Power in the Ancient World,* ed. Alan K. Bowman and Greg Woolf, 126–48. Cambridge: Cambridge University Press, 1994.

———. "The *Life of Daniel.*" In *Portraits: Biographical Representation in the Greek and Latin Literature of the Roman Empire,* ed. M. J. Edwards and Simon Swain, 175–226. Oxford: Clarendon, 1997.

Frank, Georgia. "Macrina's Scar: Homeric Allusion and Heroic Identity in Gregory of Nyssa's *Life of Macrina.*" *JECS* 8 (2000): 511–30.

———. *The Memory of the Eyes: Pilgrimage to Living Saints in Christian Late Antiquity.* Berkeley: University of California Press, 2000.

———. " 'Taste and See': The Eucharist and the Eyes of Faith in the Fourth Century," *Chruch History* 70 (2001): 619–43.

Frankfurter, David T. M. *Elijah in Upper Egypt: The Apocalypse of Elijah and Early Egyptian Christianity.* Minneapolis: Fortress, 1993.

———. "Stylites and *Phallobates*: Pillar Religions in Late Antique Syria." *VC* 44 (1990): 168–98.

Friend, A. M. "The Portraits of the Evangelists in Greek and Latin Manuscripts." Parts 1 and 2. *Art Studies: Medieval, Renaissance and Modern* 5 (1927): 115–50; 7 (1929): 3–46.

Galavaris, George. *Bread and the Liturgy: The Symbolism of Early Christian and Byzantine Bread Stamps.* Madison: University of Wisconsin Press, 1970.

Gamble, Harry Y. *Books and Readers in the Early Church: A History of Early Christian Texts*. New Haven: Yale University Press, 1995.

Gärtner, Hans Arnim. "Akrostichon." In *Der Neue Pauly: Enzyklopädie der Antike*, ed. Hubert Cancik and Helmuth Schneider.

Gilliard, Frank D. "More Silent Reading in Antiquity: Non omne verbum sonabat." *Journal of Biblical Literature* 112 (1993): 689–94.

Gleason, Maud W. *Making Men: Sophists and Self-Presentation in Ancient Rome*. Princeton: Princeton University Press, 1995.

Glenthøj, Johannes B. "The Cross and Paradise: The Robber and the Cherub in Dialogue." In *In the Last Days: On Jewish and Christian Apocalyptic and Its Period*, ed. Knud Jeppesen, Kirsten Nielsen, and Bent Rosendal, 60–77. Aarhus: Aarhus University Press, 1994.

Gottwald, Norman K. *Studies in the Book of Lamentations*. Rev. ed. London: SCM, 1962.

Grabar, André. *Les ampoules de Terre Sainte (Monza, Bobbio)*. Paris: Klincksieck, 1958.

Graf, D. E. "Akrostichis." In *Realencyclopädie der classischen Altertumswissenschaft*, ed. A. Pauly and G. Wissowa.

Grant, Robert M. *The Earliest Lives of Jesus*. New York: Harper, 1961.

———. *Eusebius as Church Historian*. Oxford: Clarendon, 1980.

Green, William Scott. "The Difference Religion Makes," *JAAR* 62 (1994): 1191–1207.

Greer, Rowan. *Theodore of Mopsuestia: Exegete and Theologian*. London: Faith Press, 1961.

Grégoire, Réginald. *Manuale di agiologia: Introduzione alla letteratura agiographica*. Fabriano: Monastero San Silvestro Abate, 1987.

Griffiths, Paul. *Religious Reading: The Place of Reading in the Practice of Religion*. New York: Oxford University Press, 1999.

Grisbrooke, W. Jardine. "Anaphora." In *The Westminster Dictionary of Worship*, ed. J. G. Davies, 10–17. Philadelphia: Westminster, 1972.

Grosdidier de Matons, José. "Aux origines de l'hymnographie byzantine: Romanos le Mélode et le Kontakion." In *Liturgie und Dichtung: Ein interdisziplinäres Kompendium I: Historische Präsentation*, ed. H. Becker and R. Kaczynski, 435–63. St. Ottilien: EOS-Verlag, 1983.

———. "Liturgie et Hymnographie: Kontakion et Canon." *Dumbarton Oaks Papers* 34/35 (1980–81): 31–43.

———. "Les *Miracula Sancti Artemii*: Note sur quelques questions de vocabulaire." In *Mémorial André-Jean Festugière: Antiquité, Païenne et Chrétienne*, ed. E. Lucchesi and H. D. Saffrey, 263–66. Geneva: Cramer, 1984.

———. *Romanos le Mélode et les origines de la poésie religieuse à Byzance*. Paris: Beauchesne, 1977.

Grossman, Peter. "The Pilgrimage Center of Abû Mînâ." In *Pilgrimage and Holy Space in Late Antique Egypt*, ed. David Frankfurter, 281–302. Leiden: Brill, 1998.

Guillaumont, Antoine. "La conception du désert chez les moines d'Egypte." *Revue de l'histoire des religions* 188 (1975): 3–21.

Guinot, Jean-Noel. *L'Exégèse de Théodoret de Cyr.* Théologie historique 100. Paris: Beauchesne, 1995.

Hackel, Sergei, ed. *The Byzantine Saint: University of Birmingham Fourteenth Spring Symposium of Byzantine Studies.* San Bernardino, Calif.: Borgo, 1983.

Hadot, Pierre. *Plotinus, or The Simplicity of Vision.* Trans. Michael Chase. Chicago: University of Chicago Press, 1993. Originally published as *Plotin ou la simplicité du regard,* 3rd. ed. (Paris: Gallimard, 1989).

Hägg, Tomas, and Philip Rousseau. "Biography and Panegyric." In *Greek Biography and Panegyric in Late Antiquity,* ed. Tomas Hägg and Philip Rousseau, 1–28. Berkeley: University of California Press, 2000.

Hägg, Tomas, and Philip Rousseau, eds. *Greek Biography and Panegyric in Late Antiquity.* Berkeley: University of California Press, 2000.

Hahn, Cynthia. "Loca Sancta Souvenirs: Sealing the Pilgrim's Experience." In *The Blessings of Pilgrimage,* ed. Robert Ousterhout, 85–96. Illinois Byzantine Studies 1. Urbana: University of Illinois Press, 1990.

Hahneman, Geoffrey Mark. *The Muratorian Fragment and the Development of the Canon.* Oxford: Clarendon, 1992.

Haines-Eitzen, Kim. "'Girls Trained in Beautiful Writing': Female Scribes in Roman Antiquity and Early Christianity." *JECS* 6 (1998): 629–46.

———. *Guardians of Letters: Literacy, Power, and the Transmitters of Early Christian Literature.* New York: Oxford University Press, 2000.

Haldon, John. "The Miracles of Artemios and Contemporary Attitudes: Context and Significance." In *The Miracles of St. Artemios: A Collection of Miracle Stories by an Anonymous Author of Seventh-Century Byzantium,* ed. Virgil S. Crisafulli and John W. Nesbitt, 33–73. Leiden: Brill, 1997.

Halleux, André de. "Héllenisme et syrianité de Romanos le Mélode." *Revue d'Histoire Ecclésiastique* 73 (1978): 632–41.

Halliburton, R. J. "The Patristic Theology of the Eucharist." In *The Study of Liturgy,* ed. Cheslyn Jones, Geoffrey Wainwright, and Edward Yarnold, 201–208. New York: Oxford University Press, 1978.

Harl, M. "Le guetteur et la cible: Les deux sens de *skopos* dans la langue religieuse des chrétiens." *Revue des études grecques* 74 (1961): 450–68.

Harpham, Geoffrey Galt. *The Ascetic Imperative in Culture and Criticism.* Chicago: University of Chicago Press, 1987.

Harrison, Verna E. F. "Word as Icon in Greek Patristic Theology." *Sobornost* 10 (1988): 38–49.

Harvey, Susan Ashbrook. *Asceticism and Society in Crisis: John of Ephesus and The Lives of the Eastern Saints.* Berkeley: University of California Press, 1990.

———. "Embodiment in Time and Eternity: A Syriac Perspective." *St. Vladimir's Seminary Quarterly* 43 (1999): 105–30.

———. *Scenting Salvation: Ancient Christianity and the Olfactory Imagination.* Berkeley: University of California Press, forthcoming.

———. "The Sense of a Stylite: Perspectives on Symeon the Elder." *VC* 42 (1988): 376–94.

———. "Spoken Words, Voiced Silence: Biblical Women in Syriac Tradition." *JECS* 9 (2001): 105–31.

———. "The Stylite's Liturgy: Ritual and Religious Identity in Late Antiquity." *JECS* 6 (1998): 523–39.

———. "Women in Early Byzantine Hagiography: Reversing the Story." In *That Gentle Strength: Historical Perspectives on Women in Christianity,* ed. Lynda L. Coon, Katherine J. Haldane, and Elizabeth W. Sommer, 36–59. Charlottesville: University Press of Virginia, 1990.

Heard, R. G. "The Old Gospel Prologues," *JThS* 6 (1955): 1–16.

Heffernan, Thomas J. *Sacred Biography: Saints and Their Biographers in the Middle Ages.* New York: Oxford University Press, 1988.

Heine, Ronald. "Reading the Bible with Origen." In *The Bible in Greek Christian Antiquity,* ed. Paul M. Blowers, 131–48. Notre Dame, Ind.: University of Notre Dame Press, 1997.

Hennecke, Edgar, and Wilhelm Schneemelcher, eds. *New Testament Apocrypha.* 2 vols. 3rd ed. Trans. R. McL. Wilson. Philadelphia: Westminster, 1965.

———. *New Testament Apocrypha.* 2 vols. Rev. 5th ed. Trans. R. McL. Wilson. Cambridge: Clark, 1992.

Henry, Patrick. "A Mirror for Justinian: The *Ekthesis* of Agapetus Diaconus." *Greek, Roman, and Byzantine Studies* 8 (1967): 281–308.

Hill, R. C. "On Looking Again at *Sunkatabasis,*" *Prudentia* 13 (1981): 3–11.

———. "St. John Chrysostom and the Incarnation of the Word in Scripture." *Compass Theology Review* 14 (1980): 34–38.

Hill, Stephen. *The Early Byzantine Churches of Cilicia and Isauria.* Birmingham Byzantine and Ottoman Monographs 1. Aldershot: Variorum, 1996.

Himmelfarb, Martha. *Ascent to Heaven in Jewish and Christian Apocalypses.* New York: Oxford University Press, 1993.

Hirschfeld, Yizhar. *The Judean Desert Monasteries in the Byzantine Period.* New Haven: Yale University Press, 1992.

Honigmann, Ernst. "Theodoret of Cyrrhus and Basil of Seleucia: The Time of Their Death." In *Patristic Studies.* Studi e testi 173. Rome: Biblioteca apostolica vaticana, 1953.

Hopkins, Keith. "Christian Number and Its Implications." *JECS* 6 (1998): 185–226.

Horrocks, Geoffrey. *Greek: A History of the Language and Its Speakers.* London: Longman, 1997.

Hunger, Herbert. "Evangelisten." *Reallexikon zur byzantinischen Kunst* 2:466–67.

———. "Romanos Melodos, Dichter, Prediger, Rhetor—und sein Publikum." *Jahrbuch der Österreichischen Byzantinistik* 34 (1984): 15–42.

Irmscher, Johannes. "Pindar in Byzanz." In *Aischylos und Pindar: Studien zu Werk und Nachwirking,* ed. Ernst Günther Schmidt, 296–302. Berlin: Akademie-Verlag, 1981.

Jackson, B. D. "The Theory of Signs in Saint Augustine's *De Doctrina Christiana.*" *Revue des Études Augustiniennes* 15 (1969): 9–49.

James, Liz. "Color and Meaning in Byzantium." *JECS* 11 (2003): 223–33.

Jauss, Hans Robert. "Theory of Genres and Medieval Literature." Trans. Timothy Bahti. In *Modern Genre Theory,* ed. David Duff, 127–47. Harlow: Pearson, 2000. First published in French, 1970.

Johnson, Barbara. "Writing." In *Critical Terms for Literary Study,* ed. Frank Lentricchia and Thomas McLaughlin, 2nd ed., 39–49. Chicago: University of Chicago Press, 1995.

Johnson, Scott. "Cult and Competition: Textual Appropriation in the Fifth-Century *Life and Miracles of Thecla.*" Unpublished paper delivered to the Byzantine Studies Conference, Columbus, Ohio, October 4, 2002.

Joly, Madeleine. "Les fondations d'Euthyme et de Sabas: texte et archéologie." In *Les saints et leur sanctuaire: textes, images et monuments,* ed. Catherine Jolivet-Lévy, Michel Kaplan, and Jean-Pierre Sodini, 49–64. Byzantina sorbonensia 11. Paris: Publications de la Sorbonne, 1993.

Jordan, M. D. "Words and Word: Incarnation and Signification in Augustine's *De doctrina christiana.*" *Augustinian Studies* 11 (1980): 177–96.

Junod, Éric, and Jean-Daniel Kaestli. *L'Histoire des actes apocryphes des apôtres du IIIe au IXe siècle: Le cas des Actes de Jean.* Geneva: Revue de théologie et de philosophie, 1982.

Kalogeras, Nikos. "Rhetoric and Emulation in the Work of Cyril of Scythopolis and the *Vita Abraamii.*" *Byzantinoslavica* 61 (2003): 1–16.

———. "The Role of the Audience in the Construction of Narrative: A Note on Cyril of Scythopolis." *Jahrbuch der österreichischen Byzantinistik* 52 (2002): 149–59.

Kaster, Robert A. *Guardians of Language: The Grammarian and Society in Late Antiquity.* Berkeley: University of California Press, 1988.

Kelly, J. N. D. *Early Christian Doctrines.* London: Black, 1958.

———. *Golden Mouth: The Story of John Chrysostom—Ascetic, Preacher, Bishop.* Ithaca: Cornell University Press, 1995.

Koskenniemi, H. *Studien zur Idee und Phraseologie des griechischen Briefes bis 400 n. Chr.* Suomalaisen Tiedeakatemian Toimituksia/Annales Academiae Scientiarum Fennicae 102.2. Helsinki: Suomalainen Tiedeakatemia, 1956.

Kraemer, Ross Shepard. *Her Share of the Blessings: Women's Religion among Pagans, Jews, and Christians in the Greco-Roman World.* New York: Oxford University Press, 1992.

Krause, Martin. "Karm Abu Mena." *Reallexikon zur byzantinischer Kunst* 3:1116–58.

———. "Menas the Miracle Maker, Saint." *The Coptic Encyclopedia* 5:1589–90.

Kresten, O., and G. Prato. "Die Miniatur des Evangelisten Markus im Codex Purpureus Rossanensis: Eine spätere Einfügung." *Römische Historische Mitteilungen* 27 (1985): 381–403.

Kropf, David Glenn. *Authorship as Alchemy: Subversive Writing in Pushkin, Scott, and Hoffmann.* Stanford: Stanford University Press, 1994.

Krueger, Derek. "Hagiography as an Ascetic Practice in the Early Christian East." *Journal of Religion* 79 (1999): 216–32.

———. *Symeon the Holy Fool: Leontius's Life and the Late Antique City.* Berkeley: University of California Press, 1996.

———. "Typological Figuration in Theodoret of Cyrrhus's *Religious History* and the Art of Postbiblical Narrative." *JECS* 5 (1997): 393–419.

———. "Writing and Redemption in the Hymns of Romanos the Melodist." *BMGS* 27 (2003): 2–44.

———. "Writing and the Liturgy of Memory in Gregory of Nyssa's *Life of Macrina.*" *JECS* 8 (2000): 483–510.

———. "Writing as Devotion: Hagiographical Composition and the Cult of the Saints in Theodoret of Cyrrhus and Cyril of Scythopolis." *Church History* 66 (1997): 707–19.

Krumbacher, K. "Die Akrostichis in der griechischen Kirchenpoesie." *Sitzungsberichte der philos.-philol. und der histor. Klasse der K. Bayer. Akad. d. Wiss.* 2 (1903): 551–692.

Kubiski, Joyce. "The Medieval 'Home Office': Evangelist Portraits in the Mount Athos Gospel Book, Stavronikita Monastery, MS 43." *Studies in Iconography* 22 (2001): 21–53.

Kuefler, Mathew. *The Manly Eunuch: Masculinity, Gender Ambiguity and Christian Ideology in Late Antiquity.* Chicago: University of Chicago Press, 2001.

Kuehn, Clement A. "Dioskoros of Aphrodito and Romanos the Melodist." *Bulletin of the American Society of Papyrologists* 27 (1990): 103–7.

Lampe, G. W. H. *A Patristic Greek Lexicon.* Oxford: Clarendon, 1961.

Leader, Zachary. *Writer's Block.* Baltimore: Johns Hopkins University Press, 1991.

Lefkowitz, Mary R. *The Lives of the Greek Poets.* Baltimore: Johns Hopkins, 1981.

Lentricchia, Frank, and Thomas McLaughlin, ed. *Critical Terms for Literary Study.* 2nd ed. Chicago: University of Chicago Press, 1995.

Leroy-Molinghen, Alice. "À propos de la Vie de Syméon Stylite." *Byzantion* 34 (1964): 375–84.

Leyerle, Blake. "Landscape as Cartography in Early Christian Pilgrimage Narratives." *JAAR* 64 (1996): 119–43.

Lietzmann, Hans. *Das Muratorische Fragment und die monarchianischen Prologe zu den Evangelien.* 2nd ed. Berlin: De Gruyter, 1933.

Lingas, Alexander. "The Liturgical Place of the Kontakion in Constantinople." In *Liturgy, Architecture, and Art in the Byzantine World: Papers of the XVIII International Byzantine Congress (Moscow, 8–15 August 1991) and other Essays Dedicated to the Memory of Fr. John Meyendorff,* ed. Constantine C. Akentiev, 50–57. St. Petersburg: Publications of the St. Petersburg Society for Byzantine and Slavic Studies, 1995.

Loerke, William. "Incipits and Author Portraits in Greek Gospel Books: Some Observations." In *Byzantine East, Latin West: Art-Historical Studies in Honor of Kurt Weitzmann,* ed. Christopher Moss and Katherine Kiefer, 377–81 and plates. Princeton: Department of Art and Archeology, 1995.

Long, Jacqueline. *Claudian's In Eutropium: Or, How, When, and Why to Slander a Eunuch.* Chapel Hill: University of North Carolina Press, 1996.

Lowden, John. "The Beginnings of Biblical Illustration." In *Imaging the Early Medieval Bible,* ed. John Williams, 9–59. University Park: Pennsylvania State University Press, 1999.

Luck, Georg. "Notes on the *Vita Macrinae* by Gregory of Nyssa." In *The Biographical Works of Gregory of Nyssa,* ed. Andreas Spira, 21–32. Cambridge, Mass.: Philadelphia Patristic Foundation, 1984.

Luttikhuizen, Gerard. "A Gnostic Reading of the Acts of John." In *The Apocryphal*

Acts of John, ed. Jan N. Bremmer, 119–52. Studies on the Apocryphal Acts of the Apostles 1. Kampen: Pharos, 1995.

Maas, Michael. *John Lydus and the Roman Past: Antiquarianism and Politics in the Age of Justinian*. London: Routledge, 1992.

MacCormack, Sabine. *Art and Ceremony in Late Antiquity*. Berkeley: University of California Press, 1981.

MacCoull, Leslie S. B. *Dioscorus of Aphrodito: His Work and His World*. Berkeley: University of California Press, 1988.

MacDonald, Dennis Ronald. *The Legend and the Apostle: The Battle for Paul in Story and Canon*. Philadelphia: Westminster, 1983.

Mango, Cyril. "History of the Templon and the Martyrion of St. Artemios at Constantinople." *Zograf* 10 (1979): 40–43.

Maraval, Pierre. "La Date de la mort de Basile de Césarée." *Études Augustiniennes* 34 (1988): 25–38.

———. "La *Vie de Sainte Macrine* de Grégoire de Nysse: continuité et nouveauté d'un genre littéraire." In *Du héros païen au saint chrétien*, ed. Gérard Freyburger and Laurent Pernot, 133–138. Paris: Études Augustiniennes, 1997.

Markus, Robert. *Saeculum: History and Society in the Theology of Saint Augustine*. Cambridge: Cambridge University Press, 1970.

———. "St. Augustine on Signs." *Phronesis* 2 (1957): 60–83. Reprinted in Robert Markus, *Signs and Meanings: World and Text in Ancient Christianity* (Liverpool: Liverpool University Press, 1996), 71–104.

———. "Trinitarian Theology and the Economy." *Journal of Theological Studies* n.s. 9 (1958): 89–102.

Marotta, Eugenio. "La basa biblica della *Vita s. Macrinae* di Gregorio di Nissa." *Vetera Christianorum* 5 (1968): 73–88.

Martinelli, Patrizia Angiolini, ed. *La Basilica di San Vitale a Ravenna*. 2 vols. Mirabilia italiae 6. Modena: Panini, 1997.

Mateos, Juan. *La Célébration de la parole dans la liturgie Byzantine*. Orientalia Christiana Analecta 191. Rome: Pontifical Institute, 1971.

———. *Le Typicon de la Grande Eglise*. Orientalia Christiana Analecta 165. Rome: Pontifical Institute, 1962.

Mathews, Thomas. *The Clash of Gods: A Reinterpretation of Early Christian Art*. Princeton: Princeton University Press, 1993.

———. *The Early Churches of Constantinople: Architecture and Liturgy*. University Park: Pennsylvania State University Press, 1971.

Mayer, Wendy. "John Chrysostom and His Audiences: Distinguishing Different Congregations at Antioch and Constantinople." *Studia Patristica* 31 (1997): 70–75.

———. "John Chrysostom: Extraordinary Preacher, Ordinary Audience." In *Preacher and Audience: Studies in Early Christian and Byzantine Homiletics*, ed. Mary B. Cunningham and Pauline Allen, 105–37. Leiden: Brill, 1998.

McCollough, C. Thomas. "A Christianity for an Age of Crisis: Theodoret of Cyrus' *Commentary on Daniel*." In *Religious Writings and Religious Systems: Systemic Analysis of Holy Books in Christianity, Islam, Buddhism, Greco-Roman Reli-*

gions, Ancient Israel, and Judaism, ed. Jacob Neusner, Ernest S. Frerichs, and A. J. Levine, 157–74. Atlanta: Scholars Press, 1989.

———. "Theodoret of Cyrus as Biblical Interpreter and the Presence of Judaism in Later Roman Syria." Ph.D diss., Notre Dame University, 1984.

McGowan, Andrew. *Ascetic Eucharists: Food and Drink in Early Christian Ritual Meals.* Oxford: Clarendon, 1999.

McKenna, John H. *Eucharist and Holy Spirit: The Eucharistic Epiclesis in Twentieth Century Theology (1900–1960).* Great Wakering: Mayhew-McCrimmon, 1975.

McKitterick, Rosamund. *The Uses of Literacy in Early Medieval Europe.* Cambridge: Cambridge University Press, 1990.

Meredith, Anthony. *The Cappadocians.* Crestwood, N.Y.: St. Vladimir's Seminary Press, 1995.

———. "A Comparison between the *Vita Sanctae Macrinae* of Gregory of Nyssa and the *Vita Plotini* of Porphyry and the *De vita Pythagorica* of Iamblichus." In *The Biographical Works of Gregory of Nyssa*, ed. Andreas Spira, 181–95. Cambridge, Mass.: Philadelphia Patristic Foundation, 1984.

———. "Gregory of Nyssa and Plotinus." *Studia Patristica* 17.3 (1982): 1120–26.

———. "Porphyry and Julian against the Christians." In *Aufstieg und Niedergang der römischen Welt.* 2.23.2, ed. Wolfgang Haase, 1120–49. Berlin: De Gruyter, 1980.

Metzger, Catherine. *Les ampoules à eulogie du Musée du Louvre.* Paris: Éditions de la Réunion des musées nationaux, 1981.

Miles, Margaret. "Image." In *Critical Terms for Religious Studies*, ed. Mark C. Taylor, 160–72. Chicago: University of Chicago Press, 1998.

Miller, Patricia Cox. *Biography in Late Antiquity: A Quest for the Holy Man.* Transformation of the Classical Heritage 5. Berkeley: University of California Press, 1983.

———. "The Blazing Body: Ascetic Desire in Jerome's *Letter to Eustochium.*" *JECS* 1 (1993): 21–45. Reprinted in Patricia Cox Miller, *The Poetry of Thought in Late Antiquity: Essays in Imagination and Religion* (Aldershot: Ashgate, 2001), 135–58.

———. "Desert Asceticism and 'The Body from Nowhere.'" *JECS* 2 (1994): 137–53. Repr. in Patricia Cox Miller, *The Poetry of Thought in Late Antiquity: Essays in Imagination and Religion* (Aldershot: Ashgate, 2001), 159–74.

———. *Dreams in Late Antiquity: Studies in the Imagination of a Culture.* Princeton: Princeton University Press, 1994.

———. "'Hagiopoiesis': Hagiography and Theological Aesthetics in Late Ancient Christianity." Unpublished paper.

———. "Poetic Words, Abysmal Words: Reflections on Origen's Hermeneutics." In *Origen of Alexandria: His World and Legacy*, ed. Charles Kannengiesser and William L. Petersen. Notre Dame, Ind.: University of Notre Dame Press, 1988. Repr. in Patricia Cox Miller, *The Poetry of Thought in Late Antiquity: Essays in Imagination and Religion* (Aldershot: Ashgate, 2001), 211–19.

———. *The Poetry of Thought in Late Antiquity: Essays in Imagination and Religion.* Aldershot: Ashgate, 2001.

———. "Strategies of Representation in Collective Biography: Constructing the Subject as Holy." In *Greek Biography and Panegyric in Late Antiquity*, ed.

Tomas Hägg and Philip Rousseau, 209–54. Berkeley: University of California Press, 2000.

Minnis, A. J. *Medieval Theory of Authorship: Scholastic Literary Attitudes in the Later Middle Ages*. 2nd ed. Philadelphia: University of Pennsylvania Press, 1988.

Mitchell, Margaret M. "The Archetypal Image: John Chrysostom's Portraits of Paul." *Journal of Religion* 75 (1995): 15–43.

———. *The Heavenly Trumpet : John Chrysostom and the Art of Pauline Interpretation*. Tübingen: Mohr Siebeck, 2000.

Momigliano, Arnaldo. "The Life of St. Macrina by Gregory of Nyssa." In *On Pagans, Jews, and Christians*, 206–21. Middletown, Conn.: Wesleyan University Press, 1987.

Mosshamer, Alden A. "Disclosing but Not Disclosed: Gregory of Nyssa as Deconstructionist." In *Studien zu Gregor von Nyssa und der christlichen Spätantike*, ed. Hubertus R. Drobner and Christoph Klock, 99–123. Supplements to *Vigiliae Christianae* 12. Leiden: Brill, 1990.

Murray, Robert. *Symbols of the Church and Kingdom: A Study in Early Syriac Tradition*. Cambridge: Cambridge University Press, 1975.

Nees, Lawrence. "Problems of Form and Function in Early Medieval Illustrated Bibles from Northwest Europe." In *Imaging the Early Medieval Bible*, ed. John Williams, 121–77. University Park: Pennsylvania State University Press, 1999.

Nelson, Robert S. *The Iconography of Preface and Miniature in the Byzantine Gospel Book*. New York: New York University Press, 1980.

O'Brien, Denis. "Comment écrivait Plotin?" In Luc Brisson et al., *Porphyre: La vie de Plotin*, 1:346–60. Paris: Vrin, 1982.

O'Meara, Dominic J. *Plotinus: An Introduction to the Enneads*. Oxford: Clarendon, 1993.

Opelt, Ilona. "Die christliche Spätantike und Pindar." *Byzantinische Forschungen* 2 (1967): 284–98.

Otero, Aurelio de Santos. "Later Acts of the Apostles." In *New Testament Apocrypha*, ed. Edgar Hennecke and Wilhelm Schneemelcher, trans. R. McL. Wilson, rev. ed., 2:426–82. Cambridge: Clark, 1992.

Ousterhout, Robert, ed. *The Blessings of Pilgrimage*. Illinois Byzantine Studies 1. Urbana: University of Illinois Press, 1990.

Oxford Dictionary of Byzantium. Ed. Alexander P. Kazhdan et al. New York: Oxford University Press, 1991.

Parker, A. S. E. "The *Vita Syncleticae*: Its Manuscripts, Ascetical Teachings and Its Use in Monastic Sources." *Studia Patristica* 30 (1997): 231–34.

Patlagean, Evelyne. "Ancient Byzantine Hagiography and Social History." In *Saints and Their Cults: Studies in Religious Sociology, Folklore and History*, ed. Stephen Wilson, 101–21. Cambridge: Cambridge University Press, 1983. Originally published as "Ancienne hagiographie byzantine et histoire sociale," *Annales* 1 (1968): 106–26.

Patrich, Joseph. *Sabas, Leader of Palestinian Monasticism: A Comparative Study in Eastern Monasticism, Fourth to Seventh Centuries*. Washington, D.C.: Dumbarton Oaks, 1995.

Patterson, Annabel. "Intention." In *Critical Terms for Literary Study*, ed. Frank Lentricchia and Thomas McLaughlin, 2nd ed., 135–46. Chicago: University of Chicago Press, 1995.

Patterson, L. G. "The Conversion of *Diastēma* in the Patristic View of Time." In *Lux in Lumine: Essays to Honor W. Norman Pittenger*, ed. R. A. Norris, 93–111. New York: Seabury, 1966.

Pease, Donald E. "Author." In *Critical Terms for Literary Study*, ed. Frank Lentricchia and Thomas McLaughlin, 2nd ed., 105–17. Chicago: University of Chicago Press, 1995.

Peeters, Paul. "Grecs hybrides et orientaux hellénisants." In *Orient et Byzance: Le tréfonds oriental de l'hagiographie byzantine*. Brussels: Société des Bollandistes, 1950.

———. "S. Syméon Stylite et ses premiers biographes." *AnBoll* 61 (1943): 29–71. Reprinted with corrections as "Un saint hellénisé par annexion: Syméon Stylite," in *Orient et Byzance: Le tréfonds oriental de l'hagiographie byzantine* (Brussels: Société des Bollandistes, 1950), 93–136.

Pépin, Jean. "L'Épisode du portrait de Plotin." In *Porphyre: La vie de Plotin*, ed. Luc Brisson et al., 2:301–30. Paris: Vrin, 1992.

Perl, Eric D. "'. . . That Man Might Become God': Central Themes in Byzantine Theology." In *Heaven on Earth: Art and the Church in Byzantium*, ed. Linda Safran, 39–57. University Park: Pennsylvania State University Press, 1998.

Petersen, William L. *The Diatessaron and Ephrem Syrus as Sources of Romanos the Melodist*. CSCO 475. Louvain: Peters, 1985.

Pettimengin, P., and B. Flusin. "Le livre antique et la dictée." In *Mémorial Andre-Jean Festugière: Antiquité paienne et chrétienne*, ed. E. Lucchesi and H. D. Saffrey, 247–62. Geneva: Cramer, 1984.

Pickstock, Catherine. *After Writing: On the Liturgical Consummation of Philosophy*. Oxford: Blackwell, 1998.

Praet, Danny. "Hagiography and Biography as Prescriptive Sources for Late Antique Sexual Morals." *Litterae Hagiologicae* 5 (1999): 2–13.

Pratsch, Thomas. *Topos Hagiographikos: Untersuchungen zur byzantinischen hagiographischen Literatur des 7.–11. Jahrhunderts* (forthcoming).

Quasten, Johannes. *Patrology*. 4 vols. Utrecht: Spectrum, 1953–86.

Raasted, Jørgen. "Kontakion Melodies in Oral and Written Tradition." In *The Study of Medieval Chant: Paths and Bridges, East and West: In Honor of Kenneth Levy*, ed. Peter Jeffery, 273–81. Woodbridge, Eng. and Rochester, N.Y.: Boydell, 2001.

———. "Zum Melodie des Kontakions Ἡ παρθένος σήμερον." *Cahiers de l'Institut du Moyen-Age Grec et Latin* 59 (1989): 233–46.

Rapp, Claudia. "Byzantine Hagiographers as Antiquarians, Seventh to Tenth Centuries." *Byzantinische Forschungen* 21 (1995): 31–44.

———. "Christians and Their Manuscripts in the Greek East in the Fourth Century." In *Scritture, libri e testi nelle aree provinciali de Bisanzio*, ed. Guglielmo Cavallo, Giuseppe de Gregorio, and Marilena Maniaci, 127–48. Spoleto: Centro italiano di studi sull'alto medioevo, 1991.

———. "'For Next to God, You Are My Salvation': Reflections on the Rise of the Holy Man in Late Antiquity." In *The Cult of the Saints in Late Antiquity and the Middle Ages: Essays on the Contribution of Peter Brown,* ed. James Howard-Johnston and Paul Antony Hayward, 63–81. Oxford: Oxford University Press, 1999.

———. "Holy Texts, Holy Men and Holy Scribes." In *The Early Christian Book,* ed. William Klingshirn and Linda Safran. Washington, D.C.: Catholic University of America Press, forthcoming.

———. "Palladius, Lausus and the *Historia Lausiaca.*" In *Novum Millenium: Studies on Byzantine History and Culture Dedicated to Paul Speck,* ed. Claudia Sode and Sarolta Takács, 279–89. Aldershot: Ashgate, 1999.

———. "Storytelling as Spiritual Communication in Early Greek Hagiography: The Use of *Diegesis.*" *JECS* 6 (1998): 431–48.

Regul, Jürgen. *Die antimarcionitischen Evangelienprologe.* Freiburg: Herder, 1969.

Reichmuth, Roland Joseph. "Typology in the Genuine Kontakia of Romanos the Melodist." Ph.D. diss. University of Minnesota, 1975.

Richard, Marcel. "Théodoret, Jean d'Antioche et les moines d'Orient." *Mélanges de Science Religieuse* 3 (1946): 147–56.

Richards, E. Randolph. *The Secretary in the Letters of Paul.* Tübingen: Mohr, 1991.

Riginos, Alice Swift. *Platonica: The Anecdotes Concerning the Life and Writings of Plato.* Leiden: Brill, 1976.

Rorem, Paul. *Biblical and Liturgical Symbols within the Pseudo-Dionysian Synthesis.* Studies and Texts 71. Toronto: Pontifical Institute of Mediaeval Studies, 1984.

Rousseau, Philip. *Basil of Caesarea.* Berkeley: University of California Press, 1994.

———. "Eccentrics and Coenobites in the Late Roman East." *Byzantinische Forschungen* 24 (1997): 35–50.

Rydén, Lennart. "Gaza, Emesa and Constantinople: Late Ancient Cities in the Light of Hagiography." In *Aspects of Late Antiquity and Early Byzantium,* ed. Lennart Rydén and Jan Olof Rosenqvist, 133–44. Swedish Research Institute in Istanbul Transactions 4. Stockholm: Almqvist and Wiksell, 1993.

Saenger, Paul. *Space between Words: The Origins of Silent Reading.* Stanford: Stanford University Press, 1997.

Satran, David. *Biblical Prophets in Byzantine Palestine: Reassessing the Lives of the Prophets.* Studia in Veteris Testamenti Pseudepigrapha 11. Leiden: Brill, 1995.

Saxer, Victor. *Bible et hagiographie: Textes et thèmes bibliques dans les Actes des martyrs authentiques des premiers siècles.* Berne: Lang, 1986.

Schäferdiek, Knut. "The Acts of John." In *New Testament Apocrypha,* ed. Edgar Hennecke and Wilhelm Schneemelcher, rev. ed., trans. R. McL. Wilson, 2:152–71. Cambridge: Clark, 1992.

Schattauer, Thomas H. "The Koinonicon of the Byzantine Liturgy: An Historical Study." *Orientalia Christiana Periodica* 49 (1983): 91–129.

Schroeder, Frederic M. "Plotinus and Language." In *The Cambridge Companion to Plotinus,* ed. Lloyd P. Gerson. Cambridge: Cambridge University Press, 1996.

Seco, Lucas F. Mateo. "'Ο εὔκαιρος θάνατος: Consideraciones en torno a la muerte en las *Homilias al Eclesiastes de Gregorio de Nisa.*" In *Gregory of Nyssa: Homilies on Ecclesiastes: An English Version with Supporting Studies,* ed. Stuart George Hall, 277–97. Berlin: de Gruyter, 1993.

Ševčenko, Ihor. "Levels of Style in Byzantine Prose." *Jahrbuch der österreichischen Byzantinistik* 31 (1981): 289–312.

Ševčenko, Nancy. "The Cave of the Apocalypse." In *Hiera Monē, Hagiou Iōannou tou Theologou—900 Chronia historikē martyrias,* 169–78. Athens: Hē Hetaireia, 1989.

Simonetti, Manlio. "La tecnica esegetica di Teodoreto nel *Commento ai Salmi.*" *Vetera Christianorum* 23 (1986): 81–116.

Smith, Jonathan Z. *To Take Place: Toward Theory in Ritual.* Chicago: University of Chicago Press, 1987.

Smyth, Herbert Weir. *Greek Grammar.* Cambridge: Harvard University Press, 1920.

Sodini, Jean-Pierre. "Les cryptes d'autel paléochrétiennes: classification." *Travaux et mémoires* 8 (1981): 440–43.

Spira, Andreas, ed. *The Biographical Works of Gregory of Nyssa.* Cambridge, Mass.: Philadelphia Patristic Foundation, 1984.

Stallman-Pacitti, Cynthia Jean. *Cyril of Scythopolis: A Study of Hagiography as Apology.* Brookline: Hellenic College Press, 1991.

Stock, Brian. *Augustine the Reader: Meditation, Self-Knowledge, and the Ethics of Interpretation.* Cambridge, Mass.: Harvard University Press, 1996.

Stout, Jeffrey. "What Is the Meaning of a Text?" *New Literary History* 1 (1982): 1–12.

Studer, Basil. "The Bible as Read in the Church." In *History of Theology: The Patristic Period,* ed. Angelo Di Bernardino and Basil Studer, trans. Matthew J. O'Connell, 1:353–73. Collegeville, Minn.: Michael Glazier, 1997.

Taft, Robert F. *A History of the Liturgy of St. John Chrysostom.* Vol. 5, *The Precommunion Rites.* Rome: Pontifical Oriental Institute, 2000.

———. *The Great Entrance: A History of the Transfer of Gifts and Other Preanaphoral Rites of the Liturgy of St. John Chrysostom.* Orientalia Christiana Analecta 200. Rome: Pontifical Instititute, 1975.

———. *The Liturgy of the Hours in East and West: The Origins of the Divine Office and Its Meaning for Today.* Collegeville, Minn.: Liturgical Press, 1986.

Taniguchi, Yuko, François Bovon, and Athanasios Antonopoulos. "The *Memorial of Saint John the Theologian (BHG* 919fb)." In *The Apocryphal Acts of the Apostles: Harvard Divinity School Studies,* ed. François Bovon, Ann Graham Brock, and Christopher R. Matthews, 333–53. Cambridge: Harvard University Press, 1999.

Taylor, Mark C., ed. *Critical Terms for Religious Studies.* Chicago: University of Chicago Press, 1998.

Thodberg, Christian. "Kontakion." *The New Grove Dictionary of Music.*

Thurn, H. *Oikonomia von der frühbyzantinischen Zeit bis zum Bilderstreit. Semasiologische Untersuchungen einer Wortfamilie.* Munich: Steinbauer und Rau, 1961.

Topping, Eva Catafygiotu. "On Earthquakes and Fires: Romanos' Encomium to Justinian." *Byzantinische Zeitschrift* 71 (1978): 22–35.

———. "Romanos, On the Entry into Jerusalem: A *Basilikos Logos.*" *Byzantion* 47 (1977): 65–91.

Trapp, M. B. "Plato's *Phaedrus* in Second-Century Greek Literature." In *Antonine Literature,* ed. D. A. Russell, 141–73. Oxford: Clarendon, 1990.

Urbainczyk, Theresa. *Theodoret of Cyrrhus: The Bishop and the Holy Man.* Ann Arbor: University of Michigan Press, 2002.

Valantasis, Richard. "Constructions of Power in Asceticism." *Journal of the American Academy of Religion* 63 (1995): 775–821.

———. *Spiritual Guides of the Third Century: A Semiotic Study of the Guide-Disciple Relationship in Christianity, Neoplatonism, Hermetism, and Gnosticism.* Harvard Dissertations in Religion 27. Minneapolis: Fortress, 1991.

van Bekkum, W. J. "Anti-Christian Polemics in Hebrew Liturgical Poetry (*Piyyut*) of the Sixth and Seventh Centuries." In *Early Christian Poetry: A Collection of Essays,* ed. J. den Boeft and A. Hilhorst, 297–308. Supplements to *Vigiliae Christianae* 22. Leiden: Brill, 1993.

van Rompay, Lucas. "Romanos le Mélode: Un poète syrien à Constantinople." In *Early Christian Poetry: A Collection of Essays,* ed. J. den Boeft and A. Hilhorst, 282–96. Supplements to *Vigiliae Christianae* 22. Leiden: Brill, 1993.

van Uytfanghe, Marc. "L'Empreinte biblique sur la plus ancienne hagiographie occidentale." In *Le monde latin antique et la Bible,* ed. Jacques Fontaine and Charles Pietri, 565–611. Bible de tous les temps 2. Paris: Beauchesne, 1985.

———. "L'Hagiographie: un 'genre' chrétien ou antique tardif?" *AnBoll* 111 (1993): 135–88.

———. *Stylisation biblique et condition humaine dans l'hagiographie mérovingienne (600–750).* Brussels: Paleis der Academiën, 1987.

Vasaly, Ann. *Representations: Images of the World in Ciceronian Oratory.* Berkeley: University of California Press, 1993.

Verghese, T. Paul. "ΔΙΑΣΤΗΜΑ and ΔΙΑΣΤΑΣΙΣ in Gregory of Nyssa: Introduction to a Concept and the Posing of a Problem." In *Gregor von Nyssa und die Philosophie,* ed. Heinrich Dörrie, Margarete Altenburger, and Uta Schramm, 243–58. Leiden: Brill, 1976.

Vikan, Gary. *Byzantine Pilgrimage Art.* Washington, D.C.: Dumbarton Oaks, 1982.

———. "Early Byzantine Pilgrimage *Devotionalia* as Evidence of the Appearance of Pilgrimage Shrines." *Jahrbuch für Antike und Christentum, Ergänzungsband* 20 (1995): 1:377–88.

———. "Pilgrims in Magi's Clothing: The Impact of Mimesis on Early Byzantine Pilgrimage Art." In *The Blessings of Pilgrimage,* ed. Robert Ousterhout, 97–107. Illinois Byzantine Studies 1. Urbana: University of Illinois Press, 1990.

Vivian, Tim. *Journeying into God: Seven Early Monastic Lives.* Minneapolis: Fortress, 1996.

von Balthasar, Hans Urs. *Presence and Thought: An Essay on the Religious Philosophy of Gregory of Nyssa.* Trans. Mark Sebanc. San Francisco: Ignatius Press, 1988. Originally published as *Présence et pensée,* 1942.

von Simson, Otto G. *Sacred Fortress: Byzantine Art and Statecraft in Ravenna.* Princeton: Princeton University Press, 1987. Originally published 1948.

Vööbus, Arthur. *History of Asceticism in the Syrian Orient: A Contribution to the History of Culture in the Near East.* Vol. 2. CSCO 197/Sub. 17. Louvain: Secrétariat du CSCO, 1960.

Wagner, M. M. "A Chapter in Byzantine Epistolography: The Letters of Theodoret of Cyrus." *DOP* 4 (1948): 119–81.

Weitzmann-Fiedler, J. "Ein Evangelientyp mit Aposteln als Begleitfiguren." In *Adolph Goldschmidt zu seinem seibenzigsten Geburtstag*, 30–34. Berlin: Würfel, 1935.

Wendel, C. "Die ΤΑΠΕΙΝΟΤΗΣ des griechischen Schreibermönches." *Byzantinische Zeitschrift* 43 (1950): 259–66.

Wengst, Klaus. *Humility: Solidarity of the Humiliated.* Trans. John Bowden. London: SCM, 1988. Originally published as *Demut: Solidarität der Gedemütigen*, 1987.

Westerink, L. G. *Anonymous Prolegomena to Platonic Philosophy: Introduction, Text, Translation, and Indices.* Amsterdam: North-Holland, 1962.

Wilken, Robert. *John Chrysostom and the Jews: Rhetoric and Reality in the Late Fourth Century.* Berkeley: University of California Press, 1983.

Williams, Rowan. "Macrina's Deathbed Revisited: Gregory of Nyssa on Mind and Passion." In *Christian Faith and Greek Philosophy in Late Antiquity: Essays in Tribute to George Christopher Stead*, ed. Lionel R. Wickham and Caroline P. Bammel, 227–46. Leiden: Brill, 1993.

Wilson, Stephen, ed. *Saints and Their Cults: Studies in Religious Sociology, Folklore, and History.* Cambridge: Cambridge University Press, 1983.

Wimbush, Vincent, and Richard Valantasis, eds. *Asceticism.* New York: Oxford University Press, 1995.

Winkler, John J. *Auctor and Actor: A Narratological Reading of Apuleius' Golden Ass.* Berkeley: University of California Press, 1985.

Wybrew, Hugh. "The Byzantine Liturgy from the *Apostolic Constitutions* to the Present Day." In *The Study of Liturgy*, ed. Cheslyn Jones, Geoffrey Wainwright, and Edward Yarnold, 209–19. New York: Oxford University Press, 1978.

Yalahom, J. "*Piyyût* as Poetry." In *The Synagogue in Late Antiquity*, ed. Lee I. Levine, 111–26. Philadelphia: American Schools of Oriental Research, 1987.

Yarnold, E. J. "The Liturgy of the Faithful in the Fourth and Early Fifth Centuries." In *The Study of Liturgy*, ed. Cheslyn Jones, Geoffrey Wainwright, and Edward Yarnold, 189–201. New York: Oxford University Press, 1978.

Young, Frances. *From Nicaea to Chalcedon: A Guide to the Literature and Its Background.* Philadelphia: Fortress, 1983.

———. "Panegyric and the Bible." *Studia Patristica* 25 (1991): 194–208.

Young, Frances M. "The God of the Greeks and the Nature of Religious Language." In *Early Christian Literature and the Classical Intellectual Tradition: In Honorem Robert M. Grant*, ed. William R. Schoedel and Robert L. Wilken, 45–74. Paris: Beauchesne, 1979.

Zanker, Paul. *The Mask of Socrates: The Image of the Intellectual in Antiquity.* Trans. Alan Shapiro. Berkeley: University of California Press, 1995.

Index

Abraham, 28, 51, 59, 107
absence, 6, 129, 140, 148, 149, 151–56; writing as compensation for, 115, 133; writing predicated on, 118. *See also* presence
acrostics, 13, 166, 169–74, 181, 184, 187
Acts of John, second-century apocryphal, 36
Acts of John by Prochoros, 37–39, 41, 61
allusion, biblical, 5, 10, 16, 18, 22, 72, 101; to biblical precursors, 35, 77; to Christ, 91
ampullae, 49
Andrew the Apostle, 36, 43, 44
anthrax, 85–86
Antony the Great. *See* Athanasius, *Life of Antony*
anxiety, 149
apostles, 26, 28, 36, 39, 45, 47, 105, 107, 150; model for emulation, 39, 95. *See also individual apostles*
asceticism, 16, 19, 29, 36, 41, 53, 61–64, 71, 72, 95–109, 112, 119, 122, 126, 131, 142, 144, 191; as artistic creation, 95; as bodily practice (and celibacy), 40; in conflict with humility, 2; as control over the body, 20; as cultivation of virtue, 39, 109; and discipline, 170–74, 197; of evangelists, 42; and food, 40, 41, 71, 95, 100, 102, 107; hagiography as, 63; and identity, 42; as mimesis, 18; as reenactment of the Bible, 34; and renunciation, 113; as sacrifice, 19; of saint, 81; writing as, 10, 11
assistance: from God, 95; from saint, 79–80, 82, 84, 97, 104
Athanasius of Alexandria, 1, 156; *Life of Antony*, 5, 13, 15, 21, 76, 103, 117, 143, 193, 194
attribute: for identification of subject, 50; as image of text, 58; of John, codex with cross, 50; —, cypress tree, 49; —, eagle, 51, 57 fig. 7, 58; of Luke, ox, 51, 56 fig. 6, 58; of Mark, lion, 52, 55 fig. 5, 58; of Matthew, angel, 52, 54 fig. 4, 58
audience, 4, 26, 27, 31, 32, 75, 79, 102, 108, 122, 136, 142, 169; assumptions of author about, 18; call on to imitate evangelists, 43; direct address to, 9, 100, 102; participation in biblical typology, 32; receiving word, 59
author, 2, 46, 47, 48, 50, 58, 82, 113, 127, 197, 204 nn. 34, 36; active role of, 46, 50; anonymous, 43, 92, 103; as ascetic, 15, 75–79, 95–109; biblical precedents for, 107, 191; as character, 71, 74, 92, 122–23; claims of inadequacy, 98, 103, 104; and classical precedents, 87; confession of, 80; as devotee, 63, 79–92; as disciple, 133; education of, 16; engaged in religious observance, 1; as eyewitness, 29, 34; as holy man, 35; identity of, 42, 91–92, 103, 135; as image of evangelists, 34; as instrument of God, 104; as mediator, 79; modesty of, 43; monastic conception of, 96; as monk, 63; as painter, 32; piety of, 71, 81; as priest, 63; reluctance (hesitation) of, 43–44; as saint, 62, 108, 187; self-abasement of, 100–101, 105; self-consciousness of, 79, 98; self-denigration of, 93; self-deprecation of, 76, 94; self-humiliation of, 104–5, 106; self-presentation of, 9, 29, 79, 84; self-representation of, 35, 169–74; as subject, 171–74, 184–88; voice of, 136; worthiness of, 98
authority, 47, 79–80, 90, 127; of biblical models, 62; canonical, 38; claim to, 28, 86; and memory, 127; and power, 93; renunciation of, 9, 44, 104, 108; of scripture, 36
authorship, 3, 61–62, 84, 86, 104, 134; act of, 27, 38, 49; as asceticism, 9, 13; as authority, 8, 92; of biblical texts, 47; credentials for, 39, 107; as cultic practice, 63, 92; as devotion, 9, 93; through dictation, 38, 60, 154; as emulation of God, 8; and holiness, 50; influence of monasticism on, 11, 96–102; as inscription, 9; as liturgy, 13, 132; models for, 35, 39, 159; and performance, 7, 8, 13, 38, 60, 62, 79, 141, 156; as reflection, 6; as

Acknowledgments

It is perhaps perilous to compose acknowledgments for a project that involved so much time looking for authors in the front and back matter of early Byzantine books. Nevertheless, it is good that modern bookmaking convention provides me a place to express gratitude to the many institutions, forums, and people who made my own practice of authorship possible.

This study benefited from the generous support provided in 1995–96 by a fellowship from the American Council of Learned Societies, in 1998–99 by a Fellowship in Byzantine Studies at Dumbarton Oaks, and in 2002–3 by a fellowship from the National Endowment for the Humanities. During each of those years I was also granted a research assignment from the University of North Carolina at Greensboro. The Department of Religious Studies at the University of Virginia welcomed me as a Visiting Scholar in 1995–96, as did the Department of Religion at Princeton University in 2002–3. I also benefited from a Stanley J. Seeger Visiting Research Fellowship in Hellenic Studies at Princeton University in 2002. UNCG awarded me faculty research grants and grants from the Kohler Fund for International Travel.

While in progress, sections of this book were presented at the Byzantine Studies Conference, meetings of the American Academy of Religion, the Society of Biblical Literature, the American Society of Church History, the American Syriac Symposium, the Congrès International des Études Byzantines, and the North American Patristics Society. I read drafts of chapters in conferences, symposia, and workshops at Dumbarton Oaks, Princeton University, the University of Minnesota, the Catholic University of America, UVA, and UNCG and delivered public lectures at King's College London, Queen's University Belfast, the University of Manchester, and the University of North Carolina at Chapel Hill. Attendants at each of these forums offered helpful insights and asked tough questions. Many hosts offered nourishing and restful hospitality and friendship.

Parts of this book were previously published in different form. Chapter 2 first appeared as "Typological Figuration in Theodoret of Cyrrhus's *Religious History* and the Art of Postbiblical Narrative," *JECS* 5 (1997): 393–419; Chapter 5 as "Hagiography as an Ascetic Practice in the Early Christian East," *Journal of Religion* 79 (1999): 216–32; Chapter 6 as "Writing and the Liturgy of Memory in Gregory of Nyssa's *Life of Macrina*," *JECS* 8 (2000): 483–510; Chapter 8 as "Writing and Redemption in the Hymns of Romanos the Melodist," *BMGS* 27 (2003): 2–44. Two sections of Chapter 4 appeared as "Writing as Devotion: Hagiographical Composition and the Cult of the Saints in Theodoret of Cyrrhus and Cyril of Scythopolis," *Church History* 66 (1997): 707–19.

I am thankful for ongoing conversation with members of the Project on Models of Piety in Late Antiquity (a.k.a. the Piety Group), a potent matrix of innovation and experimentation. I am indebted to Tony Cutler, Asen Kirin, and Glenn Peers for insight into art-historical matters. And I thank the students in my seminars at UNCG on hagiography and concepts of holiness in late antiquity and early Byzantium for their willingness to read and discuss nearly everything I put in front of them.

I am grateful for the warmth, generosity, and institutional savvy of Alice-Mary Talbot, director of Byzantine Studies at Dumbarton Oaks; Dimitri Gondicas, director of the Center for Hellenic Studies at Princeton; Charlie Orzech, former head of the Department of Religious Studies at UNCG; and Pat Bowden, our department administrator.

A number of scholars read sections of the book in draft, offering criticism and encouragement, including David Brakke, Peter Brown, Elizabeth Clark, Robert Doran, Susan Harvey, Scott Johnson, Rick Layton, Pat Miller, Bill North, and Richard Valantasis.

Virginia Burrus, Daniel Boyarin, Margaret Mullett, and Claudia Rapp read the entire manuscript, offering advice that helped me shape the book into a more coherent whole. Georgia Frank, who for many years has been a writing pal, brainstorming buddy, and true friend, read the book a number of times in its various stages.

Ancient and Byzantine writers depended on scribes and copyists for the dissemination of their work. I am indebted to Jerry Singerman, Ted Mann, and Erica Ginsburg of the University of Pennsylvania Press for their wise counsel and technical expertise and to Amanda Wall for her skilled indexing of the book.

Finally I thank my partner, Gene Rogers, for providing support, stability, and companionship. He was willing to read what I had written when I could not bear to look at it. He contributed greatly to the formation of the author. I dedicate this book to him.